THE UNIVERSITY OF
WINCHESTER

Martial Rose Library
Tel: 01962 827306

2 5 JAN 2010		
- 4 MAY 2010		
2 5 OCT 2010		
2 4 JAN 2011		

To be returned on or before the day marked above, subject to recall.

CRIMINAL LAW THEORY: DOCTRINES OF THE GENERAL PART

Criminal Law Theory:
Doctrines of the General Part

edited by
Stephen Shute
and
A.P. Simester

OXFORD
UNIVERSITY PRESS

*This book has been printed digitally and produced in a standard specification
in order to ensure its continuing availability*

OXFORD
UNIVERSITY PRESS

Great Clarendon Street, Oxford OX2 6DP

Oxford University Press is a department of the University of Oxford.
It furthers the University's objective of excellence in research, scholarship,
and education by publishing worldwide in

Oxford New York

Auckland   Cape Town Dar es Salaam   Hong Kong   Karachi
Kuala Lumpur Madrid Melbourne Mexico City   Nairobi
New Delhi Shanghai Taipei Toronto
With offices in
Argentina Austria Brazil Chile Czech Republic France Greece
Guatemala Hungary Italy Japan South Korea Poland Portugal
Singapore Switzerland Thailand Turkey Ukraine Vietnam

ISBN 0-19-924349-2

General Editor's Preface

At a time when the frontiers of the criminal law are frequently pushed outwards by governments seeking to deal with or, more likely, to be seen to be 'doing something about' issues of public concern, the so-called general part of the criminal law may be regarded as less pressing. In recent years, however, it is fair to say that scholars and indeed the higher judiciary in many common law jurisdictions have paid increasing attention to 'general part' issues. There may be no natural or convincing distinction between the special and general parts of the criminal law but, as the essays in this volume demonstrate, there are many vibrant moral and social debates which are in some way general to the criminal law. The actual and possible contours of the fault element in criminal liability and of the various defences are here analysed in the contexts of law and of principle, by scholars from various common law jurisdictions. Stephen Shute and Andrew Simester deserve great credit for conceiving and organizing the seminar on which the volume is based, and for writing an insightful introduction to the wide-ranging set of essays.

Andrew Ashworth

Preface

The origins of this book lie in a conference on the general part doctrines that was organized by the editors, in Birmingham, in November 1999. In respect of that genesis, we would like to record grateful thanks to the *Modern Law Review* and the University of Birmingham School of Law, which jointly funded the conference. All the papers presented at the conference have been included in this volume, as have some of the replies. Also included are contributions from a number of other authors who, for a variety of reasons, were unable to attend the conference but who responded positively to our request to reflect philosophically on some aspect of the general part of the criminal law. We hope that the essays in this volume, which have been written by many of the leading thinkers in the field, will help to further the understanding of the nature of the general part, and cast new light on some of the doctrines that are to be found there.

Various people have played important roles in helping us to bring this book to publication. The encouragement of the general editor of the series, Andrew Ashworth, was crucial at the inception of the project, especially in prompting us to crystallize it into a concrete book proposal. Later, John Louth at Oxford University Press provided much valuable advice. Thanks, too, are due to our families—Julia, Miranda, Winnie, and Ian—who put up with long absences while we worked on the book. Stephen Shute is also grateful to the University of Birmingham for the sabbatical leave which enabled him to devote time to editing. Finally, the editors would like to thank the contributors to this volume. Without their patience and perseverance, and above all their ideas, its completion would not have been possible.

September 2001
S.C.S.
A.P.S.

Contents

List of Contributors

Larry Alexander is Warren Distinguished Professor of Law, University of San Diego.

Peter Alldridge is Reader in Law, Cardiff Law School.

Andrew Ashworth is Vinerian Professor of English Law, University of Oxford.

Joshua Dressler is Edwin M. Cooperman Designated Professor of Law, Moritz College of Law, Ohio State University.

R. A. Duff is Professor of Philosophy, University of Stirling.

Claire Finkelstein is Professor of Law, University of Pennsylvania.

Jeremy Horder is Porjes Foundation Fellow and Tutor in Law, Worcester College, and Reader in Criminal Law, University of Oxford.

Douglas N. Husak is Professor of Philosophy, Rutgers University.

Paul H. Robinson is Edna and Ednyfed Williams Professor of Law, Northwestern University.

Stephen Shute is Professor of Criminal Law and Criminal Justice, University of Birmingham.

A.P. Simester is Professor of Legal Philosophy, University of Nottingham.

G.R. Sullivan is Professor of Criminal Law, University of Durham.

Victor Tadros is Lecturer in Law, University of Edinburgh.

1

On the General Part in Criminal Law

A.P. SIMESTER and STEPHEN SHUTE

Doug Husak argues that doctrines[1] of criminalization, such as the harm principle, rightly belong in the general part of the criminal law. We agree. The main reason why this truth may seem odd is that the general part is often thought to comprise legal doctrines that are directly justiciable, albeit cast in general form. Hence, the rules governing attempt liability may be invoked in order to convict defendants of a variety of offences—for the most part, the law of attempts subsists within the general part. But the general part also contains other types of doctrine, which need be neither legally mandatory nor even justiciable. Advisory norms, such as those collected in the 'rule of law' and in the 'harm principle',[2] are included. If this is right, it follows that we cannot simply define the general part as comprising those doctrines of the criminal law that are common to more than one type of offence. It includes those doctrines, and more.

We cannot, in this introduction, exhaustively explore the natures of the multifarious doctrines that comprise the general part in criminal law. Rather, we hope to venture remarks that touch on some of the aspects of the general part treated by the essays in this book and, in so doing, to illustrate the character and, especially, the variety of doctrines found in the general part of the criminal law.

A. THE GENERALITY OF THE GENERAL PART

There are different kinds of generalizations that can be made about the criminal law. The definitions of knowledge, belief, and recklessness, which are discussed here by Stephen Shute, Bob Sullivan, and Victor Tadros, have general application in that they apply across a range of offences in which they are part of the *mens rea* requirement. The meaning of these concepts is rightly a matter for the

---

[1] We use 'doctrine' loosely, to embrace doctrines, norms, rules, principles, etc.
[2] Advisory, in the sense that such norms are not *legally* mandatory in the hands of legislators: see section C below.

general part most obviously, though not only, because of the commonality of their deployment. Prima facie, that reason is contingent: legal inquiry into the meaning of, say, 'knowing or believing' is normally out of place in a prosecution for an offence of negligence. By contrast, doctrines governing liability for omissions and involuntary actions, discussed in this volume by Larry Alexander and Claire Finkelstein, in principle apply to offences *tout court*.

However (a point to which we shall return), even if we consider only these two sets of doctrines, separating them in this way is misleading, because the general part is never merely contingent. Consider the doctrines governing omissions liability. The general part comprises not only the directly-justiciable general rules restricting liability for omissions, and the rules concerning general exceptions to that restriction, but also their underpinning rationale. That rationale shapes the boundary of the omissions doctrines and informs their application to difficult, novel, and/or borderline cases. There are particular offences that criminalize omissions which belong to the special part of the criminal law, but even their justification must grapple with the reasons why omissions are normally special; reasons that are the provenance of the general part. Similarly, the literature on recklessness addresses not only its nature and meaning, but also the justification for incorporating it within *mens rea* elements of offences. It is not an accident of the special part that most grave offences require, at a minimum, foresight of the *actus reus* before a person commits the offence. There are rule of law and culpability-based reasons why it is generally inappropriate that inadvertent wrongdoers be labelled and punished as serious offenders.[3]

The generality of a doctrine is a condition precedent to its inclusion within the general part of the criminal law. But how general must a doctrine be before it can qualify? Some general part doctrines are clearly very general indeed. The requirement of a voluntary action—under some description[4]—operates as a principle of general application: it covers all cases where criminal liability is under consideration and tolerates no derogation. Hence it is a straightforward candidate for inclusion within the criminal law's general part. Other criminal law doctrines, although more localized in their application, are also sufficiently general to warrant inclusion. Examples include the doctrines which make up some of the fundamental precepts of legal causation, such as the doctrine that 'you must take your victim as you find him' and the doctrine that 'intended consequences are never too remote'. While these doctrines apply only to so-called 'result crimes' and not to 'conduct crimes',[5] the former are sufficiently prevalent in the criminal law to provide the necessary degree of generality.

---

[3] Although Victor Tadros's analysis of an inadvertent form of recklessness, see Chapter 10 in this volume, 'Recklessness and the Duty to Take Care'.

[4] cf. Claire Finkelstein, Chapter 7 in this volume, 'Involuntary Crimes, Voluntarily Committed'.

[5] By 'result crime', we mean crimes that specify the causing of a consequence as part of their *actus reus*. 'Conduct crimes' refer to behaviour by the defendant but not to its consequences.

There are, on the other hand, a great many other doctrines in the criminal law that are too circumscribed in their application to be properly ascribed to the general part. The traditional common law rule that 'there is no property in a corpse or in part of a corpse' might provide an example of such a doctrine, because, if it applies at all, it affects only a relatively small range of property offences. Other examples include the definitions of legal terms that form part of the *actus reus* of just one offence or at most a small handful of offences. Consider the legal definition of the term, 'penetration'. This definition is at the heart of the common law definition of sexual intercourse which in turn forms a key component of the common law definition of the crime of rape. But, despite its localized importance, the definition has little if any general application to other crimes, and like other definitions which are confined to single offences (or at most a small handful of offences)—such as the definition of the phrase 'taking and carrying away' in the common law crime of kid-napping—is rightly confined to the special part.

The crucial question, therefore, seems to be: does the doctrine apply across different ranges, or 'families', of offences?[6] If it does, it is a candidate for in-clusion in the general part. If it does not, then it can fall only within the spe-cial part. But two further points need to be stressed about this way of dividing up the terrain. First, it is easy to be drawn into thinking that, if a doctrine is not sufficiently general to be included within the general part, it is of lesser importance. That conclusion does not follow. The relationship between doctrines of the special part and doctrines of the general part is not hierarchi-cal: one cannot assume that, because a doctrine falls within the general part, it will always exclude or outweigh competing doctrines in the special part.[7] The second point is that the notion of generality is vulnerable to vagueness and there will always be difficulties at the margins in deciding into which cat-egory a particular doctrine should fall. Equally, it is important to recognize that difficulties at the periphery do not destroy the distinction's use and value, any more than they destroy the use and value of other theoretical distinctions, such as the offence/defence distinction, where there can be similar problems reaching hard and fast conclusions in marginal cases.

B. THE MOTIF OF CRIMINALITY

None of this yet establishes that the general part is anything more than a distillation of the doctrines and their rationales that are common to more than one type of offence. Perhaps it is convenient to collate those doctrines as

---

[6] For a discussion of the different ways in which a 'family' of crimes might be conceived, see John Gardner, 'On the General Part of the Criminal Law', in Antony Duff (ed.), *Philosophy and the Criminal Law* (Cambridge, 1998) 205.

[7] For discussion of some of the ways in which the special part may derogate from the general, see further section C below.

general propositions, rather than repeat them *ad nauseum* when specifying the many offences in the special part of the criminal law, but is there anything more to the general part than the avoidance of needless duplication? We think there is. For one thing, the reasons of 'convenience' should not be dismissed lightly. If a *mens rea* element such as 'knows or believes' recurs in the criminal law, its use in one offence should, *ceteris paribus*, denote the same meaning that it denotes when used in another offence. Rule of law values such as predictability and fair warning are fostered by consistency of this sort.

More significantly for present purposes, the general part contains a range of doctrines that reflect what it is about the criminal law that is distinctively *criminal*. We accept[8] *arguendo* that which is implicit in many of the essays here: that the criminal law is an institution by which the state prohibits certain types of conduct and condemns (through both conviction and sentence) and punishes persons who violate those prohibitions.[9] Such acts of prohibition, conviction, and punishment require justification: the general principles (both permissive and constraining) applicable to their justification fall within the general part. For example, in Husak's account, punishment—and, we would add, the condemnation implicit in the criminal label—presupposes culpability. From this, one may argue to the familiar maxim, *actus non facit reum nisi mens sit rea*. As a rule, crimes must be committed intentionally, recklessly, wilfully, knowingly, negligently, or with some other mental state as a result of which we can say that the defendant is culpable. The exploration of recklessness by Tadros in this volume is motivated not merely by the fact that it is a commonplace element of offences, but also by the fact that recklessness is assumed, *ceteris paribus*, to establish that a defendant is sufficiently culpable to warrant conviction. That assumption should not pass unchallenged—it should be tested in order that we can be reassured individuals are not, systematically, being defamed and falsely punished. Similarly, it is the moral imperative that the criminal law should not systematically convict blameless defendants which underpins the pervasive role of exculpatory defences in criminal law. Such defences belong in the general part not only because they cut across various offences, but also because they articulate, in justiciable form, principles that are at the core of the criminal law enterprise—and which also belong in the general part of the criminal law.

Even where they do not depend upon a claim of moral exculpation, much the same may also be said for defences of officially-induced wrongdoing. As Ashworth observes, the argument for recognizing defences of officially-

---

[8] cf. Stephen Shute, Chapter 8 in this volume, 'Knowledge and Belief in the Criminal Law' at 186.

[9] See, e.g., Douglas N. Husak, Chapter 2 in this volume, 'Limitations on Criminalization and the General Part of Criminal Law' at 23–7; R.A. Duff, Chapter 3 in this volume, 'Rule-Violations and Wrongdoings' at 53; Paul Robinson, Chapter 4 in this volume, 'The Modern General Part: Three Illusions' at 96; Joshua Dressler, Chapter 11 in this volume, 'Battered Women Who Kill Their Sleeping Tormenters: Reflections on Maintaining Respect for Human Life while Killing Moral Monsters' at 276.

induced mistake of law, entrapment, and law enforcement motivation depends, in part, upon the propositions that the integrity of the criminal justice
system is a value rightly part of the criminal law and that, in turn, it is best
given practical expression through the defences that Ashworth proposes.
Moreover, the value of integrity itself depends, in part, upon its relationship
to the nature and purposes of criminal law; hence, again, the defences
espoused by Ashworth rightly belong in the general part of the criminal law
not merely because of their generality.

It will not always be sufficient to identify a criminal law principle in order to
resolve questions about its impact upon the shape and structure of defences.
Some general part doctrines are open-ended and allow their requirements to
be met in a variety of different ways. Indeed, many of the cluster of doctrines
that protect 'rule of law' values, including integrity, take this form. While in a
liberal democracy it might be obligatory for a state to respect these values,
there may be a great many measures that can be taken to meet this obligation,
such that no particular solution is *required*. Hence, one of Ashworth's concerns is to introduce further argument about how the criminal legal system
should best respond to each of the situations he discusses. The same can be
said about the exculpatory defences at issue between Dressler and Horder.[10]
Each author subscribes to the moral imperative we identified above: that the
criminal law should not systematically convict blameless defendants. They
disagree about aspects of its implementation. Horder argues that the legal
rules governing lethal self-defence should spread equally the risks borne by putative aggressors and putative self-defenders: general part principles of equal
concern and respect, he claims, demand no less. Horder also claims that the
best way to spread these risks equally is to structure the defence so as to allow
putative self-defenders its benefit when they had no fair and reasonable opportunity to do other than use force. Horder's approach differs sharply from
that of Dressler. For Dressler, the key principle governing lethal self-defence is
that human life should be preserved if at all possible. Honouring this principle,
he argues, requires strict limits to be set on the defence. In particular, it requires that the defence be available only where a defender reasonably believes
force is *immediately necessary* to ward off the use of (unlawful) force by an aggressor. Thus Dressler favours confining the defence to narrow boundaries.
Yet both authors agree that we ought not to convict persons who lack a fair
opportunity to refrain from violating the law. Their difference is over how to
achieve that aim. For Dressler, it is best done by recognizing a broad version
of duress defence whereas, for Horder, it should be incorporated within the
law of self-defence. There is logical space for that difference only because the
general part doctrine about which they agree does not, by itself, determine
Dressler's and Horder's debate.

---

[10] Dressler, ibid.; Jeremy Horder, Chapter 12 in this volume, 'Killing The Passive Abuser: A
Theoretical Defence'.

C. Varieties of General Part Doctrine

In Chapter 2, Husak notes that the general part already contains criminalization doctrines that are relied upon by courts when interpreting statutes.[11] Such doctrines can be justiciable notwithstanding their abstraction. Consider, for example, the New Zealand case of *Nicholson*.[12] D had been in receipt of welfare benefits while unemployed. Before taking up a new job, D had informed the Department of Social Welfare by telephone that she had found employment. However, her benefit continued to be paid. She then wrote to the Department, repeating the notification. Despite this, the payments continued. Ultimately, D spent the money. She was subsequently charged with wilfully omitting to inform the Department of Social Welfare that she had commenced employment, contrary to section 127 of the Social Security Act 1964 which penalized an omission 'to do or say anything' with intent to deceive.[13] In determining that section 127 does not create a continuing duty of disclosure, the Court of Appeal asserted that there is a 'general aversion' to criminal liability for mere omissions. Further, the Court referred to the 'vice of practical uncertainty as to when the offence is complete'—better known, in English academic circles, as the principle of 'fair warning'[14]—as a reason against finding that section 127 establishes an open-ended obligation; rather, section 127 applies only to omissions that breach a 'distinct duty'[15] created elsewhere in the law.

The court's decision in *Nicholson* is an interpretive decision that draws, as aids to construction, upon rule of law doctrines about when and how to criminalize conduct—upon doctrines about criminalization. As Husak observes, these doctrines are not extraneous to the criminal law. They are internal. Indeed, in some jurisdictions these doctrines are internal because they are embedded in statutory codes. An example discussed by Robinson in Chapter 4 is section 1.02 of the Model Penal Code, which states, *inter alia*, that one of the 'general purposes of the provisions [in the Code] governing the definition of offences [is] to give fair warning of the nature of the conduct declared to constitute an offense'.[16] Where legislative effect is given to this provision there

---

[11] Chapter 2 below at 30–1.

[12] *Nicholson v Department of Social Welfare* [1999] 3 NZLR 50; noted [2000] NZLJ 191–192.

[13] The section deems it an offence if a person 'wilfully does or says anything or omits to do or say anything for the purpose of misleading or attempting to mislead any officer concerned in the administration of this Act or any other person whomsoever, for the purpose of receiving or continuing to receive (for himself or for any other person), or which results in himself or any other person receiving or continuing to receive . . . any benefit under this Act'.

[14] See, e.g., Andrew Ashworth, *Principles of Criminal Law* (3rd edn., Oxford, 1999) para. 3.5(i); A.P. Simester and G.R. Sullivan, *Criminal Law: Theory and Doctrine* (Oxford, 2000) para. 2.3.

[15] An explicit reference to A.M. Honoré's paper, 'Are Omissions Less Culpable?' in P. Cane and J. Stapleton (eds.), *Essays for Patrick Atiyah* (Oxford, 1991) 31, 33.

[16] Chapter 4 below at 77.

can be no doubt that it forms part of the law. But express legislative incorporation is not the only way rule of law doctrines can become woven into the fabric of a legal system. At least in a common law system, that can also be achieved by judicial action. Thus silence from the legislature on such matters in England has proved no bar to Lord Steyn's holding that 'in the absence of express words or a truly necessary implication, Parliament must be presumed to legislate on the assumption that the principle of legality will supplement the text'.[17]

For all that, the role of such doctrines may vary. In cases like *Nicholson*, they operate in the court's hands as justiciable principles of law, rightly constraining the interpretation of the statute. But the same principles would not have overridden a contrary interpretation, had Parliament unambiguously intended that contrary interpretation on the face of the legislation.[18] In constitutional terms, Parliament is generally unfettered by interpretive doctrines. If it had enacted: 'it is an offence wilfully to omit to notify the Department forthwith whenever D becomes aware that she is continuing to receive a benefit to which she is no longer entitled', no doubt the conclusion in *Nicholson* would have been different and D's conviction would have stood.

Thus, in Parliament's hands, the doctrines that were decisive in *Nicholson* operate instead as advisory norms of aspiration. A legislator, we may say, should not create open-ended prohibitions such as the one averred by the prosecutor in *Nicholson*. The truth that sometimes legislators do not adhere to these injunctions does not mean that they are not part of the law: rather, they are criminal law doctrines of criminalization from which the special part sometimes derogates.

Two points can be made here. First, this difference—between the operation of such doctrines in the hands of the judiciary and in the hands of the legislature—does not originate in the doctrines themselves, but reflects the constitutionally different roles of legislators and judges in making and applying criminal law. For example, even in judicial hands the general rule that offences cannot be committed by omission is not conclusive. It may be derogated from by judges, with binding effect on lower courts. The judge who does so for bad reasons errs legally; normally, the legislator who does so for equally bad reasons errs only morally. But this distinction is constitutional, not one specific to general part doctrines.

Secondly, derogation need not disclose moral or legal error. Sometimes, a general part doctrine may rightly be defeated by other, general or special,

---

[17] *B (a minor) v DPP* [2000] AC 428, at 470.

[18] But see *R v K* [2001] 3 WLR 471, at 486. In joining with a unanimous House to uphold the appellant's appeal, Lord Millett surprisingly stated that 'I do so without reluctance but with some misgiving, for I have little doubt that we shall be failing to give effect to the intention of Parliament and will reduce section 14 of the Sexual Offences Act 1956 to incoherence'. It is a justified misgiving, in so far as the interaction of general part principles and statutory interpretation can generate tension with constitutional principles of sovereignty. His Lordship's conclusion (at 487) that 'Injustice is too high a price to pay for consistency' sidesteps and does not dissolve that tension.

considerations; or it may simply not apply to parts of the criminal law. Suppose, for example, that we can formulate a criminal law duty to effect easy rescues that circumvents all the difficulties seen here by Alexander.[19] Nothing about the rationale for treating omissions as special, and for being generally averse to their criminalization, forecloses the introduction of such a duty into Anglo-American law. Most of the reasons that militate against overcriminalizing omissions are general in nature; the moral force of one's claim not to be involved in harms of which one is not the author may be little when it comes to a particular case in which D fails easily to save a drowning child, but it may be much greater in the context of generalized laws—when proscriptions of omissions *tout court* would have a far greater impact on the ability of individuals to pursue valuable, self-chosen, lives.[20] Principles of parsimony in criminalization are usually general in this fashion:[21] they show why, *ceteris paribus*, the law should be averse to prohibitions. But, as the *ceteris paribus* proviso admits, they are consistent with exceptions.

This suggests that, in theorizing about criminal law, one should not seek absolutes. Few if any doctrines of the general part are invulnerable to justified derogation. Neither is it especially profitable to look for a uniform or simple comprehensive structure to the criminal law. In part, this is because of the complex relationship between the general and the special parts. While we have denied that the relationship is hierarchical, general part doctrines do help to shape the more particular rules of the special part: but the interaction is two-way. Michael Moore has argued, for example, that omissions cannot be causes.[22] If that were true, in principle defendants could no longer be convicted of 'result crimes' by omission. But, regardless of Moore's analysis, the proposition that omissions cannot be causes does not belong within the general part because it is not true of the criminal law. Result crimes *can* be committed by omission. Where, earlier in this introduction, the general part was characterized as involving general doctrines that are not merely contingent, that was not to lose sight of the truth that, at least in part, the general part is *also* contingent. Doctrines governing the meaning of 'reckless' have their place in the general part—and essays about recklessness have their place in this volume[23]—only if recklessness is in fact a *mens rea* requirement of some particular offences. Try as academics may, the content of the general part cannot evade the shackles of legal fact.

This is not to say that apparent inconsistencies between the general and special parts are always to be resolved by revising the relevant general part doctrine. It may be, as we have noted, that a doctrine of the general part is

[19] Larry Alexander, Chapter 6 in this volume, 'Criminal Liability for Omissions: An Inventory of Issues'.

[20] cf. A.P. Simester, 'Why Omissions are Special' (1995) 1 Legal Theory 311.

[21] See, e.g., Andrew Ashworth (n. 14 above) para. 2.4; A.P. Simester and G.R. Sullivan (n. 14 above) para. 1.2(i)(b).

[22] Michael Moore, *Act and Crime* (Oxford, 1993) 267ff.

[23] See Victor Tadros, Chapter 10 in this volume, 'Recklessness and the Duty to Take Care'.

outweighed in a particular instance by other considerations. Those other considerations may themselves belong in either the general or the special part. Principles of parsimony in criminalization exist because the use of criminal prohibitions is, without further justification, onerous and undesirable. It does not follow that particular prohibitions are wrong. The injunction against murder, for instance, is justified. Moreover, its justification is both mediated by general part doctrines such as the harm principle and, at the same time, dependent upon the specific claims that murder is both harmful and wrong.

Whether countervailing considerations such as these, originating from either the general or the special part, are able to defeat a general part doctrine normally depends not only on their strength but also on the weight to be attached to the general part doctrine itself. This will, in turn, depend upon the justifications supporting that doctrine and upon the possible effects of other general or special part doctrines whose presence may augment its significance. The fact that doctrines of the general part sometimes combine in a way that allows the combination to carry greater weight than the sum of its component parts only serves to show how complicated the calculation can be.

At the same time, not every apparent inconsistency between the general and special parts dissolves upon closer inspection, or leads to revision of a general part doctrine. Suppose that, in an alternative version of *Nicholson* (say, *Nicholson₂*), D's conviction had been upheld by the Court of Appeal for failing to repeat, *per infinitum ad nauseum*, that she was now employed. Such a decision would have been open to *legal*, as well as moral, criticism, not only because the relevant general part doctrines were in principle applicable to the particular offence, and their application was not outweighed; but also because the status of those general part doctrines was not contingent upon the decision in *Nicholson₂*. Omissions doctrines have sufficient grip in legal fact to survive their violation in particular cases and, indeed, to remain a basis for criticism of those cases.

As so often with contingencies, vagueness is unavoidable. Recalling the maxim, *actus non facit reum nisi mens sit rea*, let us assume for a moment that it is a doctrine of the general part that criminal convictions are not to be inflicted upon defendants unless they are deserving of blame in respect of the *actus reus*. Bearing in mind the nature of the criminal law, the condemnatory resonance of a conviction, let us further stipulate that the doctrine is justified by compelling reasons; and that, although institutional considerations (e.g. the legal fact that 'proof' beyond reasonable doubt is sufficient to support a conviction) may result in marginal infringements of that doctrine, the reasons which underpin it do not easily admit of widespread or systematic derogation. Yet, in England and Wales, there are countless strict liability offences for which proof of a fault element is not required. So was our assumption correct? Is the general part doctrine we have just described *really* a legal doctrine as well as a moral one? The answer is probably yes, but that the doctrine does not apply to a group of offences that are loosely described as 'regulatory', or 'public welfare' offences[24]—where the element of censure accompanying a conviction is said to be relatively minor. But that answer, in turn, depends on whether a distinction can be drawn between 'regulatory' and 'truly criminal' offences, one that is not violated by English courts as a matter of course.

Strict liability doctrines supply a useful illustration of contingent, (arguably) undesirable, legal fact. The dependence of the general part upon laws should not blind us to the possibility of moral criticism, not only of specific laws, but also of general doctrines. One reason for criticizing the doctrines of strict liability is that they dispense with the culpability element that—given its public, condemnatory, nature—should be prerequisite to *any* criminal conviction. For the sake of discussion, consider some of the objections to strict liability:[25] if a clear distinction between 'regulatory' and 'truly criminal' offences cannot be drawn, or if that distinction fails to capture the public imagination, the moral authority of the criminal law is likely to be undermined by the extension of criminal liability to regulatory violations that prima facie could be controlled by civil sanctions; moreover, it is unjust to impose strict criminal liability, since the stigma of a criminal conviction should not be inflicted upon someone who is not blameworthy. These arguments exemplify a tension so often found in criminal law, in that they invoke non-contingent features of the criminal law in mounting objections[26] to its contingent doctrinal facts. Strict liability is true but wrong.

D. The Wrongness of Criminal Acts

At first glance, the 'true crime'/'regulatory offence' distinction may be likened to the one highlighted by Duff and Husak, between offences *mala in se* and offences *mala prohibita*. But while the divide in strict liability jurisprudence is correlated to the *mala in se/mala prohibita* divide, the two do not fully correspond. All regulatory offences are, we assume, *mala prohibita*, but not all offences *mala prohibita* are regulatory offences that lack a significant element of censure.

This warrants elaboration. An offence *malum in se* addresses conduct—say, øing—that is pre-legally wrong. Here, at least in part, the law acknowledges (rather than designates) the wrongfulness of that conduct through a declaration of criminalization. As Duff observes, a citizen's reasons not to ø rest primarily upon the character of øing itself, rather than upon the fact

---

[24] At least, not in England and Wales. In countries such as Canada, New Zealand, and for the most part Australia, 'strict liability' is interpreted as imposing liability on the basis of negligence, with the burden of disproving a presumption of negligence resting upon the defendant. In those jurisdictions, the blameworthiness doctrine is pervasive.

[25] cf. Chapter 2 below at 28.

[26] Or, as the case may be, endorsement—as in the case of the voluntariness doctrine, the justification of which is founded in the requirement of moral responsibility; where the need for moral responsibility is, in turn, grounded in the nature of the criminal law.

that øing is prohibited. To the extent that criminalization offers content-independent reasons not to ø, they tend to be swamped by the pre-legal reasons against øing.

By contrast, an offence *malum prohibitum* addresses conduct—say, ψing—that is not pre-legally wrong. Thus Duff distinguishes between dangerous driving (*malum in se*) and driving at 72 m.p.h. on a road where the speed limit is 70 (*malum prohibitum*).[27] The wrongness of the latter depends, in part, upon the fact that the law has prohibited it. But in saying this, we need to distinguish between different types of reason that the law may generate. One variety is prudential: the recusant who does not recognise the wrongness of ψing (or indeed of øing) may be offered incentives to refrain from so doing, in virtue of the fact that the criminal law attaches sanctions to its proscriptions. Secondly, the law may create content-independent reasons not to ψ that are grounded in the law's claim to authority. *Ceteris paribus*, individuals may have reason not to ψ to the extent that ψing would tend to undermine the authority of an otherwise valuable legal system. We cannot explore this very complex proposition here, save to note that reasons of this type are likely to be of residual importance. Much more commonly, offences *mala prohibita* invoke a third type of reason—that the offence serves, more or less indirectly, to protect or advance morally valuable ends. Suppose that a parking offence is created, not gratuitously but as an element of some more general transportation strategy. In such case the law acts as a conduit to the strategic objective. Correspondingly, individuals have grounds not to offend that rely not merely on the law's claim to be respected, but also on the value of that further objective. Similarly, but more directly, formal speed limits operate as practical *determinationes* of a more general injunction against dangerous driving.

It follows that even offences *mala prohibita* create reasons against ψing that are content-dependent. What distinguishes them from offences *mala in se* is that those reasons not to ψ are post- rather than pre-legal. What does *not* distinguish them is that offences *mala in se* are inherently morally wrong while those *mala prohibita* are inherently innocent. Certainly some acts *mala prohibita*, especially regulatory offences, are undeserving of moral condemnation. But that is by no means always true. Even though its wrongness depends on law, it is inherently wrong—because dangerous and inconsiderate—to drive, in England, on the right hand side of the road. Here the law supplies the determination of a moral norm. Indeed, as Alldridge points out in this volume, 'there is a series of offences where the fact of criminalization creates immorality';[28] for example, where the offences are designed to establish the rules by which a marketplace operates. The boundary between *mala in se* and *mala prohibita* is technical rather than 'moral': both types of offence may give rise to significant levels of censure.

---

27 See Chapter 3 below at 55.
28 Peter Alldridge, Chapter 5 in this volume, 'Making Criminal Law Known' at 109.

Against that backdrop, it is worth noticing Husak's claim that 'conduct that is innocent (such as eating pizza) cannot lose its innocence simply because a legislature has decided (and has a rational basis) to criminalize it'.[29] Suppose, as Husak conjectures, that a legislature decides to prohibit the eating of pizza on the grounds that pizza-eating is (let us concede) damaging the nation's health. Drawing upon well-known objections to strict liability, Husak claims that the criminal law ought not to criminalize 'innocent' conduct. This is unobjectionable when understood as a claim that the legislature ought to have good reasons whenever it criminalizes a type of conduct. But it is not an objection to criminalization that pizza-eating is 'innocent', in terms of what Husak calls 'extra-legal judgments of fault and innocence—those derived from somewhere other than the determinations of legislators'. *Per-se* innocent activities, like parking one's car or driving at 72 m.p.h., are frequently and legitimately criminalized; their prohibition can be justified by reference to the harm principle. The objection to criminalizing pizza-eating is not simply that pizza-eating is 'innocent'—a concern that can be addressed by a mistake of law defence—but that its prohibition would be paternalistic and unduly restrictive of individual freedom.

E. Conclusion

An informing thesis of this introduction has been negative: that the general part lacks uniformity. It is not simply the set of generalized, directly justiciable, doctrines known to criminal law. General part doctrines need not be mandatory—they may be advisory or, for that matter, permissive. They address not just adjudicators but also other officials, including legislators; the latter most obviously when they are doctrines of criminalization. Nor is the relationship between the general and special parts uniform or straightforward. Sometimes the general part is inflexible (e.g. doctrines of voluntariness, at least in principle): sometimes it admits of derogation (e.g. doctrines of omission, which allow both general and specific exceptions). The latter is typical, and criminal law judgments about the 'wrongness' ('innocence', culpability, etc.) of actions are normally the product of an interaction between the general and special parts. The proposition that murder is a culpable, harmful, wrong lies at the heart of murder's appearance in the special part; at the same time, its truth invokes permissive and mandatory general part doctrines. Murder is a qualitatively different act from, say, 'causing death' (or even 'causing death culpably'), and the reasons for that difference underpin its definition within the special part. Yet they do so legitimately only if they satisfy general part constraints that, in turn, are grounded in the nature of criminal law and the ends it serves.

---

[29] See Chapter 2 below at 29.

2

Limitations on Criminalization and the General Part of Criminal Law

DOUGLAS N. HUSAK*

In this chapter I will show how the general part of criminal law might be construed to include doctrines that place significant limitations on *criminalization*—on the kinds of conduct that may be subject to punishment in the special part of criminal law. In section A, I will explain why we need not embrace a conception of the general part that is neutral about the question of what conduct may be proscribed. In section B, I will discuss the motivation for including doctrines about criminalization in the general part of criminal law. In section C, I will describe limitations that might be derived from reflections about the nature of crime. In section D, I will suggest that the basis of hostility to strict liability might give rise to constraints on the content of offences. In section E, I will derive possible restrictions on criminalization from the need to justify punishment. In section F, I will indicate how the need to interpret and apply various defences from liability can preclude enactment of some criminal offences.

I will not endeavour to provide a detailed account of the specific laws that are incompatible with those doctrines I believe might be included in the general part. Of course, I will offer examples of how to apply the doctrines I will discuss. But the task of modifying the special part of criminal law to conform to these doctrines is a major undertaking that I will not begin here. The implications of these doctrines cannot always be developed without commitment to a normative theory that is not itself in the general part. But implications for criminalization that are theory-dependent are implications for criminalization nonetheless.

* I would like to thank Andrew Simester and Stephen Shute for providing a number of enormously valuable and helpful comments on an earlier draft of this chapter.

A. CRIMINALIZATION AND THE NATURE OF THE GENERAL PART

My topic is to explore some of the connections between the general and the special parts of criminal law. I argue that there is good reason to construe the general part to contain doctrines that have important implications for the issue of criminalization.[1] In other words, I contend that we should be able to derive from the general part substantial constraints on the kinds of conduct that can be subjected to criminal liability. Some of the limitations on criminalization I will discuss are not derived from doctrines that theorists readily locate in the general part. Thus the first step in my argument is to defend my claim that these doctrines *belong* in the general part. This defence will require a brief discussion of the nature of the general part of criminal law.

What exactly *is* the general part of criminal law? Criminal theorists have reached no consensus about this issue. Throughout recent history, commentators have provided very different rationales of what the general part of criminal law is thought to include and exclude.[2] Most scholarly contributions about the general part simply ignore this definitional dispute and proceed directly to a detailed examination of some topic or another that has long been regarded as belonging to the general part. I do not pretend to settle the definitional controversy here. My observations about the general part are designed only to show that the doctrines I will discuss—those with implications for criminalization—might be located there.[3]

Presumably, all theorists agree that the general part of criminal law consists in *general doctrines* or *generalizations*. These generalizations are (in some sense) *about* the special part of criminal law: substantive offences or crimes. Because these doctrines are generalizations about offences, any constraints on criminalization that can be derived from them will not be very direct and straightforward. They will not have the form 'the state cannot prohibit abortion' or 'the state cannot punish speech'. Restrictions like these are not generalizations about the special part, and thus could not be thought to belong to the general part of criminal law. Any implications for criminalization to be derived from doctrines in the general part must be somewhat less specific than the foregoing examples.

---

[1] No standard terminology exists to describe the various kinds of components in the general part of criminal law. These components include rules, doctrines, principles, defences, and the like. I use *doctrine* as the generic term to describe these several kinds of components.

[2] See Nicola Lacey, 'Contingency, Coherence, and Conceptualism' in Antony Duff (ed.), *Philosophy and the Criminal Law* (Cambridge, 1998) 9.

[3] I confess to some uncertainty about what is meant by saying that a given doctrine is *included* in the general part of criminal law. When criminal law is codified, the general doctrines I will cite might be law, and appear as statutes explicitly collected in a section of 'general doctrines'. See, e.g., the structure of the Model Penal Code, which is subdivided into 'General Doctrines' and 'Definitions of Specific Crimes'. When criminal law is not codified, however, the general doctrines I will cite may be law only insofar as they are components of the *best theory* of the special part of criminal law.

The nature and status of the generalizations in the general part remains open to enormous controversy. Reluctance to be precise about these generalizations is reflected in James Stephen's influential account of 'the general doctrines pervading the whole subject [of criminal law]'. According to Stephen, these general doctrines consist in a number of 'positive and 'negative' conditions, '*some* of which enter *more or less* into the definition of *nearly* all offences'.[4] Stephen's statement is virtually unintelligible. Still, theorists should sympathize with his predicament. Any account of the general part of criminal law that did not contain such imprecision would have failed to explain why Stephen focused on those doctrines he proceeded to discuss—or, I daresay, on those doctrines that theorists have discussed ever since.

In what *do* these generalizations about the special part consist? One possible answer is that the content of the general part is formulated simply by constructing inductive generalizations about the offences in the special part. To begin to construct such generalizations, we would need some criterion to identify those laws that qualify as criminal. Unless we knew which laws were criminal, we could hardly purport to generalize about them. Suppose that we adopt a *positivist* conception of the criminal law—criminal laws are whatever laws the legislature says are criminal laws. This positivistic conception of the special part yields a corresponding positivistic conception of the general part of criminal law. If the specific laws about which we generalize have whatever content the legislature chooses to give them, generalizations about such laws would be equally dependent on what the legislature has enacted. As new kinds of offences are enacted and old kinds of offences are repealed, generalizations about existing offences would have to be modified accordingly.

This positivistic conception of the special and general parts gives rise to what I call the *content-neutrality thesis*—the doctrines in the general part are *neutral* with respect to the question of what conduct may be criminalized.[5] Since the content of the general part is wholly dependent on what the legislature has enacted, it is hard to see how anything in the general part could be used to *object* to something in the special part. Theorists could point to a discrepancy between an old doctrine in the general part and a new offence in the special part, but any such conflict would have to be resolved by altering or qualifying the general doctrine. Do any theorists actually subscribe to this thesis, and hold the general part to be content-neutral? It is hard to be sure, since I am unaware of explicit discussions of whether limits on the content of

---

[4] James Stephen, *A History of the Criminal Law of England*, Vol. I (Macmillan, 1883), 3 (emphasis added).

[5] By 'conduct', I mean to include only acts, not culpability. Of course, the two are not always easy to distinguish. Clearly, however, the general part is not neutral with respect to culpability. Nor is it neutral about whether an act is required, or whether an act must be voluntary. These latter issues pertain to the *structure* of what is proscribed.

criminal offences can be derived from the general part.[6] Few criminal theorists appear to have thought about the matter, and thus have expressed no position one way or the other. At any rate, the content-neutrality thesis is worth considering and evaluating, whether or not it represents orthodoxy on the topic I investigate here.

Is the content-neutrality thesis adequate? Is the general part simply a product of inductive generalization about the offences in the special part? Can the general part really be neutral with respect to what can be included in the special part? Are there good reasons to interpret the general part so that it lacks implications for criminalization? Would changes in the special part really require theorists to revise the generalizations in the general part? Surely not. Admittedly, the content of the general part must have *some* connection to the offences in the special part. Its doctrines are not generalizations about an ideal criminal code; they are about *our* system of criminal law. Still, the content of the general part is not derived *simply* from inductive generalizations about the common features of specific offences.[7]

Many of the doctrines in the general part bear little relevance to the offences that actually make up the special part. This discrepancy becomes evident whether we begin by examining offences or by identifying doctrines. Suppose we start by examining offences. If we take as examples the criminal codes of many jurisdictions in the USA, we would come to think that the great bulk of crimes are traffic offences. Generalizations about existing crimes would necessarily reflect the characteristics of these offences. Most traffic offences, for example, are crimes of strict liability in the sense that no culpability is required for conviction. The emphasis that theorists of the general part place on culpability would be puzzling if the content of the general part were actually formed by generalizing from the statutes in existing criminal codes. Yet these very codes tend to contain 'general doctrines' that would instantly be recognizable to theorists who have written extensively about the general part of criminal law.

---

[6] I am indebted to Michael Moore for the name of the content-neutrality thesis. I am unsure, however, whether Moore actually *holds* this thesis. He describes 'what an area of law must possess if it is to have a distinction between a general part and a special part. It must possess a content-neutral theory—analogous to the theory of responsibility . . . To have such a content-neutral theory, an area of law must have a contrasting, content-laden theory . . . Criminal law has such a structure': Michael Moore, *Placing Blame* (Oxford, 1997) 34. I have reservations about attributing this thesis to Moore because I do not understand why he would believe that any distinction between a general and a special part of law *requires* the former to be neutral with respect to the latter. Why *must* the general part be neutral with respect to the special part in order to qualify as general?

[7] If I am correct that this account is inadequate, and the general part is not simply a product of inductive generalization about the special part, how *do* we arrive at the content of the general part? I do not try to answer this question here. In my more sceptical moments, I suspect that what knowledgeable theorists countenance as the general part of criminal law consists in nothing more than a hodge-podge of doctrines that have little more in common than that they have long been described as comprising the general part.

We reach this same conclusion if we start by examining doctrines. Several of the doctrines in the general part apply to only a handful of offences in the special part, and thus could hardly be thought to belong to the general part because they are generalizations about these offences. The doctrines governing causation may be the best examples of this phenomenon. All criminal theorists, to my knowledge, treat the issue of causation in the general part of criminal law. At the same time, only a small minority of offences (most notably homicide offences) are 'result crimes' that require a causal connection between conduct and result. Doctrines governing causation are in the general part, but not because they apply to nearly all offences in the special part.

More importantly, theorists use doctrines in the general part for purposes that could not be served if their content were simply a product of inductive generalization. Theorists use the general part *normatively*. No alteration in the general part is needed simply because a new kind of offence is enacted with features that provide a counterexample to a doctrine in the general part. Instead, the doctrine might well be used to form the basis of an *objection* to the inclusion of the new kind of offence. This normative function could not be served unless the doctrines in the general part were thought to constrain the features that may be included in newly enacted crimes. Normative objections would make no sense if the general part were simply an inductive generalization from existing criminal offences. If the neutrality thesis were true, and new kinds of crimes were enacted, the generalizations in the special part would have to be changed—or (as in Stephen's account) qualified to allow for exceptions.

We can take a different route to appreciating the normative dimension of the principles in the general part. Jerome Hall provided a somewhat different response to Stephen's predicament. Hall recognized that meaningful and reasonably coherent generalizations about criminal offences were possible only if theorists were *selective* in picking the crimes from which they generalized.[8] But on what basis should this process of selection take place? Which crimes should be included or excluded? Even if we agree that such laws as traffic offences should be put aside because they are 'violations' rather than 'true crimes', we still must decide on some criteria of inclusion. Suppose that this selection procedure were based on empirical data about the actual business of criminal justice—on those crimes that are actually enforced most frequently. We would not generalize from, say, blackmail, since the number of prosecutions for blackmail offences is very small.[9] By this empirical criterion, drug offences—and the offence of drug possession in particular—would be typical crimes from which to construct generalizations. But anyone familiar with the work of theorists who write about the general part of criminal law is

---

[8] See Jerome Hall, *General Principles of Criminal Law* (2nd edn., Indianapolis, 1960) 2–4.

[9] Of course, theorists have employed very different devices to identify typical crimes from which to generalize. See, e.g., George Fletcher, 'Blackmail: The Paradigmatic Crime' (1993) 141 University of Pennsylvania Law Review 1617.

aware that drug offences are rarely mentioned.[10] Entire treatises on criminal law have been published in which 'drugs' (or some comparable entry) fails to appear in the text or index.[11] Possessory offences are not regarded as paradigm crimes, but are actually treated as somewhat non-standard or deviant. Thus the selection process is not empirical, and probably has little to do with actual criminal practice. Instead, normative considerations govern the selection process. Theorists generalize from offences that contain those features we believe *should* be included in crimes in the special part of criminal law. Generalizations about these offences will necessarily incorporate those normative features that led theorists to select these crimes in the first place.

I conclude that the doctrines in the general part of criminal law are not simply inductive generalizations about the offences in the special part, but have a normative dimension. At the very least, this normative dimension is designed to place restrictions on what might be called the *structure* of crimes in the special part. Offences in the special part, whatever their content—whatever conduct they proscribe—must include a voluntary act, for example.[12] We are all familiar with the disapproval that greets crimes of strict liability, or which suspend the ordinary principles of causation.[13]

I belabour the conclusion that the general part has a normative dimension because I want to expand on it. If doctrines in the general part function to limit the structure of offences in the special part—as surely is the case—then why can't these doctrines also function to constrain the *conduct* that can be

---

[10] Among criminal theorists in the USA, the failure to construct generalizations that are sensitive to the peculiar features of drug offences probably reflects the enormous influence of the Model Penal Code. The Code itself does not include drug offences. Perhaps this omission is the best indication that its special part needs to be updated. Or perhaps this omission should remind us that drug offences are not needed. Drug offences are the sensible place to begin if we really are serious about narrowing the reach of the criminal sanction. See Douglas Husak, *Drugs and Rights* (Cambridge, 1992).

[11] Consider, e.g., the recent edition of Wayne LaFave, *Criminal Law* (3rd edn., St. Paul, 2000). He continues to subdivide offences into 'Crimes Against the Person' (ch. 7) and 'Crimes Relating to Property' (ch. 8). This organizational device provides no clear location for drug offences, which are discussed only insofar as intoxication affects *mens rea*.

[12] Perhaps *no* doctrine in the general part is without exceptions. The requirement of a voluntary act may or may not allow for exceptions, depending on how one interprets the claim that offences must *include* a voluntary act. Some theorists believe that this requirement can be manipulated to guarantee that it will have no exceptions. See Mark Kelman, 'Interpretive Construction in the Substantive Criminal Law' (1981) 33 Stanford Law Review 591.

[13] These protests are not merely hypothetical, but are raised against actual offences. Commentators have tended grudgingly to accept strict liability when used in the context of so-called regulatory offences with relatively minor penalties. But some jurisdictions impose strict liability for serious crimes that allow very severe punishments. New Jersey has enacted a variety of homicide that explicitly dispenses with a requirement of culpability. New Jersey Criminal Code, s. 2C:35–9, provides that a person who distributes a Schedule I controlled substance is 'strictly liable for a death which results from the injection, inhalation or ingestion of that substance'. This same statute provides that 'the doctrines of [that statute governing the causal relationship between conduct and result] shall not apply in a prosecution under this section'. Each of these features is inconsistent with doctrines in the general part of criminal law. Such inconsistencies are not intolerable, but should be allowed only if a special justification is provided.

criminalized? Why suppose that the normative dimension of these doctrines extends only so far, but is exhausted before it reaches the question of what conduct can be proscribed? Some of the objections to given structural features of offences form a cogent basis of opposition to the content of offences—or so I will argue. Admittedly, most (and perhaps all) of the doctrines I will cite that limit the reach of the criminal sanction allow for exceptions. But the same is true of each doctrine in the general part.[14] In short, nothing about the nature of the general part of criminal law entails that no constraints on criminalization can be found there.

Much of my motivation for locating restrictions on criminalization in the general part of criminal law stems from uncertainty about where *else* they might be located. Obviously, these restrictions cannot belong in the special part. If no such doctrines are included in the general part, they will have a hard time finding a place in criminal law at all.[15] It is an appalling prospect that professors might teach and students might learn about both the general and special parts of criminal law without paying any attention to the crucial issue of what conduct should or should not be criminalized.[16] Those who hope to find a place for the topic of criminalization within the parameters of criminal law should be receptive to my suggestion that some such limitations can be derived from the general part.[17] I have argued that nothing about how we identify the doctrines in the general part shows this hope to be misguided.

B. Overcriminalization and the Response of Criminal Theorists

I speculated that few criminal theorists appear to have thought much about what I called the content-neutrality thesis. Perhaps my conjecture is mistaken.

[14] If exceptions to a given doctrine are too numerous, we undermine the basis for including it in the general part of the criminal law we actually have. See text accompanying n.60 below.

[15] Of course, many and perhaps most restrictions on criminalization are located in other disciplines. Many such limitations are found in political philosophy. Many political theorists, for example, defend *liberalism*. Some liberals claim that the state should be *neutral* with respect to conceptions of the good. This claim gives rise to significant limitations on criminalization. For a recent discussion of the implications of this claim for drug offences, see Douglas Husak, 'Liberal Neutrality, Autonomy, and Drug Prohibitions' (2000) 29 *Philosophy & Public Affairs* 43.

[16] This 'appalling prospect' accurately describes nearly all criminal law courses taught in law schools throughout the USA today. The *Instructor's Manual* to the most widely-used casebook in criminal law (Sanford Kadish and Stephen Schulhofer, *Criminal Law and Its Processes* (6th edn., Boston, 1995)) recommends that the brief materials on 'What to Punish?' should be skipped in a one-semester course. Unfortunately, virtually all law school courses in criminal law span only a single semester.

[17] Doctrines in the general part are more likely to have implications for criminalization if they exert a 'homogenizing, rather than diversifying pressure'. For reasons to doubt that these doctrines exert homogenizing pressures, see John Gardner, 'On the General Part of the Criminal Law' in Antony Duff (ed.), *Philosophy and the Criminal Law* (Cambridge, 1998) 205. At the same time, Gardner explicitly allows doctrines in what he calls the *supervisory* general part to have a 'bearing on . . . criminalisation . . . itself': ibid. at 208.

But many criminal theorists who have made valuable contributions to our understanding of particular doctrines in the general part of criminal law have said very little about the topic of criminalization. Despite its central importance, criminalization remains the single most widely neglected issue among contemporary criminal theorists.[18]

Many contemporary debates about criminalization continue to focus on issues raised in the exchange some 40 years ago between Lord Devlin and H.L.A. Hart about 'the enforcement of morality'.[19] Few theorists are persuaded that immorality is sufficient for criminalization; most believe that harm is required.[20] This debate is seemingly relevant to so-called 'morals offences' such as homosexuality and prostitution. But much of the controversy about these offences can be attributed to disagreement about whether the proscribed conduct is really immoral.[21] These debates still engage legal philosophers.[22] But their resolution, however crucial for other purposes, may do little to address the problem of overcriminalization I will describe in this section. Much of the recent expansion of the criminal law is due to the enactment of (so-called) regulatory offences.[23] Many of these crimes appear to have little to do with morality.[24] Theorists can agree about whether the criminal law should enforce morality while continuing to disagree about whether these various offences are proper uses of the criminal sanction.

The criminal law urgently needs constraints on criminalization. In the USA, the absence of accepted constraints has led to what is frequently described as a *crisis of overcriminalization*.[25] According to some estimates,

---

[18] The work of Andrew Ashworth provides the most important exception to my generalization. In his *Principles of Criminal Law* (2nd edn., Oxford, 1995), Ashworth responds to the 'tendency' he detects in 'writings on English criminal law' to 'devote little attention to the rightness or wrongness of criminalizing certain conduct' (at 22). Although he explicitly disavows the search for 'some general theory which will enable us to tell whether or not certain conduct should be criminalized', he proceeds to 'identify some principles that may tell for or against making conduct criminal' (at 22). His efforts to defend 'minimalism' are most welcome, and cohere nicely with my endeavours here. I should point out that Ashworth's observations about the tendencies of English writers are even more trenchant about their counterparts in the USA. Textbooks in the USA that are roughly comparable to Ashworth's typically neglect the topic of criminalization altogether. For an important exception from Europe, see n.39 below.

[19] Patrick Devlin, *The Enforcement of Morals* (Oxford, 1965); and H.L.A. Hart, *Law, Liberty, and Morality* (Oxford, 1963).

[20] For the best contemporary defence of the claim that *harm* is required, see Joel Feinberg, *Harm to Others* (Oxford, 1984).

[21] Thus, Ronald Dworkin famously responds: 'What is shocking and wrong is not [Devlin's] idea that the community's morality counts, but his idea of what counts as the community's morality'. See his 'Lord Devlin and the Enforcement of Morals', in Richard Wasserstrom (ed.), *Morality and the Law* (Belmont, 1971) 55 at 69.

[22] See, e.g., Gerald Dworkin, 'Devlin Was Right: Law and the Enforcement of Morality' (1999) 40 William and Mary Law Review 927.

[23] See the examples provided in Andrew Ashworth, 'Is the Criminal Law a Lost Cause?' (2000) 116 Law Quarterly Review 225, 227–228.

[24] See nn. 116–118 below.

[25] This allegation can be traced to Sanford Kadish, 'The Crisis of Overcriminalization' (1967) 374 *Annals of the American Academy of Political and Social Science* 157.

approximately 300,000 federal regulations are punishable as crimes by the combined efforts of as many as 200 different federal agencies.[26] Perhaps 8,000 different criminal statutes exist in England.[27] These numbers are bound to rise, as criminal statutes are easily enacted but seldom repealed. The phenomenon of overcriminalization has contributed to an excessive amount of punishment. In the USA, more than 2 million persons are incarcerated in prisons and jails. This figure has quadrupled since 1980, as the rate of incarceration relative to the population has grown to 682 per 100,000 residents.[28] Since only about 8 million persons are incarcerated in the world, one-quarter of these are jailed or imprisoned in the USA. An estimated one in 20 children in the USA is destined to serve time in a state or federal prison at some point in his life.[29]

These figures are shocking. Why have criminal theorists been so complacent about the related problems of too many criminal laws and too much punishment? The lack of an adequate theory about the limits of the criminal sanction probably reflects the longstanding obsession in legal philosophy with the judiciary and, in the USA, with the Constitution. Theorists tend to address those matters that can be argued before a judge. In a criminal court in the USA, one can argue that the legislature has overstepped its bounds only by citing some constitutional doctrine that has been breached. But few of the limits on the scope of the substantive criminal law appear to have a constitutional basis.[30] Let me pause here to describe what the Constitution has to say about the limits of the criminal law. I discuss this matter both to reveal its inadequacies, and—in section E below—to begin to build a better theory of criminalization on its foundations.

Allow me to oversimplify a little. Most laws burden (that is, limit or restrict) liberties. When the constitutionality of these laws is challenged, courts respond by dividing liberties into two kinds: *fundamental* and *non-fundamental.*[31] Some liberties (e.g., speech) are fundamental because they are explicitly enumerated in the Constitution. Other liberties (e.g., marriage) are fundamental because they are said to be 'implicit in the concept of ordered liberty'. The constitutionality of legislation that burdens a fundamental liberty

---

[26] See Susan Pilcher, 'Ignorance, Discretion and the Fairness of Notice: Confronting "Apparent Innocence" in the Criminal Law' (1995) 33 American Criminal Law Review 32.

[27] A.P. Simester and G.R. Sullivan, *Criminal Law: Theory and Doctrine* (Oxford, 2000) 44.

[28] Bureau of Justice Statistics, U.S. Department of Justice, *Sourcebook of Criminal Justice Statistics* (27th edn., 2000) Table 6.19.

[29] Thomas Bonczar and Allen Beck, *Lifetime Likelihood of Going to State or Federal Prison* (Bureau of Justice Statistics, U.S. Department of Justice, 1997).

[30] As Stephen Shute points out, only five constitutional provisions directly limit the content of the substantive criminal law in the USA: the First Amendment, the Eighth Amendment, the Fourteenth Amendment, the Fifth Amendment, and sections 9[3] and 10[1] of Article 1. See his 'With and Without Constitutional Restraints: A Comparison Between the Criminal Law of England and America' (1998) 1 Buffalo Criminal Law Review 329.

[31] One oversimplification is that contemporary constitutional law now appears to divide liberties into *three* kinds. For a more detailed elaboration, see Erwin Chemerinsky, *Constitutional Law: Principles and Policies* (New York, 1997) 414–417; 533–545.

is subjected to 'strict scrutiny', and is evaluated by applying the 'compelling state interest' test. Under this test, the challenged law will be upheld only if it is necessary to achieve a compelling government purpose. In other words, the government's purpose must be essential, and the law must be necessary to accomplish that purpose. A law is not necessary unless it is the least restrictive means to attain its objective. The constitutionality of legislation that burdens a non-fundamental liberty, on the other hand, is evaluated by applying the much less demanding 'rational basis' test. Under this test, the challenged law will be upheld only if it is substantially related to a legitimate government purpose. The legitimate government purpose need not be the actual objective of the legislation—only its conceivable objective.[32] Since only those laws that lack a conceivable legitimate purpose will fail this test, courts almost never find a law to be unconstitutional when non-fundamental liberties are burdened.[33]

Virtually all criminal laws burden non-fundamental liberties and thus are assessed by the rational basis test. As a result, the state needs only some conceivable legitimate purpose to enact the great majority of criminal laws on our books today. Persons who break these laws can be punished simply because the state has a rational basis to do so. Moreover, punishments can be (and often are) severe, since courts have decided not to apply a test of proportionality to ensure that the severity of punishments reflects the seriousness of offences.[34] The rational basis test produces a startling departure from what should be demanded before punishment can be imposed. A person's life can be ruined—he can spend his remaining years in prison—simply because he engaged in conduct that the state proscribed with only a rational basis.

Of course, the state needs an extraordinary rationale to punish persons who exercise fundamental liberties. The Constitution effectively precludes the state from criminalizing marriage, prayer, or political speech, for example. Outside the narrow range of fundamental liberties, however, it is only a slight exaggeration to say that the state can decide to criminalize almost anything.[35] A hypothetical case may help to demonstrate the extent of state power in the criminal arena—and the potential injustice of this power. Suppose that legislators become dismayed at the fact that too many persons are unhealthy and overweight. Initially, they decide to facilitate the efforts of consumers to eat a better diet by enacting legislation requiring distributors of

[32] See *Federal Communications Commission v Beach Communication*, 113 S.Ct. 2096 (1993).

[33] Some have protested that judicial review under this test is 'tantamount to no review at all': ibid. at 2106 (Stevens J, concurring).

[34] See *Harmelin v Michigan* 501 U.S. 957 (1991). Capital punishment, however, is an exception to this generalization. Proportionality review is alive and well when the death sentence is imposed. See, e.g., *Coker v Georgia*, 433 U.S. 584 (1977) (capital punishment an unconstitutional punishment for rape).

[35] Of course, the rational basis test creates *some* limitations on legislation. See, e.g., *Romer v Evans*, 116 S.Ct. 1620 (1996) (mere animus toward homosexuals held not to be a rational basis for discriminating against them).

fast foods to display nutritional information on their packaging. If the constitutionality of this law were challenged, it would seem appropriate for courts to defer to legislators by invoking the rational basis test. Suppose, however, that legislators come to believe (as is probably the case) that better information has little impact on the problem of obesity. Imagine that legislators decide to prohibit—on pain of criminal liability—the consumption of a list of unhealthy foods. Suppose that pizza is placed on this list. Once again, the rational basis test would be applied to assess the constitutionality of this law. I see no constitutional difficulty with this hypothetical crime, since the liberty to eat pizza does not seem to qualify as fundamental.[36] The state has an uncontested interest in protecting health, and it is at least conceivable that proscribing the eating of pizza bears a substantial relation to that interest. Of course, many foods are more detrimental to health than pizza. In addition, not all pizzas are detrimental to health. But the fact that a criminal law is underinclusive and/or overinclusive is not regarded as a constitutional impediment under the rational basis test. In other words, a statute need not proscribe each instance of conduct that contributes to the statutory objective, and may proscribe some instances of conduct that do not contribute to the statutory objective.[37] Indeed, I see nothing in the Constitution as it is presently interpreted that precludes the state from sentencing persons to life imprisonment for the crime of eating pizza.

What is remarkable about the above theory is its complete indifference to the distinction between criminal and non-criminal legislation. It is one thing for non-criminal regulations that burden non-fundamental liberties to be evaluated by the rational basis test. But it is quite another when criminal legislation is assessed by that same test. Criminal liability is *different*—importantly dissimilar from other kinds of legal sanctions. Unless criminal liability were different, we would be at a loss to understand the exceptional protections the state affords to defendants in the context of criminal procedure. These procedural protections make sense only on the assumption that criminal law is unlike other bodies of law.[38] To a great extent, that assumption is correct. Historically, at least, the business of the criminal law has been important. But this assumption becomes increasingly problematic when criminal statutes are enacted with only a rational basis.

No one could sensibly believe that the Constitution, as so interpreted, provides an adequate theory of criminalization. We have become far too cavalier about punishment. Persons should not be punished at all (and certainly not punished severely) simply because the state has enacted a statute with only a

---

[36] Whether it is plausible to construe this liberty as fundamental depends largely on the level of generality used to describe the liberty that is burdened. The liberty to eat whatever food one prefers is a better candidate for a fundamental liberty than is the liberty to eat any given food such as pizza.

[37] See Chemerinsky (n.31 above) at 543.

[38] See William Stuntz, 'Substance, Process, and the Civil-Criminal Line' (1996) 7 Journal of Contemporary Legal Issues 1.

rational basis—a conceivable legitimate objective the statute might serve. No one should be surprised that this test has contributed to our current crisis of overcriminalization. This test provides virtually no check on the tendency to respond to any and all social problems by enacting criminal legislation.[39] In section E below, I will indicate how the deficient constitutional account I have sketched here might be used to construct a better theory of criminalization. But I do not insist that the theory I will provide is of constitutional stature.[40] I take no position on how the doctrines I will cite should be enforced. I am noncommittal about whether these doctrines—which I think should be included in the general part of criminal law—provide a basis for a court in the USA to exercise its power of judicial review and find a statute to be unconstitutional. These doctrines might be addressed directly to legislators. They describe limits that should be respected in the initial determination to employ the criminal sanction to prohibit conduct. Infringements of these doctrines might give rise to the same reaction as now takes place when the legislature enacts a law that infringes a doctrine in the general part. This reaction consists mostly in opposition from scholars, commentators, and theorists. To what extent this opposition can be expected to have a significant impact in actually reversing the trends toward overcriminalization and overincarceration is a different matter altogether.[41]

C. Limitations Derived from the Nature of Crime

I now begin my discussion of some of the limitations on criminalization that might be derived from doctrines in the general part of criminal law. The constraints I mention in this section are based on what might be called *the nature of crime*. Return to the foundational question I posed above: what *is* the criminal law? Although theorists have evaded this question more often than they have tried to answer it, the positivistic theory I mentioned above is probably the most familiar response. As Henry Hart lamented long ago, a crime seems to be 'anything which is called a crime'.[42] A better answer is needed.[43] The alternative I favour construes the criminal law as that body of law that subjects

---

[39] For a model to retard this unfortunate tendency, see Nils Jareborg, 'What Kind of Criminal Law Do We Want?' in Annika Snare (ed.), *Beware of Punishment* (Oslo, 1995) 17.

[40] Not every defect in a statute need be of constitutional stature. See Ronald Allen, 'Forward: Montana v. Egelhoff—Reflections on the Limits of Legislative Imagination and Judicial Authority' (1997) 87 Journal of Criminal Law and Criminology 633.

[41] Even when a conflict between a general doctrine and a particular offence is apparent, legislators have been able to reconcile this discrepancy simply by explicitly providing that the general doctrine should be disregarded. See, e.g., n.13 above.

[42] Henry Hart, 'The Aims of the Criminal Law' (1958) 23 Law and Contemporary Problems 401 at 404.

[43] See Claire Finkelstein, 'Positivism and the Notion of an Offense' (2000) 88 California Law Review 335.

offenders to *punishment*.[44] Support (admittedly inconclusive) for this conception of the criminal law—as that body of law that subjects offenders to punishment—can be gained by generalizing from offences in the special part.

Each statute in the Model Penal Code, for example—and statutes in codes throughout the USA that are adapted from it—contains provisions that assign it to a class that stipulates how offenders are to be sentenced.[45] If we understand these sentences as punishments, it follows that if a law is a criminal law, then it subjects offenders to punishment.[46] This conclusion would establish half of the biconditional in the conception of the criminal law I adopt here.[47] What of the other half? Why suppose that if a law subjects offenders to punishment, then that law is a criminal law? The answer stems from another doctrine already conceded to be in the general part—the principle of legality. Punishment cannot be imposed unless a crime has been committed.[48] This principle, together with the preceding conditional, establishes the conception I endorse here—a law is criminal if and only if it subjects offenders to punishment.

I readily concede the possibility that this conception must be qualified to allow for exceptions. Perhaps some laws are criminal even though they do not subject violators to punishment; perhaps some punishments are imposed for violations of laws that are not criminal.[49] To concede either or both of these possibilities does not show that the conception I have proposed is false or

---

[44] No conception of the nature of the criminal law is unproblematic. A systematic defence of the foregoing conception would require a critical assessment of alternatives and a detailed response to objections. Although I believe that no better conception is available, I will not endeavour to support that claim here.

[45] Model Penal Code, s. 1.04(1) classifies offences as felonies, misdemeanours, or petty misdemeanours. Section 1.04(5) adds a category of violations, said not to be crimes. Article 6 further subdivides offences into various degrees. The Code itself almost never uses the word 'punishment'.

[46] One commentator provides a host of citations to support his claim that 'a crime is made up of two parts, forbidden conduct and a prescribed penalty. The former without the latter is no crime': LaFave (n.11 above) at 9.

[47] A counterargument can be given. To formulate a general part, we need not only a criterion to identify what laws are criminal laws, but also a criterion to decide what to include in the content of those laws we identify as criminal. Arguably, those provisions in statutes that sort them into classes and stipulate how offenders are to be sentenced are *not* part of the content of offences. Clearly, these provisions are not *material elements* of offences. If these provisions in statutes are not part of their content, generalizations from them might not be included in the general part.

[48] Again, a counterargument can be given. Several different formulations of the principle of legality are available. Perhaps this principle states only that crimes must be created by the legislature, and says nothing about *punishment*.

[49] I will not provide examples either of criminal laws that do not subject violators to punishment, or of punishments that are imposed for conduct that is not criminal. I concede only that these are *possibilities*; no example is uncontroversial. H.L.A. Hart referred to instances of punishment imposed for non-criminal violations as 'sub-standard or secondary cases' of punishment. See his 'Prolegomenon to the Principles of Punishment' in his *Punishment and Responsibility* (Oxford, 1968) 5. Whether or not we adopt Hart's terminology, my point is that we may concede that this conception allows for exceptions while still including it in the general part of criminal law.

should be excluded from the general part.[50] Most and perhaps all of the doctrines in the general part allow for exceptions. The claim that liability to punishment is the distinctive feature of the criminal law is at least as accurate a generalization about the special part as are most of the doctrines acknowledged to belong in the general part.

Philosophers who defend the content-neutrality thesis might hold that the foregoing conception—which identifies the criminal law as that body of law that subjects offenders to punishment—has no implications whatever for the issue of what can be criminalized. According to this train of thought, a state may criminalize *any* conduct at all, simply by deciding to punish those who engage in it. But this position is problematic. Its weakness emerges by asking: *what is punishment?* More specifically, how should we decide whether given kinds of sanctions—revocation of a licence, deportation, civil commitment, termination of a benefit, and the like—are modes of punishment?[51] This question is important not only to philosophers. Persons are guaranteed a number of procedural protections when they are subjected to criminal liability and punishment, but not otherwise. Clearly, we cannot simply reply that punishment involves hard treatment, deprivation, or consequences normally regarded as unpleasant, even though these claims are true.[52] Each of the above examples satisfies this condition; this reply will not help us to decide whether and under what circumstances these sanctions are instances of punishment.

The most promising answer to this question is that punishment—whatever else it may be—expresses *condemnation*.[53] Sanctions should not be classified as modes of punishment unless they convey disapproval or blame.[54] It is hard to see how a sanction can convey disapproval or blame unless it is imposed for conduct that is disapproved and blameworthy.[55] As many commentators have noted, a tax cannot be distinguished from a fine without supposing that

[50] My proposed conception is sometimes criticized, *inter alia*, on this ground. See, e.g., Simester and Sullivan (n.27 above) at 4.

[51] The Supreme Court has struggled with this very difficult question. One commentator describes the Court's answer as 'an incoherent muddle . . . so inconsistent that it borders on the unintelligible': Wayne Logan, 'The Ex Post Facto Clause and the Jurisprudence of Punishment' (1998) 35 American Criminal Law Review 1261, at 1268 and 1280.

[52] The most well-known definition of punishment includes these components. See Hart (n.49 above) at 4–5.

[53] Arguably, the view that punishment expresses condemnation can be inferred from the 'for' relation in Hart's definition of punishment. We cannot decide whether punishment is 'for an offence' without understanding that punishment expresses condemnation. See ibid. at 5. Whether or not this view can be derived from Hart's definition, it is defended elsewhere. See Joel Feinberg, 'The Expressive Function of Punishment' (1965) 49 Monist 397; also Andrew von Hirsch, *Censure and Sanction* (Oxford, 1993).

[54] See the discussion in George Fletcher, *Basic Concepts of Criminal Law* (New York, 1998) ch. 2.

[55] In a particular case, it may be possible for a sanction to convey condemnation without being imposed for conduct that merits condemnation. Again, doctrines in the general part may have exceptions. As a general matter, however, sanctions cannot convey condemnation unless the conduct for which they are imposed is condemnable.

the latter is attached to conduct to be condemned.[56] If I am correct, the general part of criminal law should contain a doctrine with important implications for criminalization: only conduct worthy of condemnation may be punished. Of course, the implications of this doctrine for the content of the special part of criminal law cannot be developed without a normative theory of the circumstances under which conduct merits condemnation. But to say that a theory is required to trace the implications of this doctrine is a far cry from saying that it lacks implications. Not just *any* conduct can be criminalized simply by deciding to 'punish' it. Unless conduct merits condemnation, the sanction will not clearly be recognized as a punishment.

The implications of this doctrine for the special part of criminal law could range from modest to radical, depending on the theory of condemnation that is used to apply it. Some disagreements about whether and under what circumstances conduct merits condemnation seem intractable.[57] The challenge for criminal theorists is to decide what to do in the face of these disagreements, rather than to decide what to do in the unlikely event that these disagreements are finally resolved.[58] The pressing issue is to identify *whose* judgements of condemnation should be decisive in applying this doctrine.[59] But the content-neutrality thesis should be rejected, regardless of whose judgements are ultimately selected.

A tension clearly exists between the doctrine I have described and the basis I have defended for locating it in the general part of criminal law. A doctrine belongs in the general part only if it qualifies as a reasonably accurate generalization about offences in the special part. No doctrine can be an accurate generalization when exceptions become too numerous. Once the number of exceptions crosses a given threshold, perhaps we should say that the general part *should* include the doctrine I have described, rather than say that the general part actually includes this doctrine. It is hard to identify the exact point at which this doctrine (along with others) is no longer sufficiently accurate as a descriptive generalization to belong to the general part of the criminal law we already have, rather than to the general part of the criminal law we might prefer to have. The problem of overcriminalization I discussed in section B above indicates that we may have crossed this elusive threshold already. We have enacted too many criminal offences that do not seem to merit condemnation from any reasonable perspective.[60] The criminal law may well be a

---

[56] See Hart (n.49 above) at 6–8.

[57] Some research suggests that such disagreements are surprisingly infrequent in the criminal arena—at least about the relative seriousness of different crimes. See Marvin Wolfgang and N. Weiner, *Criminal Violence* (Beverly Hills, 1982).

[58] For further thoughts on this topic, see Jeremy Waldron, *Law and Disagreement* (Oxford, 1999).

[59] Several alternatives exist. See my discussion of this problem in the context of criminal law defences in section F below.

[60] See nn.116–118 below.

'lost cause'.[61] At this late stage, we may be unable to reverse the trend toward overcriminalization by applying a doctrine that allows only conduct worthy of condemnation to be punished—a doctrine we have increasingly less basis for including in the general part of the criminal law that actually exists.

D. LIMITATIONS DERIVED FROM HOSTILITY TO STRICT LIABILITY

The nature of crime is not the sole source of the doctrine that allows only conduct worthy of condemnation to be punished. This doctrine has a well-established place in the general part, as theorists have long cited it to object to the imposition of *strict liability* in the criminal law.[62] According to standard definitions, liability is strict when it dispenses with a culpability requirement for a material element of an offence, and liability without culpability is liability without blame or fault. The imposition of strict liability has attracted scholarly opposition for a straightforward reason: 'It is wrong to convict the innocent. To do so is a misuse of the criminal law, the most condemnatory institution available to society. If someone does not deserve to be convicted then they should not be. To convict innocent people violates the most basic tenet of criminal liability'.[63] These complaints about strict liability are familiar. What is less often acknowledged, however, is that the same problems that bother theorists about strict liability arise *whenever* the law punishes persons who are blameless, even while including a culpability requirement in the conduct for which they are liable. In other words, the very considerations invoked against strict liability have far more sweeping implications than theorists tend to recognize.

Return to my example of criminalizing the consumption of pizza—which I suggested would have a rational basis and thus satisfy what passes for a theory of criminalization under the Constitution of the USA. Suppose that this hypothetical statute did not attach a requirement of culpability to each material element. Commentators who oppose strict liability would protest. But amending this statute to include a culpability requirement would hardly rectify what is objectionable about it. In other words, this statute would not overcome the real problems with strict liability simply by adding a culpable state such as negligence to each material element. If negligence were required for each material element, a defendant would not be liable for the crime of consuming pizza unless a reasonable person in his situation would be aware that what he was doing was consuming, and that what he was consuming was

---

[61] See Ashworth (n.23 above). For further thoughts, see Douglas Husak, 'Retribution in Criminal Theory' (2000) 37 San Diego Law Review 959.

[62] One commentator concludes that 'the dominant view appears to be that in the Anglo-American culture, the use of strict liability crimes is arbitrary and unreasonable': Laurie Levenson, 'Good Faith Defenses: Reshaping Strict Liability Crimes' (1993) 78 Cornell Law Review 401, at 403 n.7.

[63] Simester and Sullivan (n.27 above) at 173.

pizza.[64] Amending the statute to include this (or indeed, any other) culpability requirement would represent little progress in meeting the objection to strict liability.[65] The far more serious problem is *what* conduct the statute proscribes, not the lack of culpability in proscribing it. The insertion of a culpability requirement is barely significant if the conduct should not have been criminalized in the first place. Of what importance are requirements of culpability if virtually anything can be made a criminal offence?

If objections to strict liability are sensible, there must be *some* limits on criminalization.[66] The worry that strict liability offences will punish the innocent is cogent only on the assumption that the innocent will *not* be punished if the strict liability offence is altered so that culpability is required for each element. This assumption is plausible only if the altered offence proscribes conduct that is blameworthy and worthy of condemnation. When conduct is punished that is not blameworthy, it is relatively unimportant to alter the offence so that it no longer imposes strict liability.

What exactly do commentators mean by 'innocence' when they protest that a strict liability offence punishes innocent conduct, but are satisfied that 'fault' is required whenever the offence includes a culpability requirement? They cannot be employing positivistic conceptions of innocence or fault. According to these conceptions, conduct is faulty if the legislature has decided to proscribe it, and innocent if the legislature has decided not to proscribe it. Positivism, however, is no more acceptable in this context than elsewhere. If conduct were faulty whenever the legislature proscribed it, the decision to enact a crime of strict liability, and punish conduct without a culpability requirement, would ensure that persons lack innocence when they commit the offence. But conduct that is innocent (such as eating pizza) cannot lose its innocence simply because a legislature has decided (and has a rational basis) to criminalize it.[67] *Extra-legal* judgements of fault and innocence—those

---

[64] See the definition of negligence in Model Penal Code, s. 2.02(2)(d).

[65] One way to express this point is to say that the inclusion of culpability would result in a 'formal rather than a substantive kind of fault'. See Kenneth Simons, 'When Is Strict Criminal Liability Just?' (1997) 87 Journal of Criminal Law and Criminology 1075, at 1077.

[66] Some commentators argue that the Constitution places limits on strict liability. Alan Michaels contends that 'strict liability is constitutional when, but only when, the intentional conduct covered by the statute could be made criminal by the legislature. In other words, a strict liability element runs afoul of the Constitution if the other elements of the crime, with the strict liability element excluded, could not themselves be made a crime. Otherwise, strict liability is constitutional'. See his 'Constitutional Innocence' (1999) 112 Harvard Law Review 828. In light of the breadth of the legislative power to enact crimes, this limitation is too minimal. For example, my hypothetical pizza statute would satisfy Michaels' test.

[67] *Malum prohibitum* offences may seem to create an exception to this doctrine, but appear to rest on very different rationales. As far as I am aware, no legal theorist provides an adequate account of when and under what conditions the state is permitted to create *malum prohibitum* offences. Even in such cases, however, it is doubtful that conduct loses its innocence simply because a legislature has decided to proscribe it. On some occasions, the state has compelling moral reasons to regulate conduct in some way or another, but the exact proscription itself may be arbitrary. On other occasions, the state is merely enforcing terms of fair competition; those who break the rules gain an unfair advantage.

derived from somewhere other than the determinations of legislators—are necessary if protests against crimes of strict liability make any sense.

Theorists who are reluctant to derive implications for criminalization from the general part may be hesitant to make these extra-legal judgements of fault and innocence, preferring to defer to legislative determinations. But these extra-legal judgements are needed not only to constrain legislators in enacting statutes, but also to guide courts in construing them. That is, non-positivistic conceptions of fault and innocence are required to interpret criminal statutes—whether or not these statutes include a culpability requirement. In a recent line of important cases, the Supreme Court has adopted the principle that federal statutes should be construed to preclude the conviction of blameless persons. In deciding whether a proposed interpretation is deficient on this ground, courts have examined applications of the statute to hypothetical situations far removed from the facts of the case at hand. Extra-legal judgements of fault and innocence are employed to decide whether a proposed interpretation could trap innocent persons. A given interpretation is rejected if it would criminalize the conduct of persons who are blameless according to these extra-legal judgements.[68]

This principle of statutory interpretation can be illustrated by two cases. In the first, a federal statute punishing anyone who 'knowingly acquires or . . . possesses food stamps [in an unauthorized manner]' was interpreted to require proof that the defendant 'knew that his conduct was unauthorized'.[69] The statute could have been construed so that a defendant need know only that he was acquiring or possessing food stamps, not that he also knew that the stamps he acquired or possessed were unauthorized. But this latter interpretation was rejected on the ground that it would 'criminalize a broad range of apparently innocent conduct';[70] it would allow the conviction of a person who 'possessed stamps because he was mistakenly sent them through the mail due to administrative error'.[71] The fact that the defendant himself did not acquire food stamps in this way was deemed irrelevant to how the statute should be construed.

In a second case, a federal statute proscribing the possession of a machine-gun was interpreted to require the defendant to know that his gun was a machine-gun.[72] This statute could have been construed to give rise to strict liability, inasmuch as no culpability requirement was expressly included. But this latter interpretation was rejected because it would criminalize 'blameless conduct';[73] it would allow the punishment of a person who 'inherited a gun from a relative and left it untouched in an attic or basement . . . in absolute ignorance of the gun's [automatic] firing capabilities'.[74] Again, the fact that the

---

[68] For further discussion, see Richard Singer and Douglas Husak, 'Of Innocence and Innocents: The Supreme Court and Mens Rea Since Herbert Packer' (1999) 2 Buffalo Criminal Law Review 859.

[69] *Liparota v US* 471 U.S. 419, 434 (1985).   [70] ibid. at 426.   [71] ibid.
[72] *US v Staples* 114 S.Ct. 1793 (1994).   [73] ibid. at 1800.   [74] ibid. at 1802.

defendant himself did not gain possession of his machine-gun in this manner was immaterial to how the statute should be interpreted.

As these (and several other) cases demonstrate, courts construe statutes so that only conduct that is blameworthy and merits condemnation is punished. To achieve this objective, courts resort to unwritten moral judgements to interpret statutes that Congress has written.[75] This principle of statutory construction presupposes judicial competence to recognize blameless conduct. Judges must be able to distinguish innocence from fault without legislative guidance. The judgement that someone is innocent and should not be subjected to punishment if he fails to inspect a gun he inherits from a relative is not based on a positivistic conception of innocence. Of course, such judgements are controversial—reasonable minds may disagree about them—but applications of principles of statutory construction are rarely unproblematic. If we were permitted to use only those judgements of fault and innocence made by legislatures, we would be unable to interpret criminal statutes sensibly.

Inasmuch as principles of statutory construction are included in the general part of criminal law,[76] the foregoing doctrine—which requires that statutes should be construed to protect blameless conduct—belongs there as well. This doctrine, after all, is the foundation for the widespread opposition to strict liability that has long been derived from the general part of criminal law.

E. LIMITATIONS DERIVED FROM THE JUSTIFICATION OF PUNISHMENT

Implications for criminalization are not exhausted by the doctrine that punishment expresses condemnation. Once we suppose that the criminal law is that body of law that subjects offenders to punishment, a very different argument against the content-neutrality thesis can be given. The first premise in this argument is that punishment requires a justification. This premise is beyond controversy. Theorists disagree about *how* punishment is justified, but not about *whether* a justification is needed.[77] The triviality of this step should not obscure its importance for the project of deriving constraints on criminalization from the general part of criminal law. By considering what might justify punishment, we should be able to identify some limitations on the

---

[75] See John Wiley, 'Not Guilty By Reason of Blamelessness: Culpability in Federal Criminal Interpretation' (1999) 85 Virginia Law Review 1021.

[76] See, e.g., Model Penal Code, ss. 2.02(3) and 2.02(4). The general provisions of the Code, however, do not include the doctrine of *strict construction*, even though many commentators locate it in the general part of the criminal law.

[77] They may also differ about what it is about punishment that requires a justification. Theorists struggle to decide whether and why punishment should involve 'hard treatment'. See the exchange between R.A. Duff and Andrew von Hirsch in Matt Matravers (ed.), *Punishment and Political Theory* (Oxford, 1999) 48–87.

32   *Douglas N. Husak*

kinds of conduct that may be criminalized. In other words, punishment cannot be justified without making some assumptions about the nature of the conduct for which it is imposed.[78] Theories about whether and under what conditions punishment is justified make little sense if it may be inflicted solely because a person has engaged in conduct the legislature has labelled as criminal.[79] No adequate theory would regard punishment as justified if the conduct for which it is imposed should not have been criminalized—subjected to punishment—in the first place.[80]

Although all philosophers concede that punishment requires a justification, I contend that the justificatory process is more complex than is generally supposed. This complexity results from the fact that *two* distinct interests are infringed when the state enacts proscriptions and imposes punishments. First, persons have an interest in being free to perform whatever conduct has been criminalized. Secondly, persons have an interest in being free from the punishment to which they become subject when they engage in the proscribed conduct. I want to elaborate on these two distinct interests, each of which is necessarily burdened when a state enacts and enforces criminal legislation. First, a state needs a justification to discourage given types of conduct. The state always has the alternative of doing nothing, or of employing any number of non-criminal means to reduce the incidence of the conduct. Once the decision to *criminalize* has been made, however, the state must be prepared to infringe more than the liberty to perform whatever conduct has been proscribed. In addition, the state inevitably burdens the interest in being free from punishment. All punishments, I have supposed, impose hardships or deprivations that express condemnation. What is the justification for burdening this second interest—the interest in not suffering hardship and condemnation—by punishment? We cannot answer simply that a defendant has engaged in conduct the state has good reason to discourage. To justify punishment, something is needed in addition to whatever justifies the initial decision to proscribe the behaviour in question.

My point can be expressed as a response to the deficient constitutional theory of criminalization I sketched above.[81] Recall that most criminal laws—

---

[78] Remarkably, although philosophers have written volumes defending various theories of punishment, they have largely failed to trace the implications of their theories for the issue of criminalization. They have tended to suppose that punishment could be justified without regard to the conduct for which it is imposed.

[79] Not all philosophers concur. See J.D. Mabbott, 'Punishment' (1939) *Mind* 152.

[80] See the brief discussion in Jeffrie Murphy and Jules Coleman, *The Philosophy of Law* (Totowa, 1984) 114.

[81] For an excellent response to the deficient constitutional theory, to which I am greatly indebted, see Sherry F. Colb, 'Freedom from Incarceration: Why Is This Right Different from All Other Rights?' (1994) 69 New York University Law Review 781. I differ from Colb in two important respects. First, I locate the doctrines I cite in the general part of criminal law, rather than in constitutional interpretation. Secondly, I apply these doctrines to all criminal laws, not merely to those punished by incarceration.

those burdening non-fundamental liberties—pass constitutional muster if they have a rational basis. In practice, this means that the legislature needs only a rational basis to proscribe behaviour. But the interests burdened by the criminal law are greater than the liberty to perform whatever conduct has been proscribed. When persons are punished, different and more important interests are often at stake. These two interests can be illustrated by my earlier example. Suppose that the liberty to eat pizza is not especially valuable. If so, the state would need only a minimal reason to discourage persons from exercising this liberty. This reason might support non-criminal means of discouraging the consumption of pizza—increased taxation, or bans on advertising, for example. But the interest burdened by a *criminal* law against eating pizza is greater. Persons have an interest in being free from punishment when pizza is eaten. This interest can be far more significant than the liberty to eat pizza. The state needs a much better reason—more than a mere rational basis—to justify deprivations of this important interest. Even though the state has a good reason to discourage this behaviour, it may lack a good reason to punish persons who engage in it.

I have criticized the constitutional theory I have summarized for failing to treat the criminal law as different. The same standard should not be used to evaluate both criminal and non-criminal laws. Constitutional theory may suffice to justify state actions that employ non-criminal means to discourage given kinds of conduct, but does not begin to justify inflictions of punishment. If I am correct, and the current theory is defective, why have commentators not been more vocal in contesting it? Various answers might be given; I will mention only two. First, commentators may be persuaded that *notice* suffices to justify punishment when persons perform the conduct that has been proscribed. Clearly, the state must provide adequate warning before offenders may be punished. Once fair notice has been given, persons can avoid punishment simply by not performing the conduct they have been warned is criminal. If persons engage in this conduct nonetheless, the rationale for punishment is simply that they were afforded a fair opportunity to avoid liability. But this argument, as many theorists have shown, is unsound. A punishment that is otherwise unjustified does not become justified simply because a person has been warned that it would be imposed.[82]

---

[82] Many cases typically cited to demonstrate the importance of notice actually show that notice is not at the heart of the problem. Courts in the USA frequently strike vagrancy statutes allegedly because they are vague, and fail to provide adequate notice to defendants of the conduct proscribed. Consider, e.g. the leading case of *Papachristou v City of Jacksonville* 405 U.S. 156 (1972). The statute found unconstitutional here is clearly a monstrosity. Many of its doctrines *are* vague, and provide inadequate notice. For example, the statute punished 'rogues and vagabonds . . . and habitual loafers'. But the statute also punished 'persons who use juggling'. I see no reason why this latter clause is vague; defects in the statute do not derive entirely from the inadequacy of notice. The problem with vagrancy laws cannot be rectified simply by better draftsmanship. The more obvious problem is that the statute criminalized conduct that is not condemnable.

Theorists may have been unable to recognize the deficiencies of the existing constitutional theory of criminalization for a second reason. They may have equated *proscription* with *prevention*. A criminal statute can only proscribe conduct; it cannot prevent it. Yet criminal theorists tend to use these terms interchangeably. Obviously, the extent to which proscribed conduct will actually be prevented is influenced by a host of factors. Whatever the law may say, some persons will persist in committing the offence. Therefore, in deliberating whether to enact criminal legislation, the state needs not only a good reason to proscribe the conduct in question, but also a good reason to punish persons who disregard the proscription. Conduct should not be criminalized if the proscription, but not the punishment, is justified. In such an event, non-criminal means—those that do not involve punishment—should be employed to discourage it.

The distinction between proscription and prevention is useful for many purposes. First, it helps to reveal what is often objectionable about criminal offences that are supported by a paternalistic rationale. If we focus simply on given proscriptions, we are more likely to believe that criminal legislation is actually in the interest of the persons whose liberty is infringed. Health and welfare would be markedly improved if the state effectively dissuaded persons from smoking cigarettes, for example. The problem with this narrow focus, however, is that many individuals will not be deterred; they will violate whatever criminal laws against smoking are enacted. Such persons will become subject to punishment if the state means what it says in labelling the offence as criminal. Once we realize that smokers will be punished, it is far less clear that a paternalistic rationale can justify the criminal legislation. A smoker may be better off if he quits, but not if he must be punished to make him quit. As punishments become more and more severe, we should become increasingly reluctant to believe that they can be in the interest of the persons who are punished. I conclude that the need to justify punishment should make us very sceptical of paternalistic rationales for criminal legislation that are backed by relatively severe sanctions.

In addition, recognizing that not all proscribed conduct will be prevented enables us to appreciate that some criminal statutes will do more harm than good. Consider, for example, objections to laws that subject pregnant women to drug tests and punish those whose tests are positive. The basis of protest to these laws is not that foetuses cannot be harmed by exposure to drugs. Neither is the basis of protest that women have an important liberty interest in using the drugs for which they are tested. Instead, the objection is that this law will not prevent all drug use among pregnant women, and thus may ultimately do more harm than good for the very class of persons it is designed to protect. The threat of criminal liability will dissuade some women from seeking pre-natal care, and the failure to obtain medical advice is often worse for foetuses than the effects of the drug. If the empirical basis of this objection is sound,[83] it provides a good reason to repeal (or not to have enacted) the law in question.[84]

Unfortunately, criminal laws that do more harm than good, or that injure the very persons they purport to protect, may satisfy the rational basis test. I have argued, however, that the state should require more than a rational basis to enact criminal legislation. More generally, a better theory of criminalization is needed—a theory that demands a higher standard of justification for criminal than for non-criminal laws. Of course, I cannot hope to defend the details of such a theory here. I can, however, indicate some of the directions I believe such a theory should take. A higher standard of justification is required for criminal laws because offenders are subject to punishment, and the interest in being free from punishment is entitled to more protection than we presently afford it. This interest is entitled to more protection because it is important to us that we not suffer the hardship and condemnation of punishment. What standard of justification *should* be required to burden such an important interest? Fortunately, we have ample experience in answering this question. The model we might employ to develop a theory of criminalization draws from that body of constitutional law that protects other interests acknowledged to be important. Our liberties in speech and religion are foremost among these interests. The body of law applicable to these liberties can be readily adapted to limit impositions of the criminal sanction.

Recall that constitutional law requires the state to have a compelling interest before it allows important, fundamental interests to be burdened. Generally, I see no reason why our fundamental liberties to speak or to exercise our religious beliefs are more important or entitled to a greater degree of protection than our interest in not being punished. If the interest not to be punished is of comparable value, then *all* criminal laws should be required to satisfy the same justificatory test that applies to the deprivation of our fundamental liberties. By examining what counts as an adequate reason to burden fundamental liberties such as speech and religion, we can gain insight into what should be regarded as an adequate reason to subject persons to punishment. Whether freedom from punishment *is* of comparable importance depends on many factors. Most obviously, this determination depends on the mode of punishment employed.[85] Significant interests are less clearly at stake if the

---

[83] See Hilary Surratt and James Inciardi, 'Cocaine, Crack, and the Criminalization of Pregnancy' in James Inciardi and Karen McElrath (eds.), *The American Drug Scene* (3rd edn., Los Angeles, 2001) 205.

[84] Although the doctrine that criminal laws should do more good than bad seems to be no more than a platitude, I find little explicit discussion of it in the writings of criminal theorists. But see Ashworth (n.18 above) at 33–34: 'The criminal law should not be used if it . . . causes consequences at least as bad as non-criminalization'.

[85] In addition, this determination depends on the extent to which the law infringes on a core area of the liberty that is burdened. Laws that abridge commercial speech, e.g., simply do not infringe liberties so fundamental as laws that abridge political speech. We should not be persuaded that our fundamental liberties to speak are more important than our interest in not being

state punishes criminal behaviour by a fine—even though the fine, unlike a civil sanction, expresses condemnation. Fundamental interests are unquestionably at stake, however, when the mode of punishment involves incarceration. Freedom from incarceration undoubtedly qualifies as fundamental under any plausible test to identify an interest as fundamental.[86]

The implications for criminalization are nothing short of profound. Applying the same standard of justification for criminal laws that already pertains to infringements of speech and religion would require the state to have a compelling interest in punishing persons for their conduct. Of course, the task of applying this doctrine requires a theory to decide which state interests are compelling. Attempts to identify these state interests are bound to generate enormous dispute.[87] Fortunately, some cases are easy. The clearest candidate for a compelling state interest is the protection of the individual right not to be physically harmed by violent acts. Thus I assume that the state has a compelling interest to punish persons who violate criminal laws that proscribe acts of physical violence.

Deciding that a statutory objective is compelling is only the first step in applying a higher standard of justification to criminal laws. The law must also be *necessary* to achieve this objective. No offence would be allowed in the special part of criminal law unless alternative, non-criminal means to achieve the statutory objective are inferior to it.[88] That is, the state must show that its legislative objective would be harder to achieve without resorting to punishment. The application of this doctrine to the special part of the criminal law would open up an entirely new area of research. Deciding whether and under what circumstances non-criminal sanctions are as effective as criminal sanctions would require empirical investigation that criminal theorists have seldom recognized the need to undertake.[89]

An equally important step in the justificatory process is the determination that the criminal law is *narrowly tailored* to serve the compelling state

punished by generalizing from examples of laws that infringe core areas of speech and laws that impose trivial punishments.

[86] In case there is doubt, consider situations in which the state institutionalizes persons for something other than a criminal offence, such as civil commitment of the mentally ill. Such practices must satisfy a higher standard of justification than legal rules that do not impose confinement. Presumably, however, these practices do not require the degree of justification needed for *punishment* because they fail to involve condemnation.

[87] 'As numerous commentators have pointed out, the Court's analysis of "government interests", and in particular what constitutes a compelling or important interest, is almost entirely undeveloped': Ashutosh Bhagwat, 'Purpose Scrutiny in Constitutional Analysis' (1997) 85 California Law Review 297, at 308.

[88] This principle is sometimes expressed by saying that the criminal law should be used only as a last resort. See Jareborg (n.39 above) at 22.

[89] Perhaps this dearth of empirical research is due to the fact that criminal theorists tend to be legal philosophers, and philosophers are unskilled in empirical methodology. In any event, 'there has never been a thoroughgoing examination [in the United Kingdom] of . . . whether some form of non-criminal enforcement could be devised to deal effectively with [given kinds of offences]': Ashworth (n.18 above) at 50–51. The same observation applies to the USA.

interest.[90] The requirement of narrow tailoring has at least two dimensions I will describe briefly. First and perhaps more importantly, a criminal statute must not be *overinclusive*, punishing instances of conduct beyond those needed to serve the compelling interest. Punishment must be justified for each and every person on whom it is imposed.[91] This doctrine is compromised when some persons are punished because their conduct falls under an overinclusive criminal statute.[92]

Attempts to identify overinclusive criminal statutes would give rise to tremendous controversy. The criminal laws most vulnerable to this problem are those designed to prevent a *risk* of harm rather than actual harm. Consider, to cite only one example, a statute proscribing drug possession within 1,000 feet of a school.[93] The objective of this statute, it seems clear, is to prevent school children from gaining access to drugs. Assume that this purpose is compelling. Still, the statute seems overinclusive. It punishes persons who possess drugs in prisons that happen to be located within 1,000 feet of a school. Drug use in prisons relatively close to schools would appear to pose no greater threat to school children than drug use in places farther away.[94] Empirical evidence to the contrary would be needed if this statute were subjected to the higher standard of justification I have described. For present purposes, however, I am less interested in pointing out how such an issue would be adjudicated than in indicating the kind of debate that would become relevant to criminalization if a doctrine against overinclusive criminal legislation were contained in the general part of criminal law.

In addition, the requirement of narrow tailoring would preclude the enactment of criminal laws that are *underinclusive*. To be justified, a criminal law must apply equally to each instance of conduct the state has the compelling interest to proscribe. The state must treat persons as equals in our interest in being free from punishment; it should not punish some but not others if it has a compelling interest to punish both. Underinclusive statutes are numerous. A statute punishing users of one substance because of the state interest in minimizing risks of addiction is underinclusive unless the state punishes users of other substances with a comparable addictive potential—assuming, of course, that other factors do not justify the disparate treatment of the two substances. As this example suggests, a doctrine against underinclusive legislation would help to ensure that the state is actually aiming toward the interest it alleges to

---

[90] See *Adarand Constructors Inc. v Pena* 115 S.Ct. 2097 (1995).

[91] Many commentators have argued for the importance of being 'able to say in good conscience in each instance in which a criminal sanction is imposed for a violation of law that the violation was blameworthy and, hence, deserving of the moral condemnation of the community': see Henry Hart (n.42 above) at 412.

[92] For further thoughts, see Douglas Husak, 'Reasonable Risk Creation and Overinclusive Legislation' (1998) 1 Buffalo Criminal Law Review 599.

[93] See New Jersey Criminal Code, s. 2C:35–7.

[94] See *State v Ogar* 551 A.2d 1037 (1989).

be promoted by the statute.[95] For example, a criminal law punishing building code violations in stores that distribute pornography could hardly be thought to serve the state interest in promoting safety, since building code violations are just as dangerous in stores that do not sell pornography. Such a law would be a transparent device to restrict pornography, an objective that may not be compelling.

The foregoing account simply begins the extraordinarily difficult task of deriving constraints on criminalization from the need to justify punishment. Further details would borrow from that body of law that protects interests equally important as the interest in not being punished. Applying the doctrines I have described requires independent normative theories that are enormously controversial. But the inevitable disagreements these doctrines will generate provide no reason to exclude them from the general part of criminal law. Greater controversy *should* surround the enactment of criminal laws. The state needs excellent reasons to deprive persons of their interest in being free from punishment. Applying the theory used to assess state actions that burden fundamental liberties will help to ensure that punishment is imposed sparingly, and would go a long way toward retarding the tendency to overcriminalize.

F. Limitations Derived from Criminal Law Defences

In this final section, I will briefly explore yet another limitation on criminalization that might be derived from the general part of criminal law. The limitation I will discuss emerges from efforts to interpret and apply various *defences* to criminal liability. Although theorists have disagreed about the issue,[96] I will assume that most defences should be placed in the general part.[97] Therefore, any limitations on criminalization that result from interpreting and applying these defences are derived from the general part of criminal law.

Many existing defences are required by the same doctrine I have already mentioned—that which prohibits punishing the blameless. Of course, justifications and excuses are incompatible with blame for different reasons. The

---

[95] See *City of Richmond v J.A. Croson Co.* 488 U.S. 469 (1989).

[96] Disagreement surrounds justifications rather than excuses. Justifications are available in situations where persons are permitted to engage in criminal conduct. If the special part fully described the conduct that gives rise to criminal liability, justifications would belong in the special rather than in the general part of criminal law. See Paul Robinson, *Structure and Function in Criminal Law* (Oxford, 1997) ch. 5.

[97] Some defences may pertain only to a single offence, and thus may belong in the special part, lacking sufficient generality to belong in the general part. Doctrines regarding provocation, for example, may suffice only to reduce a grade of homicide from murder to manslaughter. They typically appear in homicide statutes in the special part of criminal law. The defences I consider in this section, however, apply to virtually all offences.

former preclude blame because the *conduct* of the defendant is not wrongful; the latter because the *defendant himself* is not to blame for what he has done. The important point is that both categories of defences are required if we confine punishment only to those persons who are deserving of blame for their conduct. This doctrine also requires the creation of *new* defences from criminal liability. Ignorance of law, for example, should be a defence when it is blameless. Withholding these defences can produce punishment without fault. We might say that a *kind* of strict liability is imposed when courts do not allow a defence that precludes blame to bar liability for a given offence.[98] I describe this as a kind of strict liability, not in the formal sense that no culpability is required for each material element of an offence, but in the more meaningful sense that punishment is imposed in the absence of blame or fault.[99]

My central thesis, however, is not about the rationale for existing defences, or how this rationale might be extended to recognize new defences from criminal liability. I will argue that we cannot decide whether a number of familiar defences are available to a defendant without understanding the nature of the harm or evil sought to be prevented by the offence with which he is charged. I will describe three examples of such defences, and explain how attempts to interpret and apply them might lead to further limitations on the conduct that can be proscribed in the special part of criminal law.

First, consider the defence alternatively known as 'lesser evil', 'necessity', or 'justification generally'.[100] This defence is typically allowed when 'the harm or evil sought to be avoided is greater than that which would be caused by the commission of the offence'.[101] Next, consider the defence of consent.[102] Consent is a defence if it 'precludes the infliction of the harm or evil sought to be prevented by the law defining the offence'—unless that harm or evil is 'serious', in which case consent is not a defence at all.[103] Finally, consider the defence of *de minimis*. This defence is available when the defendant's conduct 'did not actually cause or threaten the harm or evil sought to be prevented by the law defining the offence or did so only to an extent too trivial to warrant the condemnation of conviction'.[104] Of course,

[98] For further thoughts, see Douglas Husak, 'Varieties of Strict Liability' (1995) VIII Canadian Journal of Law & Jurisprudence 189.

[99] Thus the punishment of persons who are blameless in their ignorance of law could be conceptualized as a kind of strict liability. See George Fletcher, *Rethinking Criminal Law* (Boston, 1978) at 730–731: 'The maxim that ignorance of the law is no excuse is so well entrenched in many legal systems that one is not likely to think of this form of mistake as a factor bearing on culpability . . . [Yet there is no denying that in such a case] the court imposes liability regardless of the actor's culpability in violating the statute'.

[100] This defence is available in approximately half of all Anglo-American jurisdictions. See Paul Robinson, *Criminal Law Defences*, Vol. 2 (St. Paul, 1984) 60. English law has been reluctant to recognize a general defence of necessity.

[101] Model Penal Code, s. 3.02.

[102] Sometimes, consent is relevant to criminal liability not because it is a defence, but because its absence—non-consent—is an element of the offence.

[103] Model Penal Code, s. 2.11(1) and 2.11(2)(a).   [104] Model Penal Code, s. 2.12(2).

the particular formulations of these defences vary from one jurisdiction to another. Yet it is doubtful that *any* formulation could avoid reference to the objective of the offence with which the defendant is charged and for which a defence is needed. Since the Model Penal Code formulations of these defences refer to this objective as the 'harm or evil sought to be prevented [or avoided]' by the offence, my subsequent discussion will adopt that terminology.

The difficulty in interpreting and applying these defences is evident. At least two judgements are required to decide whether these defences should be granted in particular cases in which they are invoked. First, one must identify the harm or evil the offence seeks to prevent. The second judgement is somewhat different for each of these three defences, and often requires an assessment of the magnitude or severity of the harm or evil identified in the first judgement. In the case of necessity, one must determine that the harm or evil the defendant sought to avoid is actually greater than that to be prevented by the offence; in the case of consent, one must determine that the defendant has consented to that particular harm or evil, and that this harm or evil is not serious; and in the case of *de minimis*, one must determine that the defendant did not really cause or threaten that harm or evil, or did so only to a trivial degree. Each of these complex judgements is made by law; the defendant's own views about these matters are not decisive.[105] Judges or juries should not defer to the opinion of the defendant about the first judgement that must be made in applying these defences; his conjecture about the nature of the harm or evil a given statute is designed to prevent can be mistaken. Neither should judges or juries defer to the opinion of the defendant about the second judgement that is needed; his assessment of the magnitude or severity of the harm or evil can be mistaken as well.

Suppose a defendant believes, for example, that the harm or evil to be prevented by a theft offence is trivial when he takes inexpensive office supplies from his employer. His own view of this matter should hardly be conclusive as a matter of law. But attempts to identify the nature and severity of the harm or evil a given law *is* designed to prevent can be notoriously problematic in given cases.[106] This problem is compounded, moreover, when statutes do not seem to be designed to prevent direct harm to an individual victim. A few examples of contexts in which it is especially hard to apply the foregoing defences will illustrate the interpretive difficulty.

---

[105] See Model Penal Code, Commentaries to 3.02, at 9–14. Arguably, however, the defendant's own views of these matters, even when highly idiosyncratic, are entitled to more weight than they are afforded by law at the present time.

[106] In a series of prison-break cases, courts have differed about the justifiability of escape to avoid homosexual rape by providing different characterizations of the harm or evil to be avoided by the offence. If that harm or evil includes the effect of the decision in encouraging subsequent escapes, it would be much more difficult, and perhaps impossible, for a defendant's act of escape to be justified. See *US v Bailey* 444 U.S. 394 (1980).

Consider the defence of necessity when a defendant is charged with use and/or possession of an illicit drug. Suppose he pleads a justification for using or possessing a controlled substance in the course of a religious ritual,[107] to treat a disease or illness,[108] or to display in an educational programme.[109] No one can hope to decide whether the defendant is justified in committing the offence unless he adopts a position about the nature and severity of the harm or evil the statute seeks to avoid. Suppose the offence is designed to prevent persons who possess the drug from consuming it and jeopardizing the welfare of others. If this supposition is accepted, the foregoing cases are likely to be resolved differently than if the offence is designed to reduce the likelihood that the drug will find its way into the hands of users other than the defendant. In the latter event, the defence of necessity seems less likely to succeed.

Next, turn to the defence of consent. Consider the ongoing controversy about laws requiring motorcyclists to wear helmets. Suppose this law is designed to protect the taxpaying public from the various expenses incurred when injuries in accidents are severe. If so, consent would be a plausible defence when a motorcyclist has purchased adequate insurance. Suppose, however, that this law has a paternalistic rationale, and is designed to protect the motorcyclist himself from suffering severe injuries. Insurance would be irrelevant on the latter assumption, and consent would not be a defence.

Finally, consider the defence of *de minimis*.[110] Return to the offence of drug possession. Imagine a case in which an illicit drug cannot be used to cause a psychoactive effect because its quantity is so minuscule.[111] If the offence is designed to prevent the various harms risked to oneself and others when drugs are used, the fact that the drug cannot cause these harms would seem to give rise to a *de minimis* defence. If the offence is designed to prevent some harm or evil that does not require drug consumption, however, the defence may be unavailable even though the quantity of drugs is too small for the body to detect.

Although many commentators have defended the claim that harm or evil are prerequisites for the imposition of the criminal sanction, few have noticed that we can make no sense of the foregoing defences unless their claim is adopted. Therefore, a harm or evil must be required. Still, a central difficulty in applying these defences remains—a difficulty that also complicates attempts to apply the compelling state interest test I described above. The crux

---

[107] See *Employment Division v Smith* 494 U.S. 872 (1990).
[108] See *Commonwealth v Hutchins* 575 N.E.2d 741 (Mass. 1991).
[109] See *People v Mijares* 491 P.2d 1115 (Cal. 1971).
[110] In fact, this single defence actually encompasses two distinct defences. The first obtains when the defendant did not actually cause or threaten the harm or evil sought to be prevented by the law defining the offence; the second obtains when he did cause that harm or evil, but to an extent too trivial to warrant the condemnation of conviction. The latter of these two defences is called an 'offence modification' by Robinson (n.100 above) Vol.1, at 77–82.
[111] See Note, 'Criminal Liability for Possession of Nonusable Amounts of Controlled Substances' (1977) 77 Columbia Law Review 596.

of the problem is that legislators need not articulate a rationale or objective for the criminal laws they create.[112] This problem could be rectified by a doctrine in the general part requiring the state to identify a non-trivial harm or evil for each criminal law it enacts. Such a doctrine might seem to have no implications for the special part; perhaps all we can infer about the content of specific offences is that they must be designed to prevent *some* non-trivial harm or evil. The very need to articulate a rationale, however, might go a surprisingly long way toward retarding overcriminalization. Laws generally— and bad laws in particular—might become more difficult to enact if legislators were forced to commit themselves to a harm or evil they seek to prevent. Whether or not this speculation is correct, I believe we can go somewhat further in deriving implications for criminalization from the foregoing considerations.

Suppose the general part contained a doctrine requiring that all criminal laws be designed to prevent a non-trivial harm or evil. Significant constraints on criminalization might emerge if the troublesome terms in this doctrine were defined. Clearly, accounts of both harm and evil are needed. If *any* statutory objective qualifies as a harm or evil, this doctrine would be vacuous.[113] Presumably, we can conceive of the possibility of a criminal law that is *not* designed to prevent a harm or evil. We cannot be confident that a given criminal law conforms to this doctrine unless we are able to recognize harm and evil. Unfortunately, criminal codes (like the Model Penal Code) tend to define neither of these terms.

We might begin by providing a conception of harm. Joel Feinberg defines harmful conduct 'in the relevant sense' as conduct in which 'A adversely affects B's interest and in so doing wrongs B (violates B's right)'.[114] If Feinberg's definition were adopted, all harmful conduct would wrong someone by violating his rights. Clearly, the implications of this potentially far-reaching doctrine cannot be traced without a theory of rights. Needless to say, all such theories are enormously controversial. Once again, a doctrine in the general part cannot be applied to the special part without invoking a normative theory that is outside the general part. Of course, Feinberg's particular account of harm need not be endorsed. The important point is that *any* adequate definition of harm may provide the source of significant limitations on criminalization. The same is true of evil, the prevention of which might supplement the function of the criminal law in preventing harm. A definition of evil is required unless this doctrine is vacuous. If the special part of criminal law can be used to prevent evil in addition to harm, the criminal law is compatible with *legal moralism*. But what kind of legal moralism is compatible

[112] 'This Court never has insisted that a legislative body articulate its reasons for enacting a statute': *US Railroad Retirement Board v Fritz* 449 U.S. 1, 179 (1980).
[113] Many commentators have raised this definitional failure as an objection to the harm requirement. See, e.g. Fletcher (n.99 above) at 404.
[114] Feinberg (n.20 above) at xxix.

with offences in the special part?[115] The practical question is *whose* judgement that a law actually proscribes a non-trivial harm or evil should prevail? Several alternatives exist; I will briefly mention four.

First, the judgements of legislators might be decisive. This doctrine might be satisfied as long as legislators believe that a law proscribes a non-trivial harm or evil. This positivistic alternative has the advantage of being easy to implement. The same body charged with the authority to enact criminal laws is entrusted to decide that these laws prevent a non-trivial harm or evil. As so construed, this doctrine would appear to be largely ineffective in limiting the reach of the criminal sanction, except insofar as it would help to ensure that legislatures operate in good faith. This doctrine could not be used to challenge legislative judgements if the judegments of legislatures are regarded as decisive. Still, this doctrine would have *some* implications for criminalization. Several proscriptions in the USA (as well as in the United Kingdom) do not appear to prevent a non-trivial harm or evil from *any* reasonable perspective.[116] Federal law, for example, imposes criminal penalties on persons who disturb mud in a cave on federal land.[117] Applications of the doctrine that the legislature should criminalize only conduct it believes will prevent a non-trivial harm or evil might help to retard the unwelcome trend toward creating such offences.[118]

Secondly, judgements of the community on whom criminal sanctions are imposed might be decisive in applying the doctrine that criminal laws must prevent a non-trivial harm or evil. This alternative has advantages. Empirical findings from social scientists suggest that the most effective means to maximize compliance with the criminal law is not the threat of deterrence, but the perception of the law's moral credibility among those who are subject to it.[119] The power of the criminal law to induce compliance is directly proportional to its moral credibility. If the criminal law is seen as unjust in a particular case, its power to secure future compliance is incrementally reduced. If members of a community perceive the laws as unfair, in punishing what they do not regard as a significant harm or evil, the state can hope to secure compliance only by resorting to threats. This device is expensive, inefficient, counterproductive, and sometimes unjust.

[115] For distinct versions of legal moralism, see Joel Feinberg, *Harmless Wrongdoing* (New York, 1988).

[116] 'There are many offences for which any element of stigma is diluted almost to the vanishing point': Ashworth (n.18 above) at 1. But see the reply in Stuart Green, 'Why It's A Crime to Tear the Tag Off a Mattress: Overcriminalization and the Moral Content of Regulatory Offences' (1997) 46 Emory Law Journal 1533.

[117] 16 U.S.C. ss. 4302(1), 4302(5), and 4306(a)(1).

[118] Additional examples of offences that such a doctrine would jeopardize are described in Ronald Gainer, 'Federal Criminal Code Reform: Past and Future' (1998) 2 Buffalo Criminal Law Review 45.

[119] See Paul Robinson and John Darley, *Justice, Liability & Blame* (Boulder, 1995); also Dan Kahan, 'What Do Alternative Sanctions Mean?' (1996) 65 University of Chicago Law Review 591; also the symposium in (2000) 28 Hofstra Law Review 601–797.

Thirdly, academic legal theorists and moral philosophers might be entrusted to decide whether an offence prevents a non-trivial harm or evil. Much can be said in favour of this alternative as well.[120] Why should we acquiesce when the criminal law is used to condemn conduct that is not really condemnable? Deferring to the judgements of either the legislature or the community might be a recipe for intolerance and bigotry.[121] One would hope that the (presumably enlightened) judgements of academic legal theorists and moral philosophers would be helpful in checking the uninformed prejudices and biases of the public and their elected representatives.

Finally, courts might be entrusted to decide whether a law punishes a significant harm or evil. Commentators may be reluctant to allow judges to usurp what seems like a legislative function. I have argued, however, that courts have no choice but to resort to extra-legal moral judgements in interpreting and applying criminal statutes.[122] My point here is that several criminal law defences cannot be interpreted or applied unless courts are willing to make similar judgements. It is hard to see how a court can be expected to decide whether a harm or evil is trivial, or whether and under what circumstances the harm or evil is outweighed, unless it has the authority to decide whether the statute in question proscribes a non-trivial harm or evil in the first place.

I conclude that the doctrine that criminal laws must be designed to prevent some non-trivial harm or evil—which should be included in the general part—has uncertain but nonetheless potentially important implications for criminalization. These implications have not been recognized because the general part has failed to provide a non-vacuous conception of these terms. A doctrine in the general part requiring that criminal laws be designed to prevent some non-trivial harm or evil must be given meaningful content. An unwillingness or inability to define these terms gives rise to difficulties in interpreting the defences from criminal liability I have mentioned here. We will be unable to apply these defences unless we understand the nature and severity of the harm or evil to be prevented. When adequate accounts of these terms are provided, and a rationale for all legislation is required, additional limitations on criminalization might emerge from the general part of criminal law.

G. Conclusion

I have argued against what I called the *content-neutrality thesis*, and suggested that the general part of criminal law may be construed to create significant

---

[120] See, e.g., Moore (n.6 above).

[121] For example, many commentators have expressed dismay at the decision in *Bowers v Hardwick* 478 U.S. 186 (1986), in which the presumed belief of a majority of the electorate in Georgia that homosexual sodomy is immoral was invoked to uphold a statute criminalizing sodomy.

[122] See section D above.

limitations on the kinds of conduct for which persons can be punished. The absence of such limitations has helped to contribute to the twin problems of too many criminal laws and too much punishment. Of course, I have not provided a comprehensive theory that can be invoked to retard these trends. But I have explained how we might build on the deficiencies in what passes for a theory of criminalization in constitutional law in the USA to provide the outlines of a better theory. The doctrines in this theory could be thought to belong to the general part of criminal law.

I have indicated that the following doctrines might be included in the general part and give rise to limitations on criminalization:

(1)   the criminal law is that body of law that subjects persons to punishment. Since punishment expresses condemnation, only conduct worthy of condemnation should be criminalized;

(2)   criminal laws should not punish innocent conduct, so criminal statutes should be interpreted to ensure that innocent conduct is not proscribed;

(3)   each criminal law must do more good than harm;

(4)   conduct should not be criminalized unless the state has a compelling interest in punishing those who engage in it. A criminal law must be necessary to achieve a compelling state interest; non-criminal means to prevent the conduct must be found to be inferior to the criminal alternative. The criminal law must be narrowly tailored to serve the state's compelling interest; criminal laws should be neither overinclusive nor underinclusive;

(5)   each criminal law must be designed to prevent a non-trivial harm or evil.

I make no pretence that the foregoing doctrines are original. Many commentators have argued that most of these doctrines should limit the reach of the criminal sanction. The novelty in my approach is to locate these doctrines in the general part of criminal law. Nor do I pretend that these doctrines are exhaustive. Almost certainly the general part of criminal law has additional resources to limit criminalization.[123] Even if I am mistaken about some of the foregoing doctrines, I think it is important to construe the general part of criminal law so that it contains *some* limitations on criminalization. I see no good reason for the general part to limit the structure of criminal offences without also limiting the conduct that is eligible for proscription.

But I am not so naïve as to believe that including these doctrines in the general part of criminal law will go very far toward solving the problems of overcriminalization or overincarceration I discussed in section B above. For three reasons, these doctrines might not be as helpful as one might hope. First, attempts to apply these doctrines to the special part of criminal law often require controversial normative theories that are not included in the general

---

[123] For example, the presumption of innocence almost certainly has implications for criminalization. See Finkelstein (n.43 above) at 343–349.

part. The disputes that inevitably surround such theories are bound to impede the goal of limiting the reach of the criminal sanction. Moreover, each of these doctrines allows for exceptions. The effectiveness of these doctrines in restricting criminalization depends, *inter alia*, on how we account for these exceptions. I see little point in *having* a doctrine in the general part unless we demand a good reason before we allow an exception to it. But what counts as a 'good reason' to make an exception? The details of the answer to this question will greatly affect whether the implications of these doctrines for the special part will be broad or narrow. Finally, no easy means to enforce these doctrines is available. Legislatures with no interest in retarding the recent expansion in the scope of the criminal law will find ways to evade the implications of the doctrines I have described.[124] In the current political climate on both sides of the Atlantic, public pressure to create new offences is given far more weight than the protests of criminal theorists. I have suggested that greater controversy *should* surround the enactment of new offences, but the political reality of today provides no indication that this aspiration is widely shared. A state that is not committed to ensuring that impositions of the criminal sanction meet a demanding standard of justification has ample means to undermine and circumvent the limiting implications of any doctrine in the general part of criminal law.

[124] According to Ashworth, 'political reality' is 'unpromising' for the prospect of 'restoring integrity to the criminal law'. Thus he pessimistically concludes that 'the criminal law may be a lost cause': n.23 above, at 255.

3

Rule-Violations and Wrongdoings

R.A. DUFF*

A. 'Rules for Citizens' and 'Rules for Courts'

Some moral considerations are action-guiding. They generate direct reasons for action; they concern what, as moral agents, we may, must, should, or ought to do (or not to do); they can figure in the practical reasoning of a moral agent who asks herself 'What am I to do?'. They might figure as principles: 'One ought to pay one's debts'; 'One ought not to tell lies'; 'One should help those in need'. Or they might figure as more particularized, reason-imbued descriptions of a contemplated action or of the situation: 'I owe it to her'; 'That would be dishonest'; 'He needs help'.[1] Such moral considerations identify actions as right, or wrong, or permissible, and include considerations which can *justify* otherwise or normally wrongful actions: 'I owe her this money, but I've got to give it to this desperate beggar instead'; 'That would be a lie, but it's the only way to avert disaster'; 'He needs help, but I must hurry on to a crucial meeting'.

Other kinds of moral consideration guide judgements on or reactions to actions and their agents, rather than directly guiding such actions: they concern the propriety of criticizing or blaming people (including oneself) for what they have done. Two such kinds of consideration are relevant here.

One concerns excuses: 'Yes, she was unjustifiably rude, but she was under great strain at the time, so you shouldn't blame her'; 'Yes, he lied to you, but he suffers from the paranoid delusion that you are persecuting him, so you can't blame him'; 'Yes, she walked on by when you pleaded for help, but she doesn't speak English, and thought you were propositioning her, so you can't blame her' (sometimes, the conclusion is not that we can't blame her at all, but that blame should be qualified by the factor cited). Such pleas, if successful, exculpate the agent: not by justifying the action (being rude, lying, not answering a plea for help), but by showing why the agent should not be blamed for acting thus.

---

* Thanks for helpful comments and criticisms are due to the editors, to Peter Alldridge, to Sandra Marshall, and to the other participants in the Birmingham conference.
[1] I leave aside here questions about the relationship between such particular descriptions and general principles, for instance whether such descriptions must imply suitable general principles.

The other kind of consideration renders blame or criticism inappropriate, not by showing that the agent was not blameworthy, but by showing that the would-be blamer lacks the right or the standing to blame her—to blame her to her face, perhaps to judge her conduct at all. 'Yes, he is behaving badly to his friend—but that's none of your business'; 'Yes, he lied to you—but given how often you have lied to him, you are not well placed to blame him'.

The feature common to both these kinds of case is that the factor cited as a reason for not blaming the agent is not a factor to which the agent herself could properly attend in deciding what to do. In some cases it *could not* figure in her rational deliberation about what to do: she cannot reason 'I mistakenly believe that he is propositioning me, so I should ignore his plea for help'. In other cases, it *could* figure in the agent's deliberations, but its blame-excluding force does not depend on its doing so: Jones might see the fact that Smith has regularly lied to her as a good reason to lie to him; but even if we (and she) deny this, we might still hold that Smith lacks the moral right or standing to criticize Jones for her lies to him.

The distinction between action-guiding and judgement-guiding considerations that can be found within morality has a close analogue in the criminal law. Some aspects of the criminal law define criminally wrongful actions: they declare what citizens must (or may) do (or not do); they define or identify reasons for action. Thus English criminal law declares that someone who has sexual intercourse with another person without her (or his) consent commits a crime (Sexual Offences (Amendment) Act 1976, section 1(1); Criminal Justice and Public Order Act 1994, section 141); as does one who drives a car without a licence (Road Traffic Act 1988, section 87), or sells firearms to someone under 17 (Firearms Act 1968, section 24(1)), or 'without lawful excuse' destroys or damages another's property (Criminal Damage Act 1971, section 1(1)). Such reason-giving aspects of the law include justifications for what would otherwise be criminal actions. These may appear in the law's definition of the offence (the Criminal Damage Act 1971, section 5, partially specifies 'lawful excuses' for damaging others' property),[2] or as general justificatory defences recognized by the law: in both cases they specify reasons which can properly guide an agent's actions.

In giving these examples, I have avoided two important questions. First, my descriptions of the relevant actions make no explicit reference to the agent's intentions or beliefs—to the elements normally classed as matters of *mens rea*. As we will see, it is controversial whether, or how, such elements should figure in this type of criminal law norm: all we need note here is that insofar as such norms express reasons for action, their simplest specification will omit any such explicit reference. What, according to the criminal law, gives me reason not to undertake the action is the fact that the person with whom I

---

[2] 'Lawful excuses' are typically justifications: see J. C. Smith and B. Hogan, *Criminal Law* (8th edn., London, 1996) 702–12.

would have intercourse does not consent to it, or that I would be driving without a licence, or that the person who seeks to buy a firearm from me is under 17, or that this action would damage another's property. Secondly, it is also unclear whether, or when, or how, the fact that the law defines the action as criminal should (in the law's eyes) figure as part of my reason for not undertaking it: am I to say to myself, 'She does not consent, so I shouldn't have intercourse with her', or 'She does not consent, and non-consensual intercourse is criminal, so I shouldn't have intercourse with her'; 'He is under 17, so I shouldn't sell him a firearm', or 'He is under 17, and selling firearms to anyone under 17 is criminal, so I shouldn't sell him a firearm'?

Other aspects of the criminal law serve not to define or identify reasons which are to guide citizens' actions, but to specify conditions under which an agent who has committed a crime should not be held criminally liable for it. Some such provisions specify exculpatory defences, or excuses: thus the insanity defence exempts from liability someone whose mental disorder was, whilst such as to justify his acquittal, not such as to negate the normal *mens rea* requirements for the crime; he intentionally killed a human being, but is acquitted on grounds of insanity. Other provisions concern 'non-exculpatory defences':[3] someone whose trial is barred by a statute of limitations or who legitimately claims diplomatic immunity might have committed a crime without either justification or excuse, but cannot now be held liable for it. The feature common to both these kinds of case is that the factor which saves the agent from criminal liability is *not* one which (in the law's eyes) gives her reason to commit the crime, and is therefore not one to which (in the law's eyes) she can properly attend in deciding what to do. The fact that the person whose property I contemplate destroying has consented to that destruction gives me (permissive, rather than mandatory) reason to destroy it: by contrast, the fact that I am insane in a way that brings me under the provisions of the insanity defence, or that I have diplomatic immunity, does not (in the law's eyes) give me reason to act in a way which would, were it not for that fact, render me criminally liable.

Partly in the light of the considerations noted above, some theorists argue that we should distinguish 'rules for citizens' from 'rules for courts': rules or norms that are addressed to citizens, aiming to guide, or to specify reasons that should guide, their actions from rules or norms that are addressed to criminal courts, specifying conditions under which they should or should not hold someone criminally liable. So Fletcher, drawing on German legal theory, distinguishes norms of 'wrongdoing' from norms of 'attribution'.[4] Robinson, drawing on his 'functional' account of the criminal law, argues that we should ideally have two separate criminal law codes: a 'Code of Conduct' containing the 'rules of conduct', which 'provide *ex ante* direction

---

[3] See P. H. Robinson, *Structure and Function in Criminal Law* (Oxford, 1997) 71–72.
[4] G. Fletcher, *Rethinking Criminal Law* (Boston, 1978) chs 6.6–8, 7, 9–10.

to members of the community as to the conduct that must be avoided . . . upon pain of criminal sanction', and a 'Code of Adjudication' addressed to the courts, containing 'the rules to be used in deciding whether a breach of the law's commands will result in criminal liability and, if so, the grade or degree of that liability'.[5] He also provides drafts of each code, thus engaging more seriously than have others in the task of offering a *complete* classification of the elements of the substantive criminal law into these two categories.[6]

Part of the point of such distinctions is analytical and expository clarity: if we recognize the differences in logic and in function between different aspects of the criminal law, we will gain a clearer understanding of its structure and doctrinal organization; we can then also make the law clearer to the citizens whom it binds, for instance by legislating a 'Code of Conduct'. Those who draw such distinctions are, however, typically more ambitious than that: they hope that by classifying various rules and doctrines into these two categories, we will be able to dissolve various doctrinal problems and confusions that have troubled courts and theorists. These are indeed worthy ambitions, and aspects of the distinction(s) between rules for citizens and rules for courts can indeed help towards achieving them. These distinctions are, however, seriously oversimplified by those who draw them: the complex structures of crime and criminal liability cannot be captured, without distortion, in any such stark dichotomy.

I will focus on three issues in what follows. First, in what terms do the rules for citizens, or the norms of wrongdoing, address the citizens? Robinson and Fletcher talk, as do many theorists, of the criminal law as 'prohibiting' certain kinds of conduct: but in my view this embodies an inadequate conception of how the law of a liberal polity should address its citizens. Secondly, how can this schema of two kinds of rule or norm cope with some familiar defences, such as duress? Robinson and Fletcher agree that, whilst justifications belong with the rules or norms addressed to citizens,[7] excuses belong with those addressed to courts—and that duress counts in law as an excuse rather than as a justification: but the matter is much more complicated than that. Thirdly, do the standard requirements of *mens rea* belong with the rules for citizens or with the rules for courts? Robinson and Fletcher differ on this question, and we will see that it admits of no simple answer.

---

[5] Robinson (n. 3 above) 125, 183.

[6] See also M. Dan-Cohen, 'Decision Rules and Conduct Rules: On Acoustic Separation in Criminal Law' (1984) 97 Harvard LR 625; P. Alldridge, 'Rules for Courts and Rules for Citizens' (1990) 10 Oxford Journal of Legal Studies 487. On Dan-Cohen, see R. Singer, 'On Classism and Dissonance in the Criminal Law: A Reply to Professor Dan-Cohen' (1986) 77 Journal of Criminal Law and Criminology 69.

[7] They disagree about the conditions of justification: should it suffice that the justificatory facts existed; or must the defendant have been aware of or motivated by those facts? See Fletcher (n. 4 above) 555–66; Robinson (n. 3 above) 100–124.

The first of these questions, to which I turn in the next section, is the most basic, since answers to the other two questions will depend in crucial part on an answer to it. I will sketch an account of the terms, and the tones, in which the criminal law should address the citizens: an account not of how *any* system of criminal law *must* address those whom it claims to bind (there are familiar problems with any such would-be universal and ahistorical thesis), but of how the criminal law of a polity supposedly structured by contemporary liberal values should address the citizens of that polity.[8] This account, if it is plausible, has merits and significance independently of its relation to Robinson's and Fletcher's discussions of the structure of the criminal law: but it can usefully be explained by contrast with some central features of their accounts.

B. RULES, PROHIBITIONS AND COMMANDS

According to section 1.02(a) of the Model Penal Code, the 'general purpose' of the substantive criminal law is 'to forbid and prevent conduct that unjustifiably and inexcusably inflicts or threatens substantial harm to individual or public interests'; and it is quite usual to talk of the criminal law as 'forbidding' or 'prohibiting' certain kinds of conduct—in order, as we might naturally add, to 'prevent' such conduct. From this perspective, what the law demands of and seeks from the citizens is *obedience* to its prohibitions. What ultimately matters is admittedly that the citizens refrain from crime, which need not involve *obeying* the law as distinct from behaving in a way that conforms to it: but the point of a prohibition, the aim internal to it, is to secure obedience.

To portray the law thus is to portray it as offering citizens *content-independent* reasons for action. If their reasons for refraining from conduct defined as criminal had to do solely with the nature or effects of that conduct, independently of its being defined as criminal (with its pre-legal moral wrongfulness or imprudence, for instance), their reasons would be content-dependent: they would depend on the particular content of the law, not on the fact that it was the law. In that case, however, they would not be *obeying* the law: for to obey X is to act in conformity with what X requires, *because* X requires it;[9] whereas such citizens would be acting as they do because of what it is that the law 'requires', rather than because the law requires it. To see the criminal law as prohibiting conduct, and as requiring our obedience to its prohibitions, is to see it as offering us reasons for action that are at least partly independent of its particular content: reasons that we would not otherwise

---

[8] See R. A. Duff, *Punishment, Communication, and Community* (New York, 2000) ch. 2, for a communitarian account of those liberal values: but my argument does not depend on that particular account.

[9] See H. L. A. Hart, *The Concept of Law* (2nd edn., Oxford, 1994) 19–20, 51–61.

have for acting thus; reasons having to do with the authority or power of the law itself.[10]

This is indeed how traditional legal positivism portrays the law, as a set of commands addressed to the citizens by a sovereign. It is also how the law *should* be portrayed insofar as it should be understood as a set of edicts imposed by a sovereign on her subjects.[11] But it is not how we should understand the criminal law of a liberal polity.

Consider the central kinds of criminal *mala in se*—crimes, such as murder, rape, serious assault, theft, involving conduct that is wrong independently of its being defined as criminal. (In calling such crimes 'central', I do not mean that they are the most commonly committed or punished, but that they are normatively salient: if we are to have a criminal law, it should obviously at least cover these kinds of conduct.) To say that the criminal law 'prohibits' such conduct is to say that it offers citizens reasons for refraining from it that are independent of its pre-legal wrongfulness: reasons presumably having to do either with the law's authority (citizens should obey because they recognize a general obligation to do so), or with its power (they are to obey because the threat of sanctions obliges them to do so). Many citizens might refrain from such conduct independently of the law's prohibition, because they see it to be (pre-legally) wrong. On this account of the criminal law, however, it is primarily addressed not to those who would anyway refrain from such conduct (they need no such prohibitions), but to those who might otherwise engage in it; and it offers them new reasons to refrain from it.

One point to notice about this picture concerns the motivation of those who do obey the law—those who refrain from criminal conduct because the law prohibits it. Few, if any, are likely to obey from respect for the law's authority: for what kind of person would it be who was not motivated to refrain from murder or rape by the pre-legal wrongness of such conduct, but was motivated to refrain by his respect for the law?[12] One can imagine cases in which this would be intelligible, in particular, cases in which the law makes a determinate ruling on some morally controversial or uncertain issue: someone who thinks that voluntary euthanasia is morally permissible, for instance, or that a property holder can be morally justified in using fatal force to prevent its theft, *might* be dissuaded from such conduct by respect for the law

---

[10] The reasons need not be wholly independent of the law's content: my reason for obeying the law could, for instance, be partly that it is the law, but also that what it requires is not morally wrong. I assume here that we can distinguish 'content-dependent' from 'content-independent' reasons in a way that at least makes room for the familiar claim that the law is or purports to be a source of distinctively content-independent reasons, but I recognize that explicating that distinction is problematic: see P. Markwick, 'Law and Content-Independent Reasons' (2000) 20 Oxford Journal of Legal Studies 579.

[11] See R. Cotterrell, *Law's Community* (Oxford, 1995) ch. 11, on the 'imperium' model of law; and R. A. Duff, 'Inclusion and Exclusion: Citizens, Subjects and Outlaws' (1998) 51 Current Legal Problems 241.

[12] Compare J. Raz, *Ethics in the Public Domain* (Oxford, 1994) 343–344: but Raz still talks of the law as 'prohibiting' such conduct.

that defines it as criminal. Such cases are, however, rare; in the usual run of cases, those who obey the law will more plausibly do so from fear of its threatened sanctions.

In either case, however, whether the law exerts its power or its authority over those who obey it, the more important point to notice concerns the way in which it addresses the citizens from whom it seeks obedience. It addresses them in the peremptory tones of authority or of power: it says to them either 'Act thus, because you have an obligation to obey the law'; or 'Act thus, or else you will suffer sanctions'. But these are not the tones in which the law should address the citizens of a liberal polity.

What justifies the law in 'prohibiting' murder, rape and the like is that such actions are wrong in a way that properly concerns the law: they constitute 'public' wrongs in terms of the values of the political community.[13] Those values claim to bind the citizens, as members of that normative community: they should be the citizens' own public values, as members of the polity. If the law is to address citizens, as it should, as members of that political community, it must therefore address them in terms of those values—the values which bind them as members, and which justify the law's own content. If it addresses them only in the peremptory language of authority or of power, it fails to satisfy this requirement: it addresses them as subjects rather than as citizens.

We can meet this point by portraying the law, not as *prohibiting* central criminal *mala in se*, but as *declaring* their public wrongfulness. In defining them as crimes it declares not just that they are wrongs, in terms of the community's own values; nor just that they are publicly recognized 'private' wrongs which belong in the sphere of civil law, and entitle their victims to sue *if* they wish: but that they are public wrongs which must be recognized and condemned as such by the whole political community, through the criminal law—wrongs for which the community will call their agents to account through a public criminal process, and censure them through conviction and punishment.

This is not to say that the role of the law in defining central criminal *mala in se* is *only* to declare the (public) wrongfulness of kinds of action that citizens should already recognize as wrongs. For, first, in defining such actions as public wrongs, it defines them as actions for which citizens can be called to answer: it thus requires citizens to answer for such actions (or to answer the charge that they have committed such actions) through a criminal process. This is one way in which the criminal law is a source of reasons which make a difference to what citizens ought to do: it creates a criminal process through which they are required to answer charges of what the law defines as public wrongdoing. This is also one way in which the criminal law claims authority over the citizens: it claims the authority not (as to central *mala in se*) to *make* wrong conduct that is not wrong independently of the law, but to define

---

[13] See further S. E Marshall and R. A. Duff, 'Criminalization and Sharing Wrongs' (1998) 11 Canadian Journal of Law & Jurisprudence 7.

certain wrongs as public wrongs, and so to require citizens to answer for their (alleged) commissions of such wrongs.

Secondly, even in relation to central criminal *mala in se*, the law must sometimes provide precise '*determinationes*' of values whose pre-legal meanings or implications are uncertain or controversial.[14] The law defines what counts as murder, or theft, or rape, and what can justify what would otherwise be a criminal action: in doing so, it specifies more determinate legal meanings for normative concepts whose pre-legal meanings may be less determinate, and it takes an authoritative stand on issues that may be controversial in the political community, for instance on the permissibility of euthanasia.[15] A liberal polity's law, which respects its citizens' autonomy, will as far as possible respect their different, conflicting interpretations of the community's values: where there is, as with euthanasia, reasonable disagreement about what those values (respect for life, for instance) require, it tries to avoid taking a stand that will require some citizens to act against their consciences. But this is not always possible: sometimes the law must either allow what some citizens firmly believe to be a public wrong, or declare as a public wrong what some citizens firmly believe to be permissible (or to be a private matter that should not concern the law), when both sides to the controversy found their beliefs on a not unreasonable interpretation of the value at stake. In such cases, what the law says to those who dissent from the stand it takes is not simply and unqualifiedly that the conduct in question is wrong, but rather that this is now the community's authoritative view: even if they dissent from its content, they have an obligation as members of the community to accept its authority—to obey the law, even if they are not persuaded by its content, unless and until they can secure a change in it through the normal political process.

The criminal law also, of course, defines '*mala prohibita*' as well as '*mala in se*'; and in this context there is more room to talk of the law as 'prohibiting' certain kinds of conduct, as creating new, content-independent reasons for action, and as requiring 'obedience' from the citizens. I cannot discuss the character of *mala prohibita* (or the distinction between *mala in se* and *mala prohibita*, or the question of whether these categories exhaust the content of the criminal law) here, save to note that *mala prohibita* are by no means always purely *prohibita*, i.e. kinds of conduct that are wrong *only* qua prohibited by the criminal law,[16] and from which citizens would otherwise have *no*

---

[14] See J. Finnis, 'On "The Critical Legal Studies Movement"', in J. Eekelaar and J. Bell (eds.), *Oxford Essays in Jurisprudence*, 3rd Series (Oxford, 1987) 145, at 146–147.

[15] Sometimes the law's *determinatio* reflects not so much an authoritative account of the value that is thus determined, as a concern with what courts can reasonably be expected to decide within the constraints of the trial process—the contents of the substantive criminal law are determined in part by procedural considerations.

[16] For this as the defining mark of *mala prohibita*, see e.g. G. Williams, *Criminal Law: The General Part* (2nd edn., London, 1961) 189; G. H. Gordon, *The Criminal Law of Scotland* (2nd edn., Edinburgh, 1978) 17–20; W. R. LaFave and A. W. Scott, *Criminal Law* (2nd edn., St Paul, 1986) 32–35.

reason to refrain. In many cases (including many driving offences, and many 'regulatory' offences concerning health and safety), we should rather see the law as providing more or less artificial *determinationes* of *mala in se*—*determinationes* whose artificiality might be due, for instance, to concerns with proof or enforceability, or to a concern to specify precise requirements for agents who cannot always be trusted to decide for themselves what kinds of conduct are or are not safe:[17] both kinds of factor underpin, for instance, the creation of legal speed limits (rather than relying on the *malum in se* offence of dangerous driving), and definitions of criminal 'drinking and driving' which refer to the proportion of alcohol in the blood rather than to the driver's impaired fitness.

I should note three points about my argument so far. First, I do not suggest that rejecting a simple positivist picture of the criminal law as a set of sanction-backed commands suffices by itself to justify the account I am offering. That account is, I think, independently plausible: but it can be usefully illuminated by contrasting it with the simple positivist picture.

Secondly, I do not suppose that the criminal law must speak *either* the purely peremptory language of power or authority, *or* the purely moral language that I claim is appropriate to it: it could speak initially in the moral language that identifies crimes as public wrongs, but seek to give its definitions of crimes more persuasive motivational force by adding the threat of sanctions as a deterrent.[18] All I have claimed so far is that it must at least address the citizens in that moral language, and that to talk simply of it as 'prohibiting' certain kinds of conduct does not capture this crucial point.

Thirdly, on the picture sketched here the criminal law must appeal to, and depends for its legitimacy on, the shared public values of a normative political community to which all those whom it claims to bind belong, and in which they can all make their voices heard. Some will argue that no such shared values are to be found in our contemporary societies: that they are, rather, characterized by disagreement and conflict even about the central values that, on my account, should be embodied in the criminal law.[19] All I can say here is that, whilst a liberal political community should indeed be characterized by, and should welcome, wide debate and disagreement about matters of value, the legitimacy of its criminal law does depend on there being sufficiently wide agreement in certain central values (both substantive and procedural) which

---

[17] It is in such contexts that the criminal law comes closest to claiming the kind of authority that Raz thinks is legitimate: see J. Raz, *The Morality of Freedom* (Oxford, 1986) ch. 3.

[18] Compare the suggestion that criminal punishment is to be justified partly in retributivist terms as communicating the censure that criminals deserve, and partly in deterrent terms as providing a prudential disincentive for those who are insufficiently motivated by the law's moral appeal: A. von Hirsch, *Censure and Sanctions* (Oxford, 1993) ch. 2; Duff (n. 8 above) ch. 3.3.

[19] For examples of such arguments (reflecting different starting points and arguing to very different conclusions) see A. W. Norrie, *Crime, Reason and History* (London, 1993); H. Bianchi, *Justice as Sanctuary* (Bloomington, 1994); J. Waldron, *Law and Disagreement* (Oxford, 1999).

can properly be claimed to be binding on all citizens; insofar as such agreement is lacking, the law's legitimacy is undermined.[20]

Why does any of this matter in relation to 'rules for citizens'? Do my comments amount to anything more than the trivial point that to talk of the criminal law as 'prohibiting' central *mala in se* is somewhat artificial? They do amount to more than this: thinking of the law as issuing 'prohibitions' which citizens are to 'obey' invites a particular, and distorting, way of thinking about the function that such 'prohibitions' should serve, and about how they should be formulated.

C. IDENTIFYING WRONGS

If the law is in the business of issuing prohibitions or commands, which citizens are to obey, clarity, certainty, and consistency are obvious *desiderata*: citizens must be able to understand, without doubt or confusion, what the law commands—what they must do; and they must be able to obey—which they could not do if the law's commands were mutually inconsistent. Now clarity, consistency, and certainty are virtues of a good criminal code, and *desiderata* for any tolerable system of criminal law:[21] but we must ask more carefully just what they require.

Consider two features of 'prohibitions' or 'commands'. First, they do not include, or invite a request for, content-dependent reasons. The content of a prohibition or command is not 'Do not do X, because . . .', with the 'because' clause being filled out by some reason relating to the character of X: it is either just 'Do not do X', or 'Do not do X because I tell you not to'; the reason offered concerns not the content of the prohibition, the character of X, but my authority or power thus to demand your obedience. Secondly, they neither presuppose nor seek any substantive agreement in judgements and values between the commander and the commanded: I do not suppose either that you already recognize, or that you will come to recognize, *why* (independently of my prohibition) you should not do X; I simply demand *that* you not do X. These features help to determine what will count as 'clarity' and 'certainty' in the context of prohibitions or commands.

Prohibitions are concerned with the 'that' rather than with the 'why': with making clear *that* those to whom they are addressed must not act in certain ways, rather than *why* those actions are wrong. Their addressees are not invited or expected to interpret the prohibitions in the light of the reasons that supposedly justify their content, or of the values that supposedly inform

---

[20] See further Duff (n. 8 above) chs. 2, 5.

[21] See Law Commission No. 143, *Codification of the Criminal Law* (London, 1985) paras. 1.3–9, and No. 177, *A Criminal Code for England and Wales* (London, 1989) para. 2.1. Hence the moral qualms that are rightly provoked by Dan-Cohen's commendation of a system of 'selective transmission': see Dan-Cohen (n. 6 above); Singer (n. 6 above).

them: for they are not expected or assumed to grasp or share those reasons and values. The prohibitions must therefore strive for *descriptive* clarity and certainty: they must provide clear, determinate factual specifications of the conduct they prohibit—specifications whose application avoids, as far as possible, any reliance on the normative understandings of those who are to apply them. In so far as they achieve such descriptive clarity and certainty, however, they are liable *not* to identify what their addressees could be expected to recognize as substantive *wrongs*, but rather to portray all crimes as mere *mala prohibita*; which, for the reasons noted above, is to distort the proper character and meaning of the criminal law as it concerns *mala in se*. What is wrong with murder, rape, theft, and the like as crimes is not that they are against the law, but that they are substantive pre-legal wrongs. A criminal law that is to be apt for liberal citizens must then declare them to be such wrongs in ways that make their wrongful character clear: but a law that aims to lay down 'prohibitions' or 'commands' for citizens to 'obey' will not do this, since it will have to eschew the very concepts in terms of which that wrongful character is understood.[22]

Let me illustrate and explain this claim by looking at two sections of Robinson's Draft Code of Conduct:[23]

3. Injury to a Person
You may not cause bodily injury or death to another person [subject to an exception for 'minor bodily injury' caused by conduct to which the other consents; s. 4].

24. Damage to or Theft of Property
You may not damage, take, use, dispose of, or transfer another's property without the other's consent. Property is anything of value, including services offered for payment and access to recorded information.

Each of these sections brings under one simply defined rule a range of existing offences: this simplifying and synthesizing character is, Robinson argues, one of the Code's merits.[24]

One point to note about both these sections is that they do *not* specify what Robinson counts as 'rules of conduct'. For, first, whilst 'conduct' (defined simply as 'physical acts' or 'bodily movement')[25] and its circumstances 'do contribute to the definition of the prohibited conduct, . . . result elements are not necessary to define the prohibited conduct. It is an actor's conduct, and not its results, that the criminal law prohibits'; the results brought about by that conduct are relevant, if at all, only to the issue of grading.[26] But these

---

[22] For a clear, because extreme, illustration of the line of thought I want to identify and criticize here, see R. L. Gainer, 'The Culpability Provisions of the Model Penal Code' (1988) 19 Rutgers LJ 575.

[23] Robinson (n. 3 above) 211–220.   [24] See ibid., 185–188.

[25] See ibid., 26, 51; nor need conduct prohibited by the Code of Conduct be voluntary: involuntariness blocks liability for rule-violations (see ibid., 35–38; Draft Code of Adjudication, s. 220).

[26] Robinson (n. 3 above) 128.

sections specify the prohibited conduct in terms of its results. Secondly, the requirements of 'mens rea' or 'culpability' are generally relevant not to defining the prohibited conduct, but to determining the agent's liability for a rule-violation, or the seriousness of that violation;[27] but some of the terms in section 24, as they would be understood by ordinary citizens, imply a particular intention on the part of the agent. I will comment on the exclusion of mens rea concepts from the rules of conduct later (section E below): but we must wonder why Robinson did not draft a Code of Conduct that specified what he would count as 'rules of conduct'. For instance, why should s. 3 prohibit 'caus[ing] bodily harm or injury', rather than 'acting in a way that creates a substantial unjustified risk of causing bodily injury or death'?[28]

One answer to this question (though not one that Robinson would offer) is that 'caus[ing] bodily injury or death' and 'creating a substantial unjustified risk of causing bodily injury or death' pick out different kinds of wrong; and a Code of Conduct should not just tell citizens that they must not engage in certain kinds of conduct, but identify recognizable wrongs from which citizens should refrain because they are wrongs. As I have indicated, I think that this is indeed what a criminal code should do for at least the central types of mala in se: but from this perspective there are further problems with these sections, since they conflate different kinds of wrong.

Section 3 also conflates causing bodily injury and causing death, perhaps on the grounds that in both cases we have the same kind of wrong, and that the difference between them is one of seriousness, which belongs with the grading provisions of the Code of Adjudication;[29] and it conflates all the different modes of injuring which statutes have often distinguished. Underpinning Robinson's formulation might be the 'conduct-cause-harm' model of criminal wrongdoing. We first identify a relevant kind of harm (e.g. death or bodily injury), and then identify as 'wrongs', or 'rule-violations', human actions which cause such harm. The relation between action (or 'conduct') and harm is purely contingent: the harm is identified in a way that makes no essential reference to a human action as its cause; what makes the action wrong is its causal relationship to the harm.[30] This is inadequate as a general model of criminal wrongdoing, even in the case of such 'result-crimes' as homicide: but I will not rehearse the arguments against it here.[31]

---

[27] See ibid., 129–137: only 'generally', because the definition of the rule of conduct for inchoate crimes might need to refer to some 'culpability' element.

[28] The suggested replacement is a particularized version of s. 51 of Robinson's Draft Code.

[29] See Robinson (n. 3 above) 232; Draft Code of Adjudication, s. 304.

[30] See, e.g., J. Feinberg, Harm to Others (New York, 1984) chs. 1–3.

[31] See R. A. Duff, Criminal Attempts (Oxford, 1996) 366–369. See too J. Gardner, 'Rationality and the Rule of Law in Offences Against the Person' (1994) 53 Cambridge Law Journal 502, J. Horder, 'Rethinking Non-Fatal Offences against the Person' (1994) 14 Oxford Journal of Legal Studies 335, on Law Commission No. 218, Legislating the Criminal Code: Offences against the Person and General Principles (London, 1993) (and compare ss. 70–72 of the Draft Criminal Code in Law Commission No. 177, n. 21 above): their critiques can also be applied to Robinson's Code.

Section 24 also conflates different kinds of wrong, in three ways. First, it covers both what we would ordinarily count as 'theft' and kinds of taking that we would not (morally, or under existing law) so count. If I borrow your ladder without your consent and return it undamaged, I commit no offence under English law or under the Model Penal Code, for I do not intend to deprive you of it permanently:[32] but I violate Robinson's Code of Conduct, and, if prosecuted, could avoid conviction only if the court judged my violation to be 'too trivial to warrant the condemnation of a criminal conviction'.[33] If we ask why the Code of Conduct should prohibit, as violations of the same rule, both theft and temporary non-consensual borrowing, the answer might be that Robinson wants, as far as possible, to avoid including culpability elements in the rules of conduct (the main difference between theft and illegitimate borrowing lies in the agent's intention): but the cost of this is to conflate very different kinds of wrong.

Secondly, Robinson's Code separates out the elements of some existing crimes: it includes no offence of robbery, but separate offences of theft and of 'Injury to a Person' (section 3) or 'Criminal Threat' (section 9); no burglary, but separate offences of 'Criminal Trespass' (section 25) and theft (or attempted theft; section 49).[34] This is, Robinson argues, a beneficial simplification of the proliferation of offences in existing law: we do not need a separate offence of burglary, since burglary is no more than a combination of criminal trespass and some other attempted crime; robbery is no more than a combination of criminal injury or threat and theft.[35] This is right if, but only if, the aim of the rules of conduct is simply to identify, in a descriptive and morally sanitized way, kinds of conduct which are prohibited: if citizens have already been told that they must not injure or threaten others, or take others' property without their consent, they need not also be told that they must not injure or threaten others in order to take their property without their consent. If, on the other hand, a criminal code should identify distinctive kinds of wrong that citizens are to recognize as wrongs, there is room for doubt: for burglary and robbery are, qua wrongs, more than (or different from) the sum of their parts. The wrongful character of the trespass committed by a burglar depends on the intention with which it is committed. Robbery is not just a physical attack or threat, *plus* theft: the character of the attack or the threat as a particular kind of wrong is determined in crucial part by the fact that it is made in order to steal.[36]

Thirdly, Robinson's section 24 covers both criminal damage and theft; both theft and obtaining by deception. We might (especially if we accept a

---

[32] See Theft Act 1968, ss. 1(1), 6; Model Penal Code, ss. 223.0(1), 223.2.

[33] Robinson (n. 3 above) 225; Draft Code of Adjudication, s. 201.

[34] Contrast on robbery Theft Act 1968, s. 8, Model Penal Code, s. 222.1; on burglary, Theft Act 1968, s. 9, Model Penal Code, s. 221.1.

[35] Robinson (n. 3 above) 188.

[36] See also A. P. Simester and G. R. Sullivan, *Criminal Law: Theory and Doctrine* (Oxford, 2000) 493–494 on robbery, and 507–508 on burglary.

'conduct-cause-harm' model of crime) be tempted to say that these offences are rightly classed together: in each case we find conduct that causes harm to a person's property interests—that causes them to lose, if not their property absolutely, at least the full enjoyment of and control over their property; and the particular way in which or means by which that harm is caused makes no essential difference to the character of the wrong thus committed. But if, on the other hand, we focus on the idea of wrongful *action*, we will see significant differences amongst these cases, differences not in *degree*, but in *kind*, of wrongdoing: between one who *destroys* another's property and one who 'appropriates' it for her own or another's use; between one who covertly steals another's property and one who obtains it by deceiving the victim.[37]

To note that Robinson's Code of Conduct does not separate out offences that our existing systems of criminal law distinguish is not of course yet to criticize it; indeed, he would argue that this feature is one of his Code's merits.[38] It does, however, generate a general criticism of his Code, and of the approach to clarifying the criminal law that it exemplifies, if we think both that the criminal law, as addressed to the citizens, should identify and define relevant types of 'public' wrong in terms that enable citizens to recognize them as such, and that those terms can find no place in the austerely descriptive simplicities of a Robinsonian code.

I have argued for the first of these claims already: the criminal law, in its definitions of *mala in se*, should address the citizens in terms of substantive values that already, pre-legally, demand their allegiance; it must identify crimes in terms that make clear not merely *that* such conduct is 'prohibited', but how and why it is *wrong*. This also requires the law to identify and separate out relevantly different *kinds* of wrong, so that their wrongful character can be recognized; and my first complaint about Robinson's Code is that it fails to do this.[39] But how can it be done?

It can be done, I suggest, only through the maintenance of a suitable set of 'thick' legal concepts, which connect rather closely to some of the 'thick' ethical concepts that structure our extra-legal moral thought.[40] Thick ethical concepts involve an indissoluble interweaving of fact and value: they describe

---

[37] Compare S. Shute and J. Horder, 'Thieving and Deceiving: What is the Difference?' (1993) 56 Modern Law Review 548; J. Gardner, 'On the General Part of the Criminal Law', in R. A. Duff (ed.), *Philosophy and the Criminal Law: Principle and Critique* (Cambridge, 1998) 205, at 247–249.

[38] See n. 24 above.

[39] One could also appeal here to the 'principle of fair labelling': the law's definitions of offences (and the verdicts brought against those convicted of such offences) should as far as practicable give accurate, reasonably precise specifications of the wrong committed; see A. J. Ashworth, 'The Elasticity of Mens Rea', in C. F. H. Tapper (ed.), *Crime, Proof and Punishment* (London, 1981) 45, at 53–56 (using the better notion of 'representative labelling'), *Principles of Criminal Law* (3rd edn., Oxford, 1999) 90–93. But the crucial question here is: what is it that must be fairly or representatively labelled?

[40] For 'thick' ethical concepts, see B. Williams, *Ethics and the Limits of Philosophy* (London, 1985) ch. 8.

human beings and their actions in terms of substantive and specific ethical values. Such concepts include those that identify virtues and vices (courage and cowardice, honesty and dishonesty), and those that identify different types of moral wrong: obvious examples would be murder, rape, theft, deception, defrauding, endangering. It is on these concepts that the criminal law should draw in identifying central *mala in se*: for it is in terms of such concepts that citizens can most readily recognize wrongs as wrongs.[41] The criminal law's thick legal concepts will, for various reasons, not be identical to the thick ethical concepts that structure citizens' extra-legal thought: but so long as they are closely related to some of those concepts, as specialized legal versions of them, they will enable the law to speak to citizens in the appropriate terms—in terms of what they can recognize as substantive kinds of wrong. However, it is just these kinds of concept that are missing from Robinson's Code, and that will inevitably be missing from any Code that tries to provide purified descriptive specifications of prohibited conduct. They will be missing because they are irreducibly normative concepts, whose application depends on a grasp of the substantive values they embody: they pre-suppose a set of shared values, and a shared normative language in which those values can be articulated and discussed; they are therefore radically unsuited to a criminal code which aims to provide descriptively clear and determinate specifications of 'prohibitions'.

Much more needs, of course, to be said about what kinds of thick concept are appropriate to our criminal law; about the ways in which, and the extent to which, they can diverge from our extra-legal ethical concepts; about how *mala prohibita*, both pure and impure,[42] should be understood and defined from this perspective; about the extent to which the requisite extra-legal agreement in values and in normative language exists—and about the implications of its non-existence. I cannot pursue these issues here: but my argument so far has been that if the criminal law is to address us, as it should, as citizens of a normative political community, it must speak to us in terms not simply of what is 'prohibited', but of what is wrong; and it must speak in a normative language which citizens can understand as identifying relevant kinds of wrong which should be eschewed and condemned as wrongs.

D. EXCUSES AND 'ATTRIBUTION': THE CASE OF DURESS

Robinson and Fletcher agree that we must distinguish offence definitions from defences; that among exculpatory defences we must distinguish justifications from excuses; and that whilst justifications belong to the 'rules for

---

[41] I do not suggest that such thick ethical concepts are always and wholly *pre*-legal; indeed, it would be surprising if they were *not* in part conditioned by the law's concepts.
[42] See text at n. 16 above.

citizens' (in the Code of Conduct), excuses belong to the Code of Adjudication, or the norms of attribution, which are addressed to the courts.

A 'defence', on this view, exempts the agent from liability for conduct that
satisfies the definition of a crime specified in the 'special part' of the criminal
law. Justifications exempt her from liability because her conduct was, if not
positively right or required, permissible in the law's eyes;[43] excuses exempt
her from liability because . . . what? A familiar answer is that they exempt her
because, although she committed a wrong or violated a rule of conduct, that
wrongdoing cannot fairly be attributed to her, or she cannot fairly be held liable for it: whereas justifications negate the 'wrong' in her doing, excuses
negate her responsibility or liability for the wrong that she did.[44]

My primary concern in this section is with the claim that excuses do not belong amongst the 'rules for citizens' that the law declares. This will involve
asking whether excuses do in general block the 'attribution' of an action to an
agent, rather than modifying the character of what is attributed: that is,
whether we can completely insulate the notion of 'wrongdoing', or of 'violation' of rules of conduct, from that of 'attribution', or 'liability'.[45]

Sometimes, this picture seems apt—for instance in cases in which insanity
serves as a distinctive defence.[46] In such cases insanity is clearly an excuse:[47]
the agent committed (what would otherwise count as) a crime—he intentionally killed another person; his insanity does not render his action right or permissible, but exempts him from liability and condemnation for it. His insanity
did not give him reason to do what he otherwise should not do—it did not entitle him to reason 'Since I'm insane, I can legitimately kill this person': it gives
others reasons not to hold him liable. We can see here too why we might talk
of not 'attributing' the action to him: we identify 'him', as a responsible agent
to whom actions can be appropriately attributed, with his sane self, whose action this was not. Even here we might wonder whether the notion of 'wrongdoing' can be completely insulated from that of 'attribution': an insane killer

---

[43] I take it here that we do, and the law should, count as 'justified' not only conduct that we
praise as 'the right thing' to do, but also conduct that we regard as merely permissible: see
J. Dressler, 'New Thoughts about the Concept of Justification in the Criminal Law: A Critique of
Fletcher's Thinking and *Rethinking*' (1984) 32 UCLA LR 61, at 70–75, 81–87, criticizing
Fletcher's arguments on this issue; S. Uniacke, *Permissible Killing: The Self-defence Justification
of Homicide* (Cambridge, 1994) 14–15.

[44] See Fletcher (n. 4 above) chs. 6.6–7, 10.3; Robinson (n. 3 above) 69, 81–82, 157, 197;
Alldridge (n. 6 above).

[45] See J. Dressler, 'Reflections on Excusing Wrongdoers: Moral Theory, New Excuses and the
Model Penal Code' (1988) 19 Rutgers LJ 671, n. 37.

[46] As distinct, that is, from cases in which it negates a standard *mens rea* requirement; and
from cases in which it renders the person wholly non-responsible, not answerable for anything
that he does.

[47] Some deny this: the insane whose actions lack 'rational intelligibility', like infants and
sleepwalkers, 'are not responsible for their actions and therefore need no excuses for what they
do' (J. Gardner, 'The Gist of Excuses' (1998) 1 Buffalo Criminal Law Review 575, at 589). Insanity is indeed a very different kind of excuse from such excuses as duress: but so long as we are
not misled into supposing that all excuses share just the same logic and structure, I see no reason
not to call it an excuse.

violates a Robinsonian rule of conduct, and commits what the law defines as a crime, but it is not clear that the action which cannot be attributed to him is the very kind of wrong that is attributed to the sane, non-excused killer. However, I will not pursue this issue here, since my main concern is with cases in which this picture of excuses loses its plausibility.

Consider duress, which (as a criminal defence) is standardly portrayed as an excuse.[48] If we take 'acting under duress' to mean something like 'acting under a human threat', this is surely wrong: some actions under duress are (morally and should be legally) justified by that duress. A bank clerk who hands over £10,000 of the bank's money at gun-point, or a hostage who drives a stolen car at gun-point, commits what would, absent that threat, be a wrong, but should be neither blamed nor convicted if the threat was sufficiently serious and believable: not because she has an excuse, but because in that context her action is not wrong (it is not morally wrong, and should not count as criminal)—because it is justified.[49] We might indeed sometimes commend such an agent for doing 'the right thing' in that situation, and for being clear-headed enough to see what she should do; we might think that it would have been rash or stupid, rather than heroic or courageous, to resist. In other cases we might not commend the action or admire its agent, but would at least think that giving in as this person did was not wrong—that it was morally (and so should be legally) acceptable or permissible, even if not commendable. In either case, however, there is no wrong committed by that agent for which an excuse is needed (though there is of course a wrong committed by the person who made the threat).

This might seem too hasty. It might be argued that to allow duress to justify a normally criminal action would be to permit 'the abrogation of law in the face of threats';[50] or that this would permit third parties to assist the person under duress to commit the crime, or forbid others to resist the crime;[51] none of which the law should do. But, first, neither we nor the law should require bank clerks to resist robbers at the likely cost of their own lives: they should be permitted (even expected) to hand over the money at gun-point (neither is this to abrogate the law in the face of threats—the law focuses on the threatener). Secondly, even if justifications have the implications claimed by Fletcher and

---

[48] See, e.g., Fletcher (n. 4 above) 829–835; P. Alldridge, 'Developing the Defence of Duress' [1986] Criminal LR 433, 'Rules for Courts and Rules for Citizens' (n. 6 above) at 495–499; J. Dressler, 'Exegesis of the Law of Duress: Justifying the Excuse and Searching for its Proper Limits' (1989) 62 Southern California LR 133; Robinson (n. 3 above) 69, 227 (Draft Code of Adjudication, s. 224); J. Gardner (n. 47 above).

[49] This is not to say that if the agent-victim in a case of justifying duress was actually brought to trial on a criminal charge, she would plead duress as a distinct defence; it might rather be that, in virtue of the duress, she lacked the requisite *mens rea*. But duress still justifies, renders right or permissible, what would otherwise have been a wrongful action.

[50] P. Alldridge, 'The Coherence of Defences' [1983] Criminal LR 665, at 668.

[51] On these supposed implications of justification, see Fletcher (n. 4 above) 759–762; Robinson (n. 3 above) 96.

Robinson,[52] I would think it right for another person to assist the bank clerk in giving over the money, and wrong for another to resist that giving over, *unless* that third party could effectively neutralize the threat.

Those who insist that 'duress' is an excuse, however, need not be denying any of this: they could rather be arguing that we should reserve the term 'duress' for cases in which the agent acts unjustifiably, or wrongly, under the influence of a threat, and locate cases of justified action under threat in some other legal category of justification (such as necessity, in so far as that can be a justification). Duress would then count as an excuse, in so far as it provides a defence at all. But what kind of excuse is it?

Sometimes, duress does operate rather like insanity as an excuse. Suppose that someone is subjected to torture to force him to reveal secret information, and finally gives in, in pain and terror, to avoid further agony; or he is subjected to an immediate threat which is so terrifying that he is completely panicked by it, and does what he is told to do. His conduct is not strictly involuntary (if it were, he would not be doing what he must do to avert the threat); it is indeed at least minimally intentional, in that he acts as he does in order to avert the threat. But, in excusing him, we would say that the torture or the threat rendered him incapable of rational practical thought, of ordered as opposed to disordered practical reasoning: his giving in did not display a lack of commitment to the values violated by his action; as far as we know, and as his own later response to what he has done should reveal,[53] he has a proper concern for those values; but the pressure to which he was subjected seriously impaired his capacity to guide his own actions in the light of that commitment. We wish, and he wishes, that he could have resisted (giving in was not justified): but he could not—his 'will' was 'overborne'.[54]

Even in this kind of case, duress as an excuse is not grounded in a purely factual claim that 'he could not resist' the threat. The figure of the 'reasonable person', the 'sober person of reasonable firmness',[55] should still play a normative and criterial (as distinct from evidential) role: for we should ask whether a person with the kind of commitment to the values protected by the law (and violated by this action), and with the kind and degree of courage that we can properly demand of citizens, would have been thus affected by such a threat—i.e. whether his being thus affected did or did not reveal a lack of such commitment or courage.[56]

---

[52] Which is arguable; see e.g. Dressler (n. 43 above) at 87–98.

[53] Compare Aristotle, *Nicomachean Ethics* III.1, 1110b18–24 on the significance of the agent's own response to what he has done.

[54] See *Hudson and Taylor* [1971] 2 QB 202, at 206 (Lord Widgery).

[55] *Graham* (1982) 74 Cr App R 235, at 241 (Lord Lane); see Model Penal Code, s. 2.09(1). I leave aside here the question of which of the defendant's characteristics we should ascribe to the 'reasonable' person: the short answer is that we should ascribe any characteristics that affected his response to the threat without revealing a lack of proper commitment or courage.

[56] See R. A. Duff, 'Choice, Character and Criminal Liability' (1993) 12 Law & Philosophy 345, at 357–359. Hence the significance of Aristotle's comment that 'some acts, perhaps, we cannot be

In such cases, we can certainly say that the defence of duress does not provide reasons which could properly guide the agent's actions: if he reasons to himself 'if I am so terrified by a threat that I cannot think straight, the law allows me to give in; I am thus terrified by this threat; so I'll give in', his reasoning undercuts the very claim on which he wants to rely. We can also say, with two qualifications, that we can no longer properly 'attribute' the action, or the wrong, to the agent: the action or wrong (betraying his country) is not properly 'his' as a responsible agent, because he was non-culpably rendered incapable of guiding his actions in the light of what we can suppose to be his own proper commitments.[57]

(The qualifications are, first, that we would not expect someone who had such proper commitments simply to disown the action as something that happened to him: he has still betrayed his country, and we would expect that to matter to him. Secondly, is not clear that the wrong which we do not attribute to him is just the same wrong as we attribute to someone who culpably, without duress, betrays his country; this point will become clearer shortly.)

However, other cases of duress are more problematic. It seems implausible, for instance, that the defendants in *Hudson and Taylor*,[58] who committed perjury under threat of serious injury, were so panicked by the threat that they were rendered incapable of rational thought and action; and implausible to claim that only threats which have such an effect should provide a complete defence, as distinct from mere mitigation of sentence. The exculpatory claim in such cases is, rather, that to have resisted such a threat would have required a kind or degree of 'firmness'—of courage, of commitment to the values at stake in the situation—which we cannot reasonably expect or demand of a citizen; that is, that in giving in to a threat to which even a person of 'reasonable firmness' would have given in, the agent did not display a culpable *lack* of commitment or of courage.

In *this* kind of case we can say that the agent is excused because she 'lived up to' the 'standards of character which were demanded of' her;[59] or because she 'attained . . . society's legitimate expectation of moral strength'.[60] Such claims might sound like justifications rather than excuses—as claiming not, admittedly, that her action was positively right or admirable (resistance would have been the admirable course), but at least that it was permissible: but they need not be justificatory. As Dressler and Gardner explain the defence, its point seems to be analogous to a defence of 'reasonable mistake' (of

---

forced to do, but ought rather to face death after the most fearful sufferings' (*Nicomachean Ethics* III.1, 1110a26–28).

[57] The 'gist' of duress as an excuse in such cases is thus not what Gardner takes 'the gist of excuses' to be: the agent does not claim that he 'lived up to' the 'standards of character which were demanded of' him: Gardner (n. 47 above) 598.

[58] [1971] 2 QB 202.   [59] Gardner (n. 47 above) 598.

[60] Dressler (n. 48 above) 1334.

fact): the agent's 'choice' to give in was 'deficient, but reasonable';[61] her fear of the threat was 'rationally adequate, in [her] own eyes as well as according to the applicable standards of character, for [her] to commit the wrong', but she 'mistakenly' acts for that reason.[62] This implies that the agent must, at least at the time, *think* her action justifiable: that what excuses her is the reasonableness of that mistaken thought in that situation. That might be true in some cases: in others, however, the agent might realize that she should resist, but cannot bring herself to do so; she does not think her action justified, but is too weak, or lacking in courage, to act as she realizes she should. What excuses her is that the strength or courage required to resist such a threat is more than we can reasonably demand of a citizen: we should not demand that citizens be saints,[63] but it would require a saint-like courage or firmness to resist.

This is not to say that the agent is 'permitted' not to resist (that is, justified in not resisting), or that she does no wrong in giving in—as if, as far as the law is concerned, it does not matter or is up to her whether she resists or not: she should ideally resist, and falls short of the ideal standards of commitment and courage in failing to resist. But what citizens should ideally do is more than we, or the law, can properly *demand* that they do, on pain of condemnation if they do not;[64] and that is why, whilst we do not regard such an agent's action as justified, we excuse her.

In this kind of case, however, we cannot say that the agent is excused because the wrong that she did cannot be properly 'attributed' to her. There is *a* wrong that it would indeed be inaccurate or misleading to attribute to her simply and without qualification: 'committing perjury', insofar as that bare description implies by its silence that this was *the* relevant feature of her action. Her commission of perjury is a wrong which we might instead attribute to those who threatened her and thus brought her to commit perjury, but it is not the wrong that *she* did. What she did, the action we judge, was to 'commit perjury under threat of being seriously injured': we do not condemn her for that action because, although it was wrong in the sense that in committing it she fell short of the ideals (of commitment and courage) to which she should aspire as a citizen, she did not fall short of those standards which we can properly *demand* that citizens attain.

When duress provides this kind of defence, is it still true that it does not belong among the 'rules for citizens', or that the legal definition of the defence is 'not supposed to provide any guidance to those whose actions may fall foul of

---

[61] Dressler (n. 48 above) 1367, n. 194. Dressler actually quotes Kadish (S. Kadish, 'Excusing Crime' (1987) 75 California LR 257, at 259, 262) on the action as being 'deficient, but reasonable': but his own account is focused on the agent's choice.

[62] Gardner (n. 47 above) 597, 589.   [63] See Dressler (n. 48 above) 1367, 1373.

[64] I leave aside the question of whether it is more than they can demand of themselves, or condemn themselves for failing to do: as so often, the agent's appropriate first person judgements on or responses to her own conduct do not necessarily match the appropriate second or third person judgements of responses of others.

the criminal law'?[65] Such claims now look false. The defence depends on what can be properly or reasonably *demanded* of citizens in the way of firmness, commitment, and courage: but surely the rules of conduct should give citizens 'guidance' on what is thus demanded of them. This is not to say that the law should tell them that giving in to duress is 'permitted', since it is not: resistance is an ideal to which they should aspire. But if resistance is not 'demanded', this is a matter of what demands the law makes or does not make of the citizens; and such demands must be made *to* them. If we want to use 'selective transmission' as a way of controlling conduct (to make it less likely that citizens will give in to threats that they should ideally resist), we should certainly aim to conceal from citizens the fact they will not be convicted if they give in.[66] But if the law is to respect and address the citizens as responsible agents, a basic requirement is that it must not deceive them—it must make clear to them what the law demands of them and what is liable to happen to them if they flout those demands: 'selective transmission' is intended to deceive the citizens on these matters, and therefore has no place in the law of a liberal polity.

Part of the problem here might stem from a failure to distinguish two ways in which the existence and content of the defence of duress might figure in the practical reasoning of the agent who is under threat. One possibility is that he feeds into his reasoning the fact that if he gives in, he can nonetheless hope to avoid conviction and punishment by pleading duress; this then (as he sees it) removes what would have been a reason not to give in, and might tip the balance in favour of giving in.[67] In *this* case the defence lacks moral merit:[68] the fact that I will avoid conviction is not a good reason for giving in to a threat and committing a crime; someone who regards it as a good reason thereby displays a lack of the kind of commitment to and regard for the values violated by the crime which is properly demanded of citizens. But this is not the only way in which the existence of the defence could figure in the agent's practical reasoning.

The threatened agent has asked, let us suppose, 'What should I do?'; and his answer is, appropriately, 'I should resist'. But now he asks '*Must* I resist?'—a question which expresses, in part, his reluctance thus to sacrifice or endanger himself. That is not, admittedly, a question that a hero or an ideal citizen would ask herself: *she* would just set herself to do (or try to do) what she sees she should do. But it is a question that ordinary, indeed 'reasonable',

---

[65] Gardner (n. 47 above) 597; see G. Fletcher, 'Should Intolerable Prison Conditions Generate a Justification or an Excuse for Escape?' (1979) 26 UCLA LR 1355; and references in n. 48 above.

[66] See Dan-Cohen (n. 6 above) 632–634, 637–643, 671; for criticism, see Singer (n. 6 above) 84–100.

[67] This seems to be the possibility Gardner has in mind (n. 47 above, 597); see Fletcher (n. 65 above); Alldridge (n. 6 above) 499–501.

[68] Which is not to say that it should not succeed in law: we must ask whether and how it would be in practice possible to exclude it without doing injustice to others.

citizens would probably ask, since the weakness, the reluctance to sacrifice oneself, that the question reveals is not one that shows the person who asks it to be unreasonably deficient as a citizen.

What answer should this person receive? To say 'You must resist', whilst concealing the fact that he will not be condemned if he gives in (since he would not then fall short of the standards demanded of him), seems dishonest: it implies that resistance is demanded, when it is not. What he should receive is an answer that makes clear what is demanded of him: what is demanded not so much *by* the law (as if the law was the source of the demand), but *through* the law as articulating the values of the political community and the demands of citizenship of such a polity. That answer would make clear that he *should* aspire to resist (the threat is not sufficient to justify giving in), but that resistance is not in such a case *demanded* of him; and that is just the answer that is provided by the defence of duress, if properly expressed—as a defence which thus does properly help to guide citizens' actions.

The main result of this section is that legal excuses should sometimes figure in the 'rules for citizens', since they do sometimes provide reasons which can properly guide the citizens' actions. This result follows from the account sketched earlier of the terms and tone in which the criminal law should address the citizens, and a recognition of the complexities of duress as a defence; and it illustrates one way in which the distinction between 'rules for citizens' and 'rules for courts' is somewhat porous. I turn now to another way in which that apparently clear distinction becomes less clear and determinate on closer examination.

E. Rule-Violations, Wrongdoings and *Mens Rea*

Should the normal requirements of *mens rea* or 'fault' figure in the rules or norms addressed to the citizens, or only in those addressed to the courts? For Robinson, they generally have no role in the Code of Conduct: they are relevant not to specifying the kinds of conduct which are prohibited, but to the doctrines of liability and grading by which courts are to be guided; they therefore belong in the Code of Adjudication.[69] Fletcher by contrast, finally rejects the 'objective' theory of wrongdoing, which makes such matters as intention or knowledge relevant to attribution rather than to wrongdoing, in favour of the view that wrongdoing must be defined in terms that include such matters.[70] Someone who injures another person through blameless inadvertence violates section 3 of Robinson's Code of Conduct,[71] but is saved from liability by the blamelessness of that inadvertence: on Fletcher's account, however, he commits no act of wrongdoing for which he needs to be excused or saved from liability.

[69] See Robinson (n. 3 above) 129–137, and n. 27 above.
[70] See Fletcher (n. 4 above) 475–478, 553–554, 695.
[71] As does someone whose purely involuntary movements cause injury: see n. 25 above.

Now there is at least this much to be said for Robinson's account of the content of rules of conduct: if I am laying down prohibitions, I will not normally formulate them in terms that make explicit reference to intention, recklessness, or negligence: the rule will say 'Don't Φ', not 'Don't Φ intentionally/through recklessness/through negligence'.[72] Similarly, a simple expression of many of the action-guiding norms that figure in the criminal law would make no such explicit reference: 'You do wrong if you have sexual intercourse with someone who does not consent to it or is under 13/drive a car without a licence/sell a firearm to someone under 17/destroy or damage another's property without lawful excuse'.

On the other hand, and even if we think only of how the rules of conduct can make clear to citizens what they may not do, the claim that the rules of conduct need not refer to such *mens rea* requirements seems doubtful. For without *some* indication—explicit or implicit—of a 'fault element', the prohibition's addressees will have no clear idea of how they may or may not behave. If what is prohibited is simply Φ-ing intentionally (or knowingly), they will know how to go about obeying the prohibition: they simply have to refrain from acting in ways that they intend to (or know or believe would) constitute Φ-ing. But a prohibition of 'caus[ing] bodily injury or death to another person' is far wider than that: it prohibits any conduct that actually causes injury or death.[73] To try to obey that prohibition, I must take care lest I cause injury or death; but what kind or degree of care must I take? Similarly, if what is prohibited is 'caus[ing] false alarm or panic among a gathering of persons', or 'possess[ing] stolen property',[74] I need to know what kind or degree of care I must take lest I cause such alarm, or lest I have stolen property in my possession. Am I required merely to refrain from actions that I realize might satisfy the Code's definitions (leaving aside the question of what kind or degree of risk that 'might' should involve)—in which case recklessness as awareness of risk is implicit in the Code of Conduct; or to take steps to ensure that I notice and guard against such a risk (leaving aside the question of how strenuous those steps should be)—in which case negligence is implicit in the Code of Conduct?

Suppose I know that under the Code of Adjudication I will be liable to conviction only if I am 'at least reckless as to each element of the violation as described in the Code of Conduct' except that negligence suffices for homicide under section 3 and as to the victim's age in section 14(b)–(c).[75]

---

[72] See also Fletcher (n. 4 above) 477–478.

[73] See Robinson (n. 3 above) 213 (Draft Code of Conduct, s. 3), and text at nn. 23–24 above. There are further issues, which I cannot pursue here, about the relation between ordinary action-verbs ('kill', 'injure') and the causal phrases ('cause death', 'cause injury') that Robinson prefers: can we replace action-verbs by causal phrases throughout the Code of Conduct, without significant loss of meaning? This connects to the question of the adequacy of Robinson's 'conduct-cause-harm' model of criminal wrongdoing: see at nn. 30–31 above.

[74] Robinson (n. 3 above) 216–217 (Draft Code of Conduct, ss. 32, 37(c)).

[75] ibid. 225 (Draft Code of Adjudication, s. 200(1)).

Can I properly infer from this that what is prohibited under the other sections of the Code of Conduct is only conduct that the agent intends or expects to cause, or realizes might cause, the relevant result: that the Code does not generally require me to *take* the kind of care that it is negligent not to take, but only to refrain from doing what I intend or expect to cause, or realize might cause, a relevant result? This would be at odds with Robinson's insistence that *mens rea* elements do not generally belong in the Code of Conduct, and would undermine the insulation he seeks between the question of whether a rule of conduct has been 'violated', and that of whether the violator should be held liable for that violation. But I find it hard to see how he can avoid this result.

It is not plausible to say that what is required of the citizens is that they take *every* care to avoid causing the specified results,[76] but that they are excused so long as they do not cause the result intentionally or through recklessness (or, for sections 3 and 14, through negligence). For someone who pays reasonable attention to and takes reasonable precautions against any risk that his actions might cause death or that his sexual partner is under age, and who refrains from acting in ways that he realizes might well cause injury to another's body or damage to another's property surely lives up to the standards of conduct that a Robinsonian law requires of him.

Robinson's Code of Conduct is meant to 'provide *ex ante* direction to the members of the community as to the conduct that must be avoided (or that must be performed) upon pain of criminal sanction'.[77] If a citizen seeks guidance on what conduct she must avoid in virtue of section 3 of the Code, in particular on what its implications are for driving a motor vehicle (for she knows that this activity, however carefully conducted, can cause death or injury), what should she be told? One kind of answer would talk of driving with due care and attention, of the kinds of care she should take to make her driving as safe as is reasonably possible, whilst recognizing that even such care cannot guarantee that she will not cause death or injury. Another answer would tell her that the only way to make sure that she did not violate the law, as far as this aspect of her life was concerned, would be not to drive at all. A rational criminal code would surely generate the first kind of guidance: but if Robinson's Code of Conduct excludes all fault elements, it can only generate the second kind of guidance.

If the Code of Conduct is to perform the function Robinson assigns to it, of providing '*ex ante* direction' to the citizens, it cannot be cleansed of fault requirements to the extent that he wants to cleanse it; nor can issues of 'rule violation' be separated from issues of liability as sharply as he wants to separate them.

---

[76] We do of course talk of taking 'every care' to avoid some harm: but 'every care' in such contexts means 'all reasonable care'.

[77] Robinson (n. 3 above) 125.

There is a further and deeper objection to Robinson's attempt to eliminate fault elements from the Code of Conduct, arising from the objection discussed in section C above. I argued in section C that the criminal law should not operate as a set of rules which 'prohibit' certain kinds of conduct: it should rather, in addressing the citizens, declare and define certain kinds of public wrong, in ways that enable citizens to recognize them as wrongs. 'Causing bodily injury or death', however, does not specify a recognizable kind of wrong: not just because it conflates causing injury and causing death, and different modes of causing them,[78] but because it conflates different kinds of wrong that may be done in causing death or in causing injury, and conflates wrongs with harm-causing actions that are not wrongs. If I cause death or injury to another through a non-culpable accident, they have suffered serious harm through my agency, but I have not wronged them. Even if I do wrong by causing their death or injury, the *kind* of wrong I do depends on whether I cause death or injury intentionally, or through recklessness, or through negligence. An intended killing differs from killing through recklessness not just (nor always) in degree of seriousness or wrongfulness, but in the kind of wrong it perpetrates: apart from any extrinsic differences that there may be in the agent's motivation or in the actions' context, there is the crucial intrinsic difference between attacking another's life and (wilfully, knowingly) endangering it; and between the focused, practical indifference to the lives of those whom I endanger that I display in recklessly endangering their lives and the unfocused lack of proper care that I display in negligently endangering life.[79]

These different kinds of wrong are of course connected: it would be morally strange, if not incoherent, to accept that I would do wrong in intentionally killing or injuring another, whilst recognizing no wrong in acting in ways that create a substantial and unjustified risk of causing death or injury.[80] They are, however, still different kinds of wrong; and a criminal law which is to define public wrongs in ways that will make them recognizable as wrongs by the citizens should itself incorporate a recognition of such differences—else it will fail to connect to the extra-legal moral concepts on which, I have argued, its legitimacy depends.

[78] See n. 31 above.

[79] On attacks and endangerment see further Duff (n. 31 above) 363–366; on recklessness and negligence, see R. A. Duff, '*Caldwell* and *Lawrence*: The Retreat from Subjectivism' (1983) 3 Oxford Journal of Legal Studies 77, at 90–91.

[80] But we should not be too swift to infer the wrongness of risk-taking from the wrongness of intentional action. Simester argues that if 'killing James is an unjustified action', it 'follows' that 'D should also *take care* lest she kill James'; more generally '[t]he fact that an action is harmful or to be avoided generates . . . a reason to take care lest that action be done' ('Can Negligence be Culpable?' in J. Horder (ed.), *Oxford Essays in Jurisprudence* 4th Series (Oxford, 2000) 85, at 89). Depending on our criteria of action-description, this might be true: but we should not suppose that in general if it is wrong to bring about x intentionally, I therefore have reason to avoid acting in any way such that x will or might ensue. On some views of market ethics, I should not act with the intention of ruining a competitor: but the fact that an otherwise legitimate business activity of mine will lead to her ruin need not give me any reason not to engage in that activity.

Should we then say that the declarations and definitions of wrongs that the criminal law addresses to the citizens must include the fault elements of each offence—the requirements of intention, knowledge, recklessness, or negligence that constitute conditions of liability (not to mention other possible fault elements, such as dishonesty in theft)? Unfortunately, the matter is not that simple: whilst the fact or kind of wrongdoing does often depend on such aspects of the action, this is by no means always true. One example must suffice to illustrate this point, the further ramifications of which I cannot discuss here.

Fletcher argues that mistakes of fact sometimes negate wrongdoing, but sometimes serve instead to provide an excuse for wrongdoing: mistakes about elements in the *definition* of the offence negate wrongdoing, and should secure an acquittal even if they are unreasonable; but mistakes about justificatory facts extrinsic to the definition of the offence can only provide an excuse, and therefore exculpate only if they are reasonable.[81] I am not now concerned with the general claim, but with its application to the issue of mistaken belief in consent in the context of rape, and to *Morgan* in particular.[82] Fletcher argues that a mistaken belief in the victim's consent should be reasonable or free from fault if it is to justify an acquittal; and that rather than seeing the victim's lack of consent as part of the definition of rape as a wrong, we should see her consent as a justification for what would otherwise be a wrong (for a violation of a prohibitory norm). Given his general account of wrongdoing (as satisfying the definition of an offence plus lack of justification) and attribution (as a matter of whether a wrongdoing can be attributed to the agent), he can sustain the first claim only if he can also sustain the second: but whilst the first claim is right, the second is wrong—in which case, the neat structure of Fletcher's account is undermined.

To sustain the second claim, Fletcher argues that the definition of rape should simply be 'sexual penetration':[83] the 'prohibitory norm' whose violation the other's consent justifies is a norm prohibiting sexual penetration. Now this must be a 'morally coherent' norm, one that makes sense as a moral norm to citizens of our society:[84] but it is implausible as a moral norm that could underpin the offence of rape. First, even those who think that *extramarital* sexual relations are wrong do not typically think that 'sexual penetration' *per se* violates a norm—that it 'incriminates the actor' or 'is typically sufficient to regard the act as wrongful':[85] for there is in their eyes nothing

---

[81] Fletcher (n. 4 above) ch. 9; see A. P. Simester, 'Mistakes in Defence' (1992) 12 Oxford Journal of Legal Studies 295.

[82] See Fletcher (n. 4 above) 699–707; *Morgan* [1975] 2 WLR 923; but contrast Robinson (n. 3 above) 214 (Code of Conduct, s. 14(a)).

[83] Fletcher (n. 4 above) 705. He expresses some misgivings about this, and justifies his view of *Morgan* in terms of 'forcible sexual penetration' as what must be justified or excused (at 705–707): but his final view is that the offence consists simply in sexual penetration.

[84] Fletcher (n. 4 above) 567.

[85] ibid., 562, explicating the two essential features of norm-violations.

thus intrinsically incriminating about the fact of intra-marital sexual penetration; but the law of rape covers non-consensual intra-marital sexual penetration without the victim's consent.[86] Secondly, those 'morally coherent' norms which do portray extra-marital sexual penetration as wrong or 'incriminating' do not typically portray it as the same kind of wrong as rape: what is supposedly wrong with extra-marital sexual penetration has to do with the proper role of sex in human relationships (relationships assumed in this context to be consensual), with its connection to procreation, and so on; what is wrong with rape is that it exercises a brutal power over its victim and denies her or his sexual integrity.[87] We thus cannot understand rape as a wrong by seeing it as a violation of a norm prohibiting sexual penetration, which is not justified by the other person's consent.

On Fletcher's account, a man who has sexual intercourse with a woman in the mistaken belief that she consents has violated a prohibitory norm, without justification; and since his mistake concerns a justificatory fact, rather than a defining element of the offence, he should be acquitted only if that mistake was itself 'free from fault'. Were lack of consent part of the definition of the offence, even a culpably unreasonable mistake would suffice to acquit him, since it would negate the 'intent' which is essential to the violation of the relevant norm (as it is to the violation of all prohibitory norms, except those covering negligent conduct). On my view, lack of consent is part of the definition of rape, since it is essential to the kind of wrong that rape involves: but it does not follow from this that even an unreasonably mistaken belief that the victim consents should entitle the defendant to an acquittal. For whatever the agent's beliefs, the victim was subjected to non-consensual sexual intercourse; which is to say that she suffered, at his hands, the wrong of being raped.[88] Intrinsic to that wrong is at least the man's intention to have sexual intercourse with her: but it does not necessarily involve his 'intent' as to her lack of consent. It follows that we cannot simply say, as Fletcher wants to, that the normal requirements of *mens rea* are part of the definition of every offence, of the wrongdoing that every offence must involve.

(Is this true of other offences than rape? I cannot pursue this question here, but suspect that something like this might also be true of, for instance, theft and criminal damage. That the property I take or damage belongs to another person is, I take it, part of the definition of theft and criminal damage as

---

[86] See Criminal Justice and Public Order Act 1994, s. 142.

[87] There is a strand of feminist thought, associated especially with Andrea Dworkin, which portrays all sexual penetration of women by men as having something of the character of rape: but it cannot plausibly be said that such a moral view underpins our existing laws of rape; nor, I think, is it Fletcher's view. For a subtle discussion of the character of rape as a wrong, see J. Gardner and S. Shute, 'The Wrongness of Rape', in J. Horder (ed.), *Oxford Essays in Jurisprudence*, 4th Series (Oxford, 2000) 193.

[88] Does it follow that he has 'committed rape' (cf. Lord Cross in *Morgan* [1975] 2 WLR 923, at 926)? Yes, in that he has raped her. See further R. A. Duff, *Intention, Agency and Criminal Liability* (Oxford, 1990) 167–172.

74 R.A. Duff

wrongs: if I covertly take from another person what I mistakenly believe to be my property, or deliberately destroy her property in the mistaken belief that it is mine, she has suffered a wrong of the relevant kind.)

F. CONCLUDING REMARKS

I have argued that we should not understand the criminal law as laying down 'prohibitions' or 'rules' for the citizens, which they are to 'obey': it should rather aim to declare and define 'public' wrongs, from which citizens should refrain because they recognize them as wrongs. I have also argued, on the basis of that general view of the terms in which the criminal law of a liberal polity should address its citizens, that the neat distinctions which some theorists want to draw between 'rules for citizens' and 'rules for courts' cannot be sustained: in particular, that excuses such as duress undermine such sharp distinctions; and that we cannot say either (with Robinson) that the requirements of *mens rea* should not generally figure in the 'rules of conduct', or (with Fletcher) that those requirements must always figure in the definition of the offence, and thus among the norms of wrongdoing addressed to the citizens.

I have not offered an alternative account of the structure of the criminal law, to replace those offered by such theorists as Robinson and Fletcher, neither can I claim that it is only lack of space that prevents me offering one here; nor do I suggest that the kinds of distinction that they want to draw, in particular that between wrongdoing and attribution, would have no part to play in such an account—indeed, I have argued that the specification of relevant kinds of wrongdoing is central to those aspects of the criminal law that are directly addressed to the citizens. My aim has been in part to argue that any normative account of the structure or logic of the criminal law must begin with a suitable conception of how, in what terms or tones, the criminal law should address the citizens, and to sketch what I take to be a suitable conception. I have also indicated some of the implications of that conception—partly in the hope that if those implications are anyway plausible in themselves, they will also help to render plausible the conception from which they flow. Further defence of that conception, and explorations of its further implications, are tasks for other occasions: but one result that we should not look for is the articulation of a new, logically neat and tidy, structure for the criminal law. For the point is not just that our actual criminal law is in fact much less tidy than theorists' accounts of its structure often suggest (they can recognize, but deplore, that fact), but that an adequate normative account of what the criminal law *ought* to be must also be much less tidy than such theorists would like.

4

The Modern General Part: Three Illusions

PAUL H. ROBINSON

We criminal law theorists like to think of ourselves as moving existing criminal law theory to a higher plateau of rationality, of advancing current understanding beyond that which was given us by our criminal law theory predecessors. But the truth is that our advances in rationality often are less than they appear, sometimes only advances in the appearance of rationality. This chapter gives illustrations of three illusions. As will become apparent, they are of different sorts. One illustrates the inevitable limitation of any theoretical advance; one is an example of an inevitable limitation that has been unnecessarily retained over time; and one a case of possibly cynical deception.

The focus here is upon American criminal law and its development (with some reference to the Draft Criminal Code for England and Wales), but there is nothing special about American criminal law or theory on this point. These illustrations are likely to have some form of counterpart in the criminal law theory of most systems.

A. ARTICULATING THE PURPOSES OF LIABILITY AND PUNISHMENT

1. The Problem: Policy Mush

Before the wave of American recodifications in the 1960s and 1970s, there was a growing awareness that criminal law-making operated in a policy mush. There was no articulated statement of what the criminal law was intended to do or how it was to do it. Without open agreement on even the most fundamental questions, rational debate was difficult, for every person might reason from a different set of premises; or worse, law-makers could create criminal law doctrine without reference to any set of goals.

It was this lack of a statement of purposes that was seen, well before the recodification wave, as a primary hurdle to rational criminal law-making. In 1931, the Joint Committee on the Improvement of Criminal Justice, in its brief on 'The Need for Clarification and Modernization of the Substantive Criminal Law', put near the top of its list of reasons for such clarification and modernization the 'Uncertainty in the Purposes Which the Criminal Law is Designed to Serve':

[T]here is . . . uncertainty as to the purposes which the criminal law and its various component parts are designed to serve. An example of this is to be found in the situation which has grown up in connection with the group of statutory offenses—embezzlement, writing fictitious checks, obtaining money or goods under false pretenses. Contrary to the generally recognized principle of criminal law which condemns the compromising of cases, a widespread practice has grown up of permitting the adjustment of such cases upon settlement of the money differences between offenders and complainants. This practice is freely and openly participated in by police, prosecutors and sometimes by judges upon the theory that it is proper to use the criminal law as a means of coercing a defendant into a private settlement.

Another example is to be found in the partial abandonment of the rule of the common law which provided that condonation by an injured person would not excuse the defendant. Recent statutes have declared that no prosecution for adultery shall be commenced except upon the complaint of the aggrieved spouse, and that a subsequent marriage between the defendant and the injured person shall prevent a prosecution for seduction. The point is further illustrated by the extension of certain common law crimes to cover new situations and to accomplish new purposes. So the common law crime of arson has been made to include burning a house by the owner thereof with intent to defraud an insurance company, thus accomplishing a purpose quite different from that which was envisaged by the common law definition of arson, namely the protection of the dwelling house. Again it had long been thought that the criminal law existed for the sole purpose of punishing crimes and that prevention, except through punishment, was no concern of the law, but recently a wider concept of prevention has been imported into the criminal law by provision for padlocking places wherein a certain class of crimes have been committed and are likely to be continued. The establishment of juvenile courts is another illustration of changed ideas as to the purpose the criminal law is designed to serve. The increasing individualization of the disposition or treatment of the offender, based not so much upon variations in the nature of the offence as upon the variations in the nature of the offenders, will necessitate some very radical reconstruction of our substantive criminal law.

While the present uncertainty exists as to the meaning of terms, the concepts which they represent and the purposes which the criminal law is designed to serve under present-day social, industrial and political conditions, it seems unwise to undertake the preparation of a crime definition act except in connection with a study of the whole criminal law.

The difficulty of drafting an adequate crimes definition act is but an illustration of the fact that no part of the main body of our criminal law can be effectively improved apart from a study of the problem as a whole. The existing confusion of ideas is too great.[1]

No doubt the inconsistency of the criminal law extended far beyond the kinds of specific problems that the 1931 report cites, but it is significant that

---

[1] 'Report of the Joint Committee on the Improvement of Criminal Justice' (1931) 56 *Reports of the American Bar Association* 513 (adopted and distributed 13 July 1931), App. A: The Need for Clarification and Modernization of the Substantive Criminal Law, at 527–528.

the need for a statement of purposes was recognized even when the working standards of rationality and consistency were so low.

2. The Solution: Articulated Purposes

The Model Penal Code sought to address the problem by providing section 1.02, 'Purposes, Principles of Construction'. The provision includes in one form or another all of the purposes that we now think of as part of the traditional litany—deterrence, incapacitation, rehabilitation, and desert:

(1) The general purposes of the provisions governing the definition of offenses are:
(a)   to forbid and prevent conduct that unjustifiably and inexcusably inflicts or threatens substantial harm to individual or public interests;
(b)   to subject to public control persons whose conduct indicates that they are disposed to commit crimes;
(c)   to safeguard conduct that is without fault from condemnation as criminal;
(d)   to give fair warning of the nature of the conduct declared to constitute an offense;
(e)   to differentiate on reasonable grounds between serious and minor offenses.[2]

The official commentary explains:

Section 1.02 undertakes to state the most pervasive general objectives of the Code. The statement is included for its own sake, as an explanation of the underlying legislative premises of the enactment. It is also envisaged, as Subsection (3) explicitly declares, as an aid in the interpretation of particular provisions and in the exercise of the discretionary powers vested in the courts and in the organs of the correctional administration.[3]

---

[2] *Model Penal Code and Commentaries: Official Draft and Revised Comments* (Philadelphia 1980 and 1985) (hereafter MPC), s. 1.02(1). Subsection (2) provided a similar statement of purposes for sentencing and treatment:
'(2) The general purposes of the provisions governing the sentencing and treatment of offenders are:
(a)   to prevent the commission of offenses;
(b)   to promote the correction and rehabilitation of offenders;
(c)   to safeguard offenders against excessive, disproportionate or arbitrary punishment;
(d)   to give fair warning of the nature of the sentences that may be imposed on conviction of an offense;
(e)   to differentiate among offenders with a view to a just individualization in their treatment;
(f)   to define, coordinate and harmonize the powers, duties and functions of the courts and of administrative officers and agencies responsible for dealing with offenders;
(g)   to advance the use of generally accepted scientific methods and knowledge in the sentencing and treatment of offenders;
(h)   to integrate responsibility for the administration of the correctional system in a State Department of Correction [or other single department or agency]'.
[3] MPC s. 1.02 comment at 15.

Subsection (3) directs that the statement of purposes is to guide the interpretation of the Code's provisions.[4] More than half of the American state codes now contain a statement of purposes based on this section.[5]

3. The Illusion: Undefined Interrelation

One will notice that the Model Penal Code statement of purposes includes many different purposes and does not define an interrelation among those listed. The drafters explain:

> The section ... does not undertake ... to state a fixed priority among the means to such prevention, i.e., the deterrence of potential criminals and the incapacitation and correction of the individual offender. These are all proper goals to be pursued in social action with respect to the offender, one or another of which may call for the larger emphasis in a particular context or situation. What the Code seeks is the just harmonizing of these subordinate objectives, rather than the concentration on some single target of this kind.[6]

Others suggest that the competing interests are to be 'balanced',[7] 'blended',[8] 'accommodated',[9] 'taken account of',[10] or 'deal[t] with [such that] the public interest will be served'.[11]

One may speculate that the drafters take this view in part because there was not agreement among them as to which purposes should dominate, and in part because they saw little difficulty in leaving the interrelation undefined.

---

[4] MPC s. 1.02(3) provides: '(3) The provisions of the Code shall be construed according to the fair import of their terms but when the language is susceptible of differing constructions it shall be interpreted to further the general purposes stated in this Section and the special purposes of the particular provision involved. The discretionary powers conferred by the Code shall be exercised in accordance with the criteria stated in the Code and, insofar as such criteria are not decisive, to further the general purposes stated in this Section'.

[5] MPC s. 1.02 comment at 15 note 2.

[6] The passage continues: 'It is also recognized that not even crime prevention can be said to be the only end involved. The correction and rehabilitation of offenders is a social value in itself, as well as a preventive instrument. Basic considerations of justice demand, moreover, that penal law safeguard offenders against excessive, disproportionate or arbitrary punishment, that it afford fair warning of the nature of the sentences that may be imposed upon conviction and that differences among offenders be reflected in the just individualization of their treatment': MPC s. 1.02 comment at 4 (Tent. Draft No. 2, 1954). This same approach is taken with regard to s. 7.01 ('Criteria for Withholding Sentence of Imprisonment and for Placing Defendant on Probation'). The drafters explain that 'the reasons for imprisonment are usually obvious': Model Penal Code, s. 7.01 comment at 34 (Tent. Draft No. 2, 1954).

[7] Stanley A. Cohen, 'An Introduction to the Theory, Justifications and Modern Manifestations of Criminal Punishment' (1981) 27 McGill LJ 73, at 81.

[8] Solicitor General, *Report of the Canadian Committee on Corrections—Toward Unity: Criminal Justice and Corrections* (1969) 188 (known as the Ouimet Report).

[9] Cohen (above n. 7) at 73.

[10] Herbert Wechsler, 'Sentencing, Corrections, and the Model Penal Code' (1961) 109 University of Pennsylvania LR 465, at 468.

[11] Weintraub CJ in *State v Ivan* 33 NJ 197 (1960), at 201. He concludes that one should arrive at a 'composite judgment, a total evaluation of all the facets, giving to each [purpose] the weight, if any, it merits in the context'.

Judges and administrators could 'harmonize' the purposes as needed. Professor Wechsler, during the ALI floor debate relating to section 1.02, explains:

I may say that [Section 1.02] represents a lot of work, because it really is a matter of substantive importance, what the purposes that you think to be pursued in penal law are. We . . . are an eclectic group. We are suspicious of any body who attempts to vindicate the thesis that penal law has some single, sole, exclusive objective in the world such as the reformation of offenders, or the deterrence of offenders, or any other single articulation.

We do think that its dominant and prime justification is the prevention of crime, and in that respect I do not think that we face room for large disagreement. But within that framework, there are many other values that a society must serve and that arise acutely in the context of penal law where so much is at stake for both the public and the individual.

Hence, starting with this eclectic view, we have attempted to state the major objectives that we think it right this field of law should undertake to pursue. We recognize that here as elsewhere the task of administration is largely to harmonize a group of public purposes rather than to run rough-shod in pursuit of some single one.[12]

It is argued here, however, that the failure to define the interrelation among purposes, leaving it to individual officials in the criminal justice system to 'harmonize' the purposes, undercuts much of the advance promised by the Model Penal Code's statement of purposes. Further, the provision may make things worse by creating the illusion that the system is principled, thus helping to shield decisions from criticism. The fact is that the various purposes listed frequently conflict with one another. When they do, the decision-maker is free to select that purpose which justifies the result the decision-maker prefers for whatever reason, even an inappropriate one. The result is a system that appears to be based upon principle, a system in which decision-makers can give sound reasons for their decisions, but a system that allows decision-makers uncontrolled and undisclosed discretion.

(i) The conflict among alternative purposes

The purposes enumerated in the Code's list frequently conflict. Different purposes necessarily rely on different criteria, and thus frequently suggest different sentences or statutory interpretations or formulations.

Deterrence frequently conflicts with desert and incapacitation where some abnormal condition external to the actor, such as duress, coercion, or non-justified necessity, contributes to the actor's criminal conduct. Because the conditions rather than the actor are judged responsible for the conduct, the actor may be held blameless and non-dangerous. On the other hand, the same

---

[12] Herbert Wechsler, ALI floor debate relating to section 1.02 (1954) 31 *ALI Proceedings* 47–48 (May 1954). The passage continues: 'We recognize that interpretation. This is the essential process for which we look to the courts and to judicial action. Therefore I think the measure of 1.02 is whether we have omitted anything here that a civilized system of penal law would regard as a dominant purpose, or secondly, whether we have stated purposes that we ought not to be seeking to fulfil'.

coercive conditions can create the need for a greater rather than lesser deterrent threat. Greater sanctions would provide a needed additional deterrent in the face of the added pressure to commit the offence.

If the pressure to commit the offence is so great as to be essentially irresistible, the 'special deterrence' rationale may disappear (deterrence of the offender at hand in a similar situation in the future). In such a situation, any sanction would be futile and thus an inefficient expenditure. There may remain, however, a 'general deterrent' purpose in imposing a significant sanction. In *R v Dudley and Stephens*,[13] for example, the sailors who killed the sick cabin boy in order to keep themselves alive until they could be rescued were hardly shown to be dangerous people (as long as they stayed off boats that will be adrift for weeks) and their blameworthiness was significantly reduced because of the life-threatening conditions. Further, people in their situation or they (again) in the same situation are not likely to be deterred. Nonetheless, there remains some general deterrent value in imposing a significant sanction to reaffirm to others the strong prohibition against the killing of innocent non-aggressors.[14]

The same conflict arises over mitigations like heat of passion, provocation, and mistake as to self-defence due to conditions such as those suffered by battered wives or abused children. In these cases, an otherwise normal actor reacts less than admirably when confronted with a difficult situation. Such an actor is not as dangerous or blameworthy as an actor who kills absent the mitigating conditions but, as with instances of duress, coercion, and non-justified necessity, the need for a deterrent sanction to oppose the tendency and temptation is as great if not greater. A similar conflict arises under many strict liability offences and doctrines where a defendant, who is neither blameworthy nor dangerous, is sanctioned as a means of deterring similar violations by other potential offenders.

Whenever these sorts of cases arise—an exculpating or mitigating external force or condition, or offences or doctrines of strict liability—a conflict arises in which principles of desert and incapacitation would support a reduction in the degree of liability while deterrence principles would oppose reduction.

Conflict also arises between incapacitation, on the one hand, and deterrence and desert, on the other. Consider, for example, the rationale for setting the grade and sentences for an attempt, as compared to a completed offence, and for defining the required causal relationship between an offender's conduct

---

[13] (1884) 14 QBD 273.

[14] This analysis reflects a simple deterrence goal: the goal of deterring as much crime as possible. A goal of cost-efficient deterrence would justify greater sanctions in response to greater pressures to commit the offence, only to the extent that the cost of the sanctions are less than the cost of suffering the offence. Under this efficient deterrence theory, some crime ought not to be deterred—crime that costs more to deter than it costs to suffer. See, e.g., Shavell, 'Criminal Law and the Optimal Use of Nonmonetary Sanctions as a Deterrent' (1985) 85 Columbia LR 1232, at 1244–1245. Where it is not obvious from the context, I shall generally attempt to identify in this chapter the particular theory of deterrence to which I refer.

and a prohibited result. Reduced liability for an unsuccessful attempt and a strong causal requirement reflect a conclusion of less blameworthiness and less deterrent efficiency for imposing a sanction where there is no resulting harm attributable to the offender. The absence of attributable harm does not, however, alter the offender's dangerousness. Thus, whenever cases arise under doctrines giving significance to resulting harm, a conflict arises in which desert and deterrence will take account of resulting harm while incapacitation will not.

Finally, note the conflict between desert, on the one hand, and deterrence and incapacitation, on the other. Doctrines like the insanity defence and the voluntary act requirement acquit blameless offenders even though they may be dangerous and even though their punishment might serve a general deterrent function. In a second, reverse, set of cases, doctrines like the defence for inherently unlikely attempts[15] acquit blameworthy offenders because the inherent harmlessness of the conduct suggests that both incapacitation and deterrence are unnecessary. In both sorts of cases, a conflict arises: desert leads to one result while deterrence and incapacitation lead to another.

The conflict between desert and the utilitarian-crime-control purposes of deterrence, incapacitation of the dangerous, and rehabilitation is predictable in that the factors upon which these utilitarian principles rely often are in conflict with desert.

If incapacitation determined the distribution of criminal sanctions, past employment history would be highly relevant as a predictor of future dangerousness.[16] Thus, unemployment for the preceding two years might aggravate the grade of an offence or increase the sentence imposed. Age and family situation are also useful predictors of future criminality,[17] and thus will also determine liability. Indeed, if incapacitation of the dangerous were the only distributive principle, there is little justification for waiting until an offence is

[15] An example of an inherently unlikely attempt occurs when an actor sticks pins in a voodoo doll representing the victim, honestly believing that this will cause the victim's death or injury. MPC s. 5.05(2) provides: 'If the particular conduct charged to constitute a criminal attempt, solicitation or conspiracy is so inherently unlikely to result or culminate in the commission of a crime that neither such conduct nor the actor presents a public danger warranting the grading of such offense under this Section, the Court shall . . . enter judgment and impose sentence for a crime of lower grade or degree or, in extreme cases, may dismiss the prosecution'.

[16] See, e.g., Don M. Gottfredson, Leslie T. Wilkins and Peter B. Hoffman, *Guidelines for Parole and Sentencing* (Lexington, 1978) ch. 3; Peter W. Greenwood, *Selective Incapacitation* (Santa Monica, 1982) 11–26 (known as 'the Rand study').

[17] Age has been found to be an effective predictor of future violence. See, e.g., Joseph Cocozza and Henry J. Steadman, 'Some Refinements in the Prediction of Dangerous Behavior' (1974) 131 *American Journal of Psychiatry* 1012 (cited in *State v Davis* 96 NJ 611 (1984), at 618–619, 477 A 2d 308, at 311–312). The predictive value of various aspects of an offender's family situation are discussed in Alfred Blumstein, David Farrington and Soumyo Moitra, 'Delinquency Careers: Innocents, Desisters, and Persisters' (1985) 6 Crime and Justice: An Annual Review of Research 187, 198. Greenwood identifies several other factors of predictive value: prior convictions of the instant offence type; incarceration for more than half of the preceding two years; conviction before age 16; time served in a state juvenile facility; drug use during preceding two years; and employment for less than 50 per cent of the preceding two years. Greenwood (n. 16 above) at 50.

committed; it would be more efficient to screen the general population for dangerous persons and 'convict' those in need of incapacitation.[18]

If deterrence were the distributive principle, a potential offender's perception of the probability of apprehension would be highly relevant.[19] Thus, offences with a perceived low probability of apprehension should be graded higher and punished more severely. Similarly, the perceived likelihood of conviction can be an important factor. It may be useful for deterrence to increase the likelihood of conviction by dispensing with traditional desert-based liability requirements, such as culpability or causation requirements, which significantly impede convictions. A pure deterrence principle also logically bases liability upon the extent of the publicity that a sanction receives in a particular case. Just as an advertising executive pays more to place an advertisement that reaches more people, society may efficiently spend more (i.e., impose a greater penalty at a greater cost) if imposition of a sanction will be widely communicated. Thus, news coverage should aggravate the grade of or sentence for an offence.

If rehabilitation governed distribution, the actor's amenability to reform or treatment would be central. It was in furtherance of the rehabilitative purpose that fully indeterminate sentences were imposed until the recent past.[20] The length of the sentence was to be determined by the length of time necessary for rehabilitation of the offender, which could not be determined in advance. The offender's term continued indefinitely until the offender was rehabilitated. With a pure rehabilitation principle, as with a pure incapacitation principle, there would be little reason to wait for an offence to occur. Liability would be justified if the 'offender' were shown to have an abnormality that is treatable.[21]

The utilitarian purposes not only permit or compel distribution according to factors that are likely to be judged unacceptable for desert, but also preclude the consideration of factors that are generally held to be key to desert. Even the nature of the crime committed may be of little relevance under some utilitarian purposes. As the Model Sentencing Act proudly points out:

The [Act] diminishes the major source of [sentencing] disparity—sentencing according to the particular offense. Under [the Act] the dangerous offender may be committed to a lengthy term; the non-dangerous offender may not. It makes available, for the first time, a plan that allows the sentence to be determined by the defendant's make-up, his

---

[18] One study suggests that rapists may be distinguished from non-rapists based upon their penile erection response to certain stimuli: Abel, Barlow, Blanchard and Guild, 'The Components of Rapist Sexual Arousal' (1977) 34 *Archives of General Psychiatry* 895.

[19] See, e.g., Shavell (n. 14 above) at 1235–1236.

[20] See, e.g., National Congress on Penitentiary and Reformatory Discipline, 'Statement of Principles' in *Transactions of the National Congress on Penitentiary and Reformatory Discipline* (Albany, 1871) 541–547.

[21] If a dangerous offender could not be successfully treated, application of a pure rehabilitation distributive principle would not authorize incarceration. Thus it would poorly serve even the goal of crime control.

potential threat in the future, and other similar factors, with a minimum of variation according to the offense.[22]

On the other hand, a system based upon desert might result in unnecessary inefficiency in the use of criminal sanctions to prevent crime.[23] A desert distributive principle may impose sanctions that cost more than the crime they prevent and may fail to impose sanctions where the opportunities for efficient crime prevention are great.

(ii) The exercise of undisclosed discretion

When faced with conflicting purposes, judges, officials, and legislators nonetheless must make a decision. The judge or criminal justice administrator faced with alternative interpretations of an ambiguous code provision, with some interpretations supported by one purpose and others supported by another purpose, must choose an interpretation. In doing so, he or she must choose to advance one purpose at the expense of another. The same conflict in purposes is faced by the legislator considering an addition or change to the criminal code, the sentencing guideline drafter, and the sentencing judge deciding on a sentence.

What will influence that choice? It would be surprising if the decision-maker, even one acting in good faith, did not look to his or her own values and beliefs, including his or her own views of what the proper purpose of criminal law should be. But this undercuts much of the value of having articulated purposes. Often, any of the existing choices can be justified under one or another of the purposes. The result is that decision-makers are left to decide without guidance. This discretion creates unpredictability and can create inconsistency as the decision-maker might choose to favour one purpose in one situation and another purpose in another, as is common.[24] It may be that

---

[22] National Council on Crime and Delinquency, Model Sentencing Act, reprinted in (1963) 9 Crime and Delinquency 337. There is disagreement as to whether a deterrence principle would generate liability proportionate to the seriousness of the offence. Compare, e.g., Ernest van den Haag, 'Punishment as a Device for Controlling the Crime Rate' (1981) 33 Rutgers University LR 706 (suggesting that deterrence calls for proportionality) with Alan H. Goldman, 'Beyond Deterrence Theory: Comments on van den Haag's "Punishment as a Device for Controlling the Crime Rate"' (1981) 33 Rutgers University LR 721.

[23] I say 'might' because, as I have argued elsewhere, there may be great crime control power in a desert distribution. See Paul H. Robinson and John M. Darley, 'The Utility of Desert' (1997) 91 Northwestern University LR 453.

[24] It is common for people to choose different purposes in different situations. For example, most state criminal codes maintain an insanity defence because it exculpates the blameless (and thus furthers just punishment), even though abolishing the defence might more effectively incapacitate the dangerous. Yet, the same codes sacrifice just punishment, in favour of increasing deterrence, when they recognize strict liability. At the same time, rather than increasing the threatened sanction when the temptation or inclination is greater, as a deterrence principle suggests, the same codes frequently decrease the deterrent threat, in cases of provocation, for example, because of the offender's reduced blameworthiness. Code drafters are choosing to further different purposes in different contexts. Clearly, in their own minds they have some kind of principle that

the decision-maker in fact has a private principle for how to decide among conflicting purposes—an unarticulated principle of interrelation. No matter whether such a principle is conscious or unconscious, because it is not public it will not save the system from the appearance of arbitrariness and is not open to the testing of criticism.

Indeed, undisclosed discretion may be used in a more troubling way. The decision-maker resolving conflicts among purposes may look not to his or her own view of the proper purpose of punishment but to his or her own view of how the specific case at hand ought to come out, which personal assessment may be a function of entirely inappropriate influences, even if not consciously so. The social science research suggests that people naturally tend to identify with others like themselves: the greater the similarity, the greater the identification. In a system of uncontrolled discretion, then, especially one in which the discretion is not evident, even to the decision-maker, one can expect decisions to be based on personal characteristics, such as race, gender, religion, and ethnicity.[25]

Why do we not insist that code and sentencing-guideline drafters adopt, and that judges follow, a statement of the interrelation among purposes that will direct the choice among conflicting purposes? A cynic may conclude that the use of the purposes list to justify a particular code formulation or sentence is a convenient means of rationalizing results for which the decision-maker has another, undisclosed reason.[26] And this suspicion—that the purposes list is popular as a method of justification precisely *because* it offers hidden flexibility—is fuelled by the almost universal failure to articulate a guiding principle of interrelation among alternative purposes.[27]

---

tells them when to advance one at the expense of another. But without an articulation of that principle, the law can be unprincipled and unpredictable.

The same changing choices among conflicting purposes occurs in sentencing. Rehabilitation might be the best means of avoiding future crime by a young addict who is caught selling drugs to support his habit. But a judge might rationally decide to impose a long prison term in order to further general deterrent interests. Yet, when faced with a young bank teller who embezzled money from her cash drawer, the same judge might decide to forego the general deterrent value of a long prison term and put the offender on probation, under an incapacitative theory—she is no longer dangerous because she will never again be placed in a position of trust. Each of these sentences may be justified by one of the purposes of sentencing, but they may nonetheless be the product of arbitrary or biased decision-making. Without a principle governing when one sentencing purpose is to be followed at the expense of another, judges and guideline drafters are free to choose the purpose to fit the sentence. Again, sentencing judges probably have in their own minds some kind of principle that tells them when to advance one at the expense of another. But without an articulation of that principle, the sentences can be unprincipled and unpredictable.

[25] Valerie P. Hans and Neil Vidmar, *Judging the Jury* (New York, 1986) 140–141.

[26] While Professor Kelman does not address the issue of distributive principles, he makes an analogous claim with regard to the formulation of criminal law doctrines. See Kelman, 'Interpretive Construction in the Substantive Criminal Law' (1981) 33 Stanford LR 591.

[27] For a discussion of how such a principle might be constructed, see Paul H. Robinson, 'Hybrid Principles for the Distribution of Criminal Sanctions' (1987) 82 Northwestern University LR 19–42.

B. Judging Culpability: The Individualized Objective Standard

1. The Problem: The Unfairness of the Common Law's Objective Standard

The problems inherent in the common law's use of an objective standard are well known and much discussed. For example, murder is to be reduced to manslaughter if, among other things, a reasonable person would have been similarly provoked:

> The doctrine of mitigation is briefly this: That if the act of killing, though intentional, be committed under the influence of sudden, intense anger, or heat of blood, obscuring the reason, produced by an adequate or reasonable provocation, and before sufficient time has elapsed for the blood to cool and reason to reassert itself, so that the killing is the result of temporary excitement rather than of wickedness of heart or innate recklessness of disposition, then the law, recognizing the standard of human conduct as that of the ordinary or average man, regards the offense so committed as of less heinous character than premeditated or deliberate murder. Measured as it must be by the conduct of the average man, what constitutes adequate cause is incapable of exact definition.[28]

There was much criticism of this reliance upon a purely objective standard. In the famous 1954 case of *Director of Public Prosecutions v Bedder*,[29] 17-year-old Bedder, knowing he was impotent, hired a prostitute in the hope of being able to have intercourse. When the prostitute ridiculed him for his inability to perform, he flew into a rage and killed her. The court refused to allow the jury to take Bedder's impotency into account in judging whether he might have a provocation mitigation, reducing murder to manslaughter. He was to be judged by the standard of the reasonable man, who is not impotent. The decision was attacked by scholars and ultimately led to legislation.[30]

In a famous American case, *State v Gounagias*,[31] from which the quote above is taken, the defendant was sodomized by the victim while unconscious. The sodomizer then spread the news of his accomplishment. Those who learned of it taunted and ridiculed Gounagias until he finally shot and killed his assailant two weeks after the sodomy. The court applied the common law rules to deny the mitigation because the killing was not an immediate response to sodomizing and the reasonable man would have cooled off by the time of the killing. Yet, there seems common agreement that Gounagias is easily distinguishable in blameworthiness from the unprovoked murderer and that the common law rules are too rigid, not allowing consideration of the wide variety of situations that might provoke a killing in a way that

---

[28] *State v Gounagias* 88 Wash. 304 (1915), at 311–312; 53 P 9, at 11–12.
[29] [1954] 1 WLR 1119; see also *Holmes v DPP* [1946] AC 588, at 598.
[30] See text accompanying n. 32 below.
[31] 88 Wash. 304 (1915), at 311–312; 53 P 9, at 11–12.

deserved mitigation from murder.[32] The Model Penal Code commentary describes the *Gounagias* case and its result as part of its explanation for why it adopts a broader rule.[33]

The problem of a purely objective standard is also seen in the context of recklessness and negligence. For example, whether an offender was liable for reckless murder (manslaughter) traditionally depended on whether the reasonable person would have disregarded the risk of death as the defendant did.[34] Similarly, liability for negligent homicide, where it was permitted, depended upon whether the reasonable person would have been aware of the risk.[35] (As is well known, English law does not always adopt awareness of risk as the key to the recklessness-negligence distinction; some forms of English recklessness include what Americans would call negligence.[36])

The difficulties surrounding a purely objective standard in these definitions parallel those in provocation. In *State v Williams*,[37] two loving parents failed to get medical aid for their child, believing he had only a toothache. The reasonable person would have known from the rank smell of gangrene and the baby's inability to keep food down that the situation was life-threatening. Should the lack of education and the low intelligence of the parents be taken into account in judging whether their unawareness of the risk of death was unreasonable? A purely objective standard of reasonableness would not allow it, and would hold the parents liable for negligent homicide, as they were held.[38]

2. The Solution: The Individualized Objective Standard

The Model Penal Code drafters were sympathetic to the unfairness of the purely objective standard. Citing the *Gounagias* case, they substituted a mitigation of 'extreme emotional disturbance' that individualized the objective standard:

[A] homicide which would otherwise be murder is committed under the influence of extreme mental or emotional disturbance for which there is reasonable explanation or excuse. The reasonableness of such explanation or excuse shall be determined from the viewpoint of a person *in the actor's situation under the circumstances as he believes them to be.*[39]

---

[32] For an example of criticism of the period of the objective test of provocation, see, e.g., Edwards, 'Provocation and the Reasonable Man—Another View' [1954] Criminal LR 898; Note, 'Manslaughter and the Adequacy of Provocation: The Reasonableness of the Reasonable Man' (1958) 106 University of Pennsylvania LR 1021.

[33] MPC s. 210.3 comment at 59–60.

[34] Wayne R. LaFave and Austin W. Scott, Jr., *Criminal Law* (2nd edn., St. Paul, 1986) 669–670 note 13.

[35] MPC s. 210.4 comment at 81.   [36] See, e.g., *R v Caldwell* [1982] AC 341.

[37] 4 Wash. App. 908 (1971); 484 P 2d 1167.

[38] For an influential discussion of the unfair consequences of the unindividualized objective standard in negligence, see H.L.A. Hart, *Punishment and Responsibility* (London, 1968) 152–157.

[39] MPC s. 210.3(1)(b).

The Model Penal Code mitigation uses an objective standard, as the common law doctrine does, but the objective standard is partially individualized through the requirement that the reasonableness of the explanation or excuse is to be determined 'under the circumstances as [the actor] believes them to be' and 'from the viewpoint of a person in the actor's situation'. These two phrases provide significant opportunities for a court to endow the reasonable person with the characteristics of the defendant and to place the reasonable person in the conditions under which the defendant acted. The second phrase in particular—'in the actor's *situation*'—is intended by the drafters to permit a trial judge great leeway in individualizing the reasonable person standard.[40]

Under this approach, defendants like Gounagias would be distinguished from the unprovoked murderer. His earlier sodomizing by the deceased and his public taunting would be taken into account in judging whether his liability should be mitigated to manslaughter. As Professor Wechsler explained during the ALI floor debate on the provision:

> The standard for judging the adequacy of [Common Law] provocation is the standard of the ordinary reasonable man. You don't take into account the peculiarities of the actor, whatever they may be.
>
> We tried to broaden this . . . to achieve a greater reduction, and we put it this way, that homicide which would otherwise be murder is committed under the influence of extreme mental or emotional disturbance for which there is reasonable explanation or excuse . . .
>
> Then we add, 'The reasonableness of such explanation or excuse shall be determined from the viewpoint of a person in the actor's situation under the circumstances as he believes them to be'.
>
> This is an effort . . . to make the standards somewhat more subjective than the Common Law standard of sufficiency of provocation, but on the other hand, we only say that it shall be determined from that viewpoint, not that the defendant's viewpoint governs. We ask that the men who try the man— and this usually means the jury, of course—perform the act of empathy, perhaps I should say, of trying to put themselves in the defendant's position.[41]

The English rule, at work in *Bedder*, was broadened in a somewhat different way by the Homicide Act 1957:

> Where on a charge of murder there is evidence on which the jury can find that the person charged was provoked (whether by things done or said or by both together) to lose

---

[40] See MPC s. 2.02 comment 4 at 242, quoted in the text at n. 53 below. See also ibid., comment at 242 n. 27 (noting that a similar problem exists with recklessness and that discriminations similar to those required by the negligence standard must be made).

[41] Herbert Wechsler, ALI floor debate relating to section 210.3 (1959) 36 *ALI Proceedings* 125–126. The passage continues: 'I cannot say that I can precisely tell you how this reformulation would apply to every concrete case that you can put to me, any more than you can do that with any other generalizations. But I can say that I think this is framed so as to meet what one might almost say was the traditional critique of the rigorous, inherited law of homicide and by overcoming at each point the obstacles to a decently sympathetic judgment that have appeared in the course of time'.

his self-control, the question whether the provocation was enough to make a reasonable man do as he did shall be left to be determined by the jury; and in determining that question the jury shall take into account everything both done and said according to the effect which, in their opinion, it would have on a reasonable man.[42]

While the Act keeps the reasonable person standard, the practical effect of transferring the decision to the jury is to allow the jurors to take individual characteristics into account that they otherwise would not be able to, as is borne out by subsequent cases.[43] The Draft Criminal Code for England and Wales (hereafter 'Draft Code') appears more explicitly to allow such individualization:

(a) [the defendant] acts when provoked (whether by things done or by things said or by both and whether by the deceased person or by another) to lose his self-control; and

(b) the provocation is, in all the circumstances (including any of his personal characteristics that affect its gravity), sufficient ground for the loss of self-control.[44]

The Model Penal Code drafters use the same individualization of the objective standard in their definitions of recklessness and negligence. The Code defines 'recklessly' as follows:

A person acts recklessly with respect to a material element of an offense when he consciously disregards a substantial and unjustifiable risk that the material element exists or will result from his conduct.[45]

It then goes on to provide a somewhat individualized objective standard against which the person's disregard of the risk is to judged:

The risk must be of such a nature and degree that, *considering the nature and purpose of the actor's conduct and the circumstances known to him*, its disregard involves a gross deviation from the standard of conduct that a law-abiding person would observe *in the actor's situation*.[46]

Analogous individualizing language is included in the definition of negligence.[47] (The Draft Code does not appear to provide individualization of the

---

[42] Homicide Act 1957, s. 3.

[43] See, e.g., *R v Simpson*, noted in [1957] Criminal LR 815; *DPP v Camplin* [1978] 2 WLR 679, at 682; *R v Smith* [2000] 3 WLR 654.

[44] Law Commission No. 177, *A Criminal Code for England and Wales*, Vol. 1, cl. 58 (and cl. 55, authorizing the mitigation to manslaughter); see also cl. 58 Commentary, Draft Code, Vol. 2, at 251. In a recent decision the House of Lords decided to apply such an individual (or subjective) test: see *R v Smith* [2000] 3 WLR 654.

[45] MPC s. 2.02(2)(c).   [46] ibid.

[47] MPC s. 2.02(2)(d) provides: 'A person acts negligently with respect to a material element of an offense when he should be aware of a substantial and unjustifiable risk that the material element exists or will result from his conduct. The risk must be of such a nature and degree that the actor's failure to perceive it, considering the nature and purpose of his conduct and the circumstances known to him, involves a gross deviation from the standard of care that a reasonable person would observe in the actor's situation'.

objective standard in its definition of 'recklessly',[48] although the reason for its absence is unclear given its use in provocation.)[49]

3. The Illusion: Individualize With What?

One aspect of the Model Penal Code's individualization approach is problematic. What characteristics of a defendant should be attributed to the reasonable person in judging the reasonableness of the defendant's conduct and what characteristics should not?

Clearly such things as an actor's age are relevant in assessing the reasonableness of his disturbance. But, presumably, a defendant's certifiably bad temper ought not be taken into account to lower our expectations of his resisting the provocation. That is, he ought not to be judged against the standard of the reasonable person with a similar bad temper. To individualize the objective standard fully would turn it into a purely subjective standard, which would fail to make the blameworthiness judgement the law seeks.

Yet, it is not obvious which factors should be taken into account and which should not. For example, should the law take account of a genetic predisposition toward violent reaction when provoked? If so, should it be used to alter the standard by which such an offender is judged? We are inclined to believe that people can control their temper if they choose to, but the claim of genetic predisposition clouds the issue by making it seem beyond the actor's control.[50] How is a judge to determine what characteristics are to be taken into account and which are not?

The Model Penal Code's answer to this question is not to answer, to leave the issue to the ad hoc determination of the trial judge and jury:

The critical element in the Model Code formulation is the clause requiring that reasonableness be assessed 'from the viewpoint of a person in the actor's situation'. The word 'situation' is designedly ambiguous. On the one hand, it is clear that personal handicaps and some external circumstances must be taken into account. Thus, blindness, shock from traumatic injury, and extreme grief are all easily read into the term 'situation'. This result is sound, for it would be morally obtuse to appraise a crime for mitigation of punishment without reference to these factors. On the other hand, it is

---

[48] The Draft Code definition is similar in its focus on awareness of risk: '[A] person acts . . . "recklessly" with respect to (i) a circumstance when he is aware of a risk that it exists or will exist; (ii) a result when he is aware of a risk that it will occur': Draft Code cl. 18(c). But the Draft Code does not provide the detailed decision process of the Model Penal Code for judging the culpability of the defendant's disregard of the risk. The Draft Code provides simply that taking a risk constitutes recklessness if 'it is, in the circumstances known to him, unreasonable to take the risk': ibid.

[49] Perhaps the controversy surrounding the *Caldwell* decision (n. 36 above) has deflected attention from the issue.

[50] If the genetics only create a *predisposition* toward violence, it would seem that the actor retains the ability to control his conduct. If the genetics are to be relevant, the actor must show that the influence of the genetics on his conduct is sufficiently strong that we should see him as less blameworthy.

equally plain that idiosyncratic moral values are not part of the actor's situation. An assassin who kills a political leader because he believes it is right to do so cannot ask that he be judged by the standard of a reasonable extremist. Any other result would undermine the normative message of the criminal law. In between these two extremes, however, there are matters neither as clearly distinct from individual blameworthiness as blindness or handicap nor as integral a part of the moral depravity as a belief in the rightness of killing. Perhaps the classic illustration is the unusual sensitivity to the epithet 'bastard' of a person born illegitimate. An exceptionally punctilious sense of personal honour or an abnormally fearful temperament may also serve to differentiate an individual actor from the hypothetical reasonable man, yet none of these factors is wholly irrelevant to the ultimate issue of culpability. The proper role of such factors cannot be resolved satisfactorily by abstract definition of what may constitute adequate provocation. The Model Code endorses a formulation that affords sufficient flexibility to differentiate in particular cases between those special aspects of the actor's situation that should be deemed material for the purpose of grading and those that should be ignored. There thus will be room for interpretation of the word 'situation', and that is precisely the flexibility desired. There will be opportunity for argument about the reasonableness of explanation or excuse, and that too is a ground on which argument is required. In the end, the question is whether the actor's loss of self-control can be understood in terms that arouse sympathy to the ordinary citizen. Section 210.3 faces this issue squarely and leaves the ultimate judgment to the ordinary citizen in the function of a juror assigned to resolve the specific case.[51]

An analogous problem—of selecting the factors with which to individualize an objective standard—arises in the definition of negligence,[52] and the Code deals with it in a similar fashion:

A further point in the Code's concept of negligence merits attention. The standard for ultimate judgement invites consideration of the 'care that a reasonable person would observe in the actor's situation'. There is an inevitable ambiguity in 'situation'. If the actor were blind or if he had just suffered a blow or experienced a heart attack, these would certainly be facts to be considered in a judgement involving criminal liability, as they would be under traditional law. But the heredity, intelligence or temperament of the actor would not be held material in judging negligence, and could not be without depriving the criterion of all its objectivity. The Code is not intended to displace discriminations of this kind, but rather to leave the issue to the courts.[53]

The commentary makes clear that the same analysis applies to the definition of 'recklessness' and that the same interpretation is to be given to the phrase 'in the actor's situation' in that context.[54]

This seems an inadequate resolution of the problem. Ad hoc determination means that similar cases are likely to be treated differently, that the law will be unpredictable, and that there is created the possibility of abuse of discretion by decision-makers, judge or juror. As with the 'list of purposes' innovation discussed in section A above, the individualization objective person

---

[51] See MPC s. 210.3 comment at 63.

[52] For a discussion see Paul H. Robinson, *Criminal Law* (New York, 1997) para. 4.3.

[53] MPC s. 2.02 comment 4 at 242.   [54] MPC s. 2.02 comment at 242 n. 27.

decisions may seem principled but in fact are the product of unguided and undisclosed discretion. The results may depend more on who the defendant gets as a trial judge or jury than on whether he deserves an extreme emotional disturbance mitigation, or whether he was reckless or negligent.

Unfortunately, while the Code purports to solve the problem of tailoring an objective standard to the defendant, the solution it offers masks an illusion. Behind that illusion, criminal law theory has yet to find a principle that will convincingly distinguish the characteristics that ought to be included from those that ought to be excluded when individualizing the reasonable person standard. In the absence of such a theory, let alone a workable provision implementing a theory, it is hard to see any approach other than the uncontrolled ad hoc discretion the Model Penal Code drafters have adopted.

C. Enhancing Criminal Law's Crime Control Effectiveness

1. The Problem: Dangerous Persons

Americans are sometimes criticized for being preoccupied with crime, but the fact is, even after the recent reductions, we still have the highest *per capita* rate of serious crime in the industrialized world. Our 10 homicides per 100,000 population is eight times the rate in Germany and Switzerland, for example, and 20 times the rate in England and Wales.[55]

Even with the recent declines, the overall crime rate remains nearly three times higher than it was during the decade and a half after the Second World War, when many current legislators were growing up.[56] The violent crime rate now is more than four times what it was then.[57] Homicide rates, even after the recent dramatic declines, are 50 per cent higher. Rape, robbery, and aggravated assault rates are almost quadruple.[58]

Even if crime rates dropped back to earlier levels, people still would have reason to be concerned. One reason crime rates are not higher than they are is because we have significantly altered our lifestyles to protect ourselves. Many people no longer let their children walk home from school or go out to play in the neighbourhood. Many have dead-bolts on their doors, 'The Club' on their cars, and live in security-staffed apartments and 'gated' communities.

[55] Franklin E. Zimring and Gordon Hawkins, *Crime is Not the Problem: Lethal Violence in America* (New York, 1997) 53–55; *Swiss Review of World Affairs* (3 November 1997).

[56] *Sourcebook of Criminal Justice Statistics: 1996* (Washington, DC, 1997) Table 3.106 (5078.9 per 100,000 in 1996 versus 1887.2 in 1960). Crime rates were relatively constant from the end of the Second World War until 1960. See 'Violent Crime Rates', *Uniform Crime Reports*, 1946–1960; Gary LaFree, 'Social Institutions and the Crime "Bust" of the 1990s' (1998) 88 Journal of Criminal Law and Criminology 1325, figure 3 ff.

[57] *Sourcebook of Criminal Justice Statistics: 1996* (n. 56 above) Table 3.106 (634.1 per 100,000 in 1996 versus 160.9 in 1960).

[58] ibid., Table 3.106.

Thus, we have both dramatically higher crime than 40 years ago and dramatically less freedom of action.

Given this situation, it should be no surprise that politicians have for several decades looked for ways in which criminal law could be modified more effectively to prevent crime. One obvious route to crime reduction came with the realization that a small number of repeat offenders were accounting for a disproportionate share of the offences.[59] Decision-makers reasoned that, while incapacitation normally is an expensive strategy, it would be feasible if it focused on the dangerous offenders, the high rate recidivists. Following this reasoning, the last several decades have seen many reforms aimed at incapacitating the dangerous offender.

2. The Solution: Focusing on Dangerousness

The criminal law reforms aimed at incapacitating dangerous offenders have taken several forms: altering criminal liability rules to draw into the criminal justice system more of those who are dangerous, changing the grade of some offences to increase the term an offender can be incapacitated, and revising sentencing rules to provide longer terms for dangerous offenders.

As to the first sort of 'dangerousness' reform, consider the extension of inchoate liability common among modern American criminal codes, following the lead of the Model Penal Code.[60] The Code discards the common law requirement that a person come within some proximity of completing an offence, the so-called 'proximity' test, of which the common law had several variations. It substitutes only a requirement that a person have taken a 'substantial step' toward the offence. Under the substantial-step test, it no longer matters whether the actor gets anywhere near committing a specific offence. All that matters is that the actor externalizes his intention to commit an offence, thereby revealing his dangerousness. The proximity tests are discarded because they focus on the nature of the actor's conduct rather than, as the Model Penal Code drafters explain it, 'the proper focus of attention'—'the actor's disposition' to commit a crime.[61]

The Code similarly discards the common law definition of conspiracy. It no longer requires that the actor in fact agree with another that one of them will commit an offence, instead requiring only that the actor *thought* he agreed with another.[62] This change logically follows from the drafters' view that conspiracy's purpose is 'as a basis . . . for corrective treatment of persons who

---

[59] See, e.g., Peter W. Greenwood, *Selective Incapacitation* (Santa Monica, 1982) 9.

[60] Recall that one of the Model Penal Code's stated purposes was 'to subject to public control persons whose conduct indicates that they are disposed to commit crimes': MPC s. 1.02(1)(b).

[61] ibid., at 298.

[62] Compare, e.g., *Archibold v State* 397 NE 2d 1071 (Ind. Ct. App. 1979), at 1073, to *People v Schwimmer* 66 A 2d 91 (1978), 411 NYS 2d 922; see generally Paul H. Robinson, *Criminal Law* (New York, 1997) 648.

reveal that they are disposed to criminality'.[63] There may be no real danger of that offence being committed when an actor only mistakenly believes he has conspired with another (an undercover officer, for example), but the actor's agreement shows that he is the kind of person who is willing to join in such a criminal agreement.

In each of these instances of extension of criminal liability to conduct not previously defined as criminal, the liability imposed for this newly criminalized inchoate conduct is liability equal to that for the full offence. As discussed below, the Code's general rule is that an inchoate offence is graded the same as the completed offence.

The Code similarly expands the reach of complicity liability. It drops the common law's unconvictable perpetrator defence to complicity. Thus, it no longer matters that the perpetrator had no intention of committing the crime. The drafters reason that the accomplice is equally dangerous, and therefore ought to be equally criminally liable, whether the perpetrator actually intended to commit the crime or not.[64]

With similar reasoning, the Code reduces the objective requirements of complicity, to allow liability for the full substantive offence upon proof that a person tried but failed to assist or encourage.[65] This reform is consistent, of course, with the Code's grading of attempts the same as the completed offence, reflecting its general view that resulting harm ought not be relevant to criminal liability. That the failed assister contributed nothing to the offence does not take away from the person's dangerousness revealed in trying to assist.[66]

As to the second kind of reform, relating to grading, consider the Model Penal Code's inchoate grading rule. Section 5.05(1) provides:

Except as otherwise provided in this Section, attempt, solicitation and conspiracy are crimes of the same grade and degree as the most serious offense which is attempted or solicited or is an object of the conspiracy.[67]

---

[63] MPC s. 5.03 comment at 97 (Tent. Draft No. 10).

[64] 'Under the unilateral approach of the Code, the culpable party's guilt would not be affected by the fact that the other party's agreement was feigned. He has conspired within the meaning of the definition, in the belief that the other party was with him . . . his culpability is not decreased by the other's secret intention': MPC s. 5.03(2)(b) comment at 400.

[65] MPC s. 2.06(3)(a)(ii) ('aids or agrees or attempts to aid . . .').

[66] 'It is sufficient if he solicits another to commit an offense. It is likewise sufficient if he aids the other in planning or committing the offense, or if he agrees or attempts to aid the other in such planning or commission': MPC s. 2.06 explanatory note at 297.

[67] MPC s. 5.05(1). The subsection permitted one exception: 'An attempt, solicitation or conspiracy to commit a [capital crime or a] felony of the first degree is a felony of the second degree'. The only first degree felonies in the Code are murder and aggravated kidnapping. They explain the exception this way: 'It is doubtful . . . that the threat of punishment for the inchoate crime can add significantly to the net deterrent efficacy of the sanction threatened for the substantive offense that is the actor's object, which he, by hypothesis, ignores. Hence, there is a basis for economizing in use of the heaviest and most afflictive sanctions by removing them from the inchoate crimes. The sentencing provisions for second degree felonies, including the provision for extended terms, should certainly suffice to meet whatever danger is presented by the actor': MPC s. 5.05(2) comment at 490.

A provision of this sort advances the preventive detention goal, albeit at the expense of what most persons would think was doing justice. The Model Penal Code drafters give this explanation for their inchoate grading rule:

The theory of this grading system may be stated simply. To the extent that sentencing depends upon the antisocial disposition of the actor and the demonstrated need for a corrective sanction, there is likely to be little difference in the gravity of the required measures depending on the consummation or the failure of the plan.[68]

That is, generally, a successful and a failed attempt indicate the same danger of a future offence, thus call for the same grade of liability. In the view of the drafters, the absence of resulting harm is irrelevant to liability: 'The primary purpose of punishing attempts is to neutralize dangerous individuals'.[69] (The Draft Code takes a similar approach, setting the punishment for an attempt at the same maximum as that for the substantive offence,[70] although the motivation may be simply to maximize sentencing discretion rather than a rejection of the significance of resulting harm.)

Illustrative of the third sort of reform, regarding sentencing, is the now popular 'three strikes' law, which sentences a three-time felony offender to life imprisonment.[71] The rationale for and effect of these laws is well documented: the incapacitation of dangerous offenders. Less obviously based on a preventive detention rationale is another common reform: using prior criminal record dramatically to increase the offender's term of imprisonment. Sentencing guidelines and 'three-strikes' and related habitual-offender statutes commonly double, triple, or quadruple the punishment imposed upon a repeat offender.[72] An initial portion of an imprisonment sentence may well be

---

[68] MPC s. 5.05(2) comment at 490.

[69] MPC s. 5.01 comment at 323. See also, e.g., ibid. at 298, 299, 331.

[70] Draft Code, Schedule 1, cl. 49, col. (4). The schedule sets the maximum term for offences. See Draft Code, cl. 7(3)(a)(i).

[71] See, e.g., 18 USC s. 3559 (requiring life imprisonment upon a third serious violent felony conviction). Similarly, new sentencing guidelines give great weight to an offender's prior criminal history. See, e.g., *United States Sentencing Commission Guidelines* (1997) s.4A1.1 ff; Ch. 5, Part A (Sentencing Table) (setting guideline sentence as a function of 'Offense Level' and 'Criminal History Category'. Jurisdictional reforms lower the age at which juveniles may be tried as adults. See generally United States Department of Justice, Office of Juvenile Justice and Delinquency Prevention, *Juvenile Offenders and Victims: A National Report* (Washington, DC, 1995). 'Megan's Law' statutes require community notification of a convicted sex offender: 42 USC s. 14071(d) (Wetterling Crimes Against Children and Sexually Violent Offender Registration Act). 'Sexual predator' statutes provide civil detention of sexual offenders who remain dangerous at the conclusion of their criminal commitment. See *Kansas v Hendricks* 117 S Ct 2072 (1997), at 2085–2086 (at the time the Kansas statute was challenged, in December 1996, five other states had such statutes—Arizona, California, Minnesota, Washington, and Wisconsin— and 38 states, including New Jersey and New York, filed amicus briefs urging the justices to uphold the law, which they did).

[72] Under three-strikes statutes, the criminal history often quadruples or more the sentence that would be imposed for the identical offence by the identical offender with no criminal history. A 25-year-old offender committing a felony that normally carries a 10 year sentence, for which less time than that normally would be served, can get mandatory life imprisonment without the possibility

deserved, but is followed by a purely preventive detention portion that cannot be justified as deserved punishment.

One can construct a theory that makes prior criminal record at least relevant to deserved punishment.[73] By committing another offence after having been previously convicted, an offender might be seen as 'thumbing his nose' at the system and such nose-thumbing may justify some incremental punishment over what a first offence would deserve.

But a nose-thumbing increase can hardly justify the doubling, tripling, or quadrupling, of the punishment provided by habitual offender statutes and sentencing guidelines. The nose-thumbing characteristic of the second robbery may make it more aggravated than the first, but the nose-thumbing is only one of many characteristics of the second robbery that influences its blameworthiness. It can hardly justify as much punishment as the robbery itself, and certainly not more. The victim, for example, is offended against by the robbery itself, not by the fact that it was a second-timer who performed it.

Further, if the underlying theory of these statutes were really increased desert due to the disrespect for law inherent in repeating the offence, then logically the same theory would apply to all offences. Yet, the three strikes and other habitual offender provisions typically apply only to a limited class of offences—commonly violent offences[74]—and typically take account of a criminal history of only a certain kind—again, commonly a history of violent offences.[75] It seems difficult to construct a desert theory of nose-thumbing disrespect that limits the punishment add-on in this way. In contrast, the limitation of the schemes to violent offences makes good sense under a prevention rationale, for these are the offences in greatest need of prevention.

of parole, which may mean a sentence of 45 years or more. See National Institute of Justice, '*Three Strikes and You're Out': A Review of State Legislation* (Washington, DC, 1997) Exhibit 9.

Even the less dramatic 'habitual offender' statutes, which have been in use for some time, can have a substantial effect. For example, the Model Penal Code provision, which is the structural model for such statutes, allows an 'extended term of imprisonment' for a repeat offender that essentially doubles the maximum authorized sentence: the maximum sentence for a third degree felony is increased from five years to 10; for a second degree felony, it is increased from 10 years to 20; for a first degree felony, it is increased from a maximum of 20 years to a requirement of life imprisonment: MPC s. 7.03(3) and (4). Model Penal Code sentences require the judge to give both a minimum and a maximum sentence; these sentences reflect the maximum.

Even in the absence of either three strikes or habitual offender statutes, a similar increase in punishment for dangerousness is provided by sentencing guidelines that tie the sentence in large part to the offender's criminal history. Under the United States Sentencing Commission Guidelines, for example, a level 10 offence gets 1–12 months in the absence of a criminal record, but 24–30 months for significant record; a level 19 offence gets 30–37 months, but with a record gets 63–78; a level 37 offence normally gets 18–22 years, but with a record gets between 30 years and life imprisonment. See *United States Sentencing Commission Guidelines Manual* (1997) 304.

[73] Andrew von Hirsch, Kay A. Knapp and Michael Tonry, *Past or Future Crimes: Deservedness and Dangerousness in the Sentencing of Criminals* (New Brunswick, 1985) 132–138.

[74] See National Institute of Justice, '*Three Strikes and You're Out': A Review of State Legislation* (Washington, DC, 1997) Exhibit 9 col. 2.

[75] See, e.g., Rev. Wash. Code ss. 9.94A.120(4), 9.94A.030(23) and (27).

To summarize, the current criminal justice system commonly serves more a preventive detention function than a deserved punishment function. It brings into the system persons whose conduct would not previously have been thought to be criminal, as in the extension of inchoate and complicity liability. While empirical studies suggest that people of today would not think such newly criminalized conduct warrants criminal liability and punishment,[76] such people are detained because they are thought to be dangerous. Similarly, the current criminal justice system grades offences, especially inchoate offences and complicity, to allow offenders to be kept in prison beyond the term of imprisonment justified as deserved punishment. Finally, the current criminal justice system sets sentencing rules that similarly extend terms of imprisonment past those deserved, as with 'three strikes' statutes and sentencing guidelines using prior criminal record dramatically to increase the term of imprisonment to be imposed.

3. The Illusion: Cloaking Preventive Detention as Criminal Justice

The criminal justice system has traditionally advertised itself as 'doing justice', imposing punishment on those who deserve it in the amount they deserve. Our language reflects this view. In the criminal context, we speak of a 'crime' rather than a 'violation' or 'breach', and of 'punishment' rather than of 'remedy' or 'damages' or 'sanction'. The terms 'crime' and 'punishment' carry the implication of moral condemnation that the civil terms do not. As Webster's puts it, something 'criminal' is something 'disgraceful'.[77] 'Punishment' suggests '*retributive* suffering, pain, or loss'.[78] Breaking a contract or failing adequately to fence a swimming pool may be conduct that we seek to discourage and may be a sufficient violation of rules or expectations to justify compensation of a party injured by the breach, but such conduct or omission typically lacks the moral blameworthiness, the 'disgracefulness', sufficient to merit the condemnation implicit in criminal conviction. The terminology of moral condemnation helps cultivate the moral stigmatization that sets criminal apart from civil liability or 'civil commitment'.

The criminal justice system's shift of recent decades from doing justice to providing protection from dangerous persons has produced some terminological awkwardness. It is impossible, of course, to *punish dangerousness*, within the meaning of those terms. To 'punish' is 'to cause (a person) to undergo pain, loss, or suffering *for a crime or wrongdoing*'.[79] Punishment can

---

[76] See, e.g., Paul H. Robinson and John M. Darley, *Justice, Liability and Blame: Community Views and the Criminal Law* (Boulder, 1995) Study 1 and Study 3 (finding that lay persons see the Model Penal Code's 'substantial step' test for attempt and its lack of an assistance requirement for complicity liability as inconsistent with their intuitive notions of what is an adequate basis for deserving punishment).

[77] *Webster's New Collegiate Dictionary* (7th edn., Springfield, 1965) 197.

[78] ibid. at 693 (emphasis added).

[79] *Webster's New World College Dictionary* (2nd edn., Springfield, 1959) 1180 (emphasis added).

only exist in relation to a past wrong. 'Dangerous' means 'likely to cause injury, pain, etc.',[80] that is, a threat of future harm. One can 'restrain' or 'detain' or 'incapacitate' a dangerous person, but one cannot logically 'punish' dangerousness.

Imprisonment as deserved punishment has always provided the useful side-effect of giving temporary protection from the dangerous offender. What has changed in the past decades is a shift in the criteria for assigning liability and punishment from desert to dangerousness, such that incapacitation of the dangerous is not simply a useful by-product but a primary purpose. The rules for assessing liability and punishment are increasingly set to maximize protection, even if they conflict with desert. Yet the reformers have been careful not to advertise the shift by recharacterizing the system as one of preventive detention. Instead, they have sought to maintain the increasingly false criminal *justice* image.

One might charitably conclude that the retention of the appearance of moral desert in a system that practises preventive detention is simply inertia. There was neither the opportunity or the real need to change the long-standing characterization. But a closer look at the reforms of the last decades suggest a more calculated effort to exploit the traditional image for its usefulness.

For example, recall the Model Penal Code's grading of inchoate conduct as equal to that of the substantive offence.[81] The policy logically follows from the drafters' view that the actual occurrence of resulting harm does not alter the dangerousness of the offender. Whether the harm or evil of the offence actually occurs is irrelevant; it is the person's propensity for a future offence that ought to be the system's focus.

But if the drafters believe that resulting harm should be irrelevant to grading, why did they not just drop all result elements from the Code's offence definitions and define all offences in terms of conduct and accompanying mental state? i.e.: 'Engaging in conduct by which one intends to . . .' burn a building, falsify an official document, or injure another. Why keep the result elements of offence definitions, making the Code look, at a glance, as if it takes account of resulting harm?[82]

Reformers could have taken a course, in terminology and in substance, that more openly revealed the system's growing preventive detention character.

---

[80] ibid. at 372.

[81] See text accompanying n. 62 above. Satisfying all elements other than the prohibited result, i.e., conduct and intention toward the offence, typically results in attempt liability. (This is true of offences that require intention. Every instance in which all elements of the offence are proven except the result element constitutes an attempt. See, e.g., MPC s. 5.01(b). In the few instances in which the Code punishes recklessly causing a result, recklessness is not enough in many jurisdictions to support attempt liability. See, e.g., ibid.; but see Paul H. Robinson, *Criminal Law* (New York, 1997) 28.)

[82] These issues are explored more fully in Paul H. Robinson, 'The Role of Harm and Evil in Criminal Law: A Study in Legislative Deception?' (1994) 5 Journal of Contemporary Legal Issues 299.

Why didn't they? Most jurisdictions allow civil commitment in order to detain dangerous persons who have mental illness, drug dependency, or a contagious disease.[83] Why the shyness here, in openly announcing the preventive detention of dangerous persons? One might speculate that the drafters saw value in maintaining the appearance of a criminal justice system if not its spirit. The fact is that several practical advantages exist for reformers in cloaking preventive detention as criminal justice.

First, such cloaking avoids the stigma that many people associate with the preventive detention legislation.[84] Such programmes were decried as 'Clockwork Orange'[85] and ' "Alice in Wonderland" justice' in which the punishment precedes the offence,[86] introducing a 'police state',[87] and 'fostering tyranny'.[88] It was said to be 'intellectually dishonest',[89] 'one of the most tragic mistakes we as a society could make',[90] which 'would change the complexion of American Justice'.[91] It was 'simply not the American way'.[92]

[83] For statutes authorizing detention of dangerously mentally ill persons, see, e.g., Conn. Gen. Stat. Ann. s. 17a-498 (West 1992); Idaho Code s. 66-329 (1989); La. Rev. Stat. Ann. s. 28:55 (West 1989); Mass. Ann. Laws ch. 123, s. 12 (1992); Minn. Stat. s. 253B.02, subd. 13, 17 (1990); Mo. Rev. Stat. s. 552.040 (1991); N.H. Rev. Stat. Ann. s. 135-C:34 (1991); N.J. Stat. Ann. s. 30:4-27.1 (West 1992); N.Y. Mental Hyg. Law s. 9.37 (Consol. 1993); Utah Code Ann. s. 62A-5-312 (1992); Wash. Rev. Code s. 71.05.280 (1991); Wis. Stat. s. 51.20 (1989–1990); Wyo. Stat. s. 25-10-101 (1992). For statutes authorizing detention of persons with a communicable disease, see, e.g. Ala. Code s. 22-11A-10 (tuberculosis), -14 and -18 (sexually transmitted diseases), -24 (notifiable diseases) (1992); Colo. Rev. Stat. s. 25-1-650 (1992) (communicable diseases); Del. Code Ann. tit. 16, s. 505 (1983) (communicable diseases); Fla. Stat. ch. 384.28 (1991) (sexually transmitted diseases); Haw. Rev. Stat. s. 325-8 (1985) (infectious, communicable, or other disease dangerous to public health); Iowa Code Ann. s. 139.3 (West 1989) (communicable diseases); Kan. Stat. Ann. s. 65-128 (1991) (infectious or communicable diseases); Minn. Stat. s. 144.4180 (1992) (communicable diseases); N.H. Rev. Stat. Ann. s. 141-C:11 (1990) (communicable diseases); N.C. Gen. Stat. s. 130A-145 (1992) (communicable diseases); Ohio Rev. Code Ann. s. 3707.08 (Baldwin 1989) (communicable diseases); R.I. Gen. Laws s. 23-8-4 (1989) (communicable diseases); Tenn. Code Ann. s. 68-5-104 (1992) (communicable or contagious diseases); Wis. Stat. Ann. s. 143.05 (West 1989) (communicable diseases). For statutes authorizing detention of persons with a chemical dependence, see, e.g., Cal. Welf. and Inst. Code s. 3000 to 3111 (Deering 1993); D.C. Code Ann. s. 24-601 to 24-611 (1992); Minn. Stat. s. 253B.02, subd. 14 (1990); S.C. Code Ann. ss. 44-52-50 to 44-52-210 (Law Co-op 1991).

[84] For a chronological list of preventive detention enactments, see Toborg Assoc., Inc., 'Public Danger as a Factor in Pretrial Release', reprinted in *Report on Bail Reform Act of 1984* (H.R. 98-1121) App. A at 90. The first statutes appear in Alaska and Delaware, 1967, Maryland and South Carolina, 1969, Vermont, 1967/69m and the District of Columbia, 1970. Despite the constitutional approval of pre-trial preventive detention (see *United States v Edwards* 430 A 2d 1321 (CD C App 1981) cert. den. 455 US 1022 (1982)), many jurisdictions still have refused to enact such a system. The 24 states authorizing pre-trial detention are listed in the Committee on the Judiciary's *Report on the Bail Reform Act* (H.R. 98-1121) at App. A, Table 2, 76.

[85] *Chicago Tribune*, 22 January 1987 (quoting critics).

[86] *Congressional Quarterly Weekly Report*, 30 May 1987 (quoting Professor Alan Dershowitz).

[87] e.g., *Boston Globe*, 27 May 1987; *Las Vegas Review Journal*, 17 December 1990; *Seattle Times*, 21 May 1986; *Washington Post*, 1 August 1986 (quoting Judge Jon Newman).

[88] *Seattle Times*, 3 June 1987 (citing Justice Marshall).

[89] *Houston Chronicle*, 31 May 1987.

[90] *The Record*, Northern New Jersey, 19 November 1986 (quoting New Jersey Senate President John Russo, a former prosecutor).

[91] *Time*, 8 June 1987.   [92] *Chicago Sun-Times*, 7 June 1987.

But the preventive detention legislation that prompted this outrage was controversial in large part because it provided *pre-trial* preventive detention. In contrast, most current reforms provide preventive detention only after trial and conviction, an important difference. On the other hand, part of preventive detention's bad reputation stems from an objection to its 'Alice in Wonderland' quality of having the punishment precede the offence.[93] That same objection can be made of the present post-conviction system of preventive detention, where an offender is detained past the deserved term of imprisonment in order to prevent a future offence. But by obscuring the preventive character of such extended detention by imposing it under the *criminal justice* system, the potential for controversy is reduced. Further, some of the reforms come after trial but trial for a criminal offence is defined as conduct that was previously thought not criminal and made criminal only for the purpose of gaining authority over dangerous persons, as with the extension of inchoate liability. The *entire* term of detention is based upon a preventive rather than a desert rationale.

A second, more concrete, advantage to cloaking preventive detention as criminal justice is found in the logical limitations on preventive detention that such cloaking avoids. If the justification for the detention is dangerousness, then logically the government ought to be required to show periodically the detainee's continuing dangerousness. If the dangerousness disappears, so does the justification for detention. But, if the detention is characterized as deserved punishment for a past offence, there is little reason to revisit the justification for the detention. All the factors relevant to determining deserved punishment are available at the time of sentencing: the offender's conduct and state of mind at the time of the offence and the resulting harm or evil. It is for this reason that 'determinate' and 'real time' sentencing are popular in the USA. An offender's term is set beforehand and is not subject to later modification, as parole authorities used to do.[94] Characterizing preventive detention as deserved punishment allows it to avoid periodic review by hiding behind the veil of deserved punishment for which fixed terms are appropriate.

A third and related advantage concerns the extent of intrusion on liberty. Restraint justified by prevention logically should be limited to the minimum required for the community's safety. If house arrest, an ankle bracelet, drug therapy, or other non-incarcerative conditions provide adequate protection, then greater restraint cannot be justified.[95] No such minimum-restraint principle applies in the application of deserved punishment. Indeed, Dan Kahan and others have argued that imprisonment might be preferred for punishment

---

[93] *Congressional Quarterly Weekly Report*, 30 May 1987 (quoting Professor Alan Dershowitz).

[94] Under the Federal Sentencing Reform Act 1984, for example, an offender must serve at least 85 per cent of the term imposed by the sentencing judge: 18 USC s. 3624(b).

[95] See, e.g., Norval Morris and Michael Tonry, *Between Prison and Probation: Intermediate Punishments in a Rational Sentencing System* (New York, 1990) 3, 176–220.

purposes because of its expressive power of condemnation.[96] Cloaking preventive detention as criminal justice, then, saves authorities from having to show that the detention is the least restrictive adequate for protection.

A fourth advantage of cloaking relates to conditions of confinement. When a person is detained for society's benefit rather than because of deserved punishment, logically the conditions of detention ought to be non-punitive. The civilly detained preventive detainee is not being punished, but rather suffering an intrusion of liberty for society's benefit. While financial constraints do not always make it so, the mentally ill or contagious disease detainee in principle ought to and often does enjoy noticeably better conditions than the person being punished. Where confinement is deserved punishment, the offender has little justification to complain about punitive conditions. The point of the imprisonment is to bring about suffering, within the bounds of human dignity. By cloaking preventive detention as punishment, then, the system need not justify its failure to provide non-punitive conditions of detention.

Finally, consistent with the preventive detention principle of minimum restraint, a detainee ought to have an absolute right to treatment if such can reduce the length or intrusiveness of the restraint. No similar claim to treatment is available if the justification for incarceration is punishment for a past wrong. The person incarcerated as punishment has no greater claim to government-provided treatment than any other citizen.

These, then, are some of the practical advantages to reformers of cloaking preventive detention as criminal justice. By continuing to advertise the system as 'doing justice', and shrouding the preventive mechanisms in ambiguity as to their purpose and rationale, the system can provide preventive detention without the constraints that logically would attend an explicit preventive detention system.

But, as is obvious, these practical advantages also signal unfairnesses to the persons preventively detained under the cloak of criminal justice. The logical constraints on preventive detention ought not be avoided. (There is also evidence that the current cloaking not only provides unfair detention, but also often causes ineffective preventive detention[97] and, at the same time, undermines the criminal justice system's crime control effectiveness.[98])

---

[96] See, e.g., Dan Kahan, 'What Do Alternative Sanctions Mean?' (1996) 63 University of Chicago LR 591 (discussing the 'expressive dimension' of punishment and the significance of imprisonment for moral condemnation); Dan Kahan, 'Social Influence, Social Meaning, and Deterrence' (1997) 83 Virginia LR 349, at 362–363, 382 (suggesting that the form of punishment conveys a social meaning that in turn determines the direction of social influence): 'Imprisonment is an extraordinarily potent gesture of moral disapproval; because of the symbolic importance of individual liberty in American culture, there is never a doubt that society means to condemn someone when it takes that person's freedom away'.

[97] See Paul H. Robinson, 'Punishing Dangerousness: Cloaking Preventive Detention as Criminal Justice' (2001) 114 Harvard LR, 1429.

[98] Paul H. Robinson and John M. Darley, 'The Utility of Desert' (1997) 91 Northwestern University LR 453.

D. Illusions and Criminal Law Scholarship

Here, then, are three illusions, each of a different sort. The introduction of individualization into the objective reasonable person standard was clearly an advance. It recognized a serious criticism of the previous theoretical scheme and made a useful correction. It is true that the new approach has its own theoretical weakness: we cannot provide a principled theory by which to distinguish those characteristics with which the law should individualize from those with which it should not. But our failure to move forward is more a matter of our own intellectual limitations than anything else. One might wish that more scholarly energy were being devoted to the problem, but there is little reason to think that people would not welcome a solution if it presented in itself. Here the illusion is a scholarly challenge.

The addition of an articulation of purposes for criminal liability and punishment also was an advance in its time. We are better to have had the reform than not. We see now that it too rests upon an illusion: the failure to define the interrelation among the purposes allows a decision-maker to switch among purposes as needed to give an appearance of rationality to any result the decision-maker may wish, even if it is preferred for unprincipled reasons.

When the illusion of rationality became apparent, it presented the same scholarly challenge that the individualization issue now presents. But with the passage of time since the illusion has been exposed, and especially with the passage of time since its remedy has become apparent—the articulation of a hybrid distributive principle—it is difficult to see the problem any longer as one of scholarly challenge but rather as one of scholarly weakness. We show an unflattering level of comfort with the illusion.

The third illustration also tells the story of a response to a legitimate problem: the need to reduce seriously high crime levels. But the solution offered—the use of a criminal justice system that maintains its moral desert trappings yet increasingly engages in preventive detention—is harder to justify as a principled response even from the start. It seems more a calculated than an inadvertent deception. It is conceivable that the first steps toward a preventive rationale were minor and incidental, perhaps the result of confusion in thinking more than anything else. But the history suggests that, at least with the advent of the Model Penal Code, the confusion turned into strategy. The points of potential confusion between desert and prevention were exploited for maximum effect, as in turning the ambiguity of prior convictions to blameworthiness into 'three strikes'[99] and in making results insignificant to liability

---

[99] The existence of any desert justification for increasing a sentence for repeat offenders, such as the nose-thumbing theory (see text accompanying text at nn. 75 and 76 above), creates ambiguity as to whether an increase for prior record, even if it is a 300 per cent increase, is based on desert or dangerousness; and that ambiguity helps the preventive detention portion of the term blend in with the deserved portion.

wherever it might not be noticed, as in grading attempts, yet in retaining the appearance of a system giving significance to resulting harm by keeping offences with result elements. The cloaking of preventive detention as criminal justice is not weakness but fraud. If it is a preventive detention system we are to have, then it ought to proclaim itself openly as one and be judged accordingly, subject to all the limitations that logically follow from its nature.

Illusions are not always the sign of weakness or deception. They often are an inevitable part of theoretical advance. Theorists and reformers cannot always see the full implication of new theories or reforms. Often it is only when another generation stands on their shoulders with the improved view they have been given that an illusion and its detrimental effect can be seen. Critics ought to judge less the creator of the illusion and more the theoreticians and decision-makers who discover it. Do they lack enthusiasm in their efforts to break the illusion because it serves a useful purpose? Worse, do they take the opportunity to expand and exploit the illusion?

Scholars ought not be deterred from revolutionary proposals because they cannot be sure the proposal does not hide a new illusion. Every advance has its limitations. Scholars' only obligation with regard to illusions is to search for them and to break them when discovered.

5

Making Criminal Law Known

PETER ALLDRIDGE*

A. Background

Criminal statutes, together with essays like the Model Penal Code and the various attempts at codification in England and Wales,[1] are directed, formally at least, to courts. They specify the necessary and sufficient conditions under which a conviction may be returned. If conditions C_1–C_n are satisfied, the law states, the court shall or may do x.[2] Frequently, definitions of crimes are difficult for anyone not a lawyer to understand. The case for a civic code is that it would be a good idea, therefore, if there were to be a single reliable[3] source of information as to what citizens may or may not do in those areas of their lives in which they are likely to come up against the criminal law. If we are to take seriously the idea that criminal law is to guide conduct, we should take greater care to ensure that people actually know what is required of them.[4] If a criminal offence is defined in such an obscure way that it is difficult, or even impossible, to divine any guidance as to behaviour from it, that is a reason why the offence needs to be abolished or redrawn. This simple consideration is enough to provide a powerful critique of some offences that still blemish the English statute book.[5]

---

* I am most grateful to the editors for their comments.

[1] From the nineteenth century codes through to Law Commission No. 143, *Codification of the Criminal Law* (HC 270, 1985) and Law Commission No. 177, *A Criminal Code for England and Wales* (London, HMSO, 1989).

[2] This is a necessary implication of the standard means of defining a crime: 'It is an offence to . . .'.

[3] This chapter will not deal with the legal questions arising out of reliance. See Andrew Ashworth, Chapter 13 of this volume, 'Testing Fidelity to Legal Values: Official Involvement and Criminal Justice'.

[4] This is probably best expressed in Fuller, *The Morality of Law* (New Haven, revised edn. 1969).

[5] e.g., Insolvency Act 1986, s.362: '(1) The bankrupt is guilty of an offence if he has—(a) in the 2 years before petition, materially contributed to, or increased the extent of, his insolvency by gambling or by rash and hazardous speculations, or (b) in the initial period, lost any part of his property by gambling or by rash and hazardous speculations. (2) In determining for the purposes of this section whether any speculations were rash and hazardous, the financial position of the bankrupt at the time when he entered into them shall be taken into consideration'. (The maximum penalty is two years' imprisonment: ibid., Sch. 10.)

No causal relationship is required between the gambling and the bankruptcy. No foresight or negligence is required. It is no defence that you gambled and won. A person who buys a lottery

That is the case for a code for citizens. There is a response, seldom articulated, but, nonetheless, probably the most significant reason that there is no such document. This holds that criminal law is, at the same time, too simple and too complex for the promulgation of a civic code to be worthwhile: the 'central areas' are too simple to need to be explained at all. What they boil down to is 'do not injure people or act dishonestly, and leave children alone'. All other areas of criminal law are too complex or specialized ever to be worth explaining otherwise than to and by specialists. So if a person wishes to conduct a particular type of business, or drive a car, or fill in a tax form, it is incumbent upon him/her to get adequate advice. These matters could not be dealt with in a code that was sufficiently compact to be useful.

The enormous contribution that Paul Robinson has made is to follow the argument for a code through to its production.[6] Robinson's version contemplates that the code for citizens would lay down all the prohibitions of a particular area of criminal law (offences against the person, theft, damage). In respect of any given breach or alleged breach of the criminal law the first point of reference would be the conduct rules, which would be drafted with sufficient specificity to have statutory force, and if the definition there was satisfied then the court should move to codes of adjudication and grading for all the ancillary provisions, specific immunities, and so on.

Antony Duff objects to expressions of law along the lines of Robinson's code. He holds that ' "Act thus, because you have an obligation to obey the law"; or "Act thus, or else you will suffer sanctions" . . . are not the tones in which the law should address the citizens of a liberal polity'.[7] He argues that the criminal law embodies the shared values of a political community in a declaration of the public wrongfulness of the proscribed activity. At a fairly abstract level, this has implications for the manner in which we conceive criminal law—who are its addressees, who its proponents, what values these groups have, and so on. At a more practical level, Duff's position calls into question attempts to put in place guidance directed at citizens as to how they need to behave in order to comply with the requirements of the criminal law.

This chapter is a response to both writers. I hope to show how a civic code constructed differently from Robinson's might answer some of Duff's criticism of the tone that he ascribes to Robinson's code. I shall also argue that some elements of civil law need to be included in a proper account of the distinction between justification and excuse and a code of advice for citizens,

---

ticket early in year 1, and then, late in year 2 becomes bankrupt is guilty. The only advice a lawyer could give to someone who does not want to commit a crime and is already taking all reasonable steps to avoid bankruptcy is never to gamble: but if that is what the law means then it ought to say so. Almost everyone who becomes bankrupt will be guilty of this offence, and the threat of prosecution will provide an additional club with which to beat bankrupts, with the usual risks concomitant to the granting of wide discretionary powers to prosecutors.

[6] Paul Robinson, *Structure and Function in Criminal Law* (Oxford, 1997) 211 ff.
[7] R.A. Duff, Chapter 3 in this volume, 'Rule-Violations and Wrongdoings' at 53.

and that the starting point for an account of the relationship between criminal law and citizen should be the rights (especially the human rights) of the citizen, not a conception of the major criminal proscriptions. I shall argue that we should reject the characterization of criminal law as little more than a field for the concretization of problems in linguistic philosophy, and that we should adopt a more pragmatic conception of its provenance and objectives. I will look at some of the areas of criminal law which Duff and Robinson do not regard as central, going beyond the areas from which the 'general principles' of criminal law are usually said to be derived (most frequently, and often misleadingly, offences against the person), and discuss not so much whether mental states can be removed, but whether, in laying down rules to guide conduct, we should hold a preference as between using *mens rea* and *actus reus* terms.

1. Duff's Attack

As I understand him, Duff does not attempt to undermine the entire project of providing a code of conduct for citizens, but to give it greater focus. He attacks on several fronts, from the general to the specific. On the general front, he argues that the version of law and its obligatory nature which is implied by the attempt to generate codes is misplaced because it relies upon a version of the command theory which does not properly represent the relationship between the law and the conduct of the complying citizen. More specifically, Duff attacks the classification of duress as excuse, and calls into question Robinson's attempt to strip conduct rules of requirements dealing with mental states—especially intention and recklessness, but also more complex ones like 'dishonestly' and 'corruptly'.

Duff identifies very clearly the tenets of the traditional positivist approach to criminal law proscriptions with which he takes issue: 'their addressees are not invited or expected to interpret the prohibitions in the light of the reasons that supposedly justify their content, or of the values that supposedly inform them . . . the prohibitions must therefore strive for descriptive clarity and certainty: they must provide clear, determinate factual specifications of the conduct they prohibit—specifications whose application avoids, as far as possible, any reliance on the normative understandings of those who are to apply them'.[8] He takes issue with this approach by appealing to an account of the legitimacy of criminal law as deriving from community sentiment.

Duff regards criminal law theory as a form of applied philosophy. He commences his chapter with a discussion of guiding moral reasons, averring 'a close analogue in the criminal law',[9] and makes claims for law by analogy to moral reasoning such as 'are (morally and should be legally) justified'.[10] Much of the work of British doctrinal criminal law theorists is along these

---

[8] Chapter 3 above at 56–57.   [9] Chapter 3 above at 48.   [10] Chapter 3 above at 63.

lines. It seeks accounts of the (moral or intellectual) justifiability of the criminal law, and assumes that given sufficient analysis a general account may be derived of what the criminal law principles of responsibility should be in all places for all time. In this project such cases as *Saunders and Archer*[11] and *Dudley and Stephens*[12] have the quality of fables. They are complete and can be addressed in a totally decontextualised manner. They need not be located in any particular time, place or culture. Considerations of the 'general part' of criminal law in any jurisdiction, in any epoch, can grapple with the problems of what the shocked supplier of a misdirected poisoned apple or the starving killers of a semi-comatose cabin boy should be called and how they should be treated. Historical detail, though of anecdotal interest,[13] adds nothing of importance.[14] Firmly located within that tradition, Duff presents the 'criminal law of a liberal polity' as something more or less fixed, something homogenizing which can safely ignore differences of time, location and legal culture. On this account, murder, rape, serious assault and theft are central to criminal law whenever and wherever. *Mala in se* are the core of criminal law. Within those limits it is far easier to argue for the explicatory, almost cajoling, role for criminal law in addressing citizens which Duff has in mind than for criminal law more widely defined.

I suggest that criminal law does not have the core which Duff claims, nor can it properly be sited in a liberal polity, and, to put the matter more generally, that criminal law is not, and that criminal law theory ought not to be, a means of presenting problems so as to resolve them solely as matters of applied philosophy. The appeal to community sentiment that Duff makes is dangerous because it attempts to enlist our moral approbation for the criminal law. The benefit of the detachment which underpins the basic tenet of legal positivism (that law and morals should be separated) is that it facilitates the evaluation of rules without making any assumptions about their moral quality. It also allows the widening of the area of enquiry, in terms of the prohibited behaviour and the available sanctions, of victims' and human rights, and of the international dimension of criminal law.[15]

One of the perennial problems encountered by those attempting to forge structural links between criminal law and ethical precepts is that there are some offences that apparently lack any kind of moral element. Defence of the links between law and morality usually tries to meet this by attempting to put in place a distinction between proscriptions which, for contingent reasons, 'just happen' to have been instantiated in a given society and those which form part of a core of more universally and fundamentally objectionable

---

[11] *R v Saunders and Archer* (1579) 2 Plowd 473; Fost 371.

[12] *R v Dudley and Stephens* (1884) 14 QBD 273.

[13] A.W.B. Simpson, *Cannibalism and the Common Law* (Harmondsworth, 1984).

[14] See Neil Duxbury's review of A.W.B. Simpson, *Leading Cases in the Common Law* (1996) 59 Modern Law Review 765.

[15] See too Mireille Delmas-Marty, *Les Grandes Systèmes de Politique Criminelle* (Paris, 1992) especially 15–43.

practices: between *mala prohibita* and *mala in se*. Disagreement over whether this distinction can be made to work is as old as criminal law theory. When Blackstone introduced the distinction to the literature,[16] Bentham scoffed:

Blackstone's presentation of [*mala in se*] is the first occasion of our hearing of the acute distinction between *mala in se*, and *mala prohibita*: which being so shrewd, and sounding so pretty, and being in Latin, has no sort of occasion to have any meaning to it: accordingly it has none.[17]

There is in the literature inconsistency in usage of the expressions *mala prohibita* and *mala in se*. Blackstone included currency offences as *malum in se* and treated theft inconsistently.[18] For Beccaria and Adam Smith, *mala prohibita* include smuggling.[19] There is at least one crime that has in the past been regarded as *malum in se* and is now perfectly legal.[20] Since then there have been disputes as to the sustainability of the distinction. There have been writers for[21] and writers against[22] and judges for[23] and judges against.[24] It

---

[16] 'Divine or natural duties [do not] receive any stronger sanction from being also declared to be duties by the law of the land. The case is the same as to crimes and misdemeanors, that are forbidden by the superior laws, and therefore styled *mala in se*, such as murder, theft, and perjury; which contract no additional turpitude from being declared unlawful by the inferior legislature': W. Blackstone, *Commentaries* (London, Dawsons, reprinted 1966) Vol. 1, 54, 55, 58.

[17] Jeremy Bentham, 'A Comment on the Commentaries' (1776) (reprinted in J.H. Burns and H.L.A. Hart (eds.), *Collected Works of Jeremy Bentham* (London, Athlone Press, 1977) 63).

[18] ibid., 63–64.

[19] C. Beccaria, *Of Crimes and Punishments* (2nd edn., Adolph Caso (ed.), Boston, International Pocket Library, 1992) ch. 33; Adam Smith, *The Wealth of Nations* (3rd edn., R. H. Campbell, A. S. Skinner, W. B. Todd (eds.), Oxford, Oxford University Press, 1976) Book V, ch. II.

[20] Buggery is not the only example. '[M]aintenance is not *malum prohibitum*, but *malum in se*: . . . parties shall not by their countenance aid the prosecution of suits of any kind; which every person must bring upon his own bottom and at his own expense': *Wallis v Duke of Portland* (1797) 3 Ves. 494 at 502 per Lord Loughborough LC. The crime of maintenance (including champerty) was abolished by s.13(1)(a) of the Criminal Law Act 1967.

[21] Patrick Devlin, 'Real Crimes and Quasi-Crimes' in *The Enforcement of Morals* (1965) 26–42; Patrick Fitzgerald, 'Real Crimes and Quasi-Crimes' (1965) 10 Natural Law Forum 21.

[22] Richard L. Gray, 'Note: Eliminating The (Absurd) Distinction Between *Malum In Se* And *Malum Prohibitum* Crimes' (1995) 73 Washington University Law Quarterly 1369.

[23] Some more enthusiastically than others: it was treated with some degree of ambivalence by Lord Reid in *Regazzoni v K. C. Sethia (1944) Ltd* [1958] AC 301 at 306.

[24] 'The distinction between *mala prohibita* and *mala in se* has been long since exploded. It was not founded upon any sound principle, for it is equally unfit, that a man should be allowed to take advantage of what the law says he ought not to do, whether the thing be prohibited, because it is against good morals, or whether it be prohibited, because it is against the interest of the State': *Bensley v Bignold* (1822) 5 Barn and Ald 335; 106 ER 1214 per Best J; 'I perfectly agree . . . in reprobating any distinction between *malum prohibitum* and *malum in se*, and consider it as pregnant with mischiefs. Every moral man is as much bound to obey the civil law of the land as the law of nature': *Aubert v Maze* (1801) 2 Bos & Pul 371; 126 ER 1333 per Rooke J; 'there arises the difficulty, which I regard as insoluble, of formulating a criterion which would separate cases of serious illegality from those which are not serious. Past distinctions drawn between felonies and misdemeanours, *malum in se* and *malum prohibitum*, offences punishable by imprisonment and those which are not, non-statutory and statutory offences offer no acceptable discrimen': *Jackson v Harrison* (1978) 138 CLR 438 at 455 per Mason J.

still might have some legal significance.[25] In support of the claim that there is an identifiable core to criminal law one might at least have expected reference to criminal or prison statistics, criminal justice budgets, Home Office targets or something similar, but Duff produces no such evidence. This should not simply be taken as an article of faith. Even if we ignore drugs offences[26] and eschew Marxian (especially Gramscian) accounts of criminal law and legitimation from the 1970s, the criminal law of England and Wales in the early twenty-first century is not a reflection of anything so simple and unitary as a set of shared values. For each criminalization there is a specific concatenation of events, and whilst it is sometimes possible to discern broad trends,[27] Duff's 'public wrongfulness' account does not properly describe them. For example, considering an activity *that was not criminal at all until the late 1980s*, a recent article commenced:

[Money laundering] is a serious challenge to the maintenance of law and order . . . and threatens the integrity, reliability, and stability of governments, financial institutions, and commerce.[28]

(Which makes it sound very serious indeed.) The history of criminal law contains many offences which, when first prohibited, were presented as being the embodiment of tremendous harms, and in respect of which greater investigation, enforcement, and punishment powers are required than for 'regular' crime, but which subsequently are removed from the statute book (prohibition), fall into disuse (sedition, blasphemy) or are assimilated to the body of existing offences (offences of tampering in markets). A positivist conception will take whatever the law is at any given time, and attempt to communicate its significance to its subjects as clearly as possible, without, necessarily, attempting to gain their confidence.

Nonetheless Duff portrays the law, not as prohibiting the 'central *mala in se* but as declaring their public wrongfulness'.[29] They are public wrongs that

[25] Even leaving aside Baron Bramwell's famous argument in *R v Prince* (1875) LR 2 CCR 154 at 173, there are ramifications in the law of illegal contracts and illegal wills. A court disposed to enforce part of a contract or will with some illegal terms will sometimes dismiss those illegalities as *mala prohibita* and sidestep the problems to which they would have otherwise have had to advert.

[26] Today in women's prisons in England and Wales there are about 50 times more Nigerian drug smugglers than battered women who have killed their partner. Which is 'central' to criminal law?

[27] Thus, e.g., it is open to doubt if the reversal of the rule in *Owen v Board of Trade* [1957] AC 602, by s.5 of the Criminal Justice (Terrorism and Conspiracy) Act 1998, would have happened had it not been for (a) the growth of interest in controlling sexual tourism, leading to the Sexual Offences (Conspiracy and Incitement) Act 1996 and the Sex Offenders Act 1997; and (b) the Omagh bombing in August 1998. Appeals to community values without recognition of the historical contingency of these developments ignores important respects in which law is not like philosophy. As Fish wrote: 'law is not philosophy . . .': Stanley Fish, *Doing What Comes Naturally* (Oxford, 1989) 397.

[28] Paulina Jerez, 'Proposed Brazilian Money Laundering Legislation: Analysis and Recommendations' (1997) 12 American University Journal of International Law and Policy 329.

[29] Reminiscent of Patrick Devlin, *The Enforcement of Morals* (Oxford, 1965) 27: 'Real crimes are sins with legal definitions'.

must be formally recognized and condemned by the whole political community. The way in which he deals with the standard objections to the distinction between *mala in se* and *mala prohibita* is to hold that there are few real *mala prohibita* in criminal law. Many supposed *mala prohibita* (some of which are crimes of strict liability, for example) are on Duff's account, *determinationes* of *mala in se*. Thus, for example, numerical definitions of many crimes by reference to time or speed or mass or volume might have used different quantities, and there will be no real moral distinction between two cases that fall immediately on either side of any numerical line. What the rules really provide, however, is a clear way of expressing 'too fast', 'too young', 'too long', 'too much' or whatever is in point. It is generally easier for a court to assess whether a quantitative measure has been satisfied than a qualitative one. The fact that this makes the offence one of strict liability does not relieve it of a moral quality. This analysis does indeed provide a mechanism for dealing with the argument from offences of strict liability.[30]

However, the dichotomy Duff poses, between (on the one hand) pre-legal moral wrongfulness and (on the other) its absence, does not seem to account well for a whole group of offences. There are many actions—particularly of exploitation of market conditions—which might properly give rise to disapproval, but which generate an entirely different order of condemnation in the case where it is illegal. Even for those who do not want to go the whole way with Posner[31] and assert that all criminal law is really an operation in the regulation of markets, there will be cases where the relationship between the criminal law and the market is crucial to a moral evaluation. Frequently, they arise where the issue is how the market is to be organized. There is a series of offences where the fact of criminalization creates immorality. The law lays down the 'rules of the game', and, so long as everyone knows what the rules are and plays by them, there is no real moral obloquy in using them to advantage.[32] When rules are laid down, if only because of the absence of identifiable victims, frequently the mechanism used is the criminal law. For instance, before legislation was put in place to prohibit auction rings,[33] everyone who put goods up for sale at auction was on notice that they might get a lower price if an auction ring was operating. Before 1980 (in the United

---

[30] A good example of the distinction between using *determinationes* and qualitative terms is between the law of cricket relating to interference by the wicket-keeper with the batsman attempting to play a stroke (which is, in this sense, quantitative, being determined by whether or not the wicket-keeper breaks the plane of the stumps), and the equivalent rule in baseball, which is qualitative: Official Rules of Major League Baseball, Rule 2.00: 'Defensive interference is an act by a fielder which hinders or prevents a batter from hitting a pitch', the batter then being entitled to first base.

[31] Posner's infamous account of rape is to be found in Richard Posner, 'An Economic Theory of the Criminal Law' (1985) 85 Columbia Law Review 1193 at 1194, 1198.

[32] And see Tony Honoré, 'The Dependence of Morality on Law' (1993) 13 Oxford Journal of Legal Studies 1.

[33] Auctions Rings Act 1961.

Kingdom), anyone who dealt in the Stock Exchange was on notice[34] that s/he might be selling to or buying from someone with insider information. The criminalization of auction rings and insider dealing[35] has altered their respective moral standing. Now anyone who engages in an auction ring or insider deals is representing to the world that s/he is playing by the rules when s/he is not. That immorality is not pre-legal but *post*-legal. The same kind of argument can be made in many other areas of interaction between criminal law and markets, for example, immigration offences, smuggling offences, offences for the protection of consumers or employees, offences by landlords against tenants, and offences against the regulatory structures in place relating to financial services.[36] Further, it is frequently the criminal law that lays down the extent to which particular goods and services may be bought and sold. Adoption, human organ transplants, prostitution, and surrogacy are among the private ones. In the more public sphere the criminal law lays down the extent to which jobs, votes and political services can be bought and sold. In none of these instances can the law be regarded simply as declaring the pre-legal public wrongfulness of the actions in question. I conclude that an attempt to revive the sort of distinction between *mala in se* and *mala prohibita* at least needs fuller articulation and to take account of the relationship of criminal law to market.

Duff's 'liberal polity' may seem to be ubiquitous, but even in the increasingly globalized criminal law there remain some areas in which each country can express its own sentiments. A typical piece of legislation in the modern criminal law will flow from the following set of events. In 1977, in consequence of the Lochheed scandal, the Foreign Corrupt Practices Act was put in place in the USA.[37] In 1998, under the Paris Convention of the Organisation for Economic Co-operation and Development,[38] signatory nations undertook an obligation to put in place laws equivalent to those imposed on American businesses by the Foreign Corrupt Practices Act, that is to say, a prohibition upon the bribery of overseas public officials. This is in spite of the fact that, until very recently, in England and Wales these payments were not merely lawful but a business expense deductible from tax,[39] and in spite (or because) of the fact that bribery is a normal way in which to conduct business in some of the economies towards which the legislation is directed. The UK

---

[34] Subject to the then obtaining rules of the Exchange, which were more honoured in the breach than the observance.

[35] Now to be found in Criminal Justice Act 1993, Pt V.

[36] The Financial Services and Markets Act 2000 includes (s.118) a 'civil offence' of market abuse.

[37] Foreign Corrupt Practices Act, Pub. L. No. 95–213, 91 Stat. 1494 (1977), as amended. 15 U.S.C. 78a, 78dd-1 to 78dd-3, 78ff.

[38] Convention on Combating Bribery of Foreign Public Officials in International Business Transactions: Paris, 17 December 1997 (Cm 3994, 1998).

[39] Income and Corporation Taxes Act 1988, s.577A, inserted by Finance Act 1993, s.123, Finance Act, 1994 s.141.

government will legislate shortly.[40] In the event of legislation being put in place could we talk about it embodying the 'shared values of a liberal polity'? Not at all. Like much modern criminal legislation, the move to criminalize the bribery of foreign officials has nothing to do with the shared values of a liberal polity: it has to do with the values and forces underpinning internationalization and the notion of 'the international community'. It is an exercise in the export of values about how markets should function to jurisdictions that frequently are not, and do not aspire to be, liberal polities.

It is better that we recognize criminal law is historically and culturally various, that the values it embodies are not necessarily ones which its addressee can be expected to share, and that appeals to those values may fall upon deaf ears. It will follow from that that the traditional positivist requirements of clarity and certainty should be retained, because the requirements of criminal law may well involve an order which either cannot be explained at all or one whose explanation would have to be at a level of sophistication that many addressees could not be expected to understand it. If it is to be obeyed at all, then publicity and clarity must provide the impetus. Take again, as an instance, money laundering. It is claimed that laundering causes economic harms, but the prohibition of laundering is hardly a *sine qua non* of a liberal polity, and the arguments for prohibition are so abstruse that appeal to them in any statement of what the law expects would only confuse.[41] Even the 'bad man' is entitled to clear rules. Duff's aspiration that explaining to people and asking them politely may actually alter behaviour flies in the face of the history of criminal law.

B. Producing Guidance for Citizens

I conclude, therefore, that Robinson's project is an entirely legitimate one. In some areas it might be possible for the law to attempt to explain to people why it is good for them to behave in particular ways, but an appeal to supposedly shared moral sentiment cannot always replace a requirement for a clear, authoritative, reliable statement of the normative requirements of the law. This leaves open a series of new questions, as to how the directions should be written. This chapter will deal with some of them.

1. Should a Code of Behaviour Include only Criminal Law?

One objection to Robinson's version of the core of criminal law is that it confines itself to setting out what the *criminal* law says. Failure to include in a

---

[40] And see Alldridge, 'Reforming the Criminal Law of Corruption' (2000) 11 Criminal Law Forum 287.

[41] And see Alldridge, 'The Moral Limits of the Crime of Money Laundering' (2001) 5 Buffalo Criminal Law Review 101.

code of this sort the elementary requirements of the law of torts and other pertinent areas of civil law is both to overcomplicate and to mislead. The fact that a criminal conviction might be the outcome is not the only thing a citizen will want to be informed about when deciding how to act. In trying to separate off the *criminal* law aspects of behaviour Robinson makes his code artificially and unhelpfully limited. The citizen (indeed the lawyer) may want to obey the law but might well not know whether what is in contemplation raises an issue of criminal law or not. Take, as an example, wheel-clamping on private land. A person puts up a notice saying that any car parked without permission on his/her land will be clamped and that a charge of £100 will be made to remove the clamp. A car is subsequently clamped. Under Scots law this constitutes two serious crimes.[42] Under the law of England and Wales it is not clear whether this would be a trespass to goods or theft of the car or blackmail or (under certain circumstances) a lawful distress damage feasant or a totally lawful offer and acceptance generating a contract to pay £100.[43] Any advice a code gave based solely upon criminal law would be quite misleading. It would be worse than useless to tell someone that it is lawful to attach a clamp to a car on his/her land because the offences of blackmail and theft are not constituted in English law, if there is nevertheless a tortious interference with goods in response to which the owner of the car could forcibly resist attempts to attach the clamp or lawfully get metal cutters and destroy it. A civic code must give clear advice on a matter of this sort and that can only be done if regard is had both to criminal law and civil law aspects of the question.

The most immediate matter of concern to a citizen may frequently be whether his/her behaviour may lawfully be resisted. A code of guidance should say what s/he needs to do not to be the object of lawful violence, and that will include guarantees against the invocation of self-help remedies (private defence, abatement of nuisance, distraint, recaption of chattels) for torts. A more useful civic code than Robinson's would outline the duties of citizens by reference to *all* the adverse consequences the law imposes, permits, or requires, not just those which occur in criminal courts. If a particular form of conduct may lawfully be resisted by force, then a worthwhile civic code will announce that to the citizen.

There are other reasons why a civic code should include the elementary requirements of the law of torts. The law of torts is a basic part of the general law of the land and if the objective of a civic code is to tell people in general terms what they need to do to avoid liability then it should be included. Some prohibitions can be expressed more easily and effectively by defining the unlawfulness of interference with person and property, not by reference to the law of offences against the person and theft (which are both, however they are

---

[42] i.e., theft and extortion: *Carmichael v Black* 1992 SCCR 709; 1992 SLT 897.
[43] See *Arthur v Anker* [1996] RTR 308.

adapted, unnecessarily complicated to give satisfactory guidance),[44] nor to any consequences like death or serious injury, but to the civil law of trespass.

2. Should a Code of Behaviour Include or Avoid Reference to Mental States?

Duff[45] discerns a tension between Fletcher and Robinson as to whether, when constructing conduct rules, reference to mental states could or should be excluded, and over what is meant by 'wrongdoing' if it does not mean 'such as to give rise to criminal liability, or any attribution of blame'. Why is this significant? Fletcher might have required 'wrongdoing' to trigger a right in the state to investigate, but for the purposes of a code of conduct what a citizen would need to know *at the time* of violation is whether or not force may lawfully be deployed as a response. Robinson has expressed a preference for the elimination both of liability language and grading language in the formulation of conduct rules.[46] If a prohibition can be expressed in such a way as to avoid a mental state, then certain benefits accrue. It would be easier, for example, for a police officer or a citizen to know whether or not to intervene. Also, if the crime is defined as a clear *determinatio*, then adjudication might take less time, because the issues associated with mental states are excluded from consideration.

It is far easier to eliminate *mens rea* requirements in the case of 'brazen' crimes (approximating to the civil law of trespass to person, goods, and property, where there is some clear 'line in the sand' whose crossing may physically be perceived), than in 'sneaky' crimes (where there is no such overt act).[47] This section will suggest that whilst that approach can operate relatively successfully with regard to homicides and assaults, there are many crimes whose conduct rules would have to be expressed to include a mental state: where conduct cannot be identified as wrongful without reference to *mens rea* elements. I shall use two examples, but the more general underlying claim is that there is a far larger range of offences than Robinson concedes that cannot easily be formulated as rules of conduct avoiding mental states.

First, consider the law relating to bribery and corruption, which is under review in the United Kingdom.[48] Could an offence of bribery be defined as a conduct rule without a mental element? Robinson's Code equivocates[49] on the definition of corruption (but tends toward an approach that does require

---

[44] And formulation of the norms so as to give guidance for conduct, such as how a carer should deal with the property of a person with learning difficulties, will avoid controversial questions such as whether consent negatives appropriation for the purposes of theft. See *R v Hinks* [2001] 2 AC 241.

[45] Chapter 3 above at 68.   [46] Robinson (n. 6 above) 184.

[47] This is the distinction between 'manifest' and 'subjective' criminality, seen in George Fletcher, *Rethinking Criminal Law* (Boston, 1978) ch. 3.

[48] Law Commission, Consultation Paper No. 145, *Legislating the Criminal Code: Corruption* (1997); Law Commission No. 248, *Legislating the Criminal Code: Corruption* (1998) to which is appended a draft Corruption Bill. See also Alldridge (n. 40 above).

[49] By limiting the class of person to whom it applies.

a mental state even in the conduct rule).[50] Is the core of the offence behaving for an improper motive or receiving payment? If a 'moral element' is part of the definition of the crime of bribery, the requirement for a bribe itself—that is, for money or other consideration to change hands (rather than just for a corrupt preference to be exercised)—becomes difficult to defend.[51] Conversely, there will be some cases (payments to judges) where the mere fact of paying or receiving the bribe is regarded as sufficient without inquiry into mental states. What advice can be given, for example, to company buyers as to what they can and cannot do? On the current or proposed state of English law it would be impossible to express the prohibition without a mental state. So long as the prohibition is expressed widely in the forthcoming legislation, that state of affairs will continue.

Secondly, take the large group of offences able to be committed by uttering words—a range including some assaults, 'hate-crimes', perjury, a range of offences of uttering threats and harassment, and offences of incitement and procurement.[52] It is, for example, an offence to threaten to kill someone.[53] It would be curious to have a norm saying 'You may not utter a threat to kill' when the only such utterances that are criminal are the cases where the threat is uttered and *meant* to be understood as a threat. 'Don't threaten to kill' could be taken to exclude the case of the affectionate 'I'll kill you . . .' by saying that the mental state (meaning what you say) could be regarded as being wrapped up in a 'threat': but then the mental state will not have been excluded. As the same is true, *mutatis mutandis*, in the case of any offence involving speech which has a mental element, I suggest that the mental state could not be excluded from a code of guidance dealing with these offences, and that Robinson's preference against mental states may operate satisfactorily in the cases of batteries or trespasses to goods, but that it cannot deal properly with many offences outside this sphere; that we cannot exclude mental states from all definitions in conduct rules, but that we should try to when possible, simply for the benefits in ease of comprehension that such drafting will involve. It is a practical matter, not one of principle, and one of greater

---

[50] Section 45: 'You may not offer or accept any benefit either to influence the future action of or in return for an action by a public official or servant, a party official, or a voter, unless such benefit is a legal fee or salary for such action': Robinson (n. 6 above) 218. '[T]o influence the future action of . . .' might just as well have made reference to intention, but no more complex (quasi-)mental state such as 'corruptly' is required.

[51] The Law Commission did not even demur at the suggestion (Judge Rhys Davies QC quoted in Law Commission No. 248 para. 5.41, n. 57), that 'mere gratification' might constitute a bribe. If it is not excluded then anything can amount to a bribe, and the argument for the retention of a bribe as an element of corruption is significantly weakened: Alldridge (n. 40 above).

[52] Robinson has used the example on several occasions of Henry II's alleged, 'Will no man revenge me of the injuries I have sustained from one turbulent priest?', taken as a directive to kill Beckett. We could not have a law against saying that sort of thing: what it should cover is saying it *and meaning it.*

[53] Offences Against the Person Act 1861, s.16.

practical importance than will be recognized from concentration upon a small group of offences out of which the 'general part' is supposed to grow.

3. How Should a Code of Behaviour Deal with Matters of Justification and Excuse?

The literature on codes of conduct appears alongside elaboration of the distinction between justification and excuse.[54] Duff takes the value of the distinction to be analytical and expository clarity: 'if we recognise the differences in logic and in function between different aspects of the criminal law, we will gain a clearer understanding of its structure and doctrinal organisation'.[55]

The distinction will also 'solve doctrinal problems, and dissolve confusions'. The doctrinal nuts it purports to crack are to do with liability at civil law (no civil liability for justified acts),[56] the criminal liability of accessories (no liability as accessory to justified acts, but liability possible as accessory to excused acts),[57] and the availability of force to resist (force not available to resist justified act). It may also speak to the compensation of victims of crime[58] and even verdicts at inquests.[59] Within that paradigm, a good deal of attention has centred upon the case of reasonably mistaken belief in the existence of facts which, had they existed, would have provided a justification.[60] Whether they provide a justification or excuse is, to some commentators, unclear. Other debates have centred on necessity, which in most versions is held to have both an excusatory and a justificatory incarnation, and provocation,[61] which is discussed as mitigating factor, partial excuse, or partial justification.

---

[54] Joshua Dressler, 'Justifications and Excuses: A Brief Review of the Concepts and the Literature' (1987) 33 Wayne Law Review 1155.

[55] Chapter 3 above at 50.

[56] Gustave Radbruch, 'Jurisprudence in the Criminal Law' (1936) 18 Journal of Comparative Legislation 212.

[57] See Alldridge, 'The Doctrine of Innocent Agency' (1990) 2 Criminal Law Forum 45.

[58] The current position is that compensation is payable under para. 10 of the new Criminal Injuries' Compensation Scheme: 'It is not necessary for the assailant to have been convicted of a criminal offence in connection with the injury. Moreover, even where the injury is attributable to conduct within para 8(a) [i.e., a crime of violence (including arson, fire-raising or poisoning)] of which the assailant cannot be convicted by reason of age, insanity or diplomatic immunity, the conduct may nevertheless be treated as constituting a criminal act'.

'Age, insanity or diplomatic immunity' exhausts the category of cases where a victim can recover notwithstanding there not having been a 'convictable' crime. I know of no empirical evidence on the matter, but if anything, the trauma of a woman whose mistaken attacker is acquitted on *Morgan* grounds will be worse in the case where she goes through a trial leading to his conviction, and there is no good argument for not compensating her. I thought, and think, that this is a bad thing.

[59] Two of the possible verdicts at inquests are that the deceased was lawfully and that s/he was unlawfully killed. Neither of these have any necessary consequences, but the distinction often matters to friends and relatives.

[60] See Kent Greenawalt, 'The Perplexing Borders of Justification and Excuse' (1984) 84 Columbia Law Review 1897.

[61] Joshua Dressler, 'Provocation: Partial Justification or Partial Excuse?' (1988) 51 Modern Law Review 467; Joshua Dressler, 'When "Heterosexual" Men Kill "Homosexual" Men: Reflections on Provocation Law, Sexual Advances, and the "Reasonable Man" Standard' (1995) 85 Journal of Criminal Law & Criminology 726. See, too, Chapters 11 and 12 below.

I understand most of those theorists who want to include justifications but
not excuses in rules of conduct to be saying something less sophisticated and
more necessary than does Duff: that if someone acts in a way for which s/he
would be criminally liable but for the presence of an excusing condition then
s/he acts at risk of being violently resisted, that helping him/her is unlawful,
and that bystanders are entitled to intervene with force on the side of the person who is 'in the right' (assuming that the other criteria for the use of force
are satisfied). The most immediate consequence of the distinction is simply
the availability of force to resist. Once there is a violation of a norm, then, *ceteris paribus*, force may be used to resist.

Duff is correct to say that the issue of duress is a difficult one for the theorists
who want to argue that all excuses belong to rules of conduct. He argues:[62]

(1)   that duress can be brought within the conduct rules; and
(2)   that some cases of excuses should be regarded as justification.

In earlier work I argued that the only case of duress with which the criminal law need concern itself was that of a person who simply does not have
time to reflect or to act by reference to rules.[63] Since s/he did not have time to
reflect, there was no point in trying to advise.[64] There are, however, cases of
duress in which the person acting under duress might legitimately appeal to a
rule telling him/her how to behave.[65] Duff is quite right to require us to consider more closely what the rules relating to duress say. There is a rule in the
law of duress (which is wholly unjustifiable and more honoured in the breach
than the observance) that there must be a threat of death or serious bodily
harm in order for the defence of duress to be available.[66] That is, even when
someone has acted reasonably and exercised all the firmness to be expected of
him/her in the face of other types of threats, there is still no defence of duress,
and a lawyer could so advise a client. Likewise a lawyer could advise a client
contemplating murder that, under the present state of English law, duress
would provide no defence.[67]

This does not mean, however, that conduct rules can necessarily be produced to include the defence of duress. The claim I reiterate is that the message of the criminal law to someone contemplating acting under duress is the
same as if there were no duress. *Do not do whatever it is*. Consider the person
who is placed under duress. Duff says:[68]

What he should receive is an answer that makes clear what is demanded of him: what
is demanded not so much by the law (as if the law was the source of the demand), but

---

[62] See Chapter 3 above at 63 ff.
[63] This was the rationale for the defence of duress advanced in *R v Hudson and Taylor* [1971]
2 QB 202.
[64] 'Rules for Courts and Rules for Citizens' (1990) 10 Oxford Journal of Legal Studies 487.
[65] For a modern example see *R v Abdul-Hussain* [1999] LR 570.
[66] Sir John Smith, *Criminal Law* (9th edn., London, 1999) 235–236.
[67] *R v Howe* [1987] AC 417.   [68] Chapter 3 above at 68.

through the law as articulating the values of the political community and the demands of citizenship of such a polity. That answer would make clear that he *should* aspire to resist (the threat is not sufficient to justify giving in), but that resistance is not in such a case *demanded* of him; and that is just the answer that is provided by the defence of duress, if properly expressed.

It may well be that, as Duff says,[69] the person acting under threats is morally justified. But the person at whom the gun is pointed is probably not interested in whether or not his/her conduct will receive the moral approbation or acquiescence of a jurisprude. S/he will be interested in what will happen to him/her. When talking about legal justification we are not talking about 'doing the right thing' but 'having the right to do the thing', which is by no means the same.

The answer we should expect a code of conduct to give to a duressee is rather more definite and helpful, but also more 'legal' (in the sense of conveying more information about the legal consequences of acting) than Duff suggests. The person under duress will want to know whether, if s/he goes ahead, lawful resistance may be offered, and whether people may intervene lawfully to help the 'victim'. If of a morbid disposition, s/he might want to know whether his/her life insurance policy will pay in the event of his/her being killed if it happens to contain exclusions for lawful killing, suicide, reckless endangerment of life, or death in pursuit of crime (none of these conditions is now common in life insurance policies but none is unknown either). On the current state of English law the answer to these questions is unaltered by the duress. So, even if there are cases of duress which provide a justification so far as concerns criminal liability, this need not be a conclusive argument for the inclusion of rules relating to duress in conduct rules for citizens.

The approach of looking for a simple rule, frequently embodying the civil law of trespass to land, goods, or property, gives answers to two of Duff's examples. In the example of dishonest borrowing,[70] all a code need say, and all the civil law of interference with goods does say, is 'do not move chattels without the permission of the possessor'. It need not mention dishonesty, because the right of the possessor to use force to prevent a dishonest borrowing, or to take the goods back, does not depend upon the borrowing's being dishonest. It depends upon the fact of the non-privileged interference with possession. The self-help remedy available is either private defence or recaption.[71] The significance of this is that a code of behaviour should inform the citizen when s/he is vulnerable to, and when s/he may deploy, self-help remedies—in particular, when the law permits the citizen to use force.

Duff's under-age sex case[72] also then gives no problem: even if the man is under 24 and takes all appropriate care to ensure that the girl is over 16, and

---

[69] See Chapter 3 above at 63 ff.   [70] See Chapter 3 above at 59.
[71] C.A. Branston, 'The Forcible Recaption of Chattels' (1912) 28 LQR 263; Law Reform Committee, *Eighteenth Report: Conversion and Detinue* (Cmnd 4774, 1971) paras 116–126.

so incurs no personal criminal liability, someone who did know her age and encouraged him *would* commit an offence, while someone who knew her age and forcibly prevented him from having intercourse with her (if the offence is sufficiently serious and force became necessary and reasonable) would act lawfully. The actor does not need a *moral* excuse (there is nothing with which we can reproach him)[73] and it may be misleading to call his act one of wrong-doing, but the *act* nonetheless has a legal significance different from the simple exercise of a general liberty to do something one is free to do. In Hohfeldian terms, the extra things involved are: (1) that the entire world has a duty not to assist him; and (2) the entire world has liberty to use reasonable means to cause him to desist. There may well be a better description of the actor than 'excused participant in unlawful sexual intercourse', but his legal position is quite analogous to that of one who is excused. As to the *Morgan* issue,[74] the norm directed to citizens embodying the decision in that case need not be expressed as anything more sophisticated than the (civil law) law rule prohibiting unlawful touching.[75]

4. How Should a Code of Behaviour Deal with Justification and Rights?

More generally, in dealing with excuse and justification, Duff causes us to re-consider the proposition that, when two people use violence against one another,[76] only one of them can be acting in a way which is permitted by law, or justified.[77] This proposition states the effect of the justification/excuse distinction in German law,[78] and it is the logical function that the concept is granted in the work of those people who have considered it. If two people using violence against one another are both justified then escalating levels of violence could be deployed lawfully and in circumstances such that no one could intervene to assist ether party or even just to try to stop the violence. The inarticulate premise of much of the writing which takes justification to be a legal concept distinct from, not analogous to, moral justification, simply a shorthand for the legal consequences I have outlined,[79] is that the law will not permit an escalating fight between two actors. This is the 'objective' theory of justification. One of the actors must have the right not to be hit, and the other

---

[72] See Chapter 3 above at 69.   [73] See Chapter 3 above at 72–73.

[74] See Chapter 3 above at 72.

[75] This has nothing to do with the morality of extra-marital intercourse—see Chapter 3 above at 72–73. It simply follows from the (private law) right to use reasonable force to terminate a trespass to the person.

[76] Always assuming that this is outside a boxing ring or one of the other sets of circumstances where both sides are of full age, sound mind and have given a full consent.

[77] It must be observed that as a practical matter it need not make all that much difference. There have been codes that, formally at least, have licensed such fights without the heavens falling. But we are here in pursuit of doctrinal purity.

[78] See Radbruch (n. 56 above).

[79] i.e., as to civil liability, accessories and lawful resistance: Radbruch (n. 56 above), and accompanying text.

a duty not to hit him. Why should this be so? Why might a system of criminal law be regarded as defective because it permits a fight to take place in circumstances such that it may continue indefinitely? One reason is that it follows from elementary notions about law as a means of avoiding violence. If the criminal law permits an escalating fight then life might turn out to be just as brutish and short as it would be were there no law. Secondly, consistency with how private rights to personal integrity and to property are constructed in English law is important. If we want to change what it means in English (civil and constitutional) law to have personal integrity protected by law, or to own or possess property,[80] then that should be done openly in the context of a full ventilation of those issues (and of the European Convention) rather than by fiddling with theories of justification in criminal law, which ought to be regarded as the tail, and not the dog. Thirdly (and relatively technically), it is difficult to generate a workable account of complicity, and, in this instance, of the liability of the person uttering the threats, which is consistent with the actions of the duressee being justified.[81]

5. The Missing Link

Robinson's Code is in some ways a bleak document. The underlying premise is that the Code contains a non-exhaustive list of things that the citizen may not do, and its message is that, 'if you do one of these things, you can expect to be punished, and if you don't you might still be punished'. In that sense, far more than on account of its underlying tone, the Code fails to enlist the addressee. Duff wants to enlist the citizen by invoking the political community to which s/he belongs. I suggest that a better way—a way that does not depend upon concocting the shared values of a community—is to grant the citizen some entitlements. This is the major omission both from Robinson's Code and Duff's response. Their approach is very much the English common law tradition. 'You may do anything that is not expressly forbidden', the classic statement of (negative) liberty, appears a satisfactory organizing principle for a statement of criminal law addressed to citizens, but only until it becomes clear that it is very difficult to learn whether specific behaviour is prohibited or not.

It is a matter of concern that the answer to a question like 'what is meant in English law by a right to property or personal physical integrity?' is still to be found by reference to the (civil) law of trespass to the person, land, and goods and in arcane self-help remedies. The advent of the human rights' jurisdiction should, if it is to give answers to questions citizens who are not lawyers will ask, give rise at least to a framework within which to write guidance for citizens of greater ease of access and comprehensibility. Even before making

---

[80] Compare the Scottish law of wheel-clamping, set in the context of a less absolute notion of the rights of landowners, n. 42 above.

[81] Alldridge (n. 57 above).

allowance for the rights imported by the Human Rights Act 1998,[82] the civil law rights to personal physical integrity and to property, and the liberty they generate to deploy force, should be central to any attempt to inform the citizen of his/her legal position. A code for citizens should start, not with the law of homicide, but with statements of entitlement upon which citizens can rely. The sort of structure that can offer worthwhile guidance is much more that of the European Convention on Human Rights than that of the nineteenth-century criminal codes. It should set out the entitlements of a person to be free or in lawful detention (and what rights follow from lawful detention). It should set out the right to physical integrity. A code of guidance that tells people what they *may* do tells them the law better, and gives them far better guidance, than one that tells them what they *may not do*.

C. Conclusions

The attempt to present criminal law as an exercise in moral suasion is one that should not attract us. We do not really need the criminal law to tell people not to kill one another. We need it to give them directions as to whether or not to deal inside, launder money, or take drugs (if we do not want them to do these things). It has been argued that criminal law theory should not proceed from the assumption that criminal law is, could be, or should be, nothing more than a set of universals upon whose basic precepts reasonable people, conducting a discussion with sufficient rigour, may be expected to agree. Theories about the voice of the criminal law should have regard to a wide range of offences. When discussions have considered only a few offences they have concentrated upon matters upon which such agreement seems closest, and the arguments least influenced by the outside world, but which, so far as concerns the social practice that is criminal law in England and Wales in the early twenty-first century, do not matter much. A better basis for theory is provided by recognition of a wider range of offences and the increasing significance of criminal law to markets, and by the incorporation of a human rights focus. A code of conduct for citizens would take into account civil law and constitutional rights. It would be significantly longer than Robinson's. A civic code should tell people what they may and may not do, rather than proceed from the definitions of individual offences. The advent in England and Wales of the human rights' jurisdiction gives the opportunity for just such a book, or website, or both. The code should be structured not so much around the most serious criminal offences as around the major civic rights. It should not seek primarily to enlist the moral approbation of the citizen for the rules which it expounds but rather to express those rules in terms as clear as possible.

---

[82] Robinson (n. 6 above) 183–184.

6

Criminal Liability for Omissions:
An Inventory of Issues

LARRY ALEXANDER*

It is a widely known, frequently commented upon, and often criticized fact that in Anglo-American criminal law there is no general duty to save others from harm, even when one can do so at little risk or cost to oneself.[1] It is a less widely known, rarely commented upon, and virtually never criticized fact that there are several exceptions to the 'no duty to rescue' principle. In what follows I shall devote my attention solely to these exceptions and the host of issues they raise. I do so not for lack of interest in the debate over the general principle—a debate that pits both the libertarian principle that the moral duty to aid others does not give rise to an enforceable moral right to be aided and some consequentialist considerations (various unintended effects of enforcement) against more obvious consequentialist and communitarian values. I do so rather because I have nothing novel to offer that debate. However, many of the issues that I flag regarding the exceptions to the general principle will have obvious implications for any form of criminal liability for failing to rescue others.

A. THE DOCTRINE

LaFave portrays the criminal law doctrine regarding omissions—failures to save others from harm—as follows: some criminal statutes specifically

* I wish to thank Richard Arneson, Heidi Hurd, Leo Katz, Michael Moore, and the participants at the University of North Carolina School of Law faculty workshop for their comments and criticisms, and Brian Hipp for his research assistance.

[1] For statements of the doctrinal point that there is no general duty under the criminal law to save others from harm, see Wayne R. LaFave, *Criminal Law* (3rd edn., St Paul, 2000) 215; Model Penal Code, s. 2.01(3). For some of the literature criticizing (and defending) the absence of a duty of Good Samaritanism, see Joel Feinberg, *The Moral Limits of the Criminal Law, Vol. I: Harm to Others* (Oxford, 1984) ch. 4; Patricia G. Smith, *Liberalism and Affirmative Obligation* (New York, 1998); Joshua Dressler, 'Some Brief Thoughts (Mostly Negative) About "Bad Samaritan" Laws' (2000) 40 Santa Clara LR 971; Lord Thomas Macaulay, 'Notes on the Indian Penal Code', 7 *Works* (London, The Jenson Society, 1907) 314–320; Richard Epstein, 'A Theory of Strict Liability' (1973) 2 J Legal Studies 151; Ernest J. Weinrib, 'The Case for a Duty to Rescue' (1980) 90 Yale LJ 247.

require affirmative acts, such as those requiring the filing of a tax return, the reporting of draftees for induction into the military, or the reporting by motorists of accidents in which they have been involved.[2] Duties to act enforced by the criminal law under statutes proscribing killings, batterings, burnings, and the like, however, arise only in a limited number of situations. These are situations in which the defendant and the victim have a special relationship, such as husband and wife or parent and child; those in which the defendant has a contractual duty to save the victim from harm; those in which the defendant has created the victim's peril; those in which the defendant has voluntarily assumed a duty to rescue the victim; and those in which the defendant's status as parent of children who are threatening harm to the victim, or as owner of land that is hazardous to the victim, place a duty on defendant to protect the victim from harm.[3]

LaFave's portrayal of omission liability in criminal law is orthodox. Joshua Dressler's list of exceptions to the general principle of no criminal liability for omissions is identical,[4] as is Simester and Sullivan's.[5] The Model Penal Code encapsulates the exceptions in terms of whether 'the omission is expressly made sufficient by the law defining the offense',[6] or 'a duty to perform the omitted act is otherwise imposed by law'.[7] The official commentary on these sections implies that duties 'imposed by law' include the standard exceptions to the 'no omission liability' principle.[8]

In those cases where the criminal law imposes a duty to act, the duty must be one that the defendant is physically capable of performing, and without undue risk or sacrifice.[9] Moreover, the defendant's failure to act must be accompanied by whatever *mens rea* the crime requires for its commission.

What this very orthodox presentation of the requirements for omissions liability in criminal law masks is the enormous number of issues that are either unresolved or unnoticed but that are of both practical and theoretical importance. In the following sections I shall attempt to convey a sense of both the types of issues omission liability raises and their difficulty.

B. A DROWNING

1. The Scenario

Alice, Barbara, Candy, Dana, Elise, Fran, Gina, and Victoria are attending a swimming pool party at a friend's house. Alice is boisterously running around

---

[2] LaFave (n. 1 above) 214.   [3] ibid., 214–219.

[4] Joshua Dressler, *Understanding Criminal Law* (2nd edn., New York, 1995) 89–91.

[5] A.P. Simester and G.R. Sullivan, *Criminal Law: Theory and Doctrine* (Oxford, 2000) 63–67.

[6] Model Penal Code, s. 2.01(3)(a).   [7] Model Penal Code, s. 2.01(3)(b).

[8] See American Law Institute, Comment to s. 2.01, at 222–223.

[9] See Dressler (n. 4 above) 89; LaFave (n. 1 above) 221–222; Model Penal Code, s. 2.01(1).

the side of the pool, aware that she might slip or stumble or in some other way knock someone into the pool, someone who perhaps cannot swim. And, indeed, she runs into Barbara, who is merely standing at poolside, sipping a drink. The collision with Alice sends Barbara tumbling into Victoria, who falls into the deep end of the swimming pool. Victoria cannot swim, and no one rescues her, with the obvious consequence. The question is, who is criminally liable for Victoria's death?

2. The Cases

(i) *State v Alice*

Let us assume that the facts make Alice culpable at the level of recklessness for running around the pool as she did. That is, Alice's subjective assessment of the risk of someone's drowning as a result of her conduct—which assessment was, we shall hypothesize, that the risk was at least one per cent—together with the absence of any important reason for her conduct, makes her running around the pool an act taken with conscious disregard for a substantial and unjustifiable risk.[10] If Alice were to have fallen unconscious at the moment she ran into Barbara—so that she could not have physically undertaken a rescue of Victoria—she would have been guilty of reckless homicide. And the same would be true if Alice could not rescue Victoria because she (Alice) could not swim, or because the risk to Alice from attempting a rescue were too high.

The duty to rescue Victoria imposed on Alice by virtue of her causing the peril potentially renders her crime more culpable than reckless homicide. If Alice *knows* (believes it practically certain)[11] that Victoria will drown unless Alice rescues her—or if it is Alice's 'conscious object' in not rescuing that Victoria drown;[12] if Alice *knows* that it was her conduct that caused Victoria's peril; and if Alice *knows* that she can rescue Victoria without undue risk; then, with one major caveat, we can conclude that Alice is guilty of a knowing (or purposeful) homicide (murder) for not rescuing Victoria, and not merely the reckless homicide (manslaughter) she was on the hook for when she caused Victoria to fall into the pool. (The caveat concerns whether, in order to have a duty to rescue Victoria, Alice needs to have caused Victoria's peril *culpably*, an issue we take up in considering Barbara's case. If the answer

---

[10] See Model Penal Code, s. 2.02(2)(c) (recklessness constituted by conscious disregard of a substantial and unjustifiable risk). See generally Larry Alexander, 'Insufficient Concern: A Unified Conception of Criminal Culpability' (2000) 88 California LR 931 (analysing recklessness and arguing that it subsumes the other forms of culpability). Query: can Alice discount the risk of drowning that her running is creating based on her beliefs about whether *others* will rescue anyone who is knocked into the pool?

[11] See Model Penal Code, s. 2.02(2)(b) (definition of culpable mental state of 'knowledge'); Alexander (n. 10 above) 939–942 (amalgamating 'recklessness' and 'knowledge').

[12] See Model Penal Code, s. 2.02(2)(a) (definition of culpable mental state of 'purpose'); Alexander (n. 10 above) 942–944 (amalgamating 'recklessness' and 'purpose').

is that Alice must have caused the peril culpably to have a duty to rescue, then it would seem to follow that to be guilty of murder rather than manslaughter, Alice must be aware of the facts that render her running around the pool a *culpable* cause of Victoria's peril, not just a cause *simpliciter*.)

It follows conversely that if Alice is unaware that Victoria is in peril, that she caused Victoria's peril (culpably?), *or* that she can rescue Victoria without undue risk, she cannot be held liable for failing to rescue Victoria. What authorities there are on this point generally agree that liability for failing to rescue does not attach to those who are unaware of the facts that give rise to that duty.[13] For example, in *State v Tennant*,[14] the West Virginia Supreme Court held that a defendant could not be found liable under a hit-and-run statute requiring drivers involved in accidents with injuries to stop and render aid if the defendant was unaware that his vehicle was involved in an accident.

On the other hand, so long as she is aware of the facts giving rise to the legal duty to rescue—the victim's peril, what caused it, and the safety of a rescue— a defendant need not be aware of the *legal* duty to rescue in order to be held criminally liable for failing to rescue.[15] Ignorance of the scope of the legal duty to rescue is treated like ignorance of the criminal law generally and affords no relief from liability. Thus, Alice cannot escape conviction of murder by arguing that although she knew she had culpably knocked Victoria into the pool, knew that Victoria would drown unless rescued, and knew that she (Alice) could rescue Victoria with little risk to herself, she did not know she had a legal duty to rescue Victoria.

As stated, the position on ignorance of the duty to rescue is in accord with the criminal law's general position on ignorance of the criminal law. And like that general position, it is too pat by half. Some ignorance of the criminal law is both non-culpable and consistent with good moral character.[16] And that is particularly true where the criminal law is so vague as to render it of dubious validity under the principle of legality.[17] Because the duty to rescue exists only when the rescue is 'safe' or 'easy'—and because its existence also depends on some very vague notions of status relationships and reliance—the scope of the duty is arguably so vague as to threaten its legality. But more on this when we take up the riskiness of the rescue, causation by reliance, and status relationships directly.

Thus far we have come to the following conclusions about Alice: if Alice is aware that she has created Victoria's peril, aware that Victoria will drown unless she rescues her (or wants her to drown), and aware that the rescue is not

[13] See LaFave (n. 1 above) 219–220.

[14] 173 W Va 627, 319 SE 2d 395 (1984). See also *Westrup v Commonwealth* 123 Ky 95, 93 SW 646 (1906); *Fabritz v Traurig* 583 F 2d 697 (US Ct of Apps (4th Cir), 1978); *Harding v Price* [1948] 1 KB 695.

[15] See LaFave (n. 1 above) 220.

[16] See Dan M. Kahan, 'Ignorance of Law *Is* an Excuse—but Only for the Virtuous' (1997) 96 Michigan LR 127.

[17] See Dressler (n. 4 above) 29–30.

too risky, then Alice is guilty of murder in not rescuing Victoria, despite her having been only reckless in her previous conduct. If any of these conditions fails to obtain—if Alice is unaware of Victoria's peril, unaware of her role in it, *or* unaware that rescue is low risk—then Alice's homicide can be pegged only at the level of culpability (towards death) that she displayed in running around the pool, which in this case was recklessness (manslaughter). On the other hand, Alice's knowledge or ignorance of the scope of her legal duty to rescue is immaterial. And we have raised but have not resolved the question whether Alice must be aware, not only that she has caused the peril, but that she has done so culpably, a question we shall return to when we take up in Barbara's case the question of whether causing the peril must be culpable to give rise to a duty to rescue.

But we still have not disposed of all the issues raised by Alice's case. For suppose Alice is unaware that Victoria is in peril, that she created that peril, or that she can rescue Victoria with little risk, but her lack of awareness of one or more of these facts is itself culpable? For example, suppose Alice is unaware that Victoria is drowning, but she is unaware because she *unreasonably* infers that Victoria is merely feigning drowning. How should this affect Alice's degree of culpability for the death?

If one holds the unorthodox view that I hold, namely, that inadvertent negligence is not culpable,[18] one will conclude that Alice's negligence regarding Victoria's peril does not affect her culpability, and that she remains culpable only at the level of her original conduct (recklessness). But what if one holds the orthodox view that inadvertent negligence *is* a form of culpability? Or what if Alice's unawareness of the facts giving rise to her duty to rescue Victoria is reckless (she is aware of a high risk that she may be mistaken and unjustifiably fails to investigate further)? If Alice's original recklessness plus knowledge regarding all three conditions—Victoria's peril, Alice's causation, and the risk(less)ness of the rescue—convert the potential reckless homicide (manslaughter) into a knowing homicide (murder); and if Alice's original recklessness plus her non-culpable ignorance of any of the three conditions leaves her liability for the death at the level of reckless homicide, what does Alice's original recklessness plus her *culpable* ignorance of *all*[19] of the conditions add up to? Presumably, her liability cannot be lower than her original recklessness or higher than knowledge, which she lacks. In other words, it would seem that her liability should be pegged at somewhere between her original recklessness and knowledge.[20] However, it would seem that it should

---

[18] See Alexander (n. 10 above) 949–952; Larry Alexander, 'Reconsidering the Relationship Among Voluntary Acts, Strict Liability, and Negligence in Criminal Law' (1990) 7 *Social Philosophy and Policy* 84.

[19] If Alice is culpably ignorant of one or two of the conditions, but non-culpably ignorant of the third condition, the effect is that she is under no duty to act. For she must be aware of all three conditions, meaning that *non-culpable* ignorance of *any* is sufficient to negate a duty to rescue.

[20] But see n. 25 below, where I discuss combining Alice's original recklessness liability with her liability for subsequently failing to rescue.

vary with the degree of culpability of her ignorance and with the number of conditions (one, two, or three) of which she is culpably ignorant. (The more conditions of which she is culpably ignorant, the *lower* her resultant level of culpability; for given that non-culpable ignorance of *any* of the conditions defeats omission liability altogether,[21] for each condition of which Alice is culpably ignorant, there must be one fewer condition of which she has actual knowledge, and vice versa, which means that culpable ignorance supplants, not non-culpable ignorance, but knowledge.)

So our simple grid in Alice's case—recklessness in running plus knowledge of all three conditions converts reckless homicide into knowing homicide[22]—should be supplanted with a more complex one in which *either* knowledge *or* culpable ignorance of all three conditions converts reckless homicide into a more serious homicide but not necessarily knowing homicide.[23] Otherwise, Alice's culpable ignorance of the facts giving rise to a duty to rescue will have no effect on her liability, which begins at the level of recklessness.

Of course, as we shall see in the next section, the weight of legal authority is to the effect that if one causes another's peril, one does not have to be culpable in having done so in order to be under a duty to rescue the victim. And a non-culpable actor who causes another's peril and then fails to rescue, knowing that the failure will result in harm, is guilty of a knowing harming. So perhaps if we are going to give effect to culpable failures to recognize peril, to realize one's causal implication in it, or to assess the ease of the required rescue in those cases in which Alice is not guilty of knowing homicide, we should also give effect to her recklessness in cases where she is guilty of knowing homicide, perhaps by adding the penalties of reckless endangerment and knowing homicide.

One further matter before we turn to the level of risk that Alice is legally required to run in rescuing Victoria. We have spoken of Alice's awareness or ignorance of Victoria's peril. But peril is frequently a matter of degree. It may be not certain to an onlooker that Victoria will drown if not rescued—she may make it to the shallow end of the pool—or that she will not drown (drowning is always a possibility for anyone in a swimming pool).

This point, although correct, does not complicate the analysis. If Alice believes it practically certain that Victoria will drown unless rescued, then,

---

[21] See n. 25 below.

[22] Or purposeful homicide if Alice does not believe Victoria likely to drown but fails to rescue her because she hopes Victoria drowns. See Model Penal Code, s. 2.02(2)(a) (defining the culpability level of 'purpose' by reference to defendant's 'conscious object').

[23] When the duty to rescue is premised on non-culpable behaviour, a culpable misassessment of the victim's peril should lead to conviction of the degree of crime corresponding to the degree of culpability displayed in the misassessment. See, e.g., *Cornell v State* 159 Fla 687, 32 So 2d 610 (1947), in which a grandmother was convicted of manslaughter by gross negligence for the smothering death of her grandchild. Because she fell into a drunken stupor, the defendant, who had undertaken the care of the infant and was thereby under a legal duty to rescue the child from peril, was unaware that the child being smothered. Her lack of awareness of the peril, however, was clearly culpable.

assuming all the other conditions are met, she is guilty of a knowing homicide if she fails to rescue Victoria and Victoria in fact drowns. On the other hand, if Alice estimates the risk of drowning as substantial but less than a practical certainty, we have a question like the previous issue of how to combine Alice's recklessness in causing the peril with her culpable ignorance regarding one of the duty-imposing conditions. Here, Alice has not been culpable in estimating the risk to Victoria, but has correctly estimated the risk as high enough to count as a reckless one and then failed to avert it. Arguably, Alice has a duty to rescue Victoria so long as Alice is aware of *any* risk to Victoria, given that any risk Victoria suffers as a result of Alice's reckless running is an unjustifiable one.[24] If Alice fails to rescue Victoria, believing that Victoria stands a risk of drowning that is unjustifiable, but not knowing that Victoria will drown, Alice should be culpable at a level higher than her original recklessness in running but lower than that of a knowing homicide.

One final question regarding Alice's estimation of the risk of Victoria's drowning. Suppose Alice believes that Victoria will surely drown if no one rescues her, but also believes that it is in fact quite unlikely that Victoria will drown if Alice herself fails to rescue her. She holds these two beliefs because of the presence of other people who can rescue Victoria. That is, she believes it is likely that if *she* does not rescue Victoria, someone else will, even though she does not believe anyone else has a duty to rescue Victoria. How do these beliefs affect Alice's culpability if she fails to rescue Victoria and Victoria drowns?[25]

---

[24] See Alexander (n. 10 above) 933–935, 939–942, where I argue that knowledge is just an extreme form of recklessness, and that the risk required for recklessness need only be unjustifiable, not substantial.

Query: should Alice be relieved of her duty to rescue Victoria if Victoria waves her off? One cannot consent to homicide in the standard case. Is failure to rescue within the scope of the non-waivable right against homicide?

[25] I assume throughout that Victoria drowns as a consequence of Alice's inaction. Because I would treat Alice's inaction the same if Victoria managed to survive, with or without others' aid—that is, because I do not distinguish attempts and successes for purposes of criminal punishment—Victoria's death is, for me, an immaterial fact. See Larry Alexander, 'Crime and Culpability' (1994) 5 Journal of Contemporary Legal Issues 1. Again, my view is not the orthodox one, and I therefore assume Victoria drowns in order to steer clear of an irrelevant side issue.

Of course, on my view that equates attempts and successes, things get really complicated if Alice has engaged in a completed attempt to kill Victoria and then discovers that she can rescue Victoria from the peril she created. Suppose, for example, that Alice shoots at Victoria, intending to kill her. Victoria lies wounded, and she will die if, but only if, Alice does not call for help. If Alice does not call for help, and Victoria dies, Alice is guilty of murder. But because she was already guilty of attempted murder—which I maintain should carry the same penalty as murder—Alice would appear to have no incentive in terms of potential punishment for rescuing Victoria. How the law might provide Alice with an incentive to rescue after a completed attempt while still equating attempts and successes is taken up in Larry Alexander and Kimberley D. Kessler, 'Mens Rea and Inchoate Crimes' (1997) 87 Journal of Criminal Law and Criminology 1138, at 1183–1187.

On the view that equates attempts and successes, the question of how to combine Alice's initial culpability in knocking Victoria into the pool with her subsequent culpability in not realizing the grounds for her duty to rescue Victoria (and thus not rescuing her) can be analysed in the following way: when Alice acts recklessly in running around the pool, she should be criminally

The authorities are silent on this point, as they are on the questions raised above concerning culpable ignorance of the facts giving rise to the duty to rescue and recklessness regarding the result coupled with recklessness in causing the peril. One might think, however, that if Alice herself has a duty to act, and the other onlookers do not (at least as far as Alice knows), then Alice cannot factor in the probability of their acting in assessing the risk to Victoria of her not acting. Matters are not so simple, however, when either others are under a duty to act (and Alice knows this), or others have taken actions apart from merely being present that have induced Alice to believe they will rescue Victoria. (But what if Alice is not a particularly skilled swimmer, whereas one of the bystanders is an Olympic swimmer and has rescued countless people in peril, though as yet she has made no move to rescue Victoria?)

The final issue that Alice's case raises is the issue of what makes a rescue an 'easy' one. The authorities agree that the existence of any duty to rescue depends on the rescue's being an 'easy' one, but they are remarkably silent on what that means.[26] For example, is there a material distinction between Alice's facing a risk of death or bodily injury in attempting to rescue Victoria and her facing the loss of property or time? We might easily imagine the law's imposing on Alice the duty to spend her entire life's savings to rescue Victoria but not the duty to risk her own life or health to any significant degree.[27] Nothing in the legal authorities supports such a distinction, though nothing undermines it either.

We might also understand the law's drawing distinctions in terms of risk among those whose duty to rescue is based on their own culpable behaviour (for example, Alice), those whose duty to rescue is based on a status or on non-culpable behaviour, and those whose duty to rescue is based on a contractual obligation to rescue. Thus, we might easily understand the law's requiring those who culpably cause another's peril to undertake highly risky rescues, requiring those who are non-culpable duty-possessors to undertake only minimally risky rescues, and requiring those who have contracted duties to rescue to undertake only the degree of risk they contracted to undertake. Nevertheless, nothing in the authorities suggests these distinctions, although

liable (for reckless endangerment) irrespective of whether Victoria is knocked in and irrespective of whether she is rescued. Then, when Alice culpably misassesses the situation and fails to rescue Victoria—either negligently or recklessly—she is criminally liable for negligent or reckless endangerment regardless of whether Victoria drowns. This analysis suggests that if Alice's act and her omission are combined in a single charge, the penalty should equal the combined penalties for the underlying culpable act and omission. Perhaps then the problem I raise is a product of neglecting the initial reckless act when Alice knowingly lets Victoria drown. If that reckless act is punished and the punishment is *added* to that for knowing homicide rather than subsumed within it, our problem disappears.

[26] See, e.g., LaFave (n. 1 above) 221–222; Andrew Ashworth, 'The Scope of Criminal Liability for Omissions' (1989) 105 LQR 424.

[27] Of course, in Alice's case, even if the risk to her relieves her of the duty to rescue, she still has an incentive to rescue beyond her concern for Victoria, namely, avoiding conviction for manslaughter. For although the risk will negate liability for failing to rescue, it will not negate liability based on Alice's original recklessness in running.

it would be surprising if one whose duty to rescue is contractual were held obligated to undertake a greater risk than specified or implied in the contract.[28]

The strongest case for a duty to rescue in the face of significant risk is when the defendant has culpably caused the victim's peril, as in Alice's case. But what degree of risk (and of what harms) should someone like Alice be compelled to encounter? One possibility is that culpable peril-causers like Alice should be compelled to maximize the victim's chances of escaping harm. Such a position discounts harm to the defendant to zero, which seems rather draconian in cases where the defendant is at most culpable at the level of recklessness for the victim's endangerment. (If the defendant originally acted knowingly or purposely to harm the victim, and after acting both discovered that she could save the victim from the harm and had a change of heart, failing to do so because of the risk would still leave the defendant on the hook for the highest degree of culpably harming the victim. Therefore, compelling the defendant to discount her own risk to zero in those cases puts her to no more difficult a choice than she already faces.)

Let us assume, then, that at least culpable peril-creators like Alice have to undertake some risk to rescue their victims but do not have to discount their own interests to zero. A second possibility is that they should undertake whatever risks maximize the probability of saving lives (or averting harms). In other words, the duty imposed on culpable risk-creators regarding risks involved in rescues would be to act as utilitarian maximizers, perhaps with the twist that averting more serious harms be given lexical priority over averting less serious ones in the calculus.[29]

The authorities do not suggest such a total-harm-minimization approach, even for culpable peril-creators like Alice. For in some cases on this approach, the risk persons like Alice would have to run would be very high; and a high risk to the rescuer, the authorities agree, relieves her of the duty to rescue. Suppose, for example, that the risk of Victoria's drowning if Alice does nothing is 99 per cent; that the risk of neither drowning if Alice attempts a rescue is 55 per cent; and that the risk of both drowning if Alice attempts a rescue is 45 per cent. On the approach under consideration, Alice would have a duty to rescue, even though she faces a 45 per cent chance of drowning.

If this approach is not taken, however, because it sets the risk Alice must take too high, we face the problem of having no principled way of setting the amount of risk (or sacrifice) those like Alice must encounter before she is relieved of her duty to rescue. Any point between no risk or sacrifice and the

---

[28] One court did imply that parents, whose duty to rescue their children is status based, do not have to risk death or serious injury: *State v Walden* 306 NC 466, 293 SE 2d 780 (1982). The court did not say, however, that those whose duty to rescue was based on causing the peril would have to undertake a greater risk of harm, even if their causing the peril were culpable.

[29] Query: on a lexical priority as opposed to strictly utilitarian view of averting harms, how does a very low probability of a more serious harm rank against a much higher probability of a less serious harm?

harm minimizing point will be both arbitrary as a theoretical matter and disturbingly vague as a practical matter. The former point is one on which I have devoted an entire separate article that I need not rehash here.[30] And the latter point should be obvious, for it merely describes the current situation, where the duty is described by everyone in vague terms such as 'easy' rescue and 'reasonable' efforts.[31]

There is, therefore, a real problem with legality with respect to the level of risk that eliminates the duty to rescue. Telling Alice that she is required only to take 'reasonable' or 'easy' steps to save Victoria gives her little guidance, except in obvious cases. Of course, terms like 'reasonable' are used elsewhere in the criminal law.[32] But where they define duties imposed by that law, as opposed to excuses for violating those duties,[33] they are problematic. If Alice believes that she faces a 5 per cent chance of drowning in attempting to rescue Victoria, who can blame her for being uncertain whether hers is an 'easy rescue' or a 'reasonable effort'?

(ii) State v Barbara

Barbara's case differs from Alice's in only one material respect: Barbara was not a *culpable* cause of Victoria's peril. The question her case raises is whether that difference matters.

Again, there is very little authority on the point. One case, *Commonwealth v Cali*,[34] suggests Barbara would have a duty to rescue Victoria. In *Cali*, the defendant accidentally set fire to a house, then intentionally failed to put it out in order to collect on the insurance. The court held that he was guilty of arson despite his lack of culpability in setting the fire.[35] On the other hand, in *King v Commonwealth*,[36] the defendant was held not to have a duty to aid someone he

[30] See Larry Alexander, 'Affirmative Duties and the Limits of Self-Sacrifice' (1996) 15 Law and Philosophy 65. See also Feinberg (n. 1 above) 150–157; Macaulay (n. 1 above) 318–319. My article is devoted to the *theoretical* arbitrariness of any line. Feinberg and Macaulay focus more on the problem of vagueness.

[31] See, e.g., *State v Walden* (n. 28 above); LaFave (n. 1 above) 221–222; Ashworth (n. 26 above) 432. Heidi Malm is concerned by the legality problem, whereas Feinberg and Ashworth are much less concerned by it. See H.M. Malm, 'Liberalism, Bad Samaritan Law, and Legal Paternalism' (1995) 106 *Ethics* 4, at 9–10; Feinberg (n. 1 above) 156; Ashworth (n. 26 above) 454–455. Malm also notes problems with specifying the degree of risk that rescuers must undertake that are a product of liberalism's value neutrality and respect for autonomy (ibid., 12–13, 18–24).

[32] See, e.g., the definition of negligence in Model Penal Code, s. 2.02(2)(d); Feinberg relies on the law's use of terms like 'reasonableness' in his argument for a duty to rescue. See Feinberg (n. 1 above) 155–157.

[33] See, e.g., the 'person of reasonable firmness test' for the excuse of duress found in Model Penal Code, s. 2.09(1).

[34] 247 Mass 20, 141 NE 510 (1923).

[35] In accord with *Cali* are *R v Miller* [1983] 2 AC 161, a case very similar on its facts to *Cali*; *Green v Cross*, 103 LTR (NS) 279 (KB 1910), in which a conviction for cruelty to animals was upheld in a case in which defendant had caught a dog in a legal vermin trap but then delayed releasing it; and *Van Buskirk v State*, 190 Okl Cr 38, 611 P 2d 271 (Okl Cr Ct of Apps, 1980), in which a driver was convicted of manslaughter for abandoning someone she struck accidentally.

[36] 285 Ky 654, 148 SW 2d 1044 (1941).

had wounded in lawfully defending his father from the victim's attack, though this case might be distinguishable due to the culpability of the victim. Arnold Loewy, using an example very similar to Barbara's case, concludes that the better view is to hold the non-culpable imperiller to a duty to rescue, even if she is an entirely passive cause of the peril.[37] (It is difficult to believe that Barbara's passivity after coming to the edge of the pool should matter. If, instead of being knocked by Alice into Victoria, Barbara had moved in an attempt to avoid Alice and in moving knocked Victoria into the pool, she would be a non-culpable active cause. There is no good reason why the act of jumping out of Alice's way should matter, but the act of coming to the poolside should not. Likewise, if Barbara had gone to the spot by the poolside and remained there precisely because she anticipated being knocked by Alice into Victoria and wanted that to occur, we would surely treat her as a culpable *cause* of Victoria's peril, despite her passivity just prior to the collision.[38])

Of course, Barbara's case raises the question of why innocent causes of peril should be under a duty to rescue. (Note just how many innocent causes there could be: Victoria's ride to the party; Barbara's friend who invited her; and so on.) Perhaps the thought is that, as with driving, where one's innocently driving straight down the road does not exculpate one from failing to turn the steering wheel to avoid hitting a child, an activity that imposes slight risks on others is permissible only if one is prepared to undertake at least an easy rescue in case those slight risks eventuate. Thus, going to poolside—*if it raises the risk to others of drowning*—may be permissible only if one assumes a duty to rescue those whose risks of drowning one has even slightly increased. Of course, if Barbara's standing at poolside has not, from an actuarial standpoint, increased the risk of anyone else drowning—or has done so only by decreasing the risk of other harms to the same or other people—then this rationale for imposing a duty to rescue does not apply, and we would need a different rationale for holding Barbara liable.

If culpability in causing Victoria's peril does not distinguish Alice and Barbara with respect to whether they have duties under the criminal law to rescue Victoria, then the other issues in Alice's case—awareness of Victoria's peril, awareness of her role in causing the peril, and awareness of the degree of risk and effort the rescue requires—are the same in Barbara's case, except for two differences. First, if Alice's culpability increases the risk or effort she must undertake to rescue Victoria, then Barbara will be relieved of such a duty in some circumstances in which Alice will not. Secondly, if Barbara is

---

[37] Arnold H. Loewy, *Criminal Law in a Nutshell* (3rd edn., St Paul, 2000) 159.
[38] See Larry Alexander, 'Voluntary Acts: The Child/Davidson Trilemma' (1992) 11 Criminal Justice Ethics 98. In conversation, Heidi Hurd has argued that Barbara is not a 'cause' of Victoria's peril if her passivity is innocent, but that Barbara *is* a cause if she planted herself poolside precisely because she anticipated the collision with Alice and her (Barbara's) being knocked into Victoria. However, I am not willing to accept that causation, as opposed to culpability, turns not on Barbara's physical conduct but on her state of mind.

culpably unaware of any of the facts giving rise to her duty to rescue Victoria, her liability for Victoria's death should be pegged at that level of culpability. Unlike Alice, who comes to the duty to rescue already on the hook for reckless homicide even if she is non-culpably unaware of the grounds for a duty to rescue, Barbara's baseline liability is zero because her causal contribution to the peril was non-culpable. If, therefore, she is aware of some of the conditions giving rise to the duty, but culpably unaware of others, the level of the homicide she commits in not rescuing should be no higher than her culpability in misgauging the peril, and/or her role in causing it, and/or the risk or effort a rescuer would face. Nor would culpable lack of awareness of two or three of these conditions be *more* culpable than a culpable lack of awareness of one of them. Indeed, it would be *less* culpable because she would have to *know* of the other conditions to be under the duty. (Non-culpable ignorance of any condition negates her duty to rescue.)

(Query: we have said that Barbara (or Alice), who accidentally puts Victoria in peril, will be deemed to have committed knowing homicide if she fails to rescue Victoria believing it is practically certain Victoria will die (assuming Victoria does in fact die).) She should therefore be guilty of *purposeful* homicide if she fails to rescue Victoria believing she has only slightly increased the risk that Victoria will die by knocking her into the pool (the pool, say, being very shallow) *but having as her conscious object in not pulling Victoria out that Victoria die.* Because taking what one believes is a one-in-million shot at killing another is sufficient for purposeful homicide if the shot does kill and is taken with the object of killing, where there is a duty to rescue, an omission to rescue with the object that the victim die should be sufficient for purposeful homicide even if the omitter believes it highly likely that the victim will survive—so long, that is, as she also believes that the victim is in sufficient peril to trigger the duty to rescue.[39])

(iii) State v Candy

It is time to introduce the rest of the characters who could have but did not rescue Victoria. Candy is a five-time Olympic medalist in swimming who was present at poolside when Victoria was knocked in. Just before the accident, Victoria had told Candy that although she, Victoria, was afraid of swimming pools because she could not swim, and would ordinarily not stand near the edge of a pool, she felt secure in doing so on this occasion because Candy was present and could easily rescue her. Candy did not reply to this statement. The issue then is whether Candy had a duty to rescue Victoria predicated on Candy's *causing* Victoria's peril *by inducing Victoria's reliance* that she could stand at poolside without the risk of drowning. Put differently, was Victoria entitled to rely on Candy's rescuing her in the absence of a representation by Candy to that effect?

[39] See n. 22 above.

Perhaps the answer to this question is found in the law of contractual or contract-like duties. Perhaps Candy's silence cannot be the basis of a duty to rescue, even if Candy knows that Victoria has (mis)interpreted her silence as assent to a willingness to rescue and is relying on this willingness in coming to the poolside. On the other hand, if Candy had explicitly represented that she would rescue Victoria if Victoria fell in, Candy would have a contractual or contract-like duty to rescue based on that representation. Somewhere between these polar cases would be cases in which Candy does or says things that do not ordinarily amount to representations of her willingness to rescue, but where she is aware Victoria has understood and relied upon her words or actions that way.

If contract principles, whatever they may be, determine Candy's duty with respect to Victoria's reliance on Candy, do they affect Candy's duty with respect to *others'* reliance on Candy? Suppose, in other words, Victoria has not relied on Candy—she does not even know who Candy is—but when she is knocked into the pool by Alice and Barbara, several onlookers, who *do* know who Candy is, assume, erroneously and tragically, that Candy will rescue Victoria, given how easy the rescue would be for such a strong swimmer. The onlookers were willing to rescue Victoria themselves, and would have done so had they not believed Candy would rescue her. When they realized that Candy had no intention of doing so, it was too late for them to save Victoria. In this way, Candy's presence has caused Victoria's peril, not by inducing Victoria's reliance, but by inducing that of others.

Does Candy have a duty to rescue Victoria just because she is aware that others expect her to do so and are forgoing their own rescues in reliance on her?[40] The question raised in both this and the original variant of Candy's case is one of the most nettlesome in normative philosophy: to what extent is one obligated to act because of others' readings or misreadings of one's intentions?

We can imagine a range of cases in which onlookers rely on Candy, just as we can when the issue is Victoria's reliance on Candy. At one pole is the case we have described: Candy is merely present at poolside, aware that onlookers are counting on her and forgoing their own rescues, but having done nothing other than stand at poolside to induce their reliance. At the opposite pole would be a case where Candy intends to dive in the pool and swim laps but does not intend to rescue Victoria. She realizes as she dives in and begins to swim in Victoria's direction that the onlookers are interpreting her actions as a rescue— they are cheering her on—and that if she continues swimming in Victoria's direction but does not rescue her, it will be too late for the onlookers to rescue her themselves. If Candy has no duty to rescue Victoria in this case, then she surely

---

[40] Candy must of course be aware that the onlookers are counting on her to rescue Victoria and that, if she does not, Victoria will likely drown. If she is unaware of this, just as if she is unaware that the risk of the rescue is minimal, then she has no duty to rescue, although if she is *culpably* unaware of these matters, she may be liable for homicide at the level of that degree of culpability.

has no duty to do so in the case where she merely stands at the poolside but otherwise says and does nothing. It does not follow, however, that if she has a duty to rescue in the case where she dives in and swims toward Victoria, that she has a duty in the case where she does not. Perhaps the dividing line between duty and no duty lies somewhere between these poles.

But what would be the basis for such a dividing line? The fact that Candy is *acting* in swimming toward Victoria but *not acting* in standing at poolside? This seems too slim a reed, not only because Candy at poolside can always be described in terms of action verbs—she is perhaps *talking, looking* in Victoria's direction, *contemplating* her course of action, and so forth—but also because there are cases that are clearly distinguishable in terms of action and inaction from her swimming in Victoria's direction but that intuitively seem indistinguishable from the case where she merely stands and does nothing. For example, suppose Candy had turned to look at Victoria in the pool and in turning revealed to the onlookers the back of her T-shirt, which carried the logo 'Volunteer Water Rescue Association: "Good Samaritanism is Our Sacred Duty"'. Her so turning is an action. And she is aware in all three cases that onlookers are assuming that she will rescue Victoria and are forgoing their own rescues based on that assumption. Does her revealing her T-shirt to the onlookers create a duty if her merely standing at poolside and being who she is does not?

As I said, the question of when our liberty to act is limited by how others misread and take action based on what they believe we are going to do is an extremely difficult one and one, I believe, that has received far too little philosophical examination. After all, the absence of a legally enforceable general duty to rescue could be seriously undermined if others' mere *expectation* that one will act as a Good Samaritan can create a legally enforceable duty so to act (or at least a legally enforceable duty affirmatively to apprise everyone who is so relying that one is *not* a Good Samaritan). Did Kant, aware that the citizens of Königsberg set their clocks by his regular walks around the city, have a duty either to continue those walks at the same time each day or to notify everyone that he was discontinuing them? Or was their reliance at *their* peril, not Kant's? And because its applications extend well beyond criminal law to both tort and contract law and perhaps to the coherence of the libertarian normative theory that underpins the right not to be compelled into Good Samaritanism, Candy's case by itself is worth book length treatment.[41]

---

[41] Would a principle that compelled one to rescue whenever one knows that others have forgone their own rescues in reliance on their belief that one would and could rescue—which belief was a reasonable belief given the statistical likelihood that those in the actor's circumstances intend to attempt rescues—be an acceptable principle? It makes what I am obligated to do hostage to what others who are perceived to be similar to me generally intend to do, because I must either do what is expected of me or, if there is time and opportunity, establish that I am dissimilar to most others in terms of my intentions. Perhaps that is fair when others read my intentions from the words I use, even if my intention is to use the words in an unorthodox way. Is it fair as a more general principle that extends beyond words to acts such as standing at poolside, wearing a T-shirt with a particular logo, etc.?

(iv) State v Dana

Dana, also at poolside when Victoria falls in, happens to possess a life pre-server attached to a rope. Dana tosses the preserver to Victoria, who grabs hold of it, but then Dana changes her mind about rescuing Victoria and yanks the preserver out of her grasp.

Dana's case raises three questions. First, has Dana *acted* to cause Victoria's death rather than *omitted* to save her? Secondly, if Dana has omitted to save Victoria, is she criminally liable under the exception to the 'no duty to rescue' principle for those who voluntarily begin to rescue but then do not carry through with it? Thirdly, is the exception just mentioned an independent ex-ception, or is it merely a subcategory of the exception for those who have caused or worsened the victim's peril by inducing others to forgo their own rescues?

With respect to the first question, the better view is that Dana is an omitter (to save), not an actor (to kill). It is true that yanking the life preserver out of Victoria's grasp is an act. And Dana would surely be a murderer if the life pre-server belonged not to her but to Victoria, or to someone else who had thrown it to rescue Victoria.

But consider this analogy to Dana's case. Suppose I own a life-support sys-tem. Someone needs it, but I refuse to hook him up to it. Or he hooks himself up, but I refuse to plug it in. Or the system is plugged in but shuts off period-ically, and I refuse to restart it. In each of these instances, I am a very Bad Samaritan; but in none of them am I a killer. For in none of them have I left the 'victim' worse off than he would have been in my absence, which is the most plausible criterion for distinguishing *morally* between acts and omissions.

Now Dana's case is just like these, except that at the time Dana yanks the preserver away, Victoria *would* be better off were Dana absent. But if we con-sider the entire event *and include Dana's tossing the preserver as well as her yanking it away*, Victoria is no worse off than had Dana (and her life pre-server) never existed. (I am, of course, assuming away any psychological trauma Victoria might suffer as a result of Dana's change of heart.)

Most commentators agree that switching off a life-support system that one owns and has no duty to let another use is no different from refusing to switch it on initially.[42] And we are assuming here that the victim's plight has not

<hr>

[42] See, e.g., Dressler (n. 4 above) 92–93; F.M. Kamm, *Morality, Mortality, Vol. II* (Oxford, 1996) 28–29; Judith Thomson, 'A Defense of Abortion' (1971) 1 *Philosophy and Public Affairs* 47. Michael Moore, however, disagrees with this 'normative baseline' approach to distinguish-ing between act and omission liability. See Michael S. Moore, *Act and Crime* (1993) 26–27. For Moore, Dana has killed Victoria by yanking away the life preserver and has not merely omitted to rescue her. Dana's ownership of the life preserver is, for Moore, relevant only to whether Dana has a *justification* for killing Victoria. It does not, however, make her contribution to Victoria's death one of omission. Suppose Dana is sitting poolside with her legs dangling in the water. Vic-toria then grabs onto Dana's legs to keep herself above water. At that point, on Moore's analy-sis, Dana can keep absolutely still, in which case, when Victoria no longer has the strength to

been worsened by allowing her to use the system but then removing her from it relative to her plight had she never been allowed to use the system in the first place. So Dana's overall course of conduct—throwing Victoria the life preserver and then yanking it away from her—should be treated as a failure to rescue, not as a killing, as it would be were the life preserver to belong to Victoria or to someone else who wanted Victoria to use it.

If Dana has merely failed to rescue Victoria, does she nevertheless come under the exception to the 'no duty to rescue' principle for those who have voluntarily assumed a duty to rescue another? The answer, I believe, is, and should be, 'no', for this reason: I do not believe that the category of exceptions is an independent one. Rather, I believe that all of the cases cited as establishing it are either cases in which the *victim* has relied to her detriment on defendant's implicit representation that defendant would rescue her from peril, cases in which *others* have relied on defendant's implicit representation to that effect, or cases in which defendant's initial actions in rescuing the victim coupled with the defendant's then ceasing to rescue left the victim in more peril than she had been in initially.

Take, for example, the case of *R v Instan*,[43] in which a niece had gone to live with her aunt and then refused to care for her when she became ill. The court reasoned that although the niece had no common law duty to care for her aunt, once she came to live with the aunt she acquired the duty at least to inform others that the aunt was ill and to provide food and some care.

Now why was the niece under such a duty? The most plausible basis would be a finding that the aunt had reasonably assumed that her niece would care for her in such a situation as occurred and had taken her in and provided for her based on that assumption.[44] Had the niece informed the aunt that she was assuming no obligation to care for her by coming to live with her, I believe the case would have been different. For by taking the niece in on those terms, and not seeking another person to live with her, the aunt would have indicated that she was not relying on a willingness to rescue her in choosing someone to live with her. In such a situation, the niece, having created no peril, would be no different from a stranger who observes the aunt's need for care and does nothing—the classic Bad Samaritan who is nonetheless exempt from criminal

hold on to Dana's legs and drowns, her death will be due only to an omission. But if Dana wants to pull her legs out of the water, she must do so with care that Victoria not fall off or otherwise be liable for killing her through the *act* of moving her legs.

[43] [1893] 1 QB 450.

[44] See, e.g., *Cornell v State* (n. 23 above) where the defendant was criminally liable for the death of a grandchild by omission after having agreed to take care of the grandchild. Of course, if in *Instan* there was no explicit understanding that the niece would care for her aunt, the case raises the same questions that were raised in Candy's case regarding when others have a right to rely on an unexpressed intent to rescue such that their reliance can create a duty to rescue. See n. 41 above. See also Ashworth (n. 26 above) 443–445 (arguing for a detrimental reliance or a contractual rationale for *Instan*).

liability.[45] Nor would she be different from one who gives a starving person a few bites of food but then desists before the other has eaten enough to survive.

This suggests that the most plausible basis for finding Dana criminally liable for Victoria's death would be that others relied on her throwing the life preserver to Victoria to forgo rescuing her themselves, and that when Dana withdrew the life preserver, it was then too late for them to rescue Victoria. On this view, Dana's case is merely a variant of Candy's case insofar as Candy's presence and actions induced others to rely on Candy to rescue Victoria. And we can ask in Dana's case whether her throwing the life preserver to Victoria is materially different from Candy's swimming in Victoria's direction. But properly analysed, Dana's case does not present any new considerations.[46]

(v) State v Elise

Elise has been hired by the owner of the swimming pool to serve as lifeguard at the party. She and the owner have an express contract that requires her to engage in even moderately risky and very strenuous rescues of any guests who are in danger of drowning. Elise, however, does not rescue Victoria, even though she is aware of Victoria's peril and that she can rescue Victoria with little risk or effort.

It would appear that Elise's case is a straightforward application of the contractual exception to the 'no duty to rescue' principle. The question I wish to raise is whether or to what extent the contractual exception is independent of the creation of the peril exception. For if one way that one can come under a duty to rescue through creation of the peril is by inducing either the victim or potential rescuers to rely on one's willingness to rescue, then perhaps agreeing in a contract to rescue someone is just a specific case of inducing reliance and thereby creating a peril.

We can test the latter hypothesis by imagining the following case of a contractual duty to rescue. Concerned has noted that her next-door neighbours frequently leave their small children unattended in the backyard, where they have a deep and unfenced swimming pool. Concerned does not say anything to the neighbours, but she is quite afraid for the safety of the children. Concerned speaks to her gardener and asks him if, for an additional $1 per hour,

---

[45] A more difficult case to explain on this rationale is *Stehr v State*, 92 Neb 755, 139 NW 676 (1913). There, the defendant married the mother of the victim child but did not adopt him. He allowed the boy's feet to become frozen and was criminally convicted for failing to act to bring medical attention to the boy. The case did not appear to turn on anyone's detrimental reliance on the defendant; and defendant's status as step-father was not sufficient in itself to create a legal duty to rescue.

[46] Of course, even if Dana has worsened Victoria's peril in a way that creates a duty to rescue, she, like Candy, must be aware of Victoria's peril, aware that she has worsened it, and aware that she can rescue Victoria without undue risk and effort—or, if she is unaware of any of these conditions, her lack of awareness must be culpable, and her resultant liability can be no higher than the culpability her lack of awareness evinces.

he will from time to time look over into the neighbour's backyard to see if the children are OK and, if they are in distress, call 911 or rescue them himself. He agrees to do so. If he had not agreed, Concerned would have done nothing else, except pay him only what he was currently being paid. She would not have hired a new gardener or watched the neighbour children herself. Nor do the neighbours know about Concerned's arrangement with her gardener.

Now suppose after the gardener has agreed to look in on the children as part of his duties as Concerned's gardener, he fails to take action upon observing the children in distress in the pool, with the result that the children drown. Is the gardener criminally liable for their deaths under the contractual exception, assuming, of course, that he was aware—or not culpably unaware—of the peril and of his ability to do what he had agreed to do? No one to whom I have presented this hypothetical believes that the gardener should be guilty of homicide despite his contractual obligation to rescue the children. What seems to explain this is the fact that the gardener's contract has not induced anyone's detrimental reliance and has not therefore created or worsened the children's peril.

Turn back now to the case of Elise. Suppose neither Victoria nor any of the other guests at the party knew that there was a lifeguard at the party. In other words, no one took or forwent any action in reliance on Elise's contract with the pool owner. The latter would, of course, have a civil cause of action against Elise for breach of contract when she fails to rescue Victoria. But is Elise guilty of criminal homicide—indeed, *murder*—if she was aware of Victoria's peril and the risk within the contractual limits?

If the pool owner would have hired someone else as a lifeguard had Elise not agreed to be one, then perhaps Elise did create Victoria's peril by her contract through inducing reliance by the pool owner.[47] But if Elise were merely a guest whom the owner asked to serve as lifeguard—and if, had Elise refused to serve, the owner would not have hired anyone else—then Elise's case is structurally identical to the gardener's. And if bare contractual duty is insufficient to create a duty under the criminal law in the gardener's case, it should be insufficient in Elise's as well.

Perhaps a contract can by itself create a duty to rescue under the criminal law when A promises B (for consideration?) to rescue B, even though B would not have acted in any way differently had A not made the promise. But for many, if not all, cases of criminal liability based on contract, the real basis of criminal liability would appear to be detrimental reliance, which is itself but a subcategory of causation of peril.[48]

---

[47] See *Cornell v State* (n. 23 above), where a grandmother was convicted of homicide after having agreed with the grandchild's mother to look after her grandchild and then failed to do so.

[48] Ashworth also expresses some doubts about contracts as bases for criminal liability. See Ashworth (n. 26 above) 443–445.

(vi) State v Fran

Fran was Victoria's live-in lesbian lover, and had been so for several years, with some periods of separation due to problems in the relationship. Fran was an able swimmer who could have, but did not, rescue Victoria, whom she realized was in peril but capable of being rescued (by Fran). As stated, certain status relationships, such as husband and wife and parent and child, are deemed by both conventional morality and the law to generate duties to rescue that are enforceable under the criminal law. That means, for example, that a husband who realizes (or culpably fails to realize) his wife is in danger, realizes (or culpably fails to realize) that he can rescue her with minimal risk and/or sacrifice, and realizes (or culpably fails to realize) that she *is* his wife, but who then fails to attempt to rescue her, can be criminally liable for homicide, indeed knowing homicide (murder) if he is aware of the existence of the three elements (wife's peril, his ability to rescue with low risk/effort, and wife's identity). Moreover, as was true with respect to the other exceptions to the 'no duty to rescue' principle, the defendant does not have to realize he is under a legal duty to rescue so long as he realizes (or culpably fails to realize) the existence of the facts giving rise to that legal duty.

Once we move away from the formalized relationship of husband and wife, and the quasi-formalized relationship of parent and child,[49] are there any other status relationships that give rise to a duty to rescue enforceable by the criminal law? Consider the following non-exhaustive list of relationships that *might* give rise to a duty to rescue: (1) live-in heterosexual partners whose relationship is of 10 years' or two years' or one month's duration with no or some or many interruptions; (2) live-in homosexual partners in similar circumstances; (3) a married couple who are legally separated; (4) a step-parent and step-child; (5) a foster parent and foster child; (6) a non-custodial biological parent; (7) a parent and an adult child;[50] (8) a sperm or egg donor and the resultant child; (9) a surrogate mother and child; (10) cloned and clone; (11) live-in boyfriend (girlfriend) and mother's (father's) child; (12) biological siblings;[51] (13) adoptive siblings; and (14) step-siblings. Which relationships, if any, should impose a duty under the criminal law?

Now any one of these relationships might give rise to a duty to rescue premised on an implicit or explicit agreement to do so leading to detrimental

---

[49] I label the parent-child relationship 'quasi-formalized' for reasons that will become apparent below. For being a biological parent may not be necessary in order to have a status-based duty to rescue—consider adoptive parents, who *do* have such a duty—nor may it be sufficient for such a duty. Consider sperm donors and egg donors who are not custodial parents, mothers who give their children up for adoption, and non-custodial biological fathers.

[50] This relationship of adult parent and adult child raises a question whether the child must rescue the parent as well as whether the parent must rescue the child. The same holds for the other types of parent-child relationship when the child is an adult. See Ashworth (n. 26 above) 441–442.

[51] See ibid., 442.

reliance by the victim or, more likely, other potential rescuers. In other words, cases of criminal liability that appear to rest on status relationships might really be instances of causation of peril through inducing detrimental reliance. That was the interpretation I offered of *R v Instan*, when probably neither the status of aunt and niece nor the status of housemates was sufficient to give rise to a duty to rescue.[52] Are there any relationships other than husband and wife or (custodial) parents and children that generate duties to rescue without recourse to implicit or explicit agreements to do so?[53]

The case law is sparse. A Michigan case, *People v Beardsley*,[54] held that a man's relationship to his mistress generates no duty to rescue. On the other hand, a Connecticut case, *State v Miranda*,[55] held that a long-time live-in boyfriend did have a duty to rescue his girlfriend's infant from her abuse. The rationale in the latter case is a mishmash of contractual, reliance, and status theories:

> We conclude only that . . . when defendant, who considered himself the victim's [step-] parent, established a familial relationship with the victim's mother and her children and assumed the role of a father, he assumed, under the common law, the same legal duty to protect the victim from the abuse as if he were, in fact, the victim's guardian.[56]

There are two principal dangers in extending the category of status-based duties to rescue beyond formalized marriages and biological (or formal adoptive) custodial parent-child relations. First, there is no obvious principled limitation on deeming relationships to be ones giving rise to duties to rescue. If a live-in boyfriend is in such a relationship, how about Fran, or Victoria's best friend, or her law teacher, her fellow employees, her employer, or the doorman at her apartment? Secondly, and relatedly, there is a grave problem of legality—that is, fair notice. Because even reasonable mistakes regarding whether one has a duty to rescue under the criminal law fail to exculpate, the law establishing such duties should be sufficiently clear to provide fair warning to the average person. No one who looked at the law of Connecticut in 1998 could have concluded with any confidence that Mr Miranda had a duty to rescue his girlfriend's child from her abuse, *at least purely as a matter of his relationship with the victim*. That is to say, if we disregard the evidence that he possibly led others to rely on him to rescue the child from the mother's abuse—and there is nothing in the case that supports the inference

---

52 See text at nn. 43–45 above.

53 One might try to make a case for reducing all status-based duties to duties based on causation of peril by arguing that by marriage and by assuming custody over children (rather than giving up custody), one evinces an agreement to care for the spouse or child on which all may rely. The problem with this reduction of all status-based duties to 'contractual' ones is that it does not work for some cases, such as where a mother gives birth in circumstances where it is impossible to relinquish custody of the child to others for a period of time. Even if her isolation was not her fault, she will still have a duty to care.

54 150 Mich 206, 113 NW 1128 (1907).   55 245 Conn 209, 715 A 2d 680 (1998).

56 245 Conn 209 (1998), at 226, 715 A 2d 680, at 689.

that anyone was relying on him to the detriment of the child—and focus only on the fact that he acted in a fatherly manner toward the child in various ways, nothing in the pre-existing law in Connecticut strongly supported the existence of a duty to rescue.

(vii) State v Gina

Gina was a guest at the party who realized Victoria was drowning and that she, Gina, could effect a low risk, low sacrifice rescue, but who nonetheless did nothing. However, Gina in no way contributed to Victoria's peril, either through physical causation or through inducing the detrimental reliance of Victoria on her potential rescuers. Nor did Gina contract with anyone to rescue Victoria or have any relationship with Victoria other than being a guest at the same party. In short, Gina was the classic Bad Samaritan whom the law exempts from criminal liability.

Although, as I said at the outset, I am not going to deal with whether there should be a duty imposed by the criminal law on the standard Bad Samaritan like Gina, that question raises both difficult theoretical and practical issues. On the theoretical side, there are two issues: can the moral duty to rescue be legally enforced without violating the rescuer's rights? And, if so, at what point—and why—does a rescue become so risky or difficult that the enforceable duty is extinguished? On the practical side is the question of what the consequences will be of enforcing duties to rescue of various degrees of stringency. For example, will a criminally enforceable duty to rescue lead to more rescues, or will it lead to fewer, as it might if people avoided those situations likely to give rise to such duties? Although these theoretical and practical issues have been addressed in the literature, they surely remain controversial.[57]

C. CONCLUSION

This journey through the various issues raised by omissions liability in criminal law can be summarized rather succinctly. First, insofar as one is a but-for physical cause of the victim's peril, what scant law there is appears to support liability for non-rescue, not only in cases like Alice's, where the defendant *actively* and *culpably* caused the peril, but also in cases like Barbara's, where the defendant *passively* and *innocently* caused the peril. The principal remaining issue of interest in the physical causation cases is how to combine the culpability of causing the peril (in Alice's case) with culpability in not recognizing the factual grounds for the duty to rescue (that the victim is in peril, that the defendant caused the peril, and that the rescue will not entail excessive risk or sacrifice). (The issue of how risky or difficult a rescue is required is not restricted to physical causation cases but is common to all the cases.)

---

[57] See authorities cited in nn. 1 and 30 above.

Candy's, Dana's, and Elise's cases raise the question of under what circumstances may one be deemed to have caused the victim's peril and thus have a duty to rescue where the causal path runs through the victim's or others' detrimental reliance on one's willingness to rescue. I have suggested that predicating omission liability solely on contract (Elise's case) or on assumption of the duty (Dana's case) is problematic in the former case and unjustifiable in the latter, and that examples of contractual or other voluntary assumption of duties to rescue that do justify criminal enforcement are perhaps best looked at as instances of causation of peril through detrimental reliance. On the other hand, the question of what should count as justified detrimental reliance by the victim or other potential rescuers is difficult and almost completely unexplored. (Dana's case also raises the issue of what is an 'omission', as opposed to an 'act', an issue that I believe is not particularly difficult if one shifts one's gaze from what the defendant does physically and looks instead at the normative baseline.)

Finally, Fran's case raises the issue of what statuses entail duties to rescue, and why. The law here is very murky, and under-theorized. I suggest that status-based duties to rescue should be clearly spelled out in the law, and that any other relationships should only give rise to duties to rescue where justifiable detrimental reliance—whatever it is—is shown.

My aim here has been the modest (and easy) one of raising issues that are too seldom addressed rather than solving them. I do believe this corner of the criminal law merits having more light shone on it. And I also believe that the issues one will discover there will prove to be among the more intriguing theoretical issues in the criminal law.

7

Involuntary Crimes, Voluntarily Committed

CLAIRE FINKELSTEIN *

A famous Australian case involved one Mrs Cogdon, who killed her sleeping daughter by bringing an axe down on her head.[1] Luckily for the defence, the daughter was not the only one asleep at the time. Mrs Cogdon was apparently asleep throughout the entire incident as well. For this reason the court dismissed the charges, saying that Mrs Cogdon could not be guilty of murder because she had not killed voluntarily.

Voluntariness is fundamental to responsibility. Where it is lacking, we do not treat a person as the agent of his own bodily movements. While we may speak casually of an 'involuntary action', the movements of a person asleep, in a trance, suffering an epileptic seizure, or responding reflexively are no more 'actions' than the beating of one's heart or the motion of a falling tree. What separates involuntary movement from human action is that actions are chosen, and as such they are more or less under the control of the agent.[2]

More or less. But what should we make of a case in which a person arranges in advance to do something involuntarily? Suppose that, knowing she was subject to violent acts in her sleep, Mrs Cogdon had deliberately placed the axe next to her bed, opened the door between her room and her daughter's and, just to make sure, had taken a sleeping pill to increase her chances of remaining asleep. Surely she cannot escape responsibility for her daughter's death in this case. For unlike the case where the involuntariness is unexpected, Mrs Cogdon now controls the onset of the involuntary condition itself. Something

* I wish to thank Peter Cane, Heidi Hurd, Sanford Kadish, Leo Katz, Sue Mendus, and Michael Thompson for conversations on the topic of this article as well as for comments on various drafts. Particular thanks are due to Andrew Simester and Stephen Shute, the editors of this volume, for their detailed comments on several drafts.

[1] (1950) unreported. The case was introduced into the academic literature by the discussion of it presented by Norval Morris, 'Somnambulistic Homicide: Ghosts, Spiders, and North Koreans' (1951) 5 Res Judicatae 29.

[2] When I say that actions are 'chosen', I mean to refer quite generically to the fact that actions are in some sense the product of the will. I am not assuming any particular account in the theory of action about the line between actions and non-action events, or even any particular theory about what it means to say that an action is the product of the actor's will. These issues are not important for present purposes, although I will turn to matters of action theory in the final section.

similar can be said of the person who is aware she may suffer from an involuntary condition, even if she does not seek to induce it. We might blame Mrs Cogdon for her daughter's death, for example, if she merely knew of her proclivity to perform violent acts in her sleep and did nothing to guard against it. She need not actually have tried to take advantage of that proclivity.

Exploring the problem of intended or anticipated involuntariness should provide a way of considering the nature of voluntariness more generally. What sort of thing could voluntariness be that a person's prior psychological state could affect it? In particular, does the intention to perform an involuntary act, or the knowledge that one will perform such an act, make voluntary what would otherwise be involuntary? It is hard to see how this could be, any more than a person's prior intention to become intoxicated could make his subsequent drunken movements acts of sobriety. It is hard to see, in other words, how having a certain mental state at one time could affect the voluntariness of one's actions at an entirely different time. But if intending or knowing that one will perform an involuntary act does not make the act itself voluntary, why would we blame the person who contrives to kill someone involuntarily for the resulting death?

A natural thought to have is that we blame a person who arranges to do a bad deed in an involuntary condition, not on the basis of the involuntary bodily movements themselves, but on the basis of earlier, voluntary acts that produce the later involuntary ones. In the modified Mrs Cogdon case, the argument would go, we should not seek to blame her on the basis of her somnambulatory behaviour, since that was involuntary. Rather, we blame Mrs Cogdon on the basis of her earlier, voluntary acts of procuring a murder weapon, ensuring easy access to the victim, and taking a sleeping pill. These acts produced her daughter's death, much in the way that hiring another person to kill would. Mrs Cogdon no more needs to bring the axe down on her daughter's head awake than she needs to wield the axe herself.

There are, however, several problems with looking back to a prior voluntary act to establish an agent's blameworthiness for his later involuntary conduct. The most significant of these is the fact that the earlier act and the later act are different acts. We need no technical definition of the notion of an 'act' to see that this is so. Placing an axe next to a bed simply is not the same as killing, even if the presence of the axe makes it possible to kill. Getting extremely drunk is not the same as assaulting a person, even if getting drunk causes the agent to assault. Subjecting oneself to a terrorist organization is not the same as robbing a bank, even if the organization brainwashes its subjects to rob banks. In each case, it is clear we are dealing with distinct acts from the fact that the two take place at different times and in different locations. The thing for which we wish to blame the agent is the second act, but it is only the first that the agent controls. Thus, if we wish to blame a person for doing Y, it is not clear that it will help us to focus on the fact that she did X, and that X caused Y.[3] If Y is not an action of the agent's, we cannot establish responsibility for it by showing that it was the product of something that *was* an action of the agent's. Action simply does not travel along causal lines, and ordinary morality does not accept responsibility without action.[4]

The problem of contrived involuntariness raises a series of issues in moral philosophy, but it has gone largely unnoticed among philosophers. The small amount of attention it has received has been in the criminal law context. The problem naturally arises there because the criminal law forbids holding a defendant liable for a crime unless he has voluntarily performed the precise act prohibited by law. If, for example, the definition of a crime requires the defendant to 'cause the death of another human being', or to 'unlawfully enter a building at night with the intent to commit a crime therein', he must have caused a death or entered a building voluntarily. No other voluntary act will do. The strictness of the act requirement in the criminal law helps to underscore the difficulty with trying to base responsibility on an earlier voluntary act. Does a person who was himself hypnotized to rob a bank in a trance 'enter a building with intent to commit a crime therein' *voluntarily*? It is not clear he does.

Our discussion will proceed as follows. Section A will explore the structure of the typical form in which the voluntary act problem arises in the law, namely cases in which the defendant anticipated, rather than contrived, his involuntary condition. It will consider how what is sometimes called the 'orthodox approach' to the criminal law's act requirement handles such cases. While the 'definitional' requirement I noted above is the heart of the voluntary act problem, this section will address a preliminary difficulty that poses special problems for the orthodox approach, namely the role of proximate cause. Section B will then turn to the definitional issue in detail. It will explain why an earlier voluntary act probably cannot be used to satisfy the act requirement for a crime committed while the defendant is in the grip of an involuntary condition. Section C will consider two additional potential solutions to the voluntary act problem, both of which seem, at first blush, as though they avoid the

---

[3] There is a different kind of case in which it *does* help to establish responsibility to show that the defendant performed the prohibited act in virtue of performing an earlier act that caused it. Suppose a person intentionally throws a ball and inadvertently breaks a window. If he was inattentive in doing the first thing—throwing the ball—it may not seem unfair to blame him for the second thing—breaking the window—if doing the first thing caused him to do the second thing. But this case is significantly different from our case's, since breaking a window is an action of the agent's, despite being something done unintentionally. Killing, assaulting, and robbing are not actions of any sort, unintentional or other, if they are done in an involuntary condition. While ordinary morality does not extend responsibility to non-action, it does extend it to things done unintentionally that are still actions.

[4] There are notable exceptions to this claim. For example, we sometimes blame a person for failing to act where he had a duty to act. Omission liability still requires voluntariness—the agent must have voluntarily failed to do something he had a duty to do—but the agent need not have performed any action during the time he was failing to do his duty. In what follows, I shall leave omissions to one side and simply treat them as an isolated exception to the 'no responsibility without action' principle.

causation and the definitional problems of the orthodox approach. Neither solution turns out to be entirely satisfactory. Finally, Section D will present an alternative framework for solving problems of voluntariness in the criminal law. My proposal will make use of a standard feature of philosophical action theory, namely that actions, like physical objects, are subject to different descriptions. The question we must ask, I shall argue, is whether the prior voluntary act is the *same act* as the later prohibited conduct. Is going to a hypnotist *the same act* as entering a building at night with intent to commit a crime therein? The answer will depend on whether entering a building, etc., is just another description of the act the defendant performs when he visits the hypnotist. I argue that the 'redescriptive test', as I shall call it, solves the causation problem. While it does not entirely solve the definitional problem, it will provide a helpful framework for thinking about it.

A. The Causation Problem

The problem of contrived involuntariness is the most extreme version of a more general problem, namely the problem of defendants who culpably create the conditions of their own involuntariness. The most common form in which this problem arises in the law is where the defendant is aware of a risk that the involuntary condition will occur. Like cases of contrivance, courts typically deny the involuntariness in such cases. In *People v Decina*, for example, the court denied a lack of voluntariness defence to a defendant who killed four children when he suffered an epileptic seizure while driving.[5] The court found that the defendant was aware he suffered from epilepsy, and that his decision to drive under these circumstances deprived him of the ability to claim that killing the children was involuntary. It made clear, however, that matters would have been otherwise had Decina suffered an epileptic seizure for the first time: 'To have a sudden sleeping spell, an unexpected heart or other disabling attack, without any prior knowledge or warning thereof, is an altogether different situation, and there is simply no basis for comparing such cases with the flagrant disregard manifested here'.[6]

Cases like *Decina* have led scholars to charge that the criminal law's voluntariness requirement is arbitrary. In particular, they suggest that the outcome

---

[5]   138 NE 2d 799 (1956).

[6]   138 NE 2d 799, 804. The dissent thought Decina was entitled to the defence. It thought that Decina could not be guilty of recklessly operating a vehicle, because 'recklessness' refers to the manner or style of operating the vehicle, meaning an erratic and uncontrolled pattern of vehicle movements: 138 NE 2d 799, 807 (Desmond J concurring in part and dissenting in part). This argument is confused. There is no reason to suppose that driving cannot be controlled and still be reckless. For it might be that what makes the operation of a vehicle reckless is not the manner of driving prior to the seizure, but the fact of driving at all, given the defendant's knowledge that he is subject to epileptic seizures.

of the cases depends entirely on what 'time-frame' courts adopt.[7] If courts adopt a narrow time-frame, focusing only on the defendant's conduct at the time of the criminal violation, they will exonerate the defendant, since all they perceive is a person performing a criminal act in the grip of an involuntary condition. If, on the other hand, they adopt a broad time-frame, they will find the defendant liable, since they see a defendant engaged in conduct he intends or knows will eventually produce a prohibited result. The problem, these scholars argue, is that the choice of time-frame cannot be made in any principled way.[8]

According to Michael Moore, however, the criminal law has a response to this issue, and this response, he argues, is not subject to the time-framing problem at all. According to what Moore calls the 'orthodox approach', all that is necessary to solve the problem of anticipated involuntariness is the concurrence of act and mental state that the criminal law traditionally requires. In order to determine whether the defendant should have a lack of a voluntary act defence, we need only locate some voluntary act that causes the prohibited conduct, and then ask whether that act coincides with the requisite blameworthy mental state:

Every competent teacher of elementary criminal law that I know teaches the act requirement in the following way: if, from the big bang that apparently began this show to the heat death of the universe that will end it, the court can find a voluntary act by the defendant, accompanied *at that time* by whatever culpable *mens rea* that is required, which act in fact and proximately causes some legally prohibited state of affairs, then the defendant is prima facie liable for that legal harm.[9]

Moore's approach is roughly the same as an approach we find in German law to the more general problem of contrived defences. That problem, known as *actio libera in causa*,[10] is not just limited to the involuntariness defence. It applies equally to defendants who contrive defences like self-defence and necessity. In each case, the preferred solution is to look back to an earlier act of the defendant's by which he caused himself to have a defence.[11] Applying this strategy to involuntariness, Moore would say that the reason Decina is liable

[7] See Mark Kelman, 'Interpretive Construction in the Substantive Criminal Law' (1981) 33 Stanford LR 591, at 603 ff.; see also Larry Alexander, 'Reconsidering the Relationship Among Voluntary Acts, Strict Liability, and Negligence in Criminal Law' (1990) 7 *Social Philosophy and Policy* 84, at 90–96.

[8] Kelman (n. 7 above) 603.

[9] Michael Moore, *Act and Crime* (Oxford, 1993) 35–36.

[10] See Joachim Hruschka, 'Imputation' (1986) Brigham Young University LR 669; see also Miriam Gur-Arye, *Actio Libera in Causa in Criminal Law* (Jerusalem, 1984). The Germans distinguish contrived from recklessly anticipated conditions of defence. They reserve the term *actio libera in causa* for the former, and give the label *actio illicita in causa* to the latter.

[11] While American writers are mostly unaware of the *actio libera in causa* doctrine, some have made law-reform proposals that would duplicate its effects. See Paul Robinson, 'Causing the Conditions of One's Own Defense: A Study in the Limits of Theory in Criminal Law Doctrine' (1985) 71 Virginia LR 1. On the problem of contrived justifications and excuses generally, see Leo Katz, *Ill-Gotten Gains* (Chicago, 1987) Pt I.

for manslaughter is that he performed a voluntary act (driving), which proximately caused the deaths of the children, and his act coincided with a blameworthy mental state (recklessness).[12] Had Decina suffered an epileptic seizure
for the first time, Moore would allow Decina the defence, on the grounds that
he lacked the *mens rea* required for manslaughter. For Decina, then, unanticipated involuntariness would provide him with the basis for a lack of *mens
rea* defence.

But lack of voluntariness simply is not a *mens rea*-negating defence.[13] Instead, the defence negates the *actus reus* required for the crime. We know this
because lack of voluntariness is a defence to strict liability crimes, and these
have no mental state requirement. A defendant who coasts across a double
yellow line, asleep at the wheel, has a defence to the resulting traffic violation,
even though that offence contains no *mens rea* requirement.[14] Similarly, a defendant has a defence to disorderly conduct if he committed the disorderly
acts during an epileptic seizure, even if the offence requires no *mens rea*.[15]
The defence is also available where the defendant is behind the wheel of a car
whose brakes fail,[16] or where he is attacked by a swarm of bees while driving.[17] Lack of voluntariness is thus substantially different from defences like
mistake, extreme emotional disturbance, and insanity, which either apply to
the mental state with which a criminal act was performed, or supply normative excuses that deprive an intentional mental state of culpable effect.[18] The
orthodox approach, however, would end up treating involuntariness as on a
par with the above defences. As such, it is hard to see how it can extend the
defence to strict liability crimes.

Perhaps a better way to think about the problem is to see that making room
for strict liability would saddle the orthodox approach with an unacceptable
account of causation. Imagine that the crime with which Decina had been
charged were a strict liability homicide offence. Can we now grant Decina a
defence in the case in which he did not know he suffered from epilepsy under
the orthodox approach? Since in a strict liability case, there can be no mental
state by coincidence with which one can fix a time-frame, the only grounds on
which we could grant the defence would be to say that the seizure broke the
chain of causation. That is, we would have to say that his driving was *not* the
proximate cause of the deaths of the children.[19] But this solution would make

---

[12] The actual crime under consideration was negligent homicide, but the difference is unimportant for our purposes, since we can assume that had Decina suffered an epileptic seizure for
the first time, he would not have been negligent either.
[13] Courts have been responsible for a great deal of confusion on this point, sometimes saying
the defence defeats *mens rea* and sometimes saying that it defeats *actus reus*.
[14] *Cordwell v Carley* 1984 CLD 16739 (New So. Wales, S.C.).
[15] *People v Magnus* 155 NYS 1013 (1915).
[16] *State v Kremer* 114 NW 2d 88 (Minn. 1962).
[17] *Hill v Baxter* [1958] 1 QB 277.
[18] See Model Penal Code, Comment to s. 2.04(1).
[19] Moore would probably favour this approach, since it is his preferred solution to an actual
strict liability case, *Martin v State*: Moore (n. 9 above) 36–37. See discussion below.

the orthodox approach to causation inconsistent. For if Decina's epileptic seizure broke the chain of causation in the case in which he experiences a seizure for the first time, why would it not also do so where Decina was aware of a risk of seizure in advance? Surely causal chains cannot be established or broken depending on what the actor knew or intended. When we return to the original *Decina* statute requiring recklessness, moreover, the inconsistency is particularly striking. For Decina cannot be said to have proximately caused the deaths of the children, even assuming he was reckless, if he could not have done so in a strict liability case. If Decina would not be liable in the strict liability case, he cannot be liable in the original case either. So the only way the orthodox approach can avoid ending up with an inconsistent account of causation is to insist that the involuntariness defence negates only *mens rea*. And this would require the rejection of the line of cases in which the defence is allowed in strict liability crimes.

But let us back up a moment. Why *can't* causation vary with mental state? A detractor might make the following points. First, he might suggest that the traditional test for proximate cause—foreseeability—is itself mentalistic. The proposition here would be closely related to that test. Instead of saying that proximate cause depends on foreseeability, it would be the claim that proximate cause can sometimes turn on whether the defendant anticipated the harm. Secondly, the detractor might argue that in any event the notion of proximate cause is essentially a normative concept, one that is more about tracking a defendant's responsibility for an occurrence than about some sort of physical relation between himself and it. From this vantage point there would be no difficulty saying that the fact that the defendant intended the harm could make the difference to whether he proximately caused it. And indeed, how else would we account for principles such as 'intended consequences are never too remote'? Is it not generally assumed that intention can make a difference to causal relations? If we were to allow that proximate cause could vary with mental state, there would be no difficulty here. For we could simply say that whether or not Decina caused the children's deaths depends on whether he anticipated he would kill them. With anticipation, there is causation, and without it, there is none.

But there are good reasons to reject a mentalistic account of causation, and in particular, good reasons to reject the two points raised in its favour above. First, causation should never have been conceived in terms of foreseeability in the first place. The best reason for this has to do with strict liability. If proximate cause is understood in terms of foreseeability, then strict liability effectively becomes a negligence standard, since the notion of proximate cause applies to strict liability as well as to mental state crimes.[20] Secondly, the notion of proximate cause cannot have any independent meaning from mental state on this view. For if intending a harm can serve to establish that

---

[20] See generally H.L.A.Hart and Tony Honoré, *Causation in the Law* (Oxford, 1959) 95–108.

the defendant caused the harm, this would entail that 'intention' imparts all the information we need to hold the agent responsible. Since neither Moore nor I is prepared to dispense with causation as an independent concept, neither of us is prepared to accept the normative view of causation this approach would suggest. Slogans, then, like 'intended consequences are never too remote' simply cannot be accepted. Manifestly intended consequences *can* be too remote, such as when there is an intervening event that breaks the chain of causation. In what follows, I shall assume that it is problematic to think of causation as dependent on mental state, and I shall not argue the point further.

While Moore's brief discussion of voluntariness does not advert to the orthodox approach's difficulty with causation, his writings on causation show that he is aware of it. In 'Causation and Responsibility', Moore discusses what he calls the problem of 'contrived coincidences', namely the 'purposeful exploitation of a natural event coincidence'. Imagine a defendant who foresees that a strong wind will carry a roof to where it will injure a workman, and he wants to exploit that occurrence. The law treats such cases as ones in which what would normally be an intervening cause—the strong wind—no longer breaks the chain of causation. Yet, as Moore notes later on, this is problematic, because 'it cannot be the case that the very same storm is an intervening cause, or is not, depending on the state of mind of the defendant . . . [O]ur minds do not have these kinds of telekinetic powers'.[21] The same difficulty arises where the intervening cause is not an abnormal natural event, but the independent voluntary act of another human agent. Just as we want to deprive the defendant of a defence when he exploits an abnormal, natural event, so we will want to do the same where it is based on the intervening voluntary act of another agent, if the defendant plans in advance to take advantage of that act. The problem, then, is that if we do not allow proximate cause to be a function of the defendant's mental state, we will have to give up one or the other of these conclusions. We cannot say *both* that the defendant's acts are not the proximate cause of the harm where there is an intervening abnormal event or act, *and* that the defendant's acts are the proximate cause of the harm where the defendant exploits the intervening condition.

Moore concludes that 'we ought to say that the criteria for an intervening cause do not include contrivance by the defendant'. By this, he seems to mean that where the defendant would normally be considered the cause of a prohibited act or state of affairs, his conduct remains the cause, even if he brought the event about by exploiting an abnormal intervening factor or the independent act of another agent. Thus, if the defendant would normally be responsible for the death of the workman, he remains responsible even if he brought the death about by exploiting an abnormally strong wind that

---

[21] Moore, 'Causation and Responsibility' (1999) 16 *Social Philosophy & Policy* 1, at 30.

displaces a roof. As Moore says, 'th[e] contradiction is easily eliminated if we but seize one horn of the dilemma or the other in any given case'. That is, we must simply choose whether or not the abnormal event or the intervening act of another agent is sufficient to break the chain of causation. If we conclude that the intervening abnormal event or act *does* break the chain of causation, we would not be able to reinstate causation on the grounds that the defendant exploited the event or act. So if the strong wind was sufficient to break the chain of causation in the absence of contrivance, it will be sufficient to do so where there is contrivance as well.

In light of his discussion of contrived coincidences, we can assume that Moore's *considered* solution to the voluntary act problem would be that we must bite the bullet: either the defendant's prior conduct was the proximate cause of the harm or it was not, and it makes no difference to the inquiry if he contrived the involuntariness. If Decina caused the deaths of the children in the original case (the case where he was aware of his condition), he must have caused their deaths in the case in which he suffered an epileptic seizure for the first time. Presumably, then, Moore would also deny the lack of a voluntary act defence where the defendant coasts through a red light while having a seizure, since the seizure could not break the chain of causation in that case either. If Moore were to bring his account of voluntariness into line with his account of causation, he could avoid having to say that whether the prior voluntary act was the proximate cause of the prohibited result varies with the defendant's mental state. He would, however, avoid this difficulty at the cost of encountering two other important problems.

The first problem is that the orthodox approach will now require us to make a series of extremely fine distinctions among different possible intervening involuntary conditions, and I can see no principled basis for making these distinctions. For example, if we think *Decina* was correctly decided, we must also think that in general epileptic seizures do not break the chain of causation. But Moore does not appear to accept the proposition that involuntary conditions *never* break the chain of causation. For example, he wants to allow a defence in another case, *Martin v State*, on precisely these grounds.[22] In that case, police officers forcibly removed the defendant from his home while he was intoxicated and forced him to accompany police onto a public highway. Martin was then arrested for public drunkenness, to which he raised a lack of voluntariness defence. Moore thinks the act of the officers in dragging him onto the highway breaks the chain of causation.[23] We must ask: would Moore be happy with the results of his account in the case in which Martin *knew* the police were to appear at his doorstep at a particular time, and knew also that they would drag him onto the highway? Does the behaviour of the police still break the chain of causation if Martin intentionally

---

[22] 17 So. 2d 427 (1944).   [23] Moore (n. 9 above) 36–37.

got drunk in his living room *in order* to appear on the highway in an intoxicated condition? Moore will presumably stick to his claim that Martin's getting drunk in his living room was *not* the proximate cause of his appearing
drunk on the highway. But I find this conclusion troubling. For once again, it
is hard to see what distinguishes Martin's contrived involuntariness from
Decina's.[24]

In light of Moore's admission that cases of contrived causation require us
simply to 'seize' one horn of the dilemma or other, one might wonder how
effective the orthodox approach is at combatting the arbitrariness charge
we considered above. For while it would eliminate the need to stipulate a
time-frame, Moore would now be committed to having to stipulate which
intervening factors break the chain of causation and which do not. This stipulation is every bit as arbitrary as the time-frame stipulation. Indeed, I think
it *is* the time-frame stipulation in other guise. The arbitrariness is inherent in
any account that approaches the problem of voluntariness via the notion of
proximate cause.

Notice also that the orthodox approach will be highly revisionary with respect to existing law. In effect, it will always result in the rejection of one of
the results the cases standardly yield. Depending on whether the involuntary
condition is deemed to break the chain of causation, the orthodox approach-
will either abandon the standard treatment of contrivance the case law reflects, or it will abandon the standard treatment of strict liability crimes. If the
condition *does* break the chain of causation, as in *Martin*, then contrivance
will no longer inculpate. If the condition does *not* break the chain of causation, as in *Decina*, there will be no possible defence to strict liability crimes for
unanticipated involuntariness. Both seem problematic. To abandon the line
of cases that denies the defence to defendants who contrive or anticipate the
involuntary condition would surely be too lenient. Defendants would be able
to carry out serious offences without fear of penalty, if they could somehow
arrange to do so in an involuntary state. On the other hand, to abandon the
lack of voluntariness defence in cases of strict liability seems unduly harsh.
Should a person who runs a red light while suffering an epileptic seizure for
the first time really be guilty of a criminal offence? It is one thing to deny a defence to agents who perform a prohibited act accidentally, but quite another
to deny it to agents who perform no act of any kind.

It is important to notice that the problem we are discussing is not entirely
of the orthodox approach's making. It stems from the fact that there are two
apparently incompatible lines of cases that apply to the lack of voluntariness

---

[24] Perhaps the difference lies in the fact that Decina's seizure involved his own bodily movements, whereas the intervening cause in Martin's case was the act of another agent. But the same
agent/other agent distinction seems ad hoc, given that we often are liable for results where the
causal chain passes through another agent (as in some forms of accomplice liability). Moreover,
it seems harsh to hold agents liable for *everything* their bodies do, when many bodily movements
are not in any way the product of the 'effort or determination of the actor': MPC s. 2.01.

defence: the line that says that a defendant *loses* the defence based on contrivance, and the line that makes the defence available against strict liability crimes.[25] The latter means that the defence negates *actus reus*, and that is not consistent with saying that the defendant loses the defence on mental state grounds. It looks, then, as though we must either abandon the approach to contrivance and anticipation, and say that the defendant who contrives to commit a crime in an involuntary condition can still claim the defence, or we must abandon the defence in crimes of strict liability. If we attempt to account for both lines of cases, as the orthodox approach initially attempts to do, we find ourselves committed to what I have argued is an incoherent view of causation: the view that whether or not the defendant caused the prohibited conduct or result depends on whether he intended or anticipated that result. We may put the point, then, as a challenge: is there any way to understand the voluntariness requirement in criminal law that would allow us to retain both the contrivance and the strict liability lines of cases, without running afoul of basic principles of causation?

B. THE PROBLEM OF DEFINITION

In our discussion thus far, we have implicitly treated every crime as though it were what we call a 'result' crime, namely a crime with a causal element.[26] We have done this in order to consider the hypothesis that a defendant can be held liable for a prohibited act performed involuntarily if it was caused by a prior voluntary act. This strategy, we saw, is problematic because it makes it hard to think of contrivance on the defendant's part as inculpatory without adopting an incoherent account of causation. But there is a second difficulty with this strategy that has special force for crimes whose definitions do not contain a causal element, so-called 'conduct' crimes.

Consider a crime like burglary, which requires the defendant to 'enter . . . a building or occupied structure . . . with purpose to commit a crime therein'.[27] And suppose the defendant decides to visit a hypnotist in order to be placed in a trance and told to enter a jewellery store with a weapon, demanding to be handed over its riches.[28] In order to side-step the difficulty we considered in

---

[25] Alexander makes the point forcefully by saying that the tension is a structural conflict between two important principles of the criminal law—what he calls the strict liability principle and the voluntary act principle. See Alexander (n. 7 above); see also Ingrid Patient, 'Some Remarks About the Element of Voluntariness in Offences of Absolute Liability' [1968] Criminal LR 23.

[26] We have even somewhat misleadingly done this with *Martin* (n. 22 above), despite the fact that the case quite clearly involved a conduct crime.

[27] MPC s. 221.1 (1).

[28] In order to avoid problems of complicity, we should assume that the hypnotist is himself innocent with respect to the bank robbery. Let us say, for example, that he gives the hypnotized subject commands in German, at the subject's prior request, but does not himself understand the instructions and speaks no German.

the previous section, let us assume that the trance does not break the chain of causation. It should be clear that there is a second problem with the strategy of trying to locate the voluntariness of one act in an earlier voluntary act that caused it, a problem that has nothing to do with proximate cause. This is the problem of definition: visiting a hypnotist simply is not the same act as 'entering a building'. Thus, even if seeing a hypnotist is the proximate cause of entering a building, it is *not* entering a building in the relevant sense, and so does not satisfy the *actus reus* for burglary.

As we shall see, this 'definitional' problem turns out to be far more difficult than the problem with causation. The causation problem, I shall argue, disappears on the correct account of voluntary action, for it will turn out that agency is not in fact a causal notion after all. The definitional problem, by contrast, is implicit in the very idea of a prohibition: there is *something* specific the agent is prohibited from doing, and that is usually not the same as the act by which he causes himself to do the prohibited act. In other words, causing oneself to enter a building is not itself entering a building; causing oneself to alter a writing is not itself altering a writing; causing oneself to inflict injury is not itself inflicting injury.

Granted, the problem may seem to be limited to conduct crimes, since there is a way of thinking of result crimes that avoids the difficulty altogether. Suppose a murder statute makes it a crime to 'cause the death of another human being'. And suppose a man goes to see a hypnotist in order to be placed in a trance and receive a suggestion that he poison his wife's tea. Assuming once again that the trance does not break the chain of causation, it looks as though there is no problem here: seeing a hypnotist is an act the defendant performs whereby he 'causes' the death of his wife. The defendant can satisfy the *actus reus* for murder in this case by seeing the hypnotist. The later act of poisoning the tea is not required for the defendant to satisfy the definition of the prohibited act. At least at first blush, then, the problem is serious, but only for a segment of offence definitions, namely conduct crimes.

Moore notices the definitional problem in his recent work on causation, but he dusts over it lightly. In discussing the case of a defendant who induces an innocent agent to commit a crime, for example, he correctly says that the fact that the crime is committed through the agency of an innocent does *not* break the chain of causation. But he recognizes the 'linguistic oddity' of saying that a defendant can 'rape', 'hit', 'maim', or 'take' even though it is technically someone else who did the raping, hitting, maiming, or taking. That is, Moore has noticed that even if we allow that one person can sometimes cause another person to act without breaking the chain of causation, we have a further question about whether the defendant fits the definition of the crime. Arguably, a defendant cannot fit the definition if he commits the crime through the act of another agent. The same could be said of the case in which the defendant is his own innocent agent, where he arranges for himself to commit a crime while in the grip of an involuntary condition.

Moore's answer to this problem is that there is no reason to cleave to 'stereotypes' we have about how various criminal acts are performed: 'Just as one kills by causing death, so one rapes by causing penetration, one hits by causing contact, one maims by causing disfigurement, and one takes by causing movement of the object taken'.[29] But I think Moore moves too swiftly here. For how does a defendant who induces another, whether innocent or not, to burgle a house satisfy the offence definition of 'unlawfully entering a building . . ?' It is hardly just a stereotype that a person cannot *enter* a building without physically placing his body inside it. Moreover, the innocent agent doctrine, and accomplice liability more generally, should lead us to precisely the opposite conclusion from the one Moore reaches: if a defendant could satisfy the *actus reus* for a crime like burglary without physically entering the building himself, *we would not need accomplice liability provisions in the first place*. No criminal code, for example, would need a provision like Model Penal Code section 2.06, which establishes the liability of one agent for the conduct of another. If a defendant could burgle without entering a building, we could find a person liable for burglary when he sends another person into a building on his behalf without having to invoke a special provision called 'liability for the acts of another'.[30] Thus, far from being able to use the existence of accomplice liability as support for the claim that a person can satisfy the definitions of an offence without performing the prohibited conduct, accomplice liability shows that a statute's *actus reus* is a real requirement, one that cannot be satisfied metaphorically.

Moreover, notice that Moore's definitional move effectively turns every conduct crime into a result crime. If the *actus reus* of every conduct crime can be satisfied by a defendant who causes himself (or another) to commit that act, then it is as though every offence definition contains a causal element. While this *would* avoid the definitional problem, by eliminating conduct crimes altogether, it will only serve to exacerbate the causation problem. For every time a defendant causes himself to 'kill', 'penetrate', or 'take', the problem will arise whether the defendant's act was the proximate cause of the killing, penetration, or taking. What is gained on the definitional side appears to be lost on the causal side. Even apart from its implausibility, then, Moore's definitional solution does not particularly advance the defence of the orthodox approach.

There is a final wrinkle in setting out the definitional problem we should consider. I have said that causing oneself to enter a building is not itself entering a building, but causing oneself to cause a death, I suggested, is itself causing a death. On closer inspection, however, it is not entirely clear that this

---

[29] Moore (n. 21 above) 39.

[30] It might of course be the case that accomplice liability exists as a separate doctrine for other reasons, and not to solve this definitional problem. But I suspect this is not the case. The main reason to have accomplice liability provisions, it seems to me, is that the accomplice does not satisfy the definition of the offence on the basis of his own conduct.

is so, and thus it is not entirely clear that result crimes are immune to the definitional difficulty in the way we thought. It may turn out that there are cases of contrivance where one wants to find liability, but where voluntarily causing oneself to bring about a prohibited result does not mean that one brings about that result voluntarily. In other words, causing oneself to cause is not *always* causing, in criminal law terms. Consider again the person who sees a hypnotist in order to receive a suggestion that he kill his wife by putting poison in her tea. Suppose further that being in a hypnotic trance does not break the chain of causation. Does the visit to the hypnotist *cause* the death of the wife, in the relevant sense? Upon reflection, it is not clear it does. While the visit to the hypnotist is the 'but for' cause of the death, it is not the proximate cause. And visiting a hypnotist might fail to be the proximate cause of a person's death even if there is no intervening cause that breaks the chain of causation. It might simply be too remote or incidentally related to the resulting death, quite apart from the involuntary intervention.[31]

In order to see this more clearly, it might be helpful to consider whether the defendant would be guilty of an attempt on the basis of his visit to the hypnotist. For if the hypnotic trance does not break the chain of causation, the visit to the hypnotist ought to constitute a completed attempt, since the visit must then be the last act required on the defendant's part to cause death. After the visit to the hypnotist, the remaining events are all causal, including the acts performed involuntarily. But visiting a hypnotist would almost certainly be insufficient to constitute attempted murder on a completed attempt theory if the defendant husband never did end up putting the poison in his wife's tea. Visiting a hypnotist is simply too remotely related to the potential death of the victim, and too unlikely to result in death, to count as a last-step attempt. I even doubt that it would be sufficient grounds for an attempt on a substantial step test. Seeing a hypnotist in order to kill one's wife is a little like buying a ticket on a fledgling airline company for a person one hopes will die in a crash. Thus, even where the involuntary condition itself does not break the chain of causation, there is no reason to think that causing a person to cause is the same as causing. The definitional problem we noted with conduct crimes arguably applies to result crimes as well.

---

[31] Under the American Model Penal Code, for example, this would arguably be the case. See MPC s. 2.03. Someone might reject this example and claim that visiting a hypnotist is really *not* too remote from killing one's wife. There should, however, be other examples of cases in which causing oneself to cause is simply not the same as causing. Suppose a person causes himself to delight in burning things by taking a certain medication. The medication does not render him irresponsible; it simply increases his desire to set things around him on fire. He subsequently sets fire to a building. Did the act of taking the pill cause the building to burn? I would think not, despite the fact that by taking the pill, the agent caused himself to cause the building to burn.

C. Two Possible Solutions

Before proceeding to sketch an alternative way of thinking about voluntariness in the criminal law, I wish to consider two alternatives to the orthodox approach, both of which would, if successful, surmount the difficulties with causation and definition we have discussed. I shall argue that there are nevertheless good reasons to reject both.

1. The 'Causing-the-Conditions' Solution

The first alternative is a variation on the *actio libera in causa* approach, as suggested by Paul Robinson. Like the German doctrine, Robinson's approach treats the problem of contrived involuntariness as an instance of a larger problem, namely the problem of defendants who manufacture the conditions of their own defence.[32] Robinson's primary focus is on justifications that defendants cause themselves to have, particularly justifications defendants *culpably* cause themselves to have. The question is whether the person who culpably sets a forest fire solely in order to be entitled to burn a firebreak to protect a town may avail himself of the justification he would have without the contrivance for burning the firebreak. As Robinson points out, existing criminal codes vary widely in their approach to such cases, with some denying the defence altogether on the basis of even non-culpably caused conditions, and others making no provision for depriving a defence based on full contrivance. Robinson, for his part, thinks the right approach is to grant the defence, irrespective of contrivance, but then to hold the defendant liable at the level of his culpability at the time of the earlier voluntary act:

> Where the actor is not only culpable as to causing the defense conditions, but also has a culpable state of mind *as to causing himself to engage in the conduct constituting the offense*, the state should be [sic] punish him for causing the ultimate justified or excused conduct. His punishment, however, is properly based on his initial conduct of causing the defense conditions with his accompanying scheming intention, not on the justified or excused conduct that he subsequently performs.[33]

Robinson, in short, suggests that the defendant who sets the forest fire *may* still avail himself of the lesser evils defence, despite the fact that he arranged for it in advance. But the defendant is nevertheless punishable on the basis of his earlier, culpable conduct, since he did something that he intended would require him to burn a firebreak, and *that* is not justified. This approach has the advantage of allowing us to tailor the defendant's liability to his actual culpability: if the defendant intentionally created the conditions that he knew would require him to burn a firebreak, we can hold him liable for a crime of intention or knowledge. If the defendant had instead been negligent with

---

[32] Robinson (n. 11 above) 1.   [33] ibid. at 31 (emphasis in original, citations omitted).

respect to that risk when he performed the earlier act, he can be held liable for a crime whose *actus reus* is satisfied by burning the firebreak and whose *mens rea* is negligence.

Robinson calls his solution the 'causing-the-conditions' approach to culpably caused defences. It effectively solves the problem by rejecting the concurrency requirement of the orthodox approach: it takes the *mens rea* from the earlier non-criminal act and links it to the *actus reus* performed innocently at a later time. In theory, it differs from Moore's approach because Moore retains concurrency. But the two views end up with the same results, an indirect product of the expansive view Moore takes on the second of the two problems we considered, the definitional question. About *Decina*, for example, Robinson would say that Decina retains the involuntariness defence, despite the fact that he caused the conditions of that defence. He can be held liable, however, because he performed the required prohibited act—causing a death—and he had the requisite mental state for manslaughter. To determine the *actus reus* element, Robinson is willing to accept the later, involuntary conduct, as long as the defendant also created the conditions that caused him to engage in this conduct. Moore would reach the same result, except that he would insist that the *actus reus* be satisfied on the basis of the act Decina performed at the earlier moment in time—the time at which he was reckless. Both accounts would hold Decina liable. If one would normally expect to see a difference between Robinson's and Moore's accounts in conduct crimes. For example, in the case in which I have myself hypnotized to burgle a house, Robinson would say that I may avail myself of hypnotism as a defence to the burglary, but that I am guilty on the basis of my earlier contrivance. He is willing to find me guilty on the basis of my earlier mental state, along with my involuntary act of entering a building. Since Moore restricts himself to the earlier act, one would expect him to find no liability in this case, since seeing a hypnotist should not satisfy the *actus reus* of burglary. But Moore is willing to stretch the definition of offences in conduct crimes and say that a person who causes himself to enter a building can satisfy an act requirement of 'entering a building'. The two accounts therefore give the same results in conduct crimes as well.

Another difference between Robinson's and Moore's accounts is also ultimately only superficial. Unlike Moore, Robinson reaches his results by stipulation, namely by adding a separate basis for liability to existing criminal codes. Robinson's provision would say that a defendant who creates the conditions of his own defence does not thereby forfeit the defence: if the defendant created the conditions of a justification his illegal conduct is justified, and if he created the conditions of an excuse, he is excused.[34] It would then provide:

---

[34] Robinson (n. 11 above) at 50–51.

An actor is guilty of an offense if, when acting with the culpability required by the offense definition, he causes the circumstances that justify his [or another's] engaging in the conduct that constitutes the offense or causes the conditions that excuse himself [or another] for engaging in the conduct that constitutes the offense, and he [or such other person] engages in the conduct constituting the offense.[35]

In other words, just as in the firebreak case, Robinson simply stipulates that where a contrived excuse is concerned, the defendant 'may properly be held liable for the ultimate offense on the basis of his causing the excused conduct and his accompanying culpable state of mind with respect to his commission of the ultimate offense'.[36] Now, this second divergence from Moore does make something of a difference with regard to our two problems, for this move seems to allow Robinson to avoid both the causation and the definitional problems we saw on the orthodox approach. First, with regard to causation, it is not necessary on Robinson's account to consider whether the intervening voluntary condition breaks the chain of causation, since the liability Robinson establishes is not causal. While it *is* important for Robinson that the agent cause the condition that provides his justification or excuse, it does not seem to matter whether that condition itself defeats the further causal relation between the agent's conduct and the prohibited act or result. Instead of explaining the defence of a defendant who suffers an epileptic seizure for the first time and thereby violates a criminal statute by saying that the seizure breaks the chain of causation, Robinson would give such a defendant an excuse on normative grounds: the *actus reus* of whatever offence he commits may be satisfied, but the defendant has a defence based on lack of culpability.

Secondly, the stipulative aspect of Robinson's account would probably also mean that he is impervious to the problem of definition: he simply proposes a new statutory provision as the basis for liability. In this regard, it is as though Robinson had solved the definitional problem by drafting a new offence. His provision has the same effect it would if we simply rewrote the definition of burglary to make a defendant guilty of burglary if he 'entered or caused himself to enter a building'. This solution to the definitional problem comes full circle with Moore's solution: Robinson suggests drafting a provision to accomplish what Moore thinks is already implicit in the language in which offence definitions are presently couched. But by drafting a new provision, Robinson avoids making the implausible claim that Moore does, namely that 'causing oneself to take' is conceptually the same as 'taking', and that 'causing oneself to rape' is the same as 'raping'.

It is important to see, however, that Robinson has only superficially avoided the problems with Moore's account. For the causation and definitional problems will crop up in other forms. The causation problem will appear when we go back to strict liability crimes. Suppose once again that Decina had been charged with a strict liability homicide offence. It would

---

[35] ibid. at 50.

seem to follow that if Decina innocently got in his car and drove, sub-sequently having a seizure for the first time, he would be guilty of homicide on the 'causing-the-conditions' analysis. After all, did he not cause the condition of his involuntariness defence by getting in his car and driving—precisely as he would have on Robinson's account if he had been negligent or reckless? Robinson will probably want to deny that Decina would have caused the con-ditions of his own defence in this case. But on what basis can he do so? It would be ad hoc to say that a person only causes the conditions of his own defence when he is culpable in some way, since the analysis is supposed to be separate from *mens rea*. So, once again, the problem with arbitrariness and causation we saw on Moore's account will reappear in Robinson's account in the question of when a person has *caused* the conditions of his own defence.

Secondly, where the problem of definition is concerned in particular, there is reason to think that the difficulties have only been brushed under the rug. For even if Robinson's approach achieves the desired outcome, this result is achieved on the basis of stipulation, rather than on the basis of existing doctrine. Indeed, notice that Robinson actually loses something to Moore by suggesting an entirely new provision to reach this result, since that seems to affirm that we cannot presently hold an agent liable for illegal conduct engaged in on the basis of contrived or anticipated involuntariness (a suggestion Moore would reject). Because I suspect that the legal cases of contrived involuntariness reflect a more fundamental moral problem with the notion of voluntariness, I do not think we can truly solve the problem by legislative fiat. Unfortunately we cannot solve moral difficulties by just drafting a new 'morality' provision.

Finally, while I shall not explore the matter here in any detail, someone might want to question whether the causing-the-conditions approach is even correct for justifications. Should a person who joins the police force hoping to have a chance to kill on valid law-enforcement grounds be guilty of murder on the basis of his culpable mental state in combination with his later prohib-ited act?[37] Should a person who intentionally enters a bad neighbourhood hoping for the opportunity to kill someone in self-defence be guilty of murder when he does? Allowing liability for later, prohibited conduct to be based on earlier conduct (i.e. rejecting concurrency) in the way that the causing-the-conditions analysis does creates a significant expansion of liability for what is on the face of it wholly legal conduct. Because Moore ultimately reaches the same results (albeit by a different route), this may be a drawback of his approach as well.

2. Treating a Person as His Own Accomplice

A second alternative to the orthodox approach would handle the problem of contrived involuntariness by making use of accomplice liability. We might

---

[36] Robinson (n. 11 above) at 33.   [37] I am indebted to Leo Katz for this example.

think of the person who arranges to commit a crime while in a trance as analogous to someone who hires another to burgle or kill for him, with the difference that the person who actually commits the criminal act is the defendant himself. Instead of two separate people, we just have one person in two very different states of mind. Moore himself makes a suggestion along these lines. Referring to the earlier example of the person who wants to take advantage of the storm that blows a roof off a house and onto a workman, he says that it should be 'enough for liability' that 'one has made it easier . . . for the storm to cause its harm, and one has done so with the specific intent that this happen'.[38] Moore suggests the move to accomplice liability because it is 'non-causal' in the relevant sense. If a person can be his own accomplice, it will not matter if his plan involves an involuntary act that breaks the chain of causation; the principal's act always breaks the causal link between the accomplice's conduct and the prohibited result, assuming that the principal is not an innocent agent. By invoking accomplice liability, we eliminate causation altogether.

There are, however, several problems with this suggestion. First, in a normal case of accomplice liability, the principal is also responsible for the crime. In the case of contrived involuntariness, however, we want to hold the 'accomplice' liable precisely because the 'principal' is not himself a responsible agent. Secondly, as Moore himself admits, arguably non-causal liability should only be available where the defendant *intends* the harm. In accomplice liability, for example, Moore says that 'we can relax our normal causation requirement . . . only because of the high level of culpability with which the aider acts'.[39] Thus Moore's suggestion would treat cases of contrivance differently from cases of anticipation like *Decina*. For defendants like Decina, Moore is in agreement that we cannot determine whether the involuntary condition is an intervening cause by looking at the defendant's prior mental state. Turning to accomplice liability to find a non-causal basis for liability would not entirely solve the problem even if successful, since it would not cover the range of cases we need it to cover.

There is, however, a version of Moore's appeal to accomplice liability that may be more helpful here. The form of accomplice liability where the principal is an innocent agent, such as a child or an insane person, may capture the contrived and anticipated involuntariness cases better than the ordinary accomplice doctrine.[40] First, many innocent agents are not responsible for their own conduct, and that is particularly why we must be able to hold the accomplice liable. Secondly, innocent agent liability does not require the accomplice to have the *mens rea* of intent. A person who arranges for a child or an insane person to commit a crime is as guilty of the crime as he would be had it been committed by his own hand. But a person who is merely aware that

---

[38] Moore (n. 21 above) 30.　　　　　　　　[39] ibid.
[40] I am here concerned with the paradigm case of the innocent agent—the irresponsible agent. Not all innocent agents are irresponsible, however.

a child will commit a crime, where he is responsible for the behaviour of the child, can be held liable for that crime at a level of culpability that matches his mental state.[41] The parent who is aware of a risk that his child will commit a criminal act may be liable for a crime of recklessness on the basis of the child's behaviour. Unlike ordinary accomplice liability, the innocent agent becomes an extension of the defendant's will.[42] Thirdly, innocent agent liability is *causal*: the intervening act of the innocent agent is not thought to break the chain of causation. If we think of a defendant who contrives his own involuntariness defence as an accomplice to an innocent agent, we would not need to worry that the involuntary act broke the chain of causation. And under this approach, we would still avoid the definitional problem we would face with ordinary principal liability. Liability for defendants who procure innocent agents to commit crimes is not based on the offence definitions themselves, but on separate accomplice liability provisions that create a basis for liability for the accomplice. Thus we would not lose the central advantage we might have hoped to gain by turning to accomplice liability in this context.

There are, however, a number of difficulties associated with thinking of a person as his own innocent agent. First, it is not clear that the innocent agent doctrine fits cases of contrived involuntariness very well, for precisely one of the reasons mentioned as a *benefit* above, namely that the innocent agent doctrine is causal. If we wish to maintain that involuntary conditions sometimes break the chain of causation, then we *do* ultimately need to find a basis for liability that is non-causal in order to hold people liable who contrive their defences. Secondly, the innocent agent doctrine seems unduly broad if it allows a defendant to be convicted for the conduct of an innocent agent on the basis of a lower *mens rea* than purpose or intent. In particular, holding a defendant liable for conduct he merely suspects the innocent agent will engage in is tantamount to imposing an extensive duty to rescue on defendants who learn of innocent agents who inflict harm. True, a person must have a special relationship to an innocent agent in order to be responsible for his actions. But, apart from mental state, those requirements do not seem terribly robust.[43] The natural response would be to restrict the *mens rea* for accomplices to purpose or intent. But in this context that would be problematic, since it would create an asymmetry between cases of contrived involuntariness and cases of merely anticipated involuntariness.

---

[41] See MPC s. 2.06(2): 'A person is legally accountable for the conduct of another person when: (a) acting with the kind of culpability that is sufficient for the commission of the offense, he causes an innocent or irresponsible person to engage in such conduct'.

[42] The Model Penal Code holds a defendant liable for the behaviour of an innocent agent that he causes, as long as the defendant is 'legally accountable' for the innocent agent: MPC s. 2.06(1), (2)(a).

[43] This difficulty is admittedly not specific to the innocent agent solution. Indeed, in the context of self-induced irresponsibility, the duty to rescue is arguably more palatable than it would be in an ordinary case of accomplice liability across persons, because at least here the defendant would have caused the harm to the victim in his role as innocent agent. Nevertheless, it remains an objection to the innocent agent approach.

We have explored two different approaches to the lack of a voluntary act defence that purport to avoid the problems with causation and definition we saw on the orthodox approach: first, an account that would treat lack of voluntariness as analogous to a culpably caused justification and, secondly, an account that would treat the defendant as his own innocent agent. Both approaches are problematic, as we have seen. Like these two accounts, the solution I shall present in section D seeks to avoid making the availability of the lack of voluntariness defence hinge on whether we say that the involuntary condition breaks the chain of causation. The greater difficulty will be the definitional hurdle—how to find that a defendant satisfies an offence definition on the basis of prior non-criminal conduct that causes it.

D. THE REDESCRIPTIVE TEST

According to the prevailing account of action in the philosophical literature, an action is a type of event, and events are 'particulars', meaning that they are individual items or unrepeatable things, identifiable by phrases like 'the accident that occurred on the Bay Bridge at four o'clock yesterday'. Like other particulars, such as chairs and tables, events can be described in many ways, depending on which of their various aspects enter into the description.[44] I might describe the chair on which I am sitting as a black leather object commonly found in offices, or an item to accompany a desk, or in any number of other ways, depending on its various attributes. Similarly, events can be described in terms of *their* attributes, such as the time or the place of their occurrence. A solar eclipse might be described as the event that occurred at two o'clock, or the event that was visible from such-and-such location, or the event that caused the sun's light temporarily to disappear, and so on.

Now actions can be picked out from other events by a particular feature they have: every action has at least one true description under which it is something someone did *intentionally*. For example, I might back down my driveway and run over the newspaper lying in the way. 'Running over the newspaper' is one way of describing the action I perform, but it is not the description under which my action is intentional. 'Backing down my driveway', 'releasing my foot from the brake pedal', and other descriptions do pick out things I intended to do. They consequently yield descriptions under which my action is intentional. Generally, then, we can say that an event is an action as long as there is a description of it under which it is an agent's doing something intentionally.[45]

---

[44] Jennifer Hornsby, 'On What's Intentionally Done', in Stephen Shute *et al.* (eds.), *Action, Value and Criminal Law* (Oxford, 1993) 55, 56–57. See also Donald Davidson, 'Agency', in *Essays on Actions & Events* (Oxford, 1980) 42, 55–58.

[45] This test for the identity of actions is the dominant one among philosophers, and I fully subscribe to it for present purposes.

How, then, does this framework apply to the kinds of bodily movements a person makes in her sleep or while suffering an epileptic seizure? The question is whether there is a description under which such movements can be understood as intentional. Clearly there cannot be. At the moment that the agent suffers an epileptic seizure, there is nothing she is trying to do, no purpose her movements seek to fulfil. We can now see that the expression 'involuntary action' is confused: the movements of a person experiencing an involuntary condition, like epilepsy, are not intentional under any description, and consequently they cannot be regarded as actions of any sort. This should also help clarify why I have been insisting that we cannot treat lack of voluntariness as a *mens rea* defence: to say that the person has a mental state defence *presupposes* that what she does is an action, and that would mean that there is a way of describing the defendant's behaviour under which it is something she did intentionally. Where movements performed in the grip of an involuntary condition are concerned, however, there is no possible intentional description, and thus there is no action and no prohibited action (*actus reus*) either.

Now that we have clarified the notion of voluntariness, the problem of contrived or anticipated involuntariness can also be usefully clarified. Suppose a person performs a voluntary act—visiting a hypnotist—for the purpose of committing a crime later while in an involuntary state—poisoning his wife's tea while in a trance. The question we must ask is whether the prohibited conduct, 'causing the death of another human being', is one description of the action the defendant performed at the earlier time. The question, in other words, is whether the act describable as 'seeing a hypnotist' can also be described as 'causing the death of another human being'. If so, the defendant killed voluntarily, since killing is one description of an action the defendant performed. If not, the defendant did not kill voluntarily, since 'killing' does not identify an event that has a description under which it was something done intentionally. The question, then, is how we decide whether visiting a hypnotist can be described as 'killing', when it leads to a person's death.

Here is the standard answer in the philosophy of action. A moves his index finger on a particular occasion, with the result that a gun he is holding fires, causing the death of a person he was targeting, and frightening a squirrel. The action of A's moving his finger can be redescribed in terms of each one of these consequences, respectively: A *fires a gun, kills a human being,* and *frightens a squirrel.* In describing each consequence of a person's action as something the agent *does*, we have eliminated the causal element from our description. Thus instead of causing the gun to fire, the agent can be said to have *fired* the gun. By describing an action in terms of its consequences, we expand the actor's agency. Joel Feinberg once called this phenomenon the 'accordion effect': the further down the chain of consequences we move in describing a person's act, the further we pull the accordion. In this way, we extend the scope of a person's agency to encompass the consequences of his action.

How far does a person's agency extend? Can it be extended to cover *all* of the consequences of a person's action? Philosophers writing on this topic have traditionally assumed so: they have written as though an action can be redescribed in terms of any state of affairs the action helps to produce.[46] If we take this view, then seeing the hypnotist would surely be 'causing the death of another human being', in the sense the murder statutes require, as long as seeing the hypnotist helped to produce the death. But we cannot accept this conclusion for purposes of criminal liability, since it casts the net of agency too broadly. To put the point in causal terms, it captures only (roughly) the notion of 'actual' or 'but for' causation. It does not capture the property that the further requirement of 'proximate cause' is meant to capture. Any causal term in an offence definition will normally be thought to imply the latter, and not just the former.

It should not, however, be necessary to add the rather imprecise requirement of proximate cause to this picture. For we can reach the same result on grounds of redescription alone. Roughly where the lawyer wants to say 'no proximate cause', the philosopher should notice that the redescription of an action in terms of its consequence seems to fail. Consider the following examples. Conceiving a child will (eventually) result in the child's death, but we would not want to describe it as 'killing the child'. Firing an employee may cause his minor children to starve to death. But we would not normally describe the act of firing the employee as 'starving some children to death'. Giving a depressed person a gun may result in the latter's death. But unless one wants to be rhetorical, it would be odd to describe the act of giving the gun as an act of 'killing'.[47] Contrary to what philosophers of action tend to think, then, agency does not spread from an act to *all* of its consequences, since we cannot *describe* an act in terms of all of its consequences. If a consequence of an act is just some state of affairs produced by it, then we must conclude that some of the consequences of an action are simply beyond agency's reach.

The phenomenon we have been observing seems fundamental, and yet action theorists appear to have overlooked it. It is that limitations on our own responsibility are built into the linguistic expressions we use to capture agency—the same limitations the notion of proximate cause is meant to capture. When we translate impersonal causal statements into statements of agency, we can see that the latter fail to track. Agency simply is not reliably spread along (necessary) causal lines. The result is that in any case in which we have a sequence of events, each of which is a necessary cause of the next, we will sometimes want

---

[46] Donald Davidson, 'Actions, Reasons and Causes', *Essays on Actions and Events* (Oxford, 1980) 3. I am leaving overdetermination cases to one side, where matters are vastly more complicated.

[47] Of course, there is a trivial sense in which we can redescribe an act in terms of each one of its consequences: we can simply describe it as the action that produced *that consequence*. But that is not the sort of description that spreads agency in the relevant sense, and so is not what philosophers mean when they speak of redescription as the mark of agency.

to divide that sequence up into different redescriptive segments.[48] In the cases in which causal relations do not translate into agentive relations, there appears to be a break, such that while redescription is possible on the near side of the break, we cannot redescribe in the relevant way across it. Rather than scrutinizing the obscure notion of proximate cause in order to determine whether an involuntary condition impairs responsibility, we can address the question of agency more directly. We can determine whether a defendant's voluntary performance of an earlier act is sufficient to make his performance of the later, prohibited act it causes voluntary by asking whether the earlier act can be redescribed in terms of the later one. The cases in which it can are the ones in which the performance of the prior act *is* sufficient to make the latter act voluntary. The cases in which it cannot are the ones in which the performance of the prior act is not sufficient.

Let me be clear about what the redescriptive account does and does not do. First what it *does not* do. Understanding the lack of a voluntary act defence in terms of failures of redescription does not give us any new substantive grounds for determining when the voluntariness of the earlier act carries over to the later. I am prepared to allow that something like Hart and Honoré's criteria for determining when an intervening cause breaks the chain of causation will also determine when redescription succeeds or fails: it may fail in those cases involving a wrongful intervening act of another agent, as well as where the intervening factor is an abnormal event or 'coincidence'.[49] So it is not intended to provide a new, substantive test for sorting the cases into the categories of 'liability' and 'no liability'.

What it *does* do, however, is to provide an explanation for the way we already do sort the cases. In particular, it allows us to explain why at least some of the problems we saw on the orthodox approach do not threaten to make the voluntariness requirement in criminal law entirely arbitrary, as the critics warn. On the orthodox approach, we saw that if we wish to retain both the treatment of contrivance and that of strict liability the case law reflects, we would have to say that whether the defendant's action was the cause of the prohibited harm may depend on his prior mental state. This is deeply problematic. But if we think of the relation that is broken as *agentive*, rather than *causal*, the cases may look less puzzling. For we can then say that the wrongful act of another agent or an abnormal intervening event prevents the defendant's agency from spreading from his prior voluntary act to the act prohibited by law. There is no problem with causation, since the only causal notion we require is 'but for' causation, and that is present in all the cases.

---

[48] Once again, I am here ignoring the problem of overdetermination, and simply assuming that the preliminary causal notion is 'but for' causation. Ultimately we would have to refine the underlying causal story to take such cases into account.

[49] See H.L.A. Hart and Tony Honoré, *Causation in the Law* (Oxford, 1989) 68 ff. Moore modifies Hart and Honoré's account in various respects, but these alterations are not relevant for our purposes.

In this way, we can reconcile the various cases without having to say that in one case Decina's driving is not the proximate cause of the childrens' deaths and in the other case it is. In both cases, Decina's driving is the 'but for' cause of the deaths. But in one case, the driving constitutes Decina's killing the children and in the other case it does not, given that in one case we can redescribe Decina's driving as *killing* and in the other case we cannot. On the face of it, we need not think it impossible that the two cases should differ as a function of Decina's mental state. For Decina's advance knowledge of his condition might plausibly make a difference to whether his agency spreads from driving to killing. We are thus able to retain the law's existing approach to contrivance and strict liability, without having to choose between them for each involuntary condition.

Let us now turn to the second problem we discussed, the definitional problem, and ask whether the redescriptive test allows us to make any headway here. Casting the problem in terms of redescription, instead of causation, helps make clearer the nature of the difficulty. Unfortunately, however, I do not think it will take us all the way to a solution. Indeed, it seems to drive home just how hard a problem it really is. Suppose a statute defines theft as follows: 'A person is guilty of theft if he unlawfully takes, or exercises unlawful control over, movable property of another with purpose to deprive him thereof'.[50] The voluntariness requirement as applied to this crime means that the defendant must *take or exercise control over* movable property voluntarily. Now suppose a person goes to a hypnotist and has himself programmed to take someone else's property. The question with which we have been grappling is whether the defendant's voluntary act of visiting the hypnotist is sufficient to allow us to say that he voluntarily 'takes or exercises unlawful control over' the property of another. To put the problem in terms of redescription, the question is whether seeing a hypnotist can be redescribed as *taking the jewellery*. It seems difficult to locate the defendant's satisfaction of the *actus reus* in the performance of the earlier act. For it seems implausible to say that *seeing a hypnotist* is *taking movable property*.

I think it may be correct to suppose that if the defendant hypnotizes an innocent agent to take the jewellery, we might allow that the defendant has 'taken' it when the hypnotized agent removes it from its owner. The verb 'to take' is at least somewhat flexible with regard to the manner in which a person engages in it. And arguably one might extend this to cover ordinary accomplice cases. The person who engages another person to take jewellery has arguably 'taken' the jewellery when the jewellery is taken by his associate. But this does not seem to solve the hypnotist case. For even if someone else's taking the jewellery can constitute *my* taking it, seeing a hypnotist (or even hypnotizing oneself) cannot. What makes us comfortable saying that the defendant has *taken* jewellery when someone he has commissioned takes it, is

---

[50] MPC s. 223.2(1).

that that other agent has taken it. That is, we can say the defendant engages in *taking* because his taking is parasitic on someone else's taking. The latter's act is an extension of his will. (Ironically, then, for certain verbs like 'take', it might be that a defendant can satisfy the *actus reus* without physically himself satisfying its requirements. For these offences, then, accomplice liability provisions would be redundant.) But where the 'taking' is done in a trance, there seems to be no taking at all by anyone. We cannot establish liability without special provisions. For we still need a way to say that a person voluntarily takes jewellery in virtue of having himself voluntarily programmed through hypnosis to take it, since the defendant's act of seeing a hypnotist does not itself satisfy the offence definition.

The redescriptive test allows us to see more clearly why there is a problem here, and in particular, why the problem is not limited to conduct crimes. A minimum condition for redescribing an act as one of *taking* property is that the time and place at which the act is performed are also the time and place at which the property is taken. Let us focus for the moment only on time. The time at which the defendant visits the hypnotist and the time at which the property is taken are not the same. The property is only taken after the visit to the hypnotist occurs, namely when the defendant removes it from its owner in his hypnotized state. Now compare this with a result crime. In a result crime like homicide, a time-lag between act and result *seems* to be less problematic for purposes of redescription. A person can poison another, thereby killing him, even if the latter does not die until a week after the poisoning. It is not hard to accept that the act whereby the man poisons his wife is the act whereby he kills her, even though the latter description does not emerge until she dies. But the accordion cannot be infinitely stretched to the left: if a man goes to a hypnotist to receive a suggestion that he poison his wife's tea, his act of seeing the hypnotist is *not* redescribable as an act of killing. Seeing the hypnotist is the act whereby he causes himself to perform the act whereby he kills her. The act whereby he kills her is still the act he performs when he poisons her tea.

The question still remains, then, whether the man poisons his wife's tea voluntarily when he does so in a trance. On the one hand, we probably want to say that in the case in which he has himself hypnotized to put poison in his wife's tea, he does poison her tea, and hence kills her, voluntarily. And I think we should say this, even though were someone else to decide to put him into a trance and cause him to put poison in his wife's tea, he would not have done so voluntarily. On the other hand, we probably also want to say that the moment at which he kills her is the moment at which he puts the poison in the tea, not the moment at which he visits the hypnotist. So what we *want* to be able to say is that he killed voluntarily on the basis of putting poison in the tea in an involuntary state. The problem is that we have no way of explaining how this could be so, given that at the moment that he poisons the tea he performs no action. The same goes for the contrivance version of Mrs Cogdon.

We want, on the one hand, to say that she killed her daughter voluntarily if she contrived to do so in her sleep. But she does this at the moment she brings the axe down on her daughter's head, and not a moment before. It is not clear, then, how we can say she killed voluntarily, given that at the time she wielded the axe, she was sound asleep. Similarly, I suspect that the person who has himself hypnotized to burgle *does* enter a building voluntarily. But he does this at the moment at which he enters the building, despite the fact that he is in a trance, and *not* at the moment at which he has himself hypnotized. Nevertheless, we have no easy way of understanding how this can be so, given that the defendant's seeing the hypnotist cannot be redescribed as his entering the building, and given that normally a person does not perform voluntary acts while in a trance. The causation problem may be surmounted, but the definitional puzzle, as far as I can tell, remains intact.

8

Knowledge and Belief in the Criminal Law

STEPHEN SHUTE*

Academic interest in the general part of the criminal law has deep roots. So far as Anglo-American scholarship is concerned it dates at least as far back as the first edition of Glanville Williams' ground-breaking monograph *Criminal Law: The General Part*, and probably well beyond that.[1] Yet, despite this long and illustrious pedigree, much of the analysis has centred on a limited set of doctrines. This is particularly true of discussion of the definitional general part, i.e. that part of the criminal law that specifies *how* crimes are to be defined.[2] Here a great deal of ink has been spilt on the structure and scope of the (so-called) 'general defences' of insanity, mistake, intoxication, diminished responsibility, provocation, self-defence, duress and necessity;[3] on the *mens rea* concepts of intention, recklessness and dishonesty; and on causation. But comparatively little attention has been paid to other aspects of the definitional general part. Two doctrines, in particular, have escaped detailed examination: they are the *mens rea* concepts of knowledge and belief. None of the major criminal law textbooks allots more than a page or two of text to these concepts, and coverage in the legal journals is equally sparse.[4] The purpose of this chapter is to move some way towards redressing that imbalance.

* A first draft of this chapter was presented at a conference on 'Criminal Law: Doctrines of The General Part' held at the University of Birmingham. Later drafts were read at seminars at the Universities of Nottingham and Aberdeen. The author would like to thank those who attended these events for their comments. Thanks are also due to Antony Duff, John Gardner, Jennifer Hornsby, Sally Lloyd-Bostock, Andrew Simester, J.C. Smith and Gordon Woodman, each of whom provided very helpful written comments on the chapter, and to Ralph Cunnington and Michael Kozlarek for their research assistance.

[1] (London, 1953). C.S. Kenny's *Outlines of Criminal Law*, first published in 1902 by Cambridge University Press, is arguably also an exploration of the general part.

[2] John Gardner helpfully distinguishes between the definitional general part and other aspects of the general part (in particular 'the auxiliary general part' and the 'supervisory general part') in his article 'On the General Part of the Criminal Law', in Antony Duff (ed.), *Philosophy and the Criminal Law* (Cambridge, 1998).

[3] Not all these doctrines are properly categorized as defences, let alone 'general defences'. Sanity, for example, is best seen as a precondition for responsibility, and mistake is often just a denial of *mens rea*.

[4] A notable exception is Edward Griew, 'Consistency, Communication and Codification: Reflections on Two *Mens Rea* Words', in P.R. Glazebrook (ed.), *Reshaping the Criminal Law: Essays*

There is a sense, of course, in which the terms knowledge and belief are 'ambiguous'.[5] Used in one way they refer to the psychological states of knowing or believing; used in another way they refer more narrowly to the content of what is known or believed. The focus in this chapter will largely be on the first of these usages—on knowledge and belief as psychological states. The chapter is divided into three sections. The first examines the extent to which the concepts of knowledge and belief are relied upon in the modern criminal law. The second explores our non-legal understandings of the concepts of knowledge and belief. The third compares these non-legal understandings with the ways in which judges and draftsmen have used the concepts. It also reflects upon some long-standing legal conundrums, such as the structure and role of the so-called 'wilful blindness' doctrine, and the proper relationship between knowledge and belief, on the one hand, and the related concepts of acceptance and suspicion, on the other.

A. The Prevalence of Knowledge and Belief as Doctrines of the Definitional General Part

One might easily conclude from the amount of space devoted to knowledge and belief by academic writers that neither concept has a substantial role to play in Anglo-American criminal law. Yet each does. There are, in fact, two broad ways in which the doctrines are used: first, as important *mens rea* terms in their own right ('direct usage');[6] secondly, as basic building blocks out of which more complex *mens rea* terms are constructed ('indirect usage').[7]

1. Direct Usage

When incorporated directly into the definition of an offence, the concepts of knowledge and belief are used to mark out those actions that the criminal law deems sufficiently base to warrant criminalization from those actions that it does not. Sometimes it is felt that this goal can best be achieved by coupling knowledge and belief together as alternatives. The best known example of an offence with this structure in English law is handling stolen goods, the definition

in *Honour of Glanville Williams* (London, 1978), where Griew offers some reflections on the meaning of 'recklessness' and 'belief'. See also Alan White, *Misleading Cases* (Oxford, 1991) and J. Ll. J. Edwards, *Mens Rea in Statutory Offences* (London, 1955) ch. III.

[5] See, e.g., C.J.F. Williams, *Being, Identity, and Truth* (Oxford, 1992) 97, and A.R. Lacey, *Modern Philosophy* (London, 1982) 29.

[6] *Mens rea* here does not refer to some general notion of culpability, either in a prima facie or all-things-considered form. Nor is it a catch-all phrase designed to cover every indicator of blame found in the criminal law. Rather, it refers to those *psychological* states (actual or presumed) which are incorporated into the definitions of crimes.

[7] The concepts of knowledge and belief also have an important role: (1) in defences; and (2) in the doctrines of the auxiliary general part. For reasons of space neither of these important areas will be explored here.

of which requires the prosecution to prove, *inter alia*, that the defendant *knew or believed* that the goods handled were stolen: unless knowledge or belief of this legal fact can be established a charge of handling must fail. In America the Model Penal Code also couples knowledge and belief as alternatives in its version of the handling offence.[8] But, instead of stipulating that the prosecution must prove that the defendant knew or believed that the goods handled were stolen, the Code only requires the prosecution to prove that the defendant knew the goods were stolen or believed they had *probably* been stolen.[9] I shall return later to the question of what significance, if any, this difference in wording might have for the scope of the crime. For the time being it is enough to observe that the format of the crime of handling is far from unique in English law. Other offences adopt the same structure. They include: using a false instrument (where the prosecution is required to prove that the defendant knew or believed that the instrument he was using was false);[10] assisting an offender (where the prosecution is required to prove that the defendant knew or believed that the person he was assisting was guilty of an arrestable offence);[11] and sending a false letter or other article with intent to cause distress or anxiety (where the prosecution is required to show that the defendant knew or believed that the information in the letter or other article was false).[12]

---

[8] The full definition, contained in the Theft Act 1968, s. 22(1) is: 'A person handles stolen goods if (otherwise than in the course of stealing) knowing or believing them to be stolen goods he dishonestly receives the goods, or dishonestly undertakes or assists in their retention, removal, disposal or realisation by or for the benefit of another person, or if he arranges to do so'.

[9] See s. 223.6(1), 'Receiving Stolen Property', which states that: 'A person is guilty of theft if he purposely receives, retains, or disposes of movable property of another knowing that it has been stolen, or believing that it has probably been stolen, unless the property is received, retained, or disposed with purpose to restore it to the owner. "Receiving" means acquiring possession, control or title, or lending on the security of the property'. Section 223.6(2) adds: 'The requisite knowledge or belief is presumed in the case of a dealer who: (a) is found in possession or control of property stolen from two or more persons on separate occasions; or (b) has received stolen property in another transaction within the year preceding the transaction charged; or (c) being a dealer in property of the sort received, acquires it for a consideration which he knows is far below its reasonable value. "Dealer" means a person in the business of buying or selling goods including a pawnbroker'.

[10] See the Forgery and Counterfeiting Act 1981, s. 3: 'It is an offence for a person to use an instrument which is, and which he knows or believes to be, false, with the intention of inducing somebody to accept it as genuine, and by reason of so accepting it to do or not to do some act to his own or any other person's prejudice.' See also s. 2 ('copying a false instrument'), s. 4 ('using a copy of a false instrument'), s. 5(1) ('having custody or control of a false instrument'), s. 15(1) ('passing counterfeit notes and coins'), and s. 16(1) ('having custody or control of counterfeit notes and coins').

[11] See the Criminal Law Act 1967, s. 4(1): 'Where a person has committed an arrestable offence, any other person who, knowing or believing him to be guilty of the offence or of some other arrestable offence, does without lawful authority or reasonable excuse any act with intent to impede his apprehension or prosecution shall be guilty of an offence'.

[12] See the Malicious Communications Act 1988, s. 1(1) which states, *inter alia*, that: 'Any person who sends to another person . . . a letter or other article which conveys . . . information which is false and known or believed to be false by the sender . . . is guilty of an offence if his purpose, or one of his purposes, in sending it is that it should . . . cause distress or anxiety to the recipient or to any other person to whom he intends that it or its contents or nature should be communicated'.

Given the range and diversity of actions that the law seeks to regulate, it is not surprising that different formulae—other than 'knowing or believing'—have also been relied upon. One of these is to couple knowledge not with belief but with an absence of belief as an alternative. A familiar offence that adopts this structure is the crime of perjury, which is committed when a person 'lawfully sworn as a witness or as an interpreter in a judicial proceeding wilfully makes a statement material in that proceeding, which he *knows to be false or does not believe to be true*'.[13] Other offences involving false statements[14] also conjoin knowledge with absence of belief. Schedule 4 to the Local Government (Miscellaneous Provisions) Act 1982, for example, renders it an offence for someone to make, in connection with an application for a street trading licence or street trading consent, a statement which he knows to be false in any material respect, or which he does not believe to be true.[15] Similarly, section 26(1)(c) the Immigration Act 1971 prohibits someone from making or causing to be made, to an immigration officer or other person lawfully acting in the execution of the Act, a return, statement or representation which he knows to be false or does not believe to be true.[16]

A slightly different device couples knowledge with recklessness as an alternative. An offence that takes this form is rape. Under section 1(1) of the Sexual Offences Act 1956 (as amended) a man commits rape if he has sexual intercourse with a person and at the time he '*knows* that the person does not consent to the intercourse or is *reckless* as to whether that person consents to it'.[17] A second example is the offence of making a misleading statement,

---

[13] Perjury Act 1911, s. 1(1) (emphasis added). The Model Penal Code's version of the offence of perjury omits the knowledge alternative. Thus, s. 241.1(1) of the Code states that: 'A person is guilty of perjury . . . if in any official proceeding he makes a false statement under oath or equivalent affirmation, or swears or affirms the truth of a statement previously made, when the statement is material and he does not believe it to be true'.

[14] There is some uncertainty over whether the crime of perjury extends to cases where true statements are made. Some writers have argued that criminal liability in these circumstances is possible because s. 1(1) of the Perjury Act 1911 does not expressly rule it out. On the other hand, s. 2(1) of the Perjury Act 1911, which is drafted in similar terms to s. 1(1), is headed: 'False statements on oath made otherwise than in a judicial proceeding'. This indicates that it should be confined to false statements even though the wording of the section does not expressly require that, which in turn suggests that s. 1(1) should be similarly confined. Further support for that view can be derived from *R v Millward* [1985] QB 519, at 526, where Lord Lane CJ said, *obiter*, that in the judgment of the Court of Appeal cases under s. 1(1) of the Perjury Act 1911 required the prosecution to prove, *inter alia*, that the 'statement was false'.

[15] See Sch. 4, para. 10(3) which states: 'Any person who, in connection with an application for a street trading licence or for a street trading consent, makes a false statement which he knows to be false in any material respect, or which he does not believe to be true, shall be guilty of an offence'. See also Sch. 3, para. 21 ('control of sex establishments').

[16] The section, as amended by the Immigration and Asylum Act 1999, s. 30, states that: 'A person shall be guilty of an offence . . . (a) if, without reasonable excuse, he refuses or fails to submit to examination under Schedule 2 to this Act; . . . [or] (c) if on any such examination or otherwise he makes or causes to be made to an immigration officer or other person lawfully acting in the execution of a relevant enactment a return, statement or representation which he knows to be false or does not believe to be true'.

[17] Emphasis added.

promise or forecast as to an insurance contract, contrary to section 133(1) of the Financial Services Act 1986. To be found guilty of this offence the defendant must, *inter alia*, either have *known* that the statement, promise, or forecast he made was misleading, false or deceptive or *recklessly* have made a statement, promise, or forecast which was misleading, false, or deceptive.[18]

Knowledge may also be joined with suspicion as an alternative. The offence of 'assisting another to retain the benefit of criminal conduct', for example, which was created by section 93A(1) of the Criminal Justice Act 1988 (as inserted by the Criminal Justice Act 1993, section 29(1)), is committed only if the defendant *knew or suspected* that the person he was assisting was or had been engaged in criminal conduct or had benefited from criminal conduct.[19] Similarly, the offence of 'assisting drug traffickers', which was originally created by section 24(1) of the Drug Trafficking Offences Act 1986 and is now to be found in section 50(1) of the Drug Trafficking Act 1994, can be committed only if the defendant *knew or suspected* that the person he was assisting was someone who carried on or had carried on drug trafficking or had benefited from drug trafficking.[20]

---

[18] The full definition is a follows: 'Any person who makes a statement, promise or forecast which he knows to be misleading, false or deceptive or dishonestly conceals any material facts; or recklessly makes (dishonestly or otherwise) a statement, promise or forecast which is misleading, false or deceptive, is guilty of an offence if he makes the statement, promise or forecast or conceals the facts for the purpose of inducing, or is reckless as to whether it may induce, another person (whether or not the person to whom the statement, promise or forecast is made or from whom the facts are concealed) to enter into or offer to enter into, or to refrain from entering or offering to enter into, a contract of insurance with an insurance company (not being an investment agreement) or to exercise or refrain from exercising, any rights conferred by such a contract'.

[19] The section states that 'if a person enters into or is otherwise concerned in an arrangement whereby (a) the retention or control by or on behalf of another ("A") of A's proceeds of criminal conduct is facilitated (whether by concealment, removal from the jurisdiction, transfer to nominees or otherwise); or (b) A's proceeds of criminal conduct (i) are used to secure that funds are placed at A's disposal; or (ii) are used for A's benefit to acquire property by way of investment, knowing or suspecting that A is a person who is or has been engaged in criminal conduct or has benefited from criminal conduct, he is guilty of an offence.' See also the crime of 'tipping-off' in s. 93D of the Criminal Justice Act 1988, where it must be shown that the defendant knew or suspected that a constable was acting, or was proposing to act, in connection with an investigation which was being, or was about to be, conducted into money laundering; and the crime of 'failure to disclose knowledge or suspicion of [drug] money laundering', first introduced as s. 26B of the Criminal Justice Act 1988 (as inserted by the Criminal Justice Act 1993, s. 18(1)), and now contained in s. 52(1) of the Drug Trafficking Act 1995.

[20] The full definition states that the offence is committed 'if [a person] enters into or is otherwise concerned in an arrangement whereby (a) the retention or control by or on behalf of another (call him "A") of A's proceeds of drug trafficking is facilitated (whether by concealment, removal from the jurisdiction, transfer to nominees or otherwise), or (b) A's proceeds of drug trafficking (i) are used to secure that funds are placed at A's disposal, or (ii) are used for A's benefit to acquire property by way of investment, and he knows or suspects that A is a person who carries on or has carried on drug trafficking or has benefited from drug trafficking'. See also the Criminal Justice (International Co-operation) Act 1990, s. 12(1), which renders it an offence for a person '(a) to manufacture a scheduled substance; or (b) to supply such a substance to another person, knowing or suspecting that the substance is to be used in or for the unlawful production of a controlled drug'.

A further variation is to couple knowledge with an overtly objective fault element based on belief as an alternative. Section 25 of the Firearms Act 1968 does this when it makes it an offence for a person to sell or transfer any firearm or ammunition to someone 'whom he *knows or has reasonable cause for believing* to be drunk or of unsound mind'.[21] And the same format is used in the definition of the offence of supplying an intoxicating substance contrary to section 1(1) of the Intoxicating Substance (Supply) Act 1985. Under this section it is, *inter alia*, an offence for a person to supply or offer to supply an intoxicating substance other than a controlled drug 'to a person under the age of eighteen whom he *knows, or has reasonable cause to believe*, to be under that age'.[22]

Yet another approach is to couple knowledge with an objective fault element based not on belief but on knowledge. A good example of an offence with this structure is the newly created crime of harassment, which prohibits anyone from pursuing a course of conduct that amounts to harassment of another and that the harasser '*knows or ought to know* amounts to harassment of the other'.[23] A second example is section 4 of the Unsolicited Goods and

---

[21] Emphasis added. The offence also extends to those who 'repair, prove or test any firearm or ammunition for another person' whom they know or have reasonable cause for believing to be drunk or of unsound mind. In some settings the expression 'has reasonable cause to believe' has been interpreted by the courts subjectively to mean 'has reasonable cause to believe and does believe' (see, e.g., *Liversidge v Anderson* [1942] AC 206, at 231, where Lord Atkin said that it was 'well settled' that the phrase 'reasonable cause to believe' in s. 2 of the Criminal Law Amendment Act 1922 meant that the accused had 'reasonable cause to believe and did believe'; but compare *Davis v Director of Public Prosecutions* [1988] RTR 156, at 162, where Mann J said of the same expression in s. 8 of the Road Traffic Act 1972, as substituted by the Transport Act 1981, s. 25(3), Sch. 8: 'if there is objectively determined as a matter of fact a reasonable cause to believe, put into the possession of the police constable, it is in my judgment immaterial whether the police constable actually believes, is dubious, sceptical, or, as here, disbelieving'). Here, however, the expression is offered as an alternative to knowledge, indicating that it should be interpreted objectively in a way which obviates the need to refer to the defendant's actual state of mind.

[22] Emphasis added. The full definition states that: 'It is an offence for a person to supply or offer to supply a substance other than a controlled drug—(a) to a person under the age of eighteen whom he knows, or has reasonable cause to believe, to be under that age; or (b) to a person (i) who is acting on behalf of a person under that age; and (ii) whom he knows, or has reasonable cause to believe, to be so acting, if he knows or has reasonable cause to believe that the substance is, or its fumes are, likely to be inhaled by the person under the age of eighteen for the purpose of causing intoxication'. For a further example, see the Immigration Act 1971, s. 25(1), as amended by the Asylum and Immigration Act 1996, s. 5, which makes it an offence for a person to be 'knowingly concerned in making or carrying out arrangements for securing or facilitating (a) the entry into the United Kingdom of anyone whom he knows or has reasonable cause for believing to be an illegal entrant; (b) the entry into the United Kingdom of anyone whom he knows or has reasonable cause for believing to be an asylum claimant; or (c) the obtaining by anyone of leave to remain in the United Kingdom by means which he knows or has reasonable cause for believing to include deception'. Nothing seems to turn on which of the two formulations ('has reasonable cause to believe' or 'has reasonable cause for believing') has been chosen by the draftsman.

[23] Protection from Harassment Act 1997, s. 1(1) (emphasis added). Section 2(1) states that a person who pursues a course of conduct in breach of s. 1 is guilty of an offence. Section 1(2) states that, for the purposes of s. 1, 'the person whose course of conduct is in question ought to know that it amounts to harassment of another if a reasonable person in possession of the same information would think the course of conduct amounted to harassment of the other'. The offence of 'putting people in fear of violence', created by s. 4 of the Protection from Harassment Act 1997, also uses

Services Act 1971. This makes it an offence for a person to send or cause to be sent to another person any book, magazine or leaflet (or advertising material for any such publication) which 'he *knows or ought reasonably to know* is unsolicited and which describes or illustrates human sexual techniques.'[24]

Occasionally both the above approaches are rejected in favour of a device that joins knowledge with an objective fault element based on suspicion. Section 49(2) of the Drug Trafficking Act 1994, for example, renders it an offence for a person, *knowing or having reasonable grounds to suspect* that any property is, or in whole or in part directly or indirectly represents, another person's proceeds of drug trafficking, to conceal or disguise that property, or to convert or transfer that property or remove it from the jurisdiction, for the purpose of assisting any person to avoid prosecution for a drug trafficking offence or the making or enforcement of a confiscation order.[25] And section 19(2) of the Criminal Justice (International Co-operation) Act 1990 uses the same formula when making it an offence for someone to possess a controlled drug (or to be knowingly concerned in the carrying or concealing of a controlled drug) on a ship to which the section applies, *knowing or having reasonable grounds to suspect* that the drug is intended to be imported or has been exported contrary to section 3(1) of the Misuse of Drugs Act 1971 or the law of any state other than the United Kingdom.[26]

the phrase 'knows or ought to know' and the term 'think'. The inclusion of the word 'think' is intriguing. Just as 'seeing' is not 'believing', so 'believing' is not 'thinking'. Equally, 'knowing' is not 'thinking'. One possibility, therefore, is that in this context 'thinking' is used as a synonym for 'judging'. Judging is (*inter alia*): (i) a conscious mental activity; (ii) done for reasons; and (iii) answerable to the principles of rationality. According to some, judgement is 'the fundamental way to form a belief' (see Christopher Peacocke, *Being Known* (Oxford, 1999) 238). But while this may be true, it is certainly not the only way of forming a belief.

[24] Emphasis added. The full definition in s. 4(1) provides: 'A person shall be guilty of an offence if he sends or causes to be sent to another person any book, magazine or leaflet (or advertising material for any such publication) which he knows or ought reasonably to know is unsolicited and which describes or illustrates human sexual techniques'.

[25] The full definition of the offence, which was formerly contained in s. 14(2) of the Criminal Justice (International Co-operation) Act 1990, is: 'A person is guilty of an offence if, knowing or having reasonable grounds to suspect that any property is, or in whole or in part directly or indirectly represents, another person's proceeds of drug trafficking, he (a) conceals or disguises that property; or (b) converts or transfers that property or removes it from the jurisdiction, for the purpose of assisting any person to avoid prosecution for a drug trafficking offence or the making or enforcement of a confiscation order'. See also the Criminal Justice Act 1988, s. 93C(2) (as inserted by the Criminal Justice Act 1993, s. 31); but compare s. 93C(1). Before its repeal, s. 14(3) of the Criminal Justice (International Co-operation) Act 1990 ('acquiring the proceeds of drug trafficking') also used the formula 'knowing or having reasonable grounds to suspect'. However, when a new version of this offence was introduced by s. 23(A)(1) of the Drug Trafficking Offences Act 1986, as inserted by the Criminal Justice Act 1993, s. 16(1), the words 'reasonable grounds to suspect' were omitted from the offence. The offence, without the words 'reasonable grounds to suspect', is now to be found in s. 51(1) of the Drug Trafficking Act 1994.

[26] The full definition is: 'A person is guilty of an offence if on a ship to which this section applies, wherever it may be, he (a) has a controlled drug in his possession; or (b) is in any way knowingly concerned in the carrying or concealing of a controlled drug on the ship, knowing or having reasonable grounds to suspect that the drug is intended to be imported or has been exported contrary to section 3(1) of the Misuse of Drugs Act 1971 or the law of any state other than the United Kingdom'.

All the offences mentioned thus far include knowledge as one of two alternative fault elements. But in many crimes no alternative is offered. For these offences knowledge of the relevant element is a necessary condition for liability. Four examples will suffice here. The first is section 8 of the Misuse of Drugs Act 1971, which makes it an offence knowingly to permit or suffer certain drug-related activities to take place in premises which one occupies or is concerned in managing.[27] The second is the offence (which can only be committed by a man) of knowingly living in whole or in part on the earnings of prostitution, as prohibited by section 30(1) of the Sexual Offences Act 1956.[28] The third example is to be found in section 2 of the Criminal Damage Act 1971. This prohibits a person from making to another (without lawful excuse) a threat, intending that that other will fear it will be carried out, to destroy or damage his own property in a way which he knows is likely to endanger the life of that other or a third person.[29] A fourth and final example comes from section 6 of the Criminal Law Act 1977, which makes it an offence for any person, without lawful authority, to use or threaten violence for the purpose of securing entry into any premises for himself or for any other person, provided that '(a) there is someone present on those premises at the time who is opposed to the entry which the violence is intended to secure; and (b) the person using or threatening the violence knows that that is the case'.[30]

---

[27] 'A person commits an offence if, being the occupier or concerned in the management of any premises, he knowingly permits or suffers any of the following activities to take place on those premises, that is to say: (a) producing or attempting to produce a controlled drug in contravention of section 4(1) of this Act; (b) supplying or attempting to supply a controlled drug to another in contravention of section 4(1) of this Act, or offering to supply a controlled drug to another in contravention of section 4(1); (c) preparing opium for smoking; (d) smoking cannabis, cannabis resin or prepared opium.'

[28] The full definition of this offence is: 'It is an offence for a man knowingly to live wholly or in part on the earnings of prostitution'. Section 30(2) adds: 'For the purposes of this section a man who lives with or is habitually in the company of a prostitute, or who exercises control, direction or influence over a prostitute's movements in a way which shows he is aiding, abetting or compelling her prostitution with others, shall be presumed to be knowingly living on the earnings of prostitution, unless he proves the contrary'.

[29] The full wording of s. 2 is: 'A person who without lawful excuse makes to another a threat, intending that that other would fear it would be carried out,—(a) to destroy or damage any property belonging to that other or a third person; or (b) to destroy or damage his own property in a way which he knows is likely to endanger the life of that other or a third person; shall be guilty of an offence'. See also s. 3 which makes it an offence for a person to have 'anything in his custody or under his control intending without lawful excuse to use it or cause or permit another to use it—(a) to destroy or damage any property or damage property belonging to some other person; or (b) to destroy or damage his own or the user's property in a way which *he knows is likely to endanger the life of some other person*; shall be guilty of an offence' (emphasis added).

[30] The full wording of s. 6(1) is: 'Subject to the following provisions of this section, any person who, without lawful authority, uses or threatens violence for the purpose of securing entry into any premises for himself or for any other person is guilty of an offence, provided that (a) there is someone present on those premises at the time who is opposed to the entry which the violence is intended to secure; and (b) the person using or threatening the violence knows that that is the case'.

2. Indirect Usage

While examples of direct usage of the terms knowledge and belief can be found in the definitions of a great many criminal offences, [31] this does not exhaust the criminal law's reliance on these concepts. They are also incorporated into other, more complex, *mens rea* terms. Such indirect usage can be illustrated by reflecting on two examples: intention and recklessness. [32] Consider first the concept of intention. The contours of this concept are, of course, deeply contested both in law and in philosophy, and it would be foolhardy to try to rehearse all the arguments here. Suffice it to say that many, perhaps even most, jurists consider the central case of intended action to occur when an agent has *both* a relevant desire (a motivational reason) *and* a relevant belief (an auxiliary reason). [33] If that is correct, a proper understanding of the concept of intention cannot be achieved without first having a proper understanding of the concept of belief. Remarkably, though, few of the jurists who have offered detailed accounts of the nature of intention in the criminal law have acknowledged this fact, and fewer still have felt it necessary to explain (even in outline) the form that such an account might take.

A second complex *mens rea* term that incorporates the notions of knowledge and belief is subjective recklessness. Like intention, this term, even in its subjective form, is a contested concept, and many different versions have been offered by courts and commentators. Smith and Hogan, for example, in the early editions of their textbook on criminal law, describe recklessness as 'the deliberate taking of an unjustifiable risk', [34] whereas Glanville Williams was wont to characterize it as a form of 'conscious' unjustified risk-taking which requires what he called 'advertent negligence'. [35] Comparable, but not identical, formulae have been advanced *inter alia*: (1) by the American Model Penal Code (a person is reckless with respect to a material element of an offence when he 'consciously disregards a substantial and unjustifiable risk that

[31] The terms 'knowledge' and 'belief' can also, of course, be read into statutes by necessary implication even when the statute does not include them expressly. This approach has been taken by the courts on many occasions, particularly with respect to words such as 'permits', 'possesses', 'allows', 'suffers' or 'causes'. For a recent example, see *Atkins v DPP* [2000] 2 All ER 425 (QBD) (reading the term 'knowledge' into the offence of possessing an indecent photograph, contrary to s. 160(1) of the Criminal Justice Act 1988, as amended by the Criminal Justice and Public Order Act 1994, s. 84(4)).

[32] A further example is 'dishonesty' under the test laid out by Lord Lane CJ in *R v Ghosh* [1982] QB 1053.

[33] It may be, however, that an agent's direct intentions can be *identified* solely by reference to his auxiliary reason for acting, without any need to establish his motivational reasons. For a probing analysis of these questions, see John Gardner and Heike Jung, 'Making Sense of Mens Rea: Antony Duff's Account' (1991) 11 Oxford Journal of Legal Studies 559, especially at 564–565.

[34] *Criminal Law* (4th edn., London, 1978) 52. See also 2nd edn. (London, 1965) 40; and 3rd edn. (London, 1973) 45.

[35] See Glanville Williams, *Textbook of Criminal Law* (2nd edn., London, 1983) 96; and *Criminal Law: The General Part* (London, 1953) para. 19. In Williams' view, however, simple ignorance (although not mistake) is also compatible with recklessness: see ibid., para. 40.

the material element exists or will result from his conduct');[36] (2) by the English Law Commission (a person is reckless when he is 'aware of a risk' which is, in the circumstances known to him, an unreasonable risk to take);[37] (3) by the English Court of Appeal (in the famous 1957 case of *R v Cunningham*[38] Byrne J adopted as an accurate statement of the law a definition of recklessness that, he said, had originally been put forward by Professor C.S. Kenny in the first edition of his authoritative textbook *Outlines of Criminal Law*, published in 1902: according to that definition a reckless person must have foreseen that a particular kind of harm might be done and yet have taken the risk of that harm occurring);[39] and (4) by Antony Duff ('we can define recklessness to involve the agent's realisation that his action might cause the effect in question, together with our judgment that it is unreasonable for him to take the risk of that effect occurring').[40] Although the differences between these definitions matter, relatively few criminal lawyers have paid much attention to them. For our purposes, however, the important point is that most jurists would (if pressed) acknowledge 'knowledge' and/or 'belief' as the core elements underpinning any defensible subjectivist definition of the concept of criminal recklessness.[41]

It is worth noting in passing that if knowledge and belief are the keys to recklessness, we need to know exactly what it is that the reckless person must

[36] See MPC, s. 2.02(2)(c).
[37] See Law Commission No. 177, *A Criminal Code for England and Wales* (1989) clause 18(c). See also Law Commission No. 143, *Codification of Criminal Law: A Report to the Law Commission* (1985) clause 22(a); and Law Commission No. 218, *Legislating the Criminal Code: Offences Against the Person and General Principles* (1993) clause 1(b). For earlier formulae offered by the Law Commission, see Law Commission Working Paper No. 31, *Codification of the Criminal Law: General Principles. The Mental Element in Crime* (1970) proposition 7B ('A person is reckless if, (a) knowing that there is a risk that an event may result from his conduct or that a circumstance may exist, he takes that risk, and (b) it is unreasonable for him to take it having regard to the degree and nature of the risk which he knows to be present'); and Law Commission No. 89, *Criminal Law, Report on the Mental Element in Crime* (1978) clause 4(1) ('The standard test of recklessness as to result is—Did the person whose conduct is in issue foresee that his conduct might produce the result and, if so, was it unreasonable for him to take the risk of producing it? (2) The standard test of recklessness as to circumstances is—Did the person whose conduct is in issue realise that the circumstances might exist and, if so, was it unreasonable for him to take the risk of their existence?').
[38] [1957] 2 QB 396, at 399. See also *R v Briggs* [1977] 1 All ER 475; *R v Parker* [1977] 2 All ER 37; *R v Stephenson* [1979] QB 695; and Lord Edmund-Davies' dissenting speech in *R v Caldwell* [1982] AC 341.
[39] Byrne J accepted without question J.W. Cecil Turner's claim (made in the 16th edn. of Kenny's *Outlines of Criminal Law* (Cambridge, 1952) 186, and repeated in the 10th edn. of *Russell on Crime: A Treatise on Felonies and Misdemeanours* (London, 1950) 1592) that this definition was first enunciated by Kenny in 1902. In fact, neither of the pages (pp. 47 and 168) that Turner offers as authorities (see *Russell on Crime* (10th edn.) 1592) supports his claim: on p. 47, Kenny does not really address the issue at all; and on p. 168, he states simply that for a statutory offence of malice to be made out 'there must be an intention to do the particular kind of harm that actually was done'.
[40] See 'Implied and Constructive Malice in Murder' (1979) 95 LQR 418, at 426.
[41] See, e.g., R.A. Duff, '*Caldwell* and *Lawrence*: The Retreat from Subjectivism' (1983) 3 Oxford Journal of Legal Studies 77, at 77.

have had knowledge of or have believed in. It is not enough to assert blandly that what counts is knowledge of or belief in a risk, because risks vary in a number of ways. In particular, they vary in type, extent, and character. Risks vary in type because they cannot exist in a vacuum. They must be risks as to something, be it death, bodily injury, or property damage. (Of course, as far as criminal liability is concerned, the type of risk will usually be obvious from the definition of the crime.)[42] Risks also vary in magnitude. Not all outcomes are as likely as others: the chance may be one-in-a-million or an odds-on bet. Finally, risks vary in character: some risk-taking is justifiable; other risk-taking is not. To decide which requires an overall assessment of the nature of the risk. Thus a doctor may be perfectly justified in removing a patient's diseased heart in order to prepare for a transplant operation, even though the doctor knows that the patient may die on the operating table as a result. But a sadistic surgeon may not be justified in removing the heart of a healthy man who has consented to its removal and transplantation in order to satisfy an overwhelming masochistic urge.

In light of the oft-asserted claim that the general principles of criminal liability require *mens rea* concepts to be extended to each and every element of the *actus reus*,[43] one might have expected defenders of subjective recklessness to extend the requirement of knowledge or belief to each of these different aspects of risk-taking in turn. But, although they invariably insist on knowledge of or belief in the existence of the relevant type of risk,[44] and normally also knowledge of or belief in the magnitude of that risk, they are much less likely to require knowledge of or belief in the character of the risk.[45] This omission is intriguing. Subjectivists freely claim that, to be held reckless, it is not enough for the person simply to know or believe that her activity involves some risk. Like objectivists, they acknowledge that the concept of recklessness includes what might be termed 'an unjustifiable' element: the risk must in all the circumstances have been an unjustified one to take.[46] But they are not prepared to extend their general subjectivist principles to this aspect of risk-taking. There is no requirement that the reckless person must herself have known or believed

---

[42] See, e.g., the Criminal Damage Act 1971, s. 1(1), where the relevant risk is described as the destruction or damage of another person's property.

[43] See, e.g., Smith and Hogan, *Criminal Law* (9th edn., London, 1999) 218: 'It is submitted that the ordinary principles of *mens rea* require intention or recklessness as to all the elements of the *actus reus* unless that is excluded expressly or by implication'. See also G.R. Sullivan's discussion of the so-called 'correspondence principle' in Chapter 9 of this volume, 'Knowledge, Belief and Culpability' at 216–218.

[44] See Glanville Williams, *Textbook of Criminal Law* (2nd edn., London, 1983) 189–193.

[45] See Glanville Williams, *Textbook of Criminal Law* (1st edn., London, 1978) 74, n. 2, where he states that a defendant's knowledge need only relate to the degree of risk 'not to its evaluation in terms of reasonableness, which is an objective question'.

[46] See, e.g., Geoffrey Lane LJ's comment in *R v Stephenson* [1979] QB 695, at 703 F–G, that it is not every taking of a risk that can be classed as reckless: the risk 'must be one which it is in all the circumstances unreasonable for him to take'.

that the risk was unjustified.[47] This may seem incongruous. If lack of knowledge of or belief in a risk's existence is exculpatory, why should lack of knowledge of or belief in the risk's character not perform the same function? Why, in other words, does the stoutly asserted subjectivist principle that the *mens rea* of an offence must cover all elements of the *actus reus* not apply here? One subjectivist response is to argue that when we assess a risk's character we are concerned with value judgements. Though 'intermediate between questions of fact and questions of law', these judgements—or, at least, so the argument goes—have more in common with the latter than the former.[48] They should therefore be treated as if they were questions of law, which do not require *mens rea*. The problem with this argument is that many subjectivists now regard the *ignorantia juris non excusat* doctrine as incompatible with their core theoretical positions. Andrew Ashworth, for example, maintains that the maxim 'is inconsistent with the principle of equal liberty, capacity, and opportunity', adding that 'there are strong arguments for allowing at least reasonable mistake or ignorance of law as an excuse'.[49] If Ashworth is correct, then subjectivists face a much harder task in explaining how their refusal to extend the requirement for knowledge or belief to the *actus reus* element that the risk is unjustified can be reconciled with their other central theoretical positions.[50]

After what has, of necessity, been something of a whistle-stop tour of English (and to a lesser extent American)[51] criminal law, it should now be clear that the definitional general part makes extensive use of the concepts of knowledge and belief. It follows that if we are to understand the definitional general part properly, we need a sound understanding of the nature and scope of these concepts. The section that follows seeks to contribute to that understanding.

B. KNOWLEDGE AND BELIEF AS PSYCHOLOGICAL STATES: CONSTRUCTING A COGNITIVE MAP

1. The Nature of Knowledge and Belief

There can be no doubt that beliefs are central to the human condition. Along with related cognitive states such as knowledge, beliefs help us interpret the

---

[47] See also the analysis offered by Paul H. Robinson in Chapter 4 in this volume, 'The Modern General Part: Three Illusions' at 85–91. Note that in the converse position, where the agent's action was in fact justified but the agent did not know or believe this to be the case, many subjectivists follow *R v Dadson* (1850) 4 Cox CC 358 and deny exculpation (see, e.g., Brian Hogan, 'The *Dadson* Principle' [1989] Criminal LR 679).

[48] See Glanville Williams, *Textbook of Criminal Law* (2nd edn., London, 1983) 141–145.

[49] See Andrew Ashworth, 'Belief, Intent, and Criminal Liability', in Eekelaar and Bell (eds.), *Oxford Essays in Jurisprudence: Third Series* (Oxford, 1987) 10–11. See also Ashworth, *Principles of Criminal Law* (3rd edn., Oxford, 1999) 245; and Laurence D. Houlgate, '*Ignorantia Juris*: A Plea For Justice' (1967) 78 *Ethics* 32.

[50] This does not mean, of course, that no reconciliation is possible.

[51] Other examples of statutory offences found in American law that incorporate the concepts of knowledge and/or belief as *mens rea* elements have been included in the Annex at 202 below.

way that we interact both with each other and with the world.[52] In a sense, they provide the cement that binds human communities together. But what is it to believe something? What are the concept's essential features? This section tries to respond to these questions by outlining six linked properties that beliefs might be said to possess.[53] Thereafter the focus of the section shifts, first to the concept of knowledge, and then to the relationship between knowledge and belief, on the one hand, and, on the other hand, the concepts of action and consciousness.

The first of the six characteristics of beliefs is that they are about something. This need not be true of all mental states: a feeling of depression or anxiety, for example, may, if undirected, be 'about' nothing. But beliefs have to have an object, a point of reference, a content. They are, as it were, directed *towards* something. In the philosophical literature this 'directedness' or 'aboutness' is traditionally referred to as 'intentionality'.[54]

A second characteristic of beliefs is that they are candidates for truth or falsity. Beliefs involve, in other words, the possession of a piece of information (sometimes called a 'proposition') which may be either true or false. The relationship between beliefs on the one hand and truth or falsity on the other is definitional rather than contingent.[55] It helps distinguish beliefs from other 'non-cognitive' psychological states, such as 'desire', 'hope', 'want', or 'care', which are neither true nor false but characteristically reflect a person's attitude to a given state of affairs. Beliefs are thus examples of what some philosophers have called 'cognitive states of mind'.[56]

A third and closely connected characteristic of beliefs is that there is, in an important sense, a commitment to any proposition that is the object of a belief.[57] This commitment may manifest itself in a number of ways. But it

---

[52] As Waller LJ put it in *R v Reader* (1977) 66 Cr App R 33, at 36: 'Believing is something which everybody is concerned with almost every day of their lives'.

[53] For another list of properties, see Bernard Williams, 'Deciding to Believe', in his *Problems of Self* (Cambridge, 1973).

[54] Or, sometimes, as 'Intentionality' or 'intensionality'.

[55] See John R. Searle, *The Rediscovery of Mind* (Cambridge, Massachusetts, 1992) 62.

[56] For a discussion of the distinction between 'cognitive' and 'affective' states of mind, see Anthony Kenny, *Will, Freedom and Power* (Oxford, 1975) 42–43, and *Freewill and Responsibility* (London, 1978) 46. See also Stephen Shute, 'The Second Law Commission Consultation Paper on Consent—Something Old, Something New, Something Borrowed: Three Aspects of the Project' [1996] Criminal LR 684, at 686–687. Of course, as was pointed out in the previous paragraph which explained the first characteristic of beliefs, it would be a mistake to assume that all mental states are propositional: sensations and moods, for example, do not take this form. Equally, it would be a mistake to conclude that there is no attitudinal component to beliefs. Indeed, one way of looking at beliefs is to regard them as 'truth attitudes', as the discussion of the role of 'commitment' below reveals.

[57] This is perhaps what Hume had in mind when he suggested in his *An Enquiry Concerning Human Understanding*, Section V, Part II (3rd edn., Oxford, 1975, reprinted from the posthumous edn., 1777) 40, that 'belief is nothing but a more vivid, lively, forcible, firm, steady conception of an object, than what the imagination alone is ever able to attain'. 'This variety of terms', Hume added, 'is intended only to express that act of mind, which renders realities, or what is taken for such, more present to us than fictions, causes them to weigh more in the thought, and gives them a superior influence on the passions and imagination . . . [B]elief consists

requires, at a minimum, that belief-holders have some confidence in the truth of the propositions they believe. It would be misleading to conclude, though, that every belief is a combination of two beliefs: a belief that p supplemented by a second belief that p is true. That way of explaining the concept confuses what is in essence a relationship of identity with one of co-terminacy. For having a belief that p is *one and the same thing* as having confidence that p is true. There is therefore no need to postulate a second, supplementary, belief in the truth of p in order to make sense of the idea.[58]

A fourth characteristic of beliefs is that they and their contents are always in principle open to reassessment and revision. One's beliefs should not therefore be seen as static, as the contents of a kind of mental museum of propositions that have been placed there because they were thought to be true. Rather, beliefs have a dynamic aspect, and are always available for change. Under normal conditions, as soon as a belief-holder comes to regard one of her beliefs as false that belief dies and (usually) a new belief forms in its place.[59] What might produce such a change that amounts—quite literally— to a change in mind? One possibility is that the belief-holder re-evaluates the evidence upon which her belief is based: as a result of that re-evaluation her former belief may wither on the vine. Another possibility is that the belief-holder acquires some new evidence of sufficient cogency to cause her to lose confidence in her former belief. A third possibility is that the belief simply fades away with the passage of time without any conscious re-evaluation on the part of the belief-holder having taken place.[60]

A fifth characteristic of beliefs—a corollary of the second characteristic— is that they are fallible. Part of what it is to believe something is, as we have seen, to be committed to the idea that the content of one's belief is true. But it does not follow from this that all beliefs are correctly held. The fact that I believe it is cloudy in Birmingham today doesn't mean that it *is* cloudy. Of course, if I were to say to someone during a trans-Atlantic telephone conversation, 'it's cloudy in Birmingham today', then (other things being equal) that person would have a reason to believe what I told her. Our every-day interpretative practices work in that way: when we try to understand assertions of this kind we operate on the assumption that they are, by and large, correct.

not in the peculiar nature or order of ideas, but in the *manner* of their conception, and in their *feeling* to the mind' (emphasis in the original). See also Joseph Raz, 'Two Views of the Nature of the Theory of Law: A Partial Comparison', in Jules Coleman (ed.), *Hart's Postscript: Essays on the Postscript to the Concept of Law* (Oxford, 2001) 22, who similarly argues that we 'are committed to our beliefs'.

[58] The position outlined here is similar to Bernard Williams' claim that 'To believe so and so is one and the same as to believe that that thing is true' (see 'Deciding to Believe' in his *Problems of Self* (Cambridge, 1973) 137). It applies equally to higher order beliefs (i.e. beliefs about one's belief in the truth of p).

[59] I say 'under normal conditions' to allow for the possibility that there may be pathological cases where a person's belief survives even though the rational basis for it has gone.

[60] The first two possibilities are applicable to 'evidence-based beliefs' only. It may be that some beliefs (such as perceptual beliefs) are not evidence-based.

This does not mean, however, that they are. I may have been mistaken or I may have lied.

A sixth characteristic of beliefs is that they form part of a *holistic* system. They depend for their identity, in other words, upon their place within a network of other beliefs and states of mind. As Donald Davidson put it, 'we make sense of particular beliefs only as they cohere with other beliefs, with preferences, with intentions, hopes, fears, expectations, and the rest'.[61]

With these six characteristics in place we can now consider the second cognitive state of mind that forms the subject matter of this chapter, 'knowledge'. The term 'know' can, of course, carry a number of different meanings.[62] The discussion here, though, will centre on knowledge as a psychological state. When used in that way, knowledge is parasitic on belief:[63] one cannot know something unless one also believes it. Belief is thus a necessary condition for knowledge. But it is not a sufficient condition. If a belief is to count as knowledge at least three further conditions must be satisfied:[64] first, the proposition forming the subject matter of the belief must be true,[65] not just believed to be true; secondly, the person whose belief it is must be justified in holding that belief; and, thirdly, the belief-holder must have a degree of commitment to her belief over and above the commitment required for beliefs *per se*. That commitment need not be unshakeable or unquestioned. The fact that I consider it necessary in certain circumstances to examine one of my beliefs in order to reassure myself of its veracity does not, in and of itself, stand in the way of my belief counting as knowledge. On the other hand, unless I have a fairly robust attitude of scepticism towards certain forms of contradictory evidence that might otherwise unseat my belief, it would be inappropriate to count that belief as knowledge.[66]

Commitment thus forms one of the ways in which cognitive states of mind can be differentiated. It is a scalar notion and some cognitive states require more of it than others. This can be seen if we consider a third cognitive state,

---

[61] *Essays on Actions and Events* (Oxford, 1980) 221. Beliefs are also subject to what has been called 'the ideal of integration'. See Michael E. Bratman, 'Practical Reasoning and Acceptance in a Context' (1992) 101 *Mind* 1, at 4: 'Other things equal one should be able to agglomerate one's various beliefs into a larger, overall view; and this larger view should satisfy demands for consistency and coherence'.

[62] One of these is 'know-how', which is having the ability to do certain sorts of things For an interesting discussion of this meaning, see Gilbert Ryle, *The Concept of Mind* (London, 1949) ch. 2. Another sense of the word 'know' is 'acquaintance knowing', which refers to the knowledge I have of those people or places I know.

[63] For a contrary view, see Alan White, *The Nature of Knowledge* (Lanham, 1982).

[64] For an argument that knowledge requires yet further conditions, see Edmund Gettier, 'Is Justified True Belief Knowledge?', in A. Phillips Griffiths (ed.), *Knowledge and Belief* (Oxford, 1967). For further discussion of Gettier's argument, see Linda Zagzebski, 'What is Knowledge?', in John Greco and Ernest Sosa (eds.), *The Blackwell Guide to Epistemology* (Massachusetts, 1999).

[65] If truth and falsity are situated on a continuum it may be enough for a proposition to count as knowledge if it is approximately true. But not if it is false.

[66] See A. Kenny, *What is Faith?* (Oxford, 1992) 30–31.

'acceptance'.[67] When I 'accept' a proposition for some particular purpose, such as action, argument, or deliberation, I work on the assumption that the proposition is true. But I need have no strong commitment to its being so. I might, for example, be willing to accept for the purposes of argument that the universe is expanding, while at the same time harbouring grave doubts about that proposition's truth. As a general rule, then, we are less committed to that which we believe than we are to that which we know, but we are more committed to that which we believe than we are to that which we accept.[68]

A final point about knowledge concerns its relationship to propositions about the future. Some writers take the view that things that have yet to occur cannot properly form the subject matter of knowledge. The English Law Commission, for example, comes close to endorsing this view when, in the introductory paragraphs of its *A Criminal Code for England and Wales*, it claims (without elaboration) that: 'In the strictest sense of the word one cannot "know" that something will be the case in the future'.[69] Yet such a

---

[67] The notion of acceptance is discussed further in section C3 below.

[68] For a different understanding of the concepts of acceptance and belief, see L. Jonathan Cohen, *An Essay on Belief and Acceptance* (Oxford, 1992). Cohen's thesis is that beliefs are simply dispositions to feel that a given proposition is true: the feeling, it seems, merely 'exemplifies' the belief. Beliefs are said to carry with them no commitment on the part of belief-holder (p. 31). Like occurrent feelings, they are 'passive' (involuntary). Acceptances, on the other hand, are said to be 'a policy for reasoning' (p. 5). They are 'active' (voluntary) not 'passive'. While they carry no conceptual implications about feelings, they do require commitment. In this author's view, Cohen's analysis of beliefs and (though to a lesser degree) acceptances is unconvincing. The first difficulty is (to use Robert Audi's words) that 'a disposition to believe something does not imply an actual belief of it, not even a dispositional one, as opposed to one manifesting itself in consciousness' (see *The Structure of Justification* (Cambridge, 1993) 147). Dispositions are in fact, at best, nascent beliefs. A second concern is that by denying commitment any conceptual role in our understanding of the concept of belief, Cohen's analysis turns the true relationship between belief and acceptance on its head. Cohen is right, however, to think that acceptances can involve an exercise of will: one can decide to 'accept' something (see text at n. 89 below). In contrast, 'there is something necessarily bizarre about the idea of believing at will': see Bernard Williams, 'Deciding to Believe', in his *Problems of Self* (Cambridge, 1973) 149. See also Joseph Raz, 'When We Are Ourselves', in his *Engaging Reason* (Oxford, 1999). For other, equally problematic, dispositional explanations of belief, see: Edward Griew: 'A person will typically be said to believe a proposition ("*p*") when he is *disposed to say*: "Yes, it is 'to my mind' the case that" *p*', 'Consistency, Communication and Codification: Reflections on Two *Mens Rea* Words', in P.R. Glazebrook (ed.), *Reshaping the Criminal Law: Essays in Honour of Glanville Williams* (London, 1978) 70, emphasis added; and Alan White: 'Believing that *p* is normally a disposition to behave as if *p* or appropriately to *p*, where "behaving" covers both acting and reacting, both in word and deed, with both external and internal responses, both cognitively and emotionally', *Misleading Cases* (Oxford, 1991) 133. For a further problematic (and highly stipulative) interpretation of acceptance, which takes acceptance to be primarily an 'affective' state of mind, see Alan C. Michaels, 'Acceptance: The Missing Mental State' (1998) 71 Southern California Law Review 953, at 962. According to Michaels, 'Acceptance defines a particular level of indifference towards a result or a circumstance—a particular level of not caring. The accepting actor is the actor who actually has this particular level of indifference, the actor who does not care in this special way'.

[69] See Law Commission No. 177 (n. 37 above) para. 8.11. John Henry Wigmore, *The Principles of Judicial Proof* (Boston, Mass., 1913) 96, offered a similar view. Wigmore claimed that: 'The term Belief is used commonly when the impression is thought of as bearing on a past, present, or future external fact, Consciousness when thought of as bearing on past action, and Knowledge when thought of in connection with a present or past external fact'.

restriction is hard to defend. While it is true that many things we believe are incapable of being known, either because they are false or because, for the time being at least, no adequate justification for believing them can be given, it seems wrong to conclude that all beliefs about the future must necessarily fail on one or other of these grounds. Consider my belief that there will be daylight in New York tomorrow. Is this belief, in principle, any less true or more difficult to justify than my belief that there was daylight in New York 100 years ago, or my belief that there is daylight in New York today? If not, then (unless it fails on some other ground, and no other grounds are canvassed by the Commission) my belief as to the future is no less capable in principle of counting as knowledge (whether described strictly or otherwise) than my beliefs about the present or the past. Interestingly, this view receives support from the drafting of at least one English offence—conspiracy. Section 1(2) of the Criminal Law Act 1977 states that a person shall not be guilty of conspiracy to commit an offence for which liability may be incurred without knowledge on the part of the person committing it of any particular fact or circumstance necessary for its commission unless 'he and at least one other party to the agreement intend or know that that fact or circumstance *shall or will exist at the time when the conduct constituting the offence is to take place*'.[70]

2. The Relationship between Knowledge and Belief and Action and Consciousness

We can now turn to the relationship between beliefs and actions. The exact nature of this relationship is, of course, a matter of vigorous debate. The classic Humean view argues that no belief or set of beliefs is, on its own, sufficient to produce an action. Something more—usually a 'desire'—is required to get things going. But, whatever the merits of this claim, both Humeans and non-Humeans agree that beliefs (including beliefs which amount to knowledge) have an important role in guiding action. One writer, Antony Duff, even goes so far as to make this the mainstay of his suggestion that knowledge can helpfully be divided into three subcategories: explicit knowledge, tacit knowledge, and latent knowledge.[71] For Duff the key feature of explicit knowledge is that it involves some conscious mental process: it is knowledge to which a person 'consciously adverts'. Tacit knowledge, in contrast, is knowledge that guides an agent's actions without it being consciously adverted to. Such knowledge, Duff suggests, might be called suppressed or subconscious

---

[70] Emphasis added. See also Chapter 9 below at 215.
[71] '*Caldwell* and *Lawrence*: The Retreat from Subjectivism' (1983) 3 OJLS 77, at 80. A four-way categorization would have been better. The danger with a three-way classification is that it gives the impression that knowledge to which a person 'consciously adverts' *must* be action guiding.

knowledge.[72] It is the kind of knowledge that governs a driver's actions and reactions without his consciously 'contemplating his surroundings or actively calling his latent knowledge to mind'. Latent knowledge is the third category in Duff's schema. Another term for it, although not one used by Duff himself, might be background knowledge. Duff illustrates this category by means of an example, again drawn from driving. A driver, Duff suggests, may have latent knowledge of the general risks which driving involves, such that, on other occasions, he would be conscious of the risks his present driving creates. On this occasion, however, he may have no explicit or tacit knowledge of those risks, either because he is not conscious of the facts, such as speed, weather, or traffic flow, in virtue of which his driving is dangerous, or because, although he is conscious of these facts, he has not seen them in the light of his latent knowledge, and so has not appreciated their significance.

Duff's analysis, which must apply *mutatis mutandis* to many other cognitive states of mind,[73] usefully focuses our attention on the relationship between knowledge, belief, and action.[74] It also incorporates two other important ideas. The first is that at any one time much of what we know or believe resides only in our subconscious mind. The second is that consciousness is a discrete type of mental phenomenon, separate and distinct from knowledge or belief. Both claims are controversial. An apparent counterargument to the second is that conscious beliefs are best viewed as beliefs about which the belief-holder has a particular kind of further (or second-order) belief: they are beliefs that the belief-holder believes herself to hold. This account of the nature of consciousness obviates the need to regard consciousness as a mental state distinct from knowledge or belief. It therefore has the advantages of simplicity and economy. Yet, ironically, that strength is also its Achilles' heel, for the parsimonious use of terminology opens the door to two interconnecting objections. The first of these is that the account fails to

---

[72] However, Duff goes on to say, without explanation, that he suspects that this definition is misleading. This is certainly true of the soubriquet 'suppressed knowledge': not all subconscious knowledge has been suppressed.

[73] But not to 'perception' which can never be latent in Duff's sense of the word: see John Searle, *Intentionality* (Cambridge, 1983) ch. 2.

[74] Other philosophers subdivide unconscious beliefs according to how readily they yield their identities to the belief-holder. Robert J. Ackermann, for example, distinguishes '*non-conscious*' (or '*behavioral*') beliefs—beliefs which though non-consciously held are nonetheless capable of being formulated by the human agent on due reflection—from '*unconscious*' beliefs—beliefs which 'can influence behaviour over a long period of time but which resist recognition by the agent' (see *Belief and Knowledge* (New York, 1972) 6). Freud also subdivides unconscious beliefs. He separates (i) 'pre-conscious' mental states (those which, like Duff's 'tacit' knowledge or belief, are readily accessible to the subject) from (ii) 'unconscious' mental states (those which though not readily accessible to the subject are recoverable in principle if the right procedures—hypnosis, psychoanalysis, etc.—are adopted). Freud's unconscious mental states differ from what some call 'sub-personal' mental states. These control breathing, digestion, etc., and are not in principle accessible to consciousness. For further discussion of such distinctions, see Michael Moore, *Law and Psychiatry: Rethinking the Relationship* (Oxford, 1984) 126–140, and *Act and Crime* (Oxford, 1993) 151–152.

explain why second-order beliefs have the power to make their holders conscious of the propositions they contain (i.e. propositions about first-order beliefs) when first-order beliefs do not have that power. The second objection stems from the possibility that second-order beliefs might themselves be subconsciously held. If (as we are told) first-order beliefs differ from second-order beliefs only in respect of the propositions they contain, and if (as seems plausible) first-order beliefs may be subconsciously held, it follows that the idea that second-order beliefs might also be subconsciously held must be seriously entertained. Yet, if second-order beliefs can be subconsciously held, the account runs into trouble. For in order to cling onto the claim that consciousness is no more than the holding of second-order beliefs, we are forced to accept the unattractive proposition that a *subconsciously* held second-order belief can make a person conscious of a first-order belief that would otherwise be subconsciously held. Because this idea is very hard to swallow[75] it is tempting to retreat to a higher tier of beliefs to solve the difficulties. But ultimately that strategy also fails. For however many tiers of belief are postulated, the question remains: what is it about higher order beliefs that allows their holders but not the holders of lower order beliefs to be conscious of the propositions (i.e. propositions about first-order beliefs) they contain? The only way this question can be adequately answered, it seems, is by introducing into the analysis a new mental phenomenon, consciousness, which was the very move that the notion of higher order beliefs was meant to forestall.

So, despite William of Ockham's warning against multiplying entities, there are times when reducing several phenomena to types of one phenomenon merely distorts what one is seeking to understand. None of this, though, should blind us to the fact that the foregoing argument is entirely negative in its effect. It suggests that we should reject an explanation of consciousness based solely on second-order beliefs.[76] But it does not establish the positive claim that consciousness is a discrete mental state, separate and distinct from knowledge or belief. Nor does it establish that beliefs can be subconsciously held. My own suspicion is that the validation of these propositions, although not their investigation or clarification, lies largely beyond the scope of philosophy, or for that matter medical science. For the most part we simply have to take them on trust. It is, however, always reassuring when such ideas fit comfortably with our everyday intuitions, and that—at least in respect of the second claim—would appear to be the case here. For we are perfectly at ease with the thought that at any one time some of our beliefs are conscious while others reside in our subconscious mind. Indeed, some would go so far as to say that these ideas have become so engrained in post-Freudian Western culture that they now form part of our modern day concept of the self. This

---

[75] Although it is swallowed by David M. Rosenthal: see his 'Two Concepts of Consciousness', in Rosenthal (ed.), *The Nature of Mind* (Oxford, 1991).

[76] Second-order beliefs may still be a *necessary* condition for a belief being conscious. In any event, they are essential for 'introspection'.

does not, of course, mean that they are true. It means only that many of our social practices, including those that form the criminal law, are predicated on their being true.

Once we concede that consciousness is an important mental phenomenon, and that knowledge and belief can be both consciously and subconsciously held, it becomes easier to allow a third proposition: that consciousness can be a matter of degree. Like the other ideas we have considered, this claim has considerable intuitive appeal. We have no difficulty accepting that we can be conscious of several different things at once, or that our degree of consciousness of these things may vary. Furthermore, both these propositions are compatible with the apparently contradictory claim that 'the possession of consciousness is not a matter of degree'.[77] This is because the latter refers to *possession* of consciousness whereas the former refer to the *consciousness* we possess. John Searle, one of the few writers to have recognized this point explicitly, put it thus: 'Consciousness is an on/off switch: a system is either conscious or not. But once conscious, the system is a rheostat: there are different degrees of consciousness'.[78]

Finally, two other features of consciousness are worthy of comment. The first is that our consciousness of any particular belief may be fleeting or longlasting. The second is that the method by which we become conscious of our beliefs may vary. Sometimes we obtain access to our latent knowledge and beliefs by an exercise of our will. On other occasions beliefs just come into our conscious minds without our willing them to do so: it is as if they arrived from nowhere.

C. KNOWLEDGE AND BELIEF AS LEGAL TERMS: MAKING SENSE OF THE LAW

1. Knowledge

We can now return to the use made of these concepts by the criminal law. How far does this mirror the conceptual understandings outlined above? Let us begin with offences where knowledge is a necessary condition of liability. Some of these offences (such as 'permitting' drug related activities to take place on one's premises, contrary to section 8 of the Misuse of Drugs Act 1971; or 'living' on the earnings of prostitutes, contrary to section 30 of the Sexual Offences Act 1956)[79] identify the proscribed activity by means of an action verb which is then qualified by the addition of the adverb 'knowingly'. Others identify the proscribed activity by linking an action verb to knowledge of some quite different proposition (for example, threatening to damage

---

[77] See Colin McGinn, *The Character of Mind* (Oxford, 1982) 13 (emphasis removed).
[78] *The Rediscovery of the Mind* (Cambridge, Massachusetts, 1992) 83.
[79] See n. 27 and n. 28 above.

one's own property knowing that someone's life is likely to be endangered, contrary to section 2 of the Criminal Damage Act 1971; or using violence to secure entry into premises knowing that someone on the premises is opposed to the entry, contrary to section 6 of the Criminal Law Act 1977).[80] Yet, whichever mode of expression is adopted, all offences which incorporate 'knowledge' of a specified proposition as a necessary element for their commission appear to require that the 'known' proposition be true. They therefore meet the first of the three additional requirements of the concept of knowledge outlined above.[81]

The definitional status of the other two requirements of knowledge—justification and commitment—is, however, less clear-cut. If taken seriously, the justification requirement would allow someone charged with an offence requiring knowledge to rebut that charge by showing that his belief, while true, was only true fortuitously.[82] Yet there is no indication that the criminal law is willing to entertain such an argument.[83] Nor is there evidence that it will allow defendants to argue that they were insufficiently committed to their beliefs for them to count as knowledge. In short, the criminal law seems to require nothing more of a belief for it to count as knowledge than that it be correct.[84]

2. Knowledge and Belief as Alternatives: the Place of 'Acceptance' and 'Suspicion'

Why, then, do some offences include knowledge and belief as alternatives? One possibility is that the term 'belief' is introduced into the definitions of certain crimes to allow for situations where the stipulated belief was untrue. The problem with this explanation is that few, if any, of the crimes that include knowledge and belief as alternatives leave that possibility open. Take the offence of 'using a false instrument', contrary to section 3 of the Forgery and Counterfeiting Act 1981.[85] The *mens rea* for this offence is, *inter alia*, that

---

[80] See n. 29 and n. 30 above.

[81] See section B1 above. The same conclusion may be drawn where knowledge is not a necessary condition for criminal liability but is coupled with belief, recklessness, absence of belief, suspicion, or an objective fault requirement as an alternative.

[82] It is an interesting question what difference, if any, the justification requirement makes to moral assessment.

[83] Glanville Williams certainly ruled it out. See *Criminal Law: The General Part* (2nd edn., London, 1983) 169: 'it cannot be said that the accused had no knowledge ... merely because he was essentially right only by accident'. The definition of the term 'knowingly' provided by s. 2.02(2)(b) of the Model Penal Code also seems to block an argument of this kind: 'A person acts knowingly with respect to a material element of an offense when: (i) if the element involves the nature of his conduct or the attendant circumstances, he is aware that his conduct is of that nature or that such circumstances exist; and (ii) if the element involves a result of his conduct, he is aware that it is practically certain that his conduct will cause such a result'. Section 1.13(13) states that equivalent terms, such as 'knowing' or 'with knowledge', shall have the same meaning.

[84] For a discussion of the 'wilful blindness' doctrine, see section C3 below.

the defendant knew or believed that the instrument he was using was false. The *actus reus* is, *inter alia*, that the instrument he used was in fact false. Hence, once the *actus reus* element is established, it is clear that a defendant who 'believed' that the instrument he was using was false will also (in the eyes of the law) be regarded as having 'known' that that instrument was false. This is because, from the law's perspective, a correct belief is all that there is to knowledge. It follows that the 'belief' limb of the offence of using a false instrument is redundant: any defendant who could properly be convicted on the basis of 'belief' could also be convicted on the basis of 'knowledge'.

Given that the same is true of other offences that couple knowledge and belief as alternatives,[86] we plainly need a different explanation for why the law might choose such a formula. One possibility is that the interpretation placed by the law on the term belief is, like that placed upon the term knowledge, less demanding than our normal conceptual understandings would lead us to expect. In particular, it is possible that the law extends the term belief (but not the term knowledge) to include cognitive states that are conceptually distinct from beliefs but are deemed by the law to be sufficiently close to them to warrant inclusion. Potential candidates are 'acceptance' and 'suspicion'.

Let us consider first 'acceptance'. Some authors have claimed that acceptance is 'the crucial feature' of knowledge and belief.[87] If intended as a general proposition this view cannot easily be sustained. While acceptances are certainly close cousins of beliefs, they are not features of them nor are they identical to them. Acceptances require, as we have seen, less by way of commitment than beliefs. They also engage with the will in a different way. Beliefs are 'passive'. They cannot be acquired directly through an act of will. There is a sense in which they 'just happen to us'.[88] In contrast, acceptances are 'active': they do respond to the will.[89] A further difference is that acceptances are far more sensitive to context than beliefs. The rational person can accept something in one context while refusing to accept it in another. But, subject

---

[85] See n. 10 above.

[86] See, e.g., the following statement by Lord Hailsham of St Marylebone LC in *Haughton v Smith* [1974] 2 WLR 1, at 5: 'In my view, it is plain that, in order to constitute the offence of handling, the goods specified in the particulars of offence must not only be believed to be stolen, but actually continue to be stolen goods at the moment of handling'.

[87] See A.P. Simester and Winnie Chan, 'Intention Thus Far' [1997] Criminal LR 704, at 716: 'The crucial feature [of knowledge or belief] is *acceptance*'. This claim, with its emphasis, is repeated in Simester and Brookbanks, *Principles of Criminal Law* (Wellington, 1998) 102, in a section of the *Mens Rea* chapter headed 'Knowledge'. However, it is omitted from Simester and Sullivan, *Criminal Law* (Oxford, 2000) 136. It is unclear what the authors had in mind when using the term 'acceptance'. Whereas in the preceding sentence acceptance is distinguished from 'thinking that [something] exists with provable certainty', in the next sentence it is stated that, to be found guilty of an offence requiring knowledge or belief, a defendant 'must accept, or "assume", or have no serious doubt, at the time he acts, that the circumstance is present'.

[88] This does not mean, however, that we have no influence over what we believe.

[89] See also the brief discussion of this point in n. 68 above. The quotation marks in the preceding sentence have been used to indicate that it may be a mistake to identify the active/passive distinction too closely with the will: see Joseph Raz, 'When We Are Ourselves', in his *Engaging Reason* (Oxford, 1999).

to some limited but important qualifications, it is not rational for a person's beliefs to vary across contexts in this way.[90]

Nonetheless, despite these differences, both cognitive states—acceptance and belief—play a similar role in our practical reasoning. This is because when I accept a proposition for a particular purpose that proposition operates *as if it were* one of my beliefs. Acceptances, in other words, are simulacra for beliefs. There are therefore good grounds for treating them as if they were beliefs for legal purposes.[91] 'Suspicions', in contrast, are not simulacra for beliefs.[92] Along with 'inklings' and 'doubts' they play a much more tangential role in our practical reasoning. The grounds for including them within the legal definition of belief are accordingly weaker.

Interestingly, the law reflects these considerations. It readily concludes that a person who worked on the assumption that a thing was true shall, in the eyes of the law, be deemed to have believed that thing;[93] but it is very reluctant to extend its definition of belief as far as suspicion, even when that suspicion is strongly held. That this is so can be seen from the recent decision in *R v Forsyth*.[94] The case arose out of the collapse of Mr Asil Nadir's 'Polly Peck' empire. At first instance Mrs Elizabeth Forsyth, the Chairman and director of one of Nadir's companies, was convicted on two counts of handling stolen goods. However, on appeal that conviction was quashed. One ground for the decision was that the direction given by the trial judge (Tucker J) might have led the jury 'to find the appellant guilty without finding that she actually believed the money was stolen'.[95] Tucker J's direction had been based on the 1980s handling case of *R v Hall*.[96] Indeed, so concerned had he been to ensure that the jury should get the law on handling right that he had taken the precaution of having the *Hall* direction typed out and handed to each jury

[90]   See Robert C. Stalnaker, *Inquiry* (Cambridge, Massachusetts, 1984) 80–81 (note that Stalnaker's use of the term 'acceptance' differs in many important respects from that found here; for Stalnaker 'acceptance' is a 'technical term' (p. 79) which serves to pick out 'a natural class of propositional attitudes about which one can usefully generalize'). See also Michael E. Bratman, 'Practical Reasoning and Acceptance in a Context' (1992) 101 *Mind* 1.

[91]   This is true both where the defendant does not believe the proposition and where he disbelieves it. For examples of cases where a person accepts something she does not believe, see Michael E. Bratman, 'Practical Reasoning and Acceptance in a Context' (1992) 101 *Mind* 1, at 6–8.

[92]   One can have degrees of suspicion but suspicions are not, as some writers have asserted (see H.H. Price, *Belief* (London, 1969) 39, and M. Wasik and M.P. Thompson, '"Turning a Blind Eye" As Constituting Mens Rea' (1981) 32 NILQ 328, at 335) 'degrees of belief'. It should be remembered, however, that 'commitment', one of the characteristics of belief discussed above, does admit of degrees.

[93]   See, e.g., *R v Simpson* [1978] 2 NZLR 221. See also *R v Forsyth* [1997] 2 Cr App R 299, at 320, where Beldam LJ even went as far as to say (falsely) that 'The ordinary meaning of belief is the mental acceptance of a fact as true or existing'.

[94]   [1997] 2 Cr App R 299. See also *Grundy v The Queen* (Tasmanian Supreme Court) (1993) CCA 60/1993, per Underwood J (discussing the crime of receiving stolen goods): 'Although the relevant section speaks of knowledge, the question is one of belief . . . Suspicion is insufficient'.

[95]   [1997] 2 Cr App R 299, at 321.

[96]   (1985) 81 Cr App R 260.

member. Unfortunately, by stressing that 'mere' suspicion was not enough to establish belief, the direction gave the impression that real or weighty suspicion might suffice. Hence, in the Court of Appeal's view, it amounted to misdirection; for, as Beldam LJ forcefully put it, 'It is beyond question that even great suspicion is not to be equated with belief'.[97]

We now have a possible insight into why the term belief is provided as an alternative to the term knowledge in the definition of many criminal offences. The reason is that, for legal purposes, belief includes acceptance, whereas knowledge does not. Put another way, the law regards the relationship between knowledge and belief, on the one hand, and belief and acceptance, on the other hand, as non-transitive. Thus, for legal purposes, two propositions appear to hold: first, that knowledge is nothing more than true belief, and secondly, that belief includes acceptance. But, because the law deems the relationship between these propositions to be non-transitive, it blocks any inference that knowledge must therefore include acceptance. Consequently, a draftsman who wishes to ensure that acceptance is a sufficient *mens rea* for the commission of a crime cannot rely on the term knowledge to do the work. He can, however, achieve that goal by including the term belief as an alternative.[98]

---

[97] [1997] 2 Cr App R 299, at 318–319. A draftsman who wishes to include 'suspicion' within the *mens rea* of an offence should therefore do so explicitly, as in s. 93(A) of the Criminal Justice Act 1988 and s. 50(1) of the Drug Trafficking Act 1994 (discussed in text at nn. 19 and 20 above). The concept of 'suspicion' has also been used by draftsmen in relation to defences. For example, s. 4(2) of the Knives Act 1977 states that it is a defence for a person charged with an offence under s. 2 (i.e. with publishing any written, pictorial or other material in connection with the marketing of any knife which '(a) indicates, or suggests, that the knife is suitable for combat; or (b) is otherwise likely to stimulate or encourage violent behaviour involving the use of the knife as a weapon') to prove 'that he did not know or suspect, and had no reasonable grounds for suspecting, that the material (a) amounted to an indication or suggestion that the knife was suitable for combat; or (b) was likely to stimulate or encourage violent behaviour involving the use of the knife as a weapon'. A second example is s. 28(2) of the Misuse of Drugs Act 1971 which states that it shall be a defence in any proceedings for an offence to which the section applies for the accused to prove 'that he neither knew of nor suspected nor had reason to suspect the existence of some fact alleged by the prosecution which it is necessary for the prosecution to prove if he is to be convicted of the offence charged'. (See also the Misuse of Drugs Act 1971, s. 5.) The concept also appears in the Sexual Offences Act 1956 in relation to offences involving 'defectives'. Section 29(2), for example, makes it clear that it is not an offence for a person to cause or encourage the prostitution of a woman who is a defective if that person 'does not know and has no reason to suspect her to be a defective'. See also ss. 14(4), 15(3) and 21(2). Concerning powers of arrest, the Theft Act 1968, s. 25(4), authorizes any person to arrest without warrant 'anyone who is, and whom he, with reasonable cause, suspects to be, committing an offence under this section [i.e. going equipped for stealing]'. See also the Police and Criminal Evidence Act 1984 where the expressions 'reasonable grounds for suspecting' and 'reasonable grounds for doubting' are used. The term also appears in s. 16(A)(1) of the Prevention of Terrorism (Temporary Provisions) Act 1989: 'A person is guilty of an offence if he has any article in his possession in circumstances giving rise to a reasonable suspicion that the article is in his possession for a purpose connected with the commission, preparation or instigation of acts of terrorism to which this section applies'.

[98] Contrast the following (false) assertion about the law: 'Strictly speaking ... "belief" is simply a degree of knowledge rather than an alternative fault element' (W. Wilson, *Criminal Law* (London, 1998) 163).

This argument explains why draftsmen might wish to include the term belief as an alternative to the term knowledge in the definition of many criminal offences. By doing so they are able to widen the scope of the offence to include acceptance. But it does not explain the strong tendency found amongst common law draftsmen to use the formula 'knows or believes' in the definition of many criminal offences in preference to relying on 'belief' alone as the relevant *mens rea*. It is hard to see what would be lost by employing the latter strategy. According to the law, knowledge is nothing more than true belief, and for this reason a draftsman's decision to substitute the term 'believes' for the formula 'knows or believes' in the definition of a criminal offence will leave the scope of that offence unaffected. Oddly, though, this is a drafting technique that is rarely used.

3. Other Possible Extensions to the Legal Definition of Belief

The next question is whether the common law augments the concept of belief in other ways. Two issues will be discussed here. First, does the legal definition of belief in some specified thing (p) extend to beliefs that p is 'possible', 'likely', 'more likely than not', 'highly likely', etc? Secondly, does the legal definition of belief include what some lawyers term 'wilful blindness'?

Our non-legal understandings of the nature of belief draw a clear distinction between a 'belief that-it-might-be-that p' and a 'belief that p': not only is a belief that-it-might-be-that p not a belief that p, it cannot imply a belief that p. There are therefore good reasons for the law to be wary about extending its legal definition of belief generally to include beliefs that a thing is 'possible', 'likely', 'more likely than not', or 'highly likely' etc. If we turn to the common law, this is exactly what we find. The following statement by Waller LJ in *R v Reader*, made again in the context of a case involving the crime of handling stolen goods, provides an illustration:[99]

> We are clearly of opinion that to have in mind that it is more likely that [the goods] are stolen than that they are not, which is the test which the judge told the jury to apply, is not sufficient to comply with the terms of the section. To believe that the goods are probably stolen is not to believe that the goods are stolen, and in our view this was a misdirection by the learned judge and one which was not a misdirection which was in favour of the appellant but against him. The jury were being told to accept a lower state of guilty mind than the section actually requires.

However, the fact that the legal definition of belief does not extend generally to include beliefs that p is 'possible', 'likely', 'more likely than not', 'highly likely', etc., creates no bar to the same result being achieved through the wording of a particular statutory provision.[100] An example of a crime that has been drafted in a way that achieves this outcome is the Model Penal

---

[99] (1977) 66 Cr App R 33, at 36.
[100] For the position in relation to recklessness, see section A2 above.

Code's offence of receiving stolen property. The definition provided by the Code, it will be recalled, states that a person is guilty of the offence 'if he purposely receives, retains, or disposes of movable property of another knowing that it has been stolen, *or believing that it has probably been stolen*'.[101]

The above considerations apply equally to knowledge. While some writers hold that one cannot 'know' that something *will* be the case in the future (a view that was challenged in section B1, above), it does not follow that one cannot know that something *may* be the case in the future, or that something *may* be the case in the present. Furthermore, just as a belief that-it-might-be-that p is not a belief that p and cannot imply a belief that p, so knowledge that-it-might-be-that p is not knowledge that p and cannot imply knowledge that p. There are therefore good reasons why the law should decline to extend its definition of knowledge generally to include knowledge that p is 'possible', 'likely', 'more likely than not', 'highly likely', etc. This result can, nonetheless, be achieved in particular offences by appropriate drafting if that is thought desirable. An example of an offence drawn from English law which does just that is the crime of making a threat to destroy or damage one's own property, contrary to section 2 of the Criminal Damage Act 1971.[102] This prohibits a person from making to another (without lawful excuse and intending that the other will fear it would be carried out) a threat to destroy or damage his own property in a way which he knows *is likely* to endanger the life of that other or a third person. A second example, created by section 1(1) of the Intoxicating Substance (Supply) Act 1985, is the offence of supplying or offering to supply an intoxicating substance (other than a controlled drug) to a person who is acting on behalf of a person under the age of 18 when the defendant '*knows or has reasonable cause to believe* that the substance is, or its fumes are, *likely* to be inhaled by the person under the age of eighteen for the purpose of causing intoxication'.[103]

The second question is whether the legal definitions of belief and knowledge include what some term 'wilful blindness'. Despite its nineteenth century roots,[104] the *locus classicus* of the wilful blindness doctrine is usually thought to be Devlin J's difficult judgment in *Roper v Taylor's Garages*.[105] In

---

[101] Section 223.6(1) (emphasis added): see n. 9 above.   [102] See n. 29 above.

[103] Emphasis added. See n. 22 above.

[104] It has been claimed that, so far as it is possible to tell, 'the first occasion in which judicial approval was given to the notion that some lesser degree of knowledge than actual knowledge would suffice to establish *mens rea*' was *R v Sleep* (1861) 30 LJMC 170 (see J. Ll. J. Edwards, 'The Criminal Degrees of Knowledge' (1954) 17 Modern Law Review 294, at 298, note omitted). So far as American law is concerned, the Model Penal Code's version of the wilful blindness doctrine is generally thought to be contained in s. 2.02(7), a strangely-worded provision which states: 'When knowledge of the existence of a particular fact is an element of an offense, such knowledge is established if a person is aware of a high probability of its existence, unless he believes that it does not exist'. Although the Commentary claims this subsection 'deals with the situation that British commentators have denominated "wilful blindness" or "connivance"', it seems probable that there are substantial differences between the two doctrines.

[105] [1951] 2 TLR 284, at 288–289.

Roper Devlin J suggested that 'shutting [one's] eyes to an obvious means of knowledge' or 'deliberately refraining from making inquiries, the results of which the person does not care to have' (dubbed by Devlin J 'knowledge of the second degree') is, in law, 'actual knowledge'. This, he said, could be distinguished from 'merely neglecting to make enquiries' ('knowledge in the third degree'), which is 'not knowledge at all'.[106] These words stored up a host of problems for judges and juries. By dint of a legal fiction, 'wilful blindness' was deemed to be actual knowledge. But the exact scope of the rule remained unclear. Was it enough to establish that the defendant 'deliberately refrained from making inquiries, the results of which he did not care to have'?[107] Or were there other conditions that needed to be met? Must, for example, the means of obtaining the knowledge have been (as Devlin J indicated) 'obvious'? Must the means also have been 'easy' to employ, and must the defendant have been 'at fault' in not employing them?[108] And what, if anything, had to be true of the defendant's mental state? Must he have 'known' at the time enquiries could have been made what their outcome would be,[109] or what their outcome was likely to be? Or would it be enough if he merely 'suspected' that result?[110]

The longer these and other issues remained unresolved the more unsatisfactory the doctrine became. Indeed, by 1984, Lord Lane CJ considered that mistakes in this area of the law were commonplace.[111] Accordingly, he suggested in *R v Moys* that juries should be told that suspicion, even when coupled with the fact that the defendant had shut his eyes to the circumstances, was not enough to establish knowledge or belief.[112] But 'old concepts tend to

---

[106] The latter notion, he added, came within the legal conception of constructive knowledge that, generally speaking, had no place in criminal law.

[107] In *Taylor v Kenyon* [1952] 2 All ER 726, at 727, Lord Goddard CJ omitted the word 'deliberately' from the formula: '[The defendant] admitted in court that he had suspected he might have been disqualified, but he made no inquiry. This seems to me to be a clear case of a man shutting his eyes to the obvious and refraining from getting information which he did not want to get'. The definition of 'knowingly' in the English Draft Criminal Code also omits the word 'deliberately' from its wilful blindness formula: see Law Commission No. 177 (n. 37 above) clause 18(a): '[A person acts] "knowingly" with respect to a circumstance not only when he is aware that it exists or will exist, but also when he avoids taking steps that might confirm his belief that it exists or will exist'. However, in the Commentary (at para. 8.10), the Law Commission states that clause 18(a) is trying to capture, in a short form of words, the essence of the common law position. This, it says, is that a person can be treated as knowing something if, 'being pretty sure that it is so, he deliberately avoids making an examination or asking questions that might confirm the fact—he avoids taking advantage of an available means of "actual knowledge"'.

[108] As has been suggested by M. Wasik and M.P. Thompson, '"Turning a Blind Eye" As Constituting *Mens Rea*' (1981) 32 NILQ 328, especially at 330–331.

[109] Suggested in the New Zealand case of *R v Crooks* [1981] 2 NZLR 53, at 58, by Mahon J.

[110] Suggested by Lord Widgery CJ in *Atwal v Massey* (1971) 56 Cr App R 6, at 8, and by Lord Bridge of Harwich in *Westminster City Council v Croyalgrange Ltd* (1986) 83 Cr App R 155, at 164.

[111] *R v Moys* (1984) 79 Cr App R 72, at 76.

[112] ibid., at 76. He added, though, that the jury could take these matters into account evidentially when deciding whether or not the necessary knowledge or belief existed.

recur'[113] and in *R v Hall* new life appeared to be breathed into the wilful blindness doctrine.[114] The Court of Appeal was therefore forced to make another attempt to put it to rest in *R v Forsyth* when it ruled that the guidance in *Moys* was not only 'clearer and more readily understandable by a jury' than that in *Hall*, but avoided 'the potential for confusion' that was inherent in a *Hall* direction. It is very much to be hoped that this latest attempt to excise the wilful blindness doctrine from the law will be successful. Now that suspicion, even great suspicion, has been held not to be the equivalent of belief, the wilful blindness doctrine looks increasingly anomalous. Furthermore, if the legislature wishes to extend the scope of a criminal offence to include those who deliberately shut their eyes in order to avoid believing something, it has most of the tools it needs at its disposal. It can (and does) couple knowledge with recklessness, with suspicion, with absence of belief, and with an objective fault requirement based on knowledge, belief, or suspicion. Absent such a formula, however, it is presumptuous of the judiciary to try to achieve the same result by fiat. To do so also erodes the allegiance that the judiciary ought properly to show to the values protected by the rule of law.[115]

4. Consciousness

Finally, we should pay some attention to the role given to consciousness in the criminal law. In this area there is little agreement amongst jurists. In particular, there is no consensus as to whether knowledge or belief may be latent, or tacit, or must be explicit for criminal liability to be established. A number of different approaches may be distinguished. The first requires what Duff terms explicit knowledge, that is knowledge (or belief) to which the defendant consciously adverts. There are strong and weak versions of this position. According to the strong version the relevant knowledge or belief must have been at the forefront of the defendant's conscious mind; according to the weak version it is enough if the defendant were minimally conscious of the relevant knowledge or belief. The strong version has some academic supporters, most notably Wasik and Thompson.[116] Yet the English Law Commission recently

---

[113] *R v Forsyth* [1997] 2 Cr App R 299, at 320, per Beldam LJ.

[114] (1985) 81 Cr App R 260.

[115] There is, of course, conceptual space for (some of) the various doctrines of wilful blindness, even allowing for the fact that the legislature can couple knowledge with recklessness, suspicion, absence of belief, or an objective fault requirement based on knowledge, belief, or suspicion. This is particularly true if the objective is to isolate the purposive character of many wilful blindness doctrines. The problem is that it is almost impossible for the criminal law to fill that conceptual space without confusion. There is therefore a good rule of law argument against it trying to do so.

[116] See M. Wasik and M.P. Thompson, '"Turning a Blind Eye" As Constituting *Mens Rea*' (1981) 32 NILQ 328, at 342: 'We have argued that D should only be found to have the mental element required for the offence charged if, at the time of the *actus reus*, or at some previous time closely connected with the *actus reus*, the necessary mental element was at the forefront of his mind'.

gave credence to the weak version when, as part of a spirited defence of a *Cunningham*-type test for recklessness, it argued that the rules of subjective liability require only a 'modest degree of awareness'.[117] Despite their differences, however, advocates of both versions appear to agree that, so long as *actus reus* and *mens rea* coincide (at least approximately), then knowledge or belief need not have been adverted to by the defendant for any length of time: even a fleeting 'awareness' will do. *A fortiori*, the two camps also agree that the defendant need not have ruminated or reflected on the matter.

The second approach, in contrast, rejects the idea that knowledge or belief must have been consciously held for criminal liability to be made out. There are at least three versions of this position. One endorses what one might call a 'capacity approach' to knowledge and belief. It holds that a defendant knows or believes something if she is capable of bringing that thing to her conscious mind. A second version is less demanding. Although it extends the concepts of knowledge and belief to their latent forms, that is to knowledge or belief which is neither explicit nor action-guiding, it does not stipulate that (at the time the offence was committed) the defendant must have had the capacity to bring the relevant fact to her conscious mind. A third version argues that the crucial question is not whether the knowledge or belief was consciously or subconsciously held but whether it played a role in guiding the defendant's actions. If it did, then (be it consciously *or* subconsciously held) it should count for the purposes of the law; if it did not, then (at least for legal purposes) it should be ignored.

Given the paucity of cases to have addressed this matter directly, it is very difficult to state with confidence which of these accounts best matches the current law. One of the few relevant authorities is *R v Bello*,[118] where the Court of Appeal was asked to consider the meaning of section 24(1)(b)(i) of the Immigration Act 1971. This makes it an offence for someone to remain knowingly in the country beyond the time limited by the leave to enter that the person had been granted.[119] The appellant claimed that he had been wrongly convicted of the offence. He argued that his mother's death had 'destroyed his memory' and rendered him incapable of thinking of anything for a very long period. As a result, he said, he was not in a state to know that he was in the country after his permit had expired. The Court of Appeal rejected his argument. Observing that, despite being upset by his mother's death, he had nonetheless been 'capable of living a normal life', Lord Lane CJ, who gave the judgment of the Court, offered the following general statement on the relationship between knowledge and consciousness:

[117] Law Commission No. 218 (n. 37 above) para. 14.24. In a companion statement in the same paragraph the Commission asserts that *Cunningham*-type recklessness demands only a 'comparatively low level of cognition'.

[118] (1978) 67 Cr App R 288.

[119] Section 24(1) states: 'A person who is not a patrial shall be guilty of an offence . . . in any of the following cases . . . (b) if, having only a limited leave to enter or remain in the United Kingdom, he knowingly . . . (i) remains beyond the time limited by the leave'.

A man can do an act knowingly even though at the moment when he does it the relevant fact is not actually in his mind. If he has the capacity to restore the fact to his mind, then on the face of it we would have thought the requirement of 'knowingly' is satisfied.[120]

This statement would, at first blush, appear to endorse a version of the 'capacity approach' to knowledge (and hence to belief).[121] It certainly gives no indication that the knowledge or belief must have guided the defendant's actions for criminal liability to be established. Nonetheless, *Bello* may not be the last word on the matter. One reason for this is that a number of academic commentators have argued forcefully that the approach taken in *Bello* cuts against the basic tenets of subjectivism. That view is held, for example, by Antony Duff, who claims that when criminal liability moves away from explicit or tacit knowledge subjectivism is abandoned.[122] Wasik and Thompson take a similar view. They argue that *Bello* is inconsistent 'with the spirit of subjective liability in modern criminal law'. Unlike Duff, however, Wasik and Thompson claim that the same will be true of any approach that accepts something less than the strong version of explicit knowledge outlined above.[123]

There is also a second reason to doubt the *Bello* doctrine. This derives from the fact that Lord Lane himself introduced an important qualification to it when he said that if a man has the capacity to restore a fact to his mind then, *on the face of it*, the requirement of 'knowingly' is satisfied. By adding the italicized words, Lord Lane left the door open for defendants to argue that the *Bello* doctrine merely lays down an evidential presumption and does not establish a legal rule. Put another way, the qualification allows scope for defendants to assert that 'having the capacity to restore the fact to his mind' bears the same evidential relationship to 'knowledge' that (at least in some people's view) 'foresight of a virtual certainty' bears to 'intention'. Hence, however unsatisfactory that may be, it seems that the authority of the *Bello* dicta will remain in doubt until the matter is revisited by the appellate courts.[124]

---

[120] (1978) 67 Cr App R 288, at 290.

[121] I say 'a version of the "capacity approach"' because Lord Lane's use of the word 'restore' might be taken to mean that the relevant fact must have previously been in the defendant's *conscious* mind for the *Bello* doctrine to apply.

[122] See '*Caldwell* and *Lawrence*: The Retreat from Subjectivism' (1983) 3 OJLS 77, at 80–81. For this reason Duff now prefers a bipartite division between 'actual' knowledge and 'latent' knowledge—the former being knowledge which is used to guide actions, whether explicit or not; the latter being knowledge which is not (at the moment) being used in this way: see *Intention, Agency and Criminal Liability* (Oxford, 1990) 159–160.

[123] See M. Wasik and M.P. Thompson, ' "Turning a Blind Eye" As Constituting *Mens Rea*' (1981) 32 NILQ 328, at 332.

[124] The *Bello* case was referred to by the Court of Appeal (Civil Division) in *Immigration Appeal Tribunal v Maheswary Chelliah* [1985] Imm AR 192, where Kerr LJ made the following *obiter* remark: 'There is no rule of law, so far as I am aware, which requires, in order to establish guilt of such an offence [under s. 24(1)(b) of the Immigration Act 1971], proof that the accused not only had knowledge of the relevant fact but also that on a particular day, or when doing a particular act, he summoned that knowledge from his memory and consciously adverted to it. If

D. CONCLUSION

This chapter was written with three broad, interconnected goals: to reveal the extent to which the definitional general part of the criminal law relies on the psychological states of knowledge and belief; to analyse the structure of these psychological states; and, in the light of that investigation, to try to make better sense of the criminal law. The first section of the chapter showed that, despite the lack of attention paid to them by many legal authors, the psychological states of knowledge and belief lie at the heart of modern criminal jurisprudence: indeed they are relied on to such an extent (both directly and indirectly) that it is plausible that a proper understanding of the criminal law cannot be attained without a good grasp of what they entail. In the second section of the chapter an attempt was made to illuminate our non-legal understandings of these concepts. This was done by outlining six defining characteristics of beliefs: that they are directed towards something; that they are candidates for truth and falsity; that they necessitate a certain level of commitment; that they are always in principle open to revision and reassessment; that they are fallible; and that they depend for their identity upon their place within a network of other beliefs and states of mind. The section also cast light on the nature of our concept of knowledge and on the relationship between belief and knowledge and action and consciousness. In the final section of the chapter the analytical structure developed in the second section was used to explore some of the law's peculiarities. Amongst the conclusions reached were: (1) that the richness of our everyday concept of knowledge is not reflected in the criminal law, since for legal purposes nothing more is required of a belief for it to count as knowledge than that it be correct; (2) that a special legal meaning is given to the term belief in that, while suspicion is excluded, acceptance is not; (3) that the legal definition of belief that p does *not* extend generally to a belief that p is 'possible', 'likely', 'more likely than not', 'highly likely', etc., although that result can be (and is) achieved through the wording of particular statutory provisions; (4) that the judicially-created doctrine of 'wilful blindness' has become increasingly anomalous and represents an unwarranted usurpation by the judiciary of the authority of the legislature; and (5) that, despite the Court of Appeal's decision in *R v Bello*, there is still considerable uncertainty as to whether knowledge or belief must be explicit or tacit or may be latent for criminal liability to be established.

More work clearly remains to be done in this area. There is, for example, an urgent need to examine the extent to which these psychological states

the law made any such requirement it is difficult to see how, in the ordinary case, the burden of proof could be discharged'. But compare Lord Hope of Craighead's somewhat confusing remarks in *R v Forbes (Giles)* [2001] 3 WLR 428, at 433, concerning the decision in *R v Hussain* [1969] 2 QB 567: 'What had to be proved was that he was knowingly, and to that extent consciously and deliberately, concerned in co-operating in what he must have known was an operation of getting prohibited goods into this country'.

matter morally. There is also a need to analyse whether the criminal law is right to rely on them as heavily as it does. But those are projects for another day. In the meantime, it is hoped that this chapter has moved the debate forward by clarifying the nature of the concepts of knowledge and belief and explaining their role in modern criminal law.

Annex: Examples of Statutory Offences in the USA that Incorporate 'Knowledge' and/or 'Belief' as Mens Rea Elements

1. 'Knowledge' as a *Mens Rea* Element

(1) *Gross sexual imposition contrary to section 213.1(2) of the Model Penal Code.*[125] Section 213.1(2) states that 'a male who has sexual intercourse with a female not his wife commits a felony . . . if (b) he knows that she suffers from a mental disease or defect which renders her incapable of appraising the nature of her conduct; or (c) he knows that she is unaware that a sexual act is being committed upon her or that she submits because she mistakenly supposes that he is her husband'.

(2) *Sexual assault contrary to section 213.4 of the Model Penal Code.* Section 213.4 states (*inter alia*) that 'a person who has sexual contact with another not his spouse, or causes such other to have sexual conduct with him, is guilty of sexual assault, a misdemeanour, if: (1) he knows that the contact is offensive to the other person; or (2) he knows that the other person suffers from a mental disease or defect which renders him or her incapable of appraising the nature of his or her conduct; or (3) he knows that the other person is unaware that a sexual act is being committed'.

2. 'Knowledge' and 'Belief' as Alternative *Mens Rea* Elements

(3) *Fraudulent transfers contrary to section 15A:14-10(e) of the New Jersey Statutes Annotated (West 1984).* Section 15A:14-10(e) states that 'Every transfer made and every obligation incurred by a corporation which is or will thereby be rendered insolvent, within four months prior to the commencement of a receivership action by or against the corporation, is fraudulent as to the then existing and future creditors: (1) if made or incurred in contemplation of the commencement of the action or in contemplation of liquidation of all or the greater portion of the corporation's property, with intent to use the consideration obtained for the transfer or obligation to enable any creditor of the corporation to obtain a greater percentage of a debt than some other creditor of the same class; and (2) if the transferee or obligee of the

---

[125] The definition of 'knowingly' in the Model Penal Code is to be found in s. 2.02(2)(b).

transfer or obligation, at the time of the transfer or obligation, knew or believed that the corporation intended to make that use of the consideration'.

(4) *Intimidating former witnesses contrary to section 9A.72.110(2) of the Revised Code of Washington (2000)*. Section 9A.72.110(2) states that 'A person is guilty of intimidating a witness if the person directs a threat to a former witness because of the witness's role in an official proceeding'. Section 9A.72.110(3)(c) states that for the purposes of the section a 'former witness' means (*inter alia*) '(iii) A person whom the actor knew or believed may have been called as a witness if a hearing or trial had been held; or (iv) A person whom the actor knew or believed may have provided information related to a criminal investigation or an investigation into the abuse or neglect of a minor child'.

3. 'Knowledge' and 'Recklessness' as Alternative *Mens Rea* Elements

(5) *Interference with custody of children contrary to section 212.4(1) of the Model Penal Code*. Section 212.4(1) states that a person commits an offence 'if he knowingly or recklessly takes or entices any child under the age of 18 from the custody of its parent, guardian or other lawful custodian, when he has no privilege to do so'.

(6) *Interference with custody of committed persons contrary to section 212.4(2) of the Model Penal Code*. Section 212.4(2) states that a person is guilty of a misdemeanour 'if he knowingly or recklessly takes or entices any committed person away from lawful custody when he is not privileged to do so'.

4. 'Knowledge' and an Objective 'Belief'-Based Fault Element as Alternative *Mens Rea* Elements

(7) *Receiving stolen property contrary to section 13A-8-16(a) of the Code of Alabama (1994)*. Section 13A-8-16(a) states that 'A person commits the crime of receiving stolen property if he intentionally receives, retains or disposes of stolen property knowing that it has been stolen or having reasonable grounds to believe it has been stolen, unless the property is received, retained or disposed of with intent to restore it to the owner'.

(8) *Unlawful possession of a listed chemical contrary to title 46, section 893.149(1)(b) of the Florida Statutes (2000)*. Title 46, section 893.149(1) states that 'It is unlawful for any person to knowingly or intentionally: . . . (b) Possess or distribute a listed chemical knowing, or having reasonable cause to believe, that the listed chemical will be used to unlawfully manufacture a controlled substance'.

(9) *Sale, etc., of alcoholic liquor to persons under age contrary to section 123.47.1 of the Code of Iowa (Supp. 2001)*. Section 123.47.1 states that 'A person shall not sell, give, or otherwise supply alcoholic liquor, wine, or beer to any person knowing or having reasonable cause to believe that person to be under legal age'.

(10) *Fraud in obtaining accommodation contrary to section 21:21A of the Louisiana Revised Statutes Annotated (West Supp. 2001).* Section 21:21.A states that 'No person shall: . . . (5) obtain accommodations, food, property or services by the use of a credit card, knowing or having reasonable cause to believe that such card has been revoked, or was obtained, is retained, or is being used fraudulently'.

(11) *Sale, transfer, etc., of stolen regulated firearm contrary to article 27, section 446 of the Annotated Code of Maryland (1996).* Article 27, section 446 states that it is unlawful for any person 'to possess, sell, transfer or otherwise dispose of any stolen regulated firearm, knowing or having reasonable cause to believe same to have been stolen'.

(12) *Sale, etc., of motor vehicle master keys for illegal use contrary to chapter 266, section 140 of the General Laws of the Commonwealth of Massachusetts (2000).* Chapter 266, section 140 states that 'Whoever sells or offers to sell or solicits offers to purchase a master key designed to fit more than one motor vehicle knowing, or having reasonable cause to believe, that said key will be used for an illegal purpose' shall be guilty of an offence.

(13) *Illegal transfers of intercepting devices contrary to section 626A.18 of the Minnesota Statutes (1983).* Section 626A.18 states that 'No person shall receive an electronic, mechanical or other device, knowing or having reasonable cause to believe that such electronic, mechanical or other device has been sold or transported in violation of the provisions of [specified sections of the Minnesota penal code]'.

(14) *Endangering life or property by breaking employment contract contrary to section 613.100 of the Nevada Revised Statutes (2000).* Section 613.100 states that 'Every person who shall wilfully and maliciously, either alone or in combination with others, break a contract of service or employment, knowing or having reasonable cause to believe that the consequence of his so doing will be to endanger human life or to cause grievous bodily injury or to expose a valuable property to destruction or serious injury, shall be guilty of a misdemeanor'.

(15) *Harboring or aiding certain persons contrary to section 14-259 of the General Statutes of North Carolina (1999).* Section 14-259 states that 'It shall be unlawful for any person knowing or having reasonable cause to believe, that any person has escaped from prison, jail, reformatory, or from the criminal insane department of any State hospital, or from the custody of any peace officer who had such person in charge, or that such person is a convict or prisoner whose parole has been revoked, or that such person is a fugitive from justice or is otherwise the subject of an outstanding warrant for arrest or order of arrest, to conceal, hide, harbor, feed, clothe or otherwise aid and comfort in any manner to any such person'.

(16) *Spreading contagion contrary to section 3701.81(A) of the Ohio Revised Code Annotated (Anderson 1999).* Section 3701.81(A) states that 'No person, knowing or having reasonable cause to believe that he is suffering

from a dangerous, contagious disease, shall knowingly fail to take reasonable measures to prevent exposing himself to other persons, except when seeking medical aid'.

(17) *Receiving stolen property contrary to title 21, section 1713.A of the Oklahoma Statutes (Supp. 2001)*. Title 21, section 1713.A states that 'Every person who buys or receives, in any manner, upon any consideration, any personal property of any value whatsoever that has been stolen, embezzled, obtained by false pretense or robbery, knowing or having reasonable cause to believe the same to have been stolen, embezzled, obtained by false pretense, or robbery, or who conceals, withholds, or aids in concealing or withholding such property from the owner, shall be guilty of a felony'.

(18) *Buying illegally taken fish contrary to section 506.025 of the Oregon Revised Statutes (1999)*. Section 506.025 states that 'Whenever the commercial fishing laws state that it is unlawful to buy any food fish, illegally taken, this prohibition means that it is unlawful to buy, knowing or having reasonable cause to believe that the fish have been illegally taken or transported within this state, or unlawfully imported or otherwise unlawfully brought into this state'.

(19) *False reports concerning bombs or other explosive devices contrary to section 61-6-17(a) of the West Virginia Code (2000)*. Section 61-6-17(a) states that 'Any person who shall impart or convey or cause to be imparted or conveyed any false information, knowing or having reasonable cause to believe such information to be false, concerning the presence of any bomb or other explosive device in, at, on, near, under or against any dwelling house, structure, improvement, building, bridge, motor vehicle, vessel, boat, railroad car, airplane or other place, or concerning an attempt or alleged attempt being made or to be made to so place or explode any such bomb or other explosive device, shall be guilty of a misdemeanor'.

5. 'Knowledge' and an Objective 'Knowledge'-Based Fault Element as Alternative *Mens Rea* Elements

(20) *Unlawful possession or sale of gravestones and gravesite items contrary to section 635:7 of the New Hampshire Revised Statutes Annotated (1996)*. Section 635:7 states that 'No person shall possess or sell, offer for sale or attempt to sell, or transfer or dispose of any monument, gravestone, marker, or other structure, or any portion or fragment thereof, placed or designed for a memorial of the dead, or any fence, railing, gate, plot delineator, or curb, knowing or having reasonable cause to know that it has been unlawfully removed from a cemetery or burial ground'.

(21) *Sale or offer to sell unauthorized recordings contrary to section 570.230 of the Missouri Revised Statutes (1999)*. Section 570.230 states that 'No person shall advertise, or offer for sale, resale, or sell or resell, or cause to be sold, resold or process for such purposes any article that has been produced

in violation of [specified sections of the Missouri penal code], knowing or having reasonable grounds to know, that the sounds thereon have been so transferred without the consent of the owner'.

6. 'Knowledge' and an Objective 'Belief'-Based Fault Element and a 'Suspicion'-Based Fault Element as Alternative *Mens Rea* Elements

(22) *Harboring or concealing persons contrary to section 792 of the United States Code (2000).* 18 U.S.C. section 792 states that 'Whoever harbors or conceals any person who he knows, or has reasonable grounds to believe or suspect, has committed, or is about to commit, an offense under [specified sections of the code]' is guilty of an offense.

7. 'Does Not Believe to be True' as a *Mens Rea* Element

(23) *Perjury contrary to section 241.1 of the Model Penal Code.* Section 241.1 states that a person is 'guilty of perjury ... if in any official proceeding he makes a false statement under oath or equivalent affirmation, or swears or affirms the truth of a statement previously made, when the statement is material and he does not believe it to be true'.

(24) *Perjury contrary to section 1621(2) of United States Code (2000).* 18 U.S.C. section 1621(2) states (*inter alia*) that a person commits the crime of perjury if 'in any declaration, certificate, verification, or statement under penalty of perjury ... [he] wilfully subscribes as true any material which he does not believe to be true'.

(25) *Perjury contrary to section 11.56.200(a) of the Alaska Statutes (Michie 2000).* Section 11.56.200(a) states that 'A person commits the crime of perjury if the person makes a false sworn statement which the person does not believe to be true'.

(26) *Deception contrary to article 27, section 340(b)(1) of the Annotated Code of Maryland (Supp. 2000).* (See also section 708-800 of the Hawaii Revised Statutes (1999) and section 13A-8-1 of the Code of Alabama (1994).) Article 27, section 340(b)(1) defines 'deception' (*inter alia*) as 'knowingly to: (i) Create or confirm in another an impression which is false and which the offender does not believe to be true'.

(27) *Deception contrary to section 31.0(1)(A) of the Texas Penal Code Annotated (West 2001).* Section 31.01(1)(A) defines 'deception' (*inter alia*) as 'creating or confirming by words or conduct a false impression of law or fact that is likely to affect the judgment of another in the transaction, and that the actor does not believe to be true'.

9

Knowledge, Belief, and Culpability

G.R. SULLIVAN

Stephen Shute's valuable paper in this volume informs us of the extensive role played by the terms knowledge and belief in determining the culpability of defendants.[1] As Shute relates, an offence may explicitly require proof of knowledge or may be interpreted to require such proof. Additionally, knowledge may be paired explicitly with belief as alternative forms of culpability. Yet, as his chapter shows, these terms feature in assessments of culpability on a much larger scale than this. For example, questions pertaining to knowledge and belief may arise when determining the presence of intent or recklessness. In all of these contexts, the concept of knowledge may seem the dominant term. On closer examination, however, we often find that talk of knowledge is more accurately identified as talk about belief. Indeed, the more attention we give, in legal contexts, to the terms 'knowledge and belief', the more indistinct the boundary between them seems to be.

The reason for this lack of sharp demarcation is familiar. Like intent, knowledge and belief are used to designate the culpability required for offences but they are, of course, words of ordinary language most frequently used in nonjudgemental contexts. In normal speech we may give an approximate description of knowledge as a true belief based on reliable data and of belief as a psychological disposition to take something to be true yet without any implication that the thing believed is true. But, as we shall see, in legal contexts, findings of knowledge may be made with scant regard for the epistemological basis of the agent's conviction. Indeed, it is scarcely an exaggeration to say that any true belief held with conviction may constitute knowledge in the eye of the law. Assurance on the part of the agent that something is or will be the case may be sufficient for legal findings of culpability expressed in terms of knowledge if it turns out that the agent's state of conviction reflects the true facts. When assessing culpability, one may disregard the empirical adequacy of an agent's true beliefs. Accordingly, while this chapter divides for convenience under two main headings, respectively concerned with knowledge and belief, there is considerable interpenetration regarding the matters raised in each section.

[1] Stephen Shute, Chapter 8 in this volume, 'Knowledge and Belief in the Criminal Law'.

Shute provides an excellent general discussion of the legal and philosophical issues that arise in the search for reliability and consistency in the use of these terms. No attempt will be made here to reprise that ground. The primary focus of this chapter will be on the pressures upon and distortions of ordinary usage that arise when interpretations of ordinary language terms are the coinage of culpability findings. Subsidiary issues to be canvassed include the possibility of knowledge of the resolution of events as yet unresolved; the degree to which knowledge or beliefs relating to facts extraneous to the definitional elements of the offence charged should feature in determining liability for the offence; and the relevance for criminal liability of knowledge and beliefs concerning applicable normative standards.

A. Knowledge and Issues of Culpability

1. Epistemology

As Shute informs us, in making findings that an agent possessed requisite knowledge, courts will not investigate the adequacy of the empirical basis of the agent's state of conviction that something is or will be the case.[2] In law, if D has a belief based on *some* relevant data that Φ obtains and that belief is in fact true, she will be taken to know that Φ.

But can we entirely disconnect questions of epistemology from findings of knowledge, even in legal discourse?[3] Consider D, who is sold a stolen video-recorder by E, his workmate. D believes he has acquired a stolen recorder because he assumes that the price asked by E is much lower than the normal retail price. In fact the price asked by E is higher than the shop-price. Here we might be inclined to say that while D *believed* (correctly as it turned out) that the item was stolen he did not *know* it to be stolen. The assumption on which his true belief was based does not verify the stolen character of the goods.

In that example, characterizing D's state of mind as one of knowledge or belief is of no moment in terms of D's criminal liability: either knowledge or belief is a sufficient form of culpability for the offence of handling stolen goods.[4] But consider the following scenario. D places some fuel-soaked rags and a lighted match through the letterbox of a house. He is convinced that this will cause the house to burn down, entailing, he believes, the death of V, the sleeping occupant. The evidence is that, other things equal, D's inadequate *modus operandi* would not have started a fire sufficient to endanger V's

---

[2] Chapter 8 above at 191.

[3] Shute takes the disconnection to be complete in legal discourse when he states, 'In short, the criminal law seems to require nothing more of a belief for it to count as knowledge than it be correct': Chapter 8 above at 191. While there is academic support for this view, there is no definitive authority in English law.

[4] Theft Act 1968, s. 22.

life. As things turned out, because of an unknown gas-leak in the house, the lighted match caused an explosion, destroying the house and killing V.

Assume that D did not directly intend to kill V: D was set on destroying the house as a means to a fraudulent insurance claim; the success or otherwise of that claim was not dependent on killing V, only on the destruction of the house. Under current English law, in the absence of a direct intent to kill or cause serious bodily harm, D may be guilty of murder only if:

(a) death or serious harm to V was a virtually certain consequence of D's conduct; and

(b) D *knew* that death or serious harm to V was the virtually certain consequence of his conduct.[5]

It may well be that condition (a) is satisfied: the presence of gas and a lighted match may have made it virtually certain that an explosion sufficiently potent to cause V's death would occur. But it can hardly be said that condition (b) is satisfied: D's state of conviction concerning V's death is not based on the salient facts. That said, given that D believes death is certain, the fact that he does not know that he will kill V appears to have little or no bearing on his culpability.[6] Crucial to any moral evaluation of D's conduct is that D has killed V in circumstances where he was virtually certain that his conduct would have this effect. The fact that the causal pathway leading to V's death contained features not known to D does not seem to diminish his culpability to any extent.[7] His culpability is not most cogently expressed in terms of the concept of knowledge, at least in the core sense of that term. It seems more accurate to say that he acted in the *conviction* rather than in the knowledge that V would die. In terms of culpability, there seems to be little difference between a conviction well or poorly founded. If that is so, there may be reason to dispense with knowledge as a term of culpability and to focus on what D *believed*. In ordinary discourse, knowledge is inextricably bound to questions of cognition and epistemology and not especially attuned to issues of culpability. What seems more central to questions of blame is the degree of assurance with which D believes a particular outcome will materialize. D's beliefs about outcomes are just as germane to his culpability as is his well-founded knowledge of outcomes. Accordingly, we should anticipate that in legal discourse the borderland between knowledge and belief will be indistinct.

---

[5] *R v Woollin* [1999] 1 AC 82. For condition (b) courts employ the term 'appreciated' rather than knew; in this context these two terms may be regarded as synonymous. In formal terms, these two conditions are the gateway for a finding of *intent* rather than knowledge in the language employed in the law of murder. But as side-effects play no part in the motivation of conduct, they fall beyond the scope of intentionality and are best accommodated within the domain of knowledge/awareness: John Finnis, 'Intention and Side-Effects' in R. G. Frey and Christopher W. Morris (ed.), *Liability and Responsibility: Essays in Law and Morals* (Cambridge, 1991) 32.

[6] Compare J. C. Smith and B. Hogan, *Criminal Law* (9th edn., London, 1999) 55.

[7] On unanticipated and deviant causal pathways and moral responsibility for outcomes see Jonathan Bennett, *The Act Itself* (Oxford, 1995) 50–54.

2. Forms of Knowledge: Explicit, Tacit, and Latent[8]

The form of knowledge that fits most comfortably with issues of culpability in the criminal law is what Duff has usefully described as *explicit* knowledge—things consciously adverted to at the time the *actus reus* of the offence occurs. Consider, for example, D, who is smuggling drugs into the United Kingdom for the first time. As he enters the green channel, he is acutely aware of the heroin hidden in his suitcase. We have here the clearest possible case of knowingly evading a restriction on importation.[9] Six months later, D has made many successful drug-smuggling trips and is now quite relaxed when passing through customs. He gives no thought to the drugs in the case; his mind is on other things. But, again, we are seemingly confronted with a clear case of knowing importation. Were he to be approached by a customs officer, his mind would immediately engage with the drugs in his possession. He has *tacit* knowledge of the presence of drugs and that seems to be enough.[10]

Imagine, however, that D is passing through customs some three years later. He has ceased smuggling drugs some two years previously. However, a packet of heroin is to be found in the concealed panel of his case. He had omitted to remove it some considerable time ago and has now forgotten about its presence. The most that can be claimed is that he has *latent* knowledge of the drugs. It is by no means clear, in terms of authority or principle, whether this latent knowledge should suffice as the culpability for the offence of knowingly evading a restriction on importation.[11]

In *Bello*,[12] D was charged with knowingly remaining in the United Kingdom beyond the time limit allowed by his conditions of entry. He claimed that because of the pressure of stressful events associated with the recent death of his mother he had at no time adverted to the fact that his period of leave had expired. As Shute explains,[13] in a judgment not notable for its clarity, the Court of Appeal seemingly took the view that even if D's account had been

---

[8] This tripartite classification is taken from Antony Duff, '*Caldwell and Lawrence*: The Retreat from Subjectivism' (1983) Oxford Journal of Legal Studies 77, at 80. My account of these categories of knowledge differs in some regards from Duff's. For the purposes of our discussion here 'explicit knowledge' refers to situations where D is consciously aware of those matters germane to the *actus reus* of the offence at the time of the commission of the offence. 'Tacit knowledge' refers to those matters which are not to the forefront of D's consciousness but with which he can immediately engage by the exercise of his own volition or by way of response to stimuli. 'Latent knowledge' refers to those objects of knowledge which fall within the repertoire of things that D knows but which he can only recover by introspection or assistance.

[9] Contrary to the Customs and Excise Management Act 1979, s. 170.

[10] It may well be too that the phrase 'knowing evasion of a prohibition on importation' may include conduct occurring before the point of entry into the United Kingdom, although such a view is likely to incur jurisdictional difficulties.

[11] Cases of latent knowledge most clearly illustrate the difference between 'intent' and 'knowledge' as terms of culpability. The linkage between intent strictly so called and conduct is conceptual and explanatory whereas the things that a person knows, even knowledge relating to the definitional elements of an offence with which he is charged, may have no explanatory bearing on conduct.

[12] (1978) 67 Cr App R 288 (CA).   [13] Chapter 8 above at 199–200.

credible it would not have afforded a defence because he was capable of re-calling the fact of his expired leave had he applied his mind to that matter. Contrast *Russell*,[14] where it was held that D would not be in knowing pos-session of an offensive weapon if, at the time of his arrest in his car, he had for-gotten the fact of its existence (notwithstanding that D himself had some months earlier taped the weapon to the underside of his dashboard).

Bello then, it seems, is a case of tacit knowledge—the fact that his leave had expired while not constantly at the forefront of his mind was still something that, as it might be put, was with him, something with which he could in-stantly engage. In *Russell*, by contrast, D had lost contact with the fact that he was in possession of an offensive weapon—on reacquaintance with the weapon's existence he was reminded of a fact he no longer explicitly or tac-itly knew. Nonetheless, D had *latent* knowledge of the weapon. He was not suffering from any form of amnesia. When the police officer found the knife taped to the underside of the dashboard the presence of the knife in his car was not a fathomless mystery to D. He was reminded of the knife and why, at one time, it seemed a good idea to have a knife with him.

Our discussion of *Bello* and *Russell* suggests that for the purposes of the criminal law either explicit or tacit knowledge will provide proof of know-ledge whereas latent knowledge will not suffice.[15] One may be struck by the thinness of the line dividing tacit from latent knowledge. Indeed, it may merely differentiate between persons possessed of differing cognitive capa-cities with little purchase on questions of culpability and social protection. There may be good reason for the acquittal in *Russell*, in that the social threat posed by the possession of a weapon no longer obtained in his case: the knife was no longer kept by him in order to use should need arise. *Mutatis mutan-dis*, the same may be said of the retired drug smuggler in our earlier example: the heroin remaining in his case is more in the nature of evidence of past crimes than the stuff of current offending. To the extent, if at all, that these considerations should provide an excuse they are imperfectly captured by a distinction between tacit and latent knowledge.

This point may be reinforced by an example from an everyday context. Sup-pose that X is preoccupied with finishing a paper within a deadline. He glances at the clock and, with some consternation, notes that it is 2.40 pm and in-stantly remembers the faculty meeting he should be attending which started at 2.30 pm. He should accept a rebuke for being late but understandably might resent censure expressed in terms of knowingly not attending the start of the meeting.[16] Clearly, though, he has tacit knowledge of the time of the

[14] (1984) 81 Cr App R 315 (CA).

[15] The decision in *Russell* is queried in *R v Martindale* [1986] 3 All ER 25 and *R v McAlla* (1988) 87 Cr App R 372. These latter decisions, however, take *Russell* to be a case about the mental element required to establish 'possession', whereas at issue in *Russell* was 'knowing' pos-session.

[16] Duff (n. 8 above) regards censure in such cases as being based on an objective appraisal of conduct rather than upon a finding of culpability on subjective grounds.

meeting—it is a matter that he instantly engages with upon looking at the clock. Contrast Y, who also should be at the meeting but is sound asleep in his chair after a good lunch. He wakes up, glances at the clock at 2.40 pm, and goes back to sleep. Later he remembers about the meeting when rebuked by a colleague for not attending. Y's case is one of latent knowledge. These differing categories of knowledge applicable to X and Y respectively do not track our moral intuitions about these cases, which are likely to consist of findings of condonable lateness in the case of X and dereliction of duty in the case of Y.

This account suggests that a more clear-cut division needs to be made between explicit knowledge, on the one hand, and tacit or latent knowledge on the other. Within the latter category there are persons some of whom should and some of whom should not be censured for acts or omissions when in possession of either tacit or latent knowledge of relevant facts. Differentiation between candidates for censure or non-censure in this category is best done by departing from a subjective approach and by addressing the issue in terms of objective standards of conduct. Clearly there should not be any excuse to a charge of smuggling drugs merely because one was not adverting consciously to the possession of drugs at the point of entry into the country if the drugs had earlier been acquired to import them.[17] Less obvious is the situation where the drugs are, in effect, moribund, forgotten items, not destined for use or commerce. Similarly, there may be compelling or uncompelling reasons to excuse remaining in a country when leave to stay has expired.[18] And so on. In cases where explicit knowledge of contravening a prohibition can be proved, culpability will be prima facie established and, typically, any ground of justification or excuse undercut. But neither tacit nor latent knowledge are sure guides to the presence of a sufficient culpability. Where knowledge is designated as the culpability for an offence, it should be construed as requiring explicit knowledge. Such a constraint would inhibit the conviction of some persons who are deserving of criminal censure. However, for those cases, it would be better to depart explicitly from a knowledge standard of culpability and to formulate standards of reasonable conduct concretized in terms of the specific elements and social concerns of particular offences.[19]

---

[17] As noted in n. 10 above, in the context of the offence of knowingly evading a restriction on importation, difficulties associated with the coincidence of *actus reus* and *mens rea* may be resolvable by extending the time frame for the offence to include conduct occurring prior to the point of entry into the country.

[18] Contrast the sensitive approach of the Court of Appeal of New Zealand in *Finau v Department of Labour* [1984] 2 NZLR 396 with the notorious intransigence of the English Divisional Court in *Larsonneur* (1933) 24 Cr App R 74.

[19] An approach which assumes that failure to comply with objective standards of conduct justifies the imposition of criminal liability: see further H. L. A. Hart, 'Negligence, Mens Rea and Criminal Responsibility', in *Punishment and Responsibility* (Oxford, 1968) 138; A. P. Simester, 'Can Negligence be Culpable?' in Jeremy Horder (ed.), *Oxford Essays in Jurisprudence* (4th Series, Oxford, 2000).

3. Knowledge in the Form of Wilful Blindness

In his well-known judgment in *Roper v Taylor's Central Garages Ltd*,[20] Devlin J, as he then was, identified what he termed three 'degrees' of knowledge. The first degree is what we have termed explicit knowledge and need not further detain us. Neither need we dwell upon what he termed knowledge in the third degree, that is the knowledge a reasonable person placed in the same circumstances as D would have gleaned. Although we have argued that there is room for a more objective approach for situations where we encounter tacit or latent knowledge, it is for now, well accepted that where 'knowledge' is the requisite form of culpability, a subjective approach is taken by the criminal law. It is Devlin J's category of knowledge in the second degree that concerns us here. Within this category D will be taken to know that Φ if:

(a)   he suspects that Φ obtains;
(b)   he knows that he has the means to determine whether or not that Φ; and
(c)   he deliberately refrains from determining whether or not that Φ.

For Devlin J, if these conditions are met,[21] D will be taken to have knowledge that Φ obtains for the purposes of any criminal offence which uses knowledge as a form of culpability. Shute disputes the legitimacy of this conclusion in terms of knowledge and beliefs. He is entirely right to do so if the issue is confined to whether a person who meets the three criteria stated above possesses knowledge or belief that Φ in the lexical senses of those terms. The matter becomes more contestable if the issue is whether, *in terms of culpability*, a person who satisfies the three conditions in relation to Φ is in the same moral case as a person who has explicit knowledge of Φ.[22] It is submitted that this will very often be the case. Suppose that D is the manager of a bar which is very popular with young people. Assume that all persons are legally obliged to carry identity cards stating date of birth. D instructs his staff not to examine customers' cards as he has no wish to turn business away. Were D to be convicted for knowingly allowing underage persons to consume alcohol on licensed premises he has no cause for complaint. He has easy access to the relevant information which, for his own purposes, he would rather not have.

In terms of authority, Shute turns to a number of cases dealing with the offence of handling stolen goods. They hold that even the strongest suspicion that goods are stolen will constitute proof neither of the knowledge nor the belief that the offence requires. In their own terms these cases are correctly

---

[20] [1951] 2 TLR 284.
[21] These conditions are, perhaps, more clearly stated in the text here than they are in Devlin J's judgment which, as Shute observes in Chapter 8 above at 196–197, contains some ambiguous language. It is submitted that the conditions set out in the text provide for a defensible form of culpability.
[22] It should be stressed that Shute's concern was with the linguistic tension inherent in wilful blindness as a form of knowledge, rather than with the question whether forms of wilful blindness might be commensurate with knowledge in terms of culpability.

decided. But none of these authorities concerns the issue at hand: they do not deal with defendants who had access to the relevant information concerning the status of the goods but wilfully refused to find out the truth.[23] Neither is this surprising. It is in the nature of commerce in stolen goods that easy resolution of a buyer's suspicions will not be forthcoming from those with whom he deals. Yet should reliable means to resolve one's suspicions be available, we are faced with something more than mere suspicion. Suspicion coupled with a deliberate failure to use readily available and effective means to resolve the suspicion should be held for the purposes of the criminal law as equivalent to knowledge. Of course, it is not knowledge *per se* and an objection may be raised that it is not for judges, however sound their moral theorizing, to take words beyond their natural meaning. In response, it might be said that the rule of strict construction of criminal statutes is now a default rule and that the rule of construction for criminal statutes, as with other statutes, is their 'ordinary meaning in context'.[24] In *Westminster City Council v Croyalgrange*,[25] the House of Lords, in the context of licensing sex shops, held that 'knowledge in the second degree' fell within the purview of an offence concerning knowingly permitting unlicensed sex shops to trade. The finding was entirely appropriate. In the context of this offence, a deliberate failure to follow up doubts concerning the nature of the trade conducted on the premises, doubts that were readily resolvable, was quite the equivalent, in terms of culpability, of the most explicit form of knowledge.

4. Knowledge of Future Events

Courts have, on occasion, held that it is not possible to have knowledge of a future event. The theory goes that one can only predict, not know, the future. Accordingly D, a travel agent, was held not to have knowingly made a false trade description when he assured customers in April that the hotel swimming pool would be ready for use by August.[26]

Shute is surely correct to criticize this fallacy.[27] If I say categorically on Monday that there will be daylight in New York on Tuesday, the ensuing daylight that New York enjoys on Tuesday does not confirm any prediction I have made; it demonstrates the truth of what I said on Monday.[28] Of course, it is perfectly possible that, according to information to hand, I cannot know the truth of some particular statement about the future at the time I make it.

---

[23] It should be emphasized that Shute does not claim that the defendants had means to confirm their suspicions.

[24] See A. P. Simester and G. R. Sullivan, *Criminal Law: Theory and Doctrine* (Oxford, 2000) 45–51.

[25] [1986] 2 All ER 353 (HL).

[26] *R v Sunair Holidays* [1973] 1 WLR 1105; *Beckett v Cohen* [1973] 1 WLR 1593.

[27] Chapter 8 above at 186–187.

[28] For full explication see Alan R. White, 'Future Truths' in *Misleading Cases* (Oxford, 1991) 113.

If I were to say on Monday that it will be *sunny* in New York on Tuesday my statement may be based on incontrovertible meteorological data or it may be an uninformed guess. Whether we can know the truth of statements about the future depends upon the particular case. Yet according to the facts of the matter, it may be perfectly possible to know by April that the swimming pool will *not* be ready for August.

A converse situation sometimes occurs when courts hold that the resolution of future events may be 'known' in circumstances in which it was quite impossible to know what form the resolution would take. For example, in the law of criminal conspiracy, a conspirator must *intend* or *know* that 'facts or circumstances necessary for the commission of [the substantive offence] shall or will exist at the time when the conduct constituting the offence is to take place'.[29] Assume that D and E agree to kill V. They know that V drives home by either route A or route B. They decide that their plot is feasible only if V takes route B. They agree to meet on 1 November and to intercept and kill V should he take route B. This would be held to be a criminal conspiracy but it is hard to see, linguistically, how the *mens rea* for the offence is made out. The conspirators cannot *intend* that V take route B unless they have means of influencing which route he chooses to drive. They cannot *know* that V will take route B if there is any likelihood that V will take route A on 1 November. Convictions sustained in such cases are useful in so far as they refute any notion that, *in legal discourse*, one can never be found to have knowledge of facts relating to the future.[30] However, in so doing, they afford graphic demonstrations of how statutory language is sometimes completely overridden. The offence of conspiracy needs to be redrafted in language more suited to the realities of the offence of conspiracy.[31]

5. Knowledge and the *Actus Reus* of Offences

On first principles one should expect that when knowledge, by specification or interpretation, is the culpability requirement for an offence, proof of knowledge should extend to all definitional elements of the offence, unless a contrary intention clearly appears. Conversely, knowledge of matters going beyond the definitional particulars of the offence should not feature in deliberations concerning liability for the offence but should be matters of mitigation or aggravation at the sentencing stage. Students of English criminal law will be familiar with the fact that neither of these conditions holds: even for crimes which *ex facie* do not involve strict liability as to one or more elements of the offence, something less than proof of knowledge may suffice for one or more elements of the offence notwithstanding that proof of knowledge is taken to be the relevant culpability standard for the offence. Furthermore,

---

[29] Criminal Law Act 1977, s. 1(2).   [30] e.g. *R v O'Hadhmaill* [1996] Crim LR 509.
[31] J C Smith, 'Conspiracy under the Criminal Law Act 1977' [1977] Criminal LR 598 and 638.

knowledge of matters extraneous to the *actus reus* of the offence may be taken to be decisive on a question germane to liability for the offence.

(i) Knowledge of matters within the definitional elements of the offence

What has been termed the 'correspondence principle'[32] sets an expectation that the *mens rea* required for an offence should correspond to the terms of the *actus reus*, an expectation given a considerable boost by the recent House of Lords decision in *B v DPP*.[33] It remains to be seen whether that decision will entrench the principle across the range of offences which require *mens rea*. Certainly, at present, the principle is of imperfect application. By way of example, consider the offence of the knowing evasion of a restriction on importation.[34] The range of items subject to restriction is, of course, extensive, and we will confine attention to prohibited drugs. The maximum penalty for the offence varies according to the class of drug imported: from a combination of the decision in *Courtie*[35] and the correspondence principle,[36] one would anticipate that, for example, a conviction for importing a class A drug (the most serious drug importation offence) would require knowledge that the drug imported was a class A drug. But on the state of the authorities, including decisions of the House of Lords, nothing could be further from the truth. All that is required is a *belief* that the item in possession is an item subject to import control—a conviction for knowingly importing a class A drug will follow if the item possessed is in fact a class A drug.[37]

These decisions are influenced by the exigencies of law enforcement. They are clearly contrary to the correspondence principle and doubtful in terms of authority.[38] But should the correspondence principle be rigidly applied? A full application of the correspondence principle has the virtue of certainty and clarity. The moral value of the principle is seen most clearly when insisting, for a serious offence, that the *mens rea* must correspond to the *actus reus*: a

---

[32] Andrew Ashworth, *Principles of Criminal Law* (3rd edn., Oxford, 1999); Jeremy Horder, 'A Critique of the Correspondence Principle' [1995] Criminal LR 759; Barry Mitchell, 'In Defence of a Principle of Correspondence' [1999] Criminal LR 195; Jeremy Horder, 'Questioning the Correspondence Principle—A Reply' [1999] Criminal LR 206; A. P. Simester and G. R. Sullivan, *Criminal Law: Theory and Doctrine* (Oxford, 2000) 177–181.

[33] [2000] 1 All ER 833. In *B v DPP*, the House of Lords ruled that a requirement for *mens rea* must be read as extending to all elements of the offence including in the sphere of sexual offences the age of the victim; an element that, hitherto, had been construed as a strict liability element.

[34] Customs and Excise Management Act 1979, s. 170.   [35] [1984] AC 463.

[36] In *R v Courtie* the House of Lords decided that if proof of any given fact would determine the statutory maximum penalty available for an offence otherwise defined in general terms, the fact which determines the statutory maximum becomes a defining element of a discrete offence. Accordingly, while s. 170 of the Customs and Excise Management Act 1979 proscribes in general terms the importation of restricted items, this general proscription embraces many forms of contraband which under various statutory provisions attract greatly varying penalties. Strict application of the correspondence principle would require proof of *mens rea* in relation to any fact which determines the maximum sentence.

[37] *R v Taafe* [1984] AC 539; *R v Shivpuri* [1987] AC 1; and *R v Forbes* [2001] 4 All ER 24.

[38] *B v DPP* [2000] 1 All ER 833.

conviction for importing a class A drug should require knowledge of the nature of the drug. But what if D believes that he is importing heroin whereas in fact the packets contain cannabis? A correspondence principle purist would allow a conviction for attempted heroin importation but dismiss a charge of knowing importation of cannabis.

That would be overrefined. Departing from the correspondence principle and substituting a substantive judgement of culpability, D has *mens rea en sus* for the cannabis-related offence. It would be bizarre to become involved in importing heroin but to draw the line at cannabis![39] D has no ground of complaint should he be convicted for the cannabis offence. It is submitted that the correspondance principle should rigidly be applied to disallow the *mens rea* for a lesser offence sufficing as the *mens rea* for a more serious offence. But in the converse case, insistence on the correspondence principle becomes a dogma precluding a more substantive moral evaluation. Admittedly, following this approach may lead to a loss of clarity, should dispute arise concerning the moral equivalence of different types of offence. Issues of commensurability will arise, particularly on the matter of whether a willingness to injure propriety interests can be made equivalent to a willingness to cause injury to a person. For example, the decision in *Pembliton*[40] held that foresight of injury to the person would not provide *mens rea* for an offence of malicious damage to property. If the view is taken that vandalism is a distinctive wrong incommensurable with violence to the person, the decision is clearly correct. Less impressed would be persons of the opinion that breaking a window (the damage in *Pembliton*) was less serious than breaking a head (the target of the projectile).

Once the appropriate culpability standard has been resolved, one would anticipate that it should be applicable to all the constituent elements of the offence.[41] However, at least for the crime of attempt, this may not be the case. In *R v Khan*,[42] D was charged with attempted rape. On the face of it, the culpability required by section 1 of the Criminal Attempts Act 1981 is an intention to have intercourse in the knowledge that there is no consent to the act. It was held that, provided an intent to have intercourse was proved, it sufficed that there was recklessness as to the possibility of lack of consent. This departs from a clear requirement to prove knowledge.[43] There may well be

---

[39] In *R v Patel*, 7 August 1991 (CA), transcript 87/4351/51, Woolf LJ, as he then was, considered, *obiter*, that D would be a party to a conspiracy to import cannabis in circumstances where he had mistakenly assumed that the drug to be imported was heroin. The learned judge cogently reasoned that in the realm of the importation of drugs, a willingness to be involved in the importation of a class A drug implied a preparedness to become involved in the smuggling of lesser drugs.

[40] (1874) LR 2 CCC.

[41] Particularly in the light of the recent decision in *B v DPP* [2000] 1 All ER 833. In *R v Forbes* [2001] 4 All ER 24, the House of Lords confirmed the approach criticized in the text but, unfortunately, did not consider *B v DPP*.

[42] [1990] 2 All ER 783. See too *A-G's Reference (No. 3 of 1992)* [1994] 2 All ER 121.

[43] As the 1981 Act requires an intent to commit the substantive offence it should follow that 'knowledge' should be the standard of culpability for circumstance elements beyond the control and volition of D.

grounds on which to justify the result in *Khan* without resorting to mere recklessness as the culpability standard for circumstance elements.[44] It would
be unfortunate however if *Khan* were to be read as endorsing a doctrine to
the effect that, where intent or knowledge is specified as the *mens rea* for an
offence, recklessness will suffice as to circumstance elements of the offence
provided intent/knowledge is present as to other constituent parts of the
offence. Were there to be a general doctrine to such effect, on occasion the
culpability specified for the commission of a crime requiring proof of intent
or knowledge would be substantially diminished.[44a]

*(ii) Knowledge of matters falling outside the definitional elements of the
offence*

The argument in the previous section supports an exception to, and does not
undermine, the well-known arguments in favour of maintaining a correspondence between the *mens rea* requirement and the *actus reus* elements of an offence. A concomitant of the correspondence principle is that *mens rea* should
go to all elements of the offence as a necessary *and* sufficient condition of
liability. Thus, as a matter of principle, knowledge, or the lack of knowledge,
of matters falling outside the definitional elements of offences should go to aggravation of mitigation but *not* to liability.[45] For example, prior to the Law
Reform (Sexual Offences) Act 1967, the offence of buggery was committed irrespective of the consent or non-consent of the sexual partner. With changing
sexual mores, the presence or absence of consent made an enormous difference to culpability—indeed, other things equal, the difference between culpability and non-culpability. However, under the unreformed law, it was correct
in terms of legal principle to permit the prosecution to argue its case without
adverting to the question of D's knowledge of the non-consent of V.[46]

In cases involving the liability of principal offenders, this general rule appears
to be applied with a modicum of consistency: proof of knowledge pertains to the

---

[44] cf. G. R. Sullivan, 'Intent, Subjective Recklessness and Culpability' (1992) 12 Oxford
Journal of Legal Studies 380 where it is argued that a finding of 'wilful blindness' may have been
made with respect to the absence of consent and that wilful blindness may be regarded as the legal
equivalent of proof of knowledge; on which see section A3 above. The general applicability of
the approach taken in *Khan* may also be limited by stressing the context of liability for attempts:
in *Khan*, and also in *A-G's Reference (No. 3 of 1992)* [1994] All ER 121, it was taken to be appropriate to align as closely as possible the culpability for an attempt with the culpability required for the substantive offence.

[44a] For example, D might be found to intend permanently to deprive V of property for the purposes of theft in circumstances where D is unsure whether the property is ownerless or still belongs to V.

[45] This approach puts a premium on including elements germane to variations of culpability
within the definition of the offence, which should tend towards particularity of definition rather
than broad brush offences: see further D. A. Thomas, 'Form and Function in the Criminal Law'
in P. R. Glazebrook (ed.), *Reshaping the Criminal Law* (London, 1978) 21.

[46] With the advent of the Law Reform (Sexual Offences) Act 1967, however, even in circumstances where consent did not provide a complete defence, it nonetheless capped the maximum available sentence. Applying *R v Courtie* [1984] AC 463 (n. 36 above), the issue of consent
becomes integral to all charges of buggery and must be dealt with at the trial stage.

constituent elements of the offence (or, as discussed above, may fall short of them)[47] but does not go beyond them. Such consistency of approach is not to be found in cases involving conspirators with and accomplices to the principal offenders. Formerly, there was authority to support the view that in order to be implicated in the crime of another it was not enough to know the kind of crime the other had in mind to commit; in addition, some knowledge of circumstantial detail was required. Accordingly in *Lomas*[48] it was not enough for D to give P housebreaking equipment in the knowledge that P would be assisted to carry out burglaries. Additionally, D was required to be aware of the identity of P's victims. The idea seems to be that D is insufficiently 'in on the plot' unless such details are known. Fortunately, in cases involving forms of complicity through the provision of material assistance, this approach is no longer followed. In *Bainbridge*,[49] D became P's accomplice to burglary by supplying P with cutting equipment. D knew that P would use the equipment to break into safes; it was unnecessary for D to know that P's victim was the Stoke Newington branch of the Midland Bank. Further, in *R v Maxwell*,[50] where D was pressurized into driving a group of terrorists who were on an operation, without D's being vouchsafed any details of what kind of operation was afoot, D was found to be their accomplice on the basis that he had contemplated the possibility that the crime actually committed might be carried out. D did not have to know that such a crime would be perpetrated: it was enough for him to know that he was assisting a criminal enterprise which involved commission of one of a number of offences falling within his contemplation.

However, the older approach lingers on in cases where D becomes a member of a joint criminal enterprise, that is where his involvement goes beyond material assistance and he becomes a voluntary participant in a criminal plot. Liability in these circumstances may depend on knowledge of aspects of the crime extraneous to its definitional elements. Professor Sir John Smith has lent his authority to the view that, if D joins in an enterprise to kill V with V's consent, he should not be held a party to the killing if P kills V after V has withdrawn his consent to be killed.[51] Yet consent is irrelevant to the definition of murder. Smith's position is fortified by the decision of the House of Lords in *R v English*[52] where D and P in concert attacked V with wooden staves, whereupon P drew a knife and fatally stabbed V. That P might use a knife was not within D's contemplation. It was ruled that use of the knife was something different in kind from an attack with staves and consequently D was wholly unimplicated in the killing of V. On this view a material variation from the joint enterprise may occur notwithstanding that P still commits the very offence contemplated by D.

---

[47] See n. 42 and associated text.   [48] (1913) 9 Cr App R 220 (CCA).
[49] [1960] 1 QB 129 (CCA).   [50] [1978] 3 All ER 1140 (HL).
[51] J. C. Smith and B. Hogan, *Criminal Law* (9th edn., London, 1999) 140 approving *S v Robinson* (1968) ISA 666.
[52] [1999] 1 AC 1.

But should such variations affect liability? Suppose that D and P agree to beat V to death with wooden staves. As D and P belabour V's prone body with the staves, P tires of the work involved in this laborious method and kills V instantly by shooting him. Suppose that D was wholly unaware that P might do this. Nothing essential has changed. The joint enterprise was to kill V and changes in the *modus operandi* do not alter the essential nature of that enterprise.[53] Likewise, where D agrees with P that P should rob W, a person known to carry large sums of money, nothing of significance changes if P encounters and robs V, who also carries large sums of money. What contributes a material variation should be informed by the parameters of the offence to which the joint enterprise related.

Of course, differences about the nature of the enterprise which arise between D and P may preclude a joint enterprise or conspiracy from arising *ab initio*. If D and P agree to obtain money from V 'by the usual method' there is unlikely to be a finding of conspiracy if D takes the expression to mean theft while P understands it as a reference to blackmail. Situations may arise, too, where the identity of the victim is material and misunderstandings about the identity of the victim are inimical to proof of agreement. But where a conspiracy or joint enterprise is formed, changes in method, victim, or other circumstances which arise in the course of the implementation of the criminal project and which are uncontemplated by D should be immaterial to D's liability unless they change the nature of the offence into an offence more serious than the offence that D contemplated would be committed.

B. Belief and Issues of Culpability

For D to believe that Φ requires a degree of commitment or acceptance on D's part that Φ *is* the case (not merely that might be or could be the case). Shute considers that beliefs properly so called occur if and only if D has a *commitment* to the truth of Φ.[54] He contrasts the situation where D merely *accepts* that Φ and reckons the latter not to be a case of belief. It is true, as he points out, that we can accept facts or propositions as true for the sake of discussion or argument and our acceptance need not betoken any commitment to the truth of a presupposed fact or proposition. Yet when we use the term 'accept' in the sense that the thing asserted to be true is recognized to be correctly asserted as true, the distinction between a commitment to and acceptance of the truth of the matter asserted seems thin. In any event, Shute accepts that in legal contexts no distinction is likely to be drawn between a state of commitment and a state of acceptance when acceptance is used in this sense.

---

[53] The decision in *R v English* gains some force from the fact that as an intention to cause grievous bodily harm suffices as the *mens rea* for murder, a 'substantial variation' exception cuts down to some extent an excessively wide form of liability. The cure for that, however, is a narrower formulation of the *mens rea* for murder.

[54] Chapter 8 above at 183–187.

When we assert that D *knows* that Φ, we make a claim about the mental disposition of D and a claim concerning the state of the world. We assert both that D believes that Φ and that Φ obtains in fact. When we assert that D believes Φ we make only the claim that D accepts that Φ. There is no necessary implication as to the truth or otherwise of D's belief. If D's belief corresponds with what is taken by the tribunal of fact to be the true state of affairs, there is, as we have noted, little practical distinction in legal discourse to be drawn between states of belief and states of knowledge.[55] It is where D's belief is taken to be false that questions of belief have their own domain.

1. True Beliefs

As Shute observes, knowledge and belief are often paired as alternative forms of culpability but the practical effect of such pairing is exceedingly limited if there is a requirement that the matter believed should be true. So while a person may be convicted of handling stolen goods if she believed the goods to be stolen, the inculpatory potential of that mind-set is sharply reined in by the requirement that the goods must indeed be stolen.[56] As our earlier example demonstrated, D may handle stolen goods in a situation where it is more apt to say that she believed rather than knew the goods were stolen. But since even the strongest suspicion is, properly, not regarded as a state of belief,[57] the number of cases of true belief which do not, at one and the same time, amount in law to states of knowledge will be exceedingly small.

The same applies for exculpatory beliefs. If, for example, D defends himself against V there is no need to differentiate a case of D's believing defensive force to be required from a case of his knowing that defensive force was required, provided an actual need for defensive force had arisen.

2. False Beliefs

Beliefs held by D which are found not to correspond to the true facts may have an inculpatory or exculpatory effect.

(i) Inculpation

The inculpatory effect of false beliefs is most prominent in the law of attempts. Return to the example of D believing he has acquired a stolen video recorder because he has mistakenly assumed that the price he has been asked to pay is less than the normal retail price. As earlier discussed, if the recorder *is* stolen a conviction for handling stolen goods will follow. A conviction for

---

[55] See section A1 above. [56] Theft Act 1968, s. 22.
[57] *R v Moys* (1984) 79 Cr App R 72; *R v Forsyth* [1977] 2 Cr App R 299.

attempting to handle stolen goods will follow if the goods are not stolen.[58] Should a foolish, unfounded belief give rise to any criminal liability where no societal harm and no danger of such harm has arisen? The issue arises even more starkly where the belief may be considered deranged. Suppose that D sticks pins into a wax effigy convinced that this will cause V to die. Assuming D has no mental condition defence (and superstitious or magical beliefs will by no means entail any such defence), there is no logical bar to a conviction for attempted murder.[59]

Undoubtedly, in terms of prosecutorial decisions, liability in the latter circumstances is unlikely. But the fact that such liability is theoretically possible gives pause for thought. For this kind of case, Duff usefully proposes an 'engagement with the world' defence: liability should not ensue for conduct which has no engagement, and can have no engagement, with forces in the world as it is presently understood.[60] Duff further proposes that for the earlier case of purchasing goods believed to be stolen, liability for attempt should not ensue if the belief that the goods were stolen played no part in the practical reasoning that led D to acquire the goods.[61] These are appropriate limitations on the inculpatory effect of false beliefs. The accepted justification of liability for impossible attempts is that D, with requisite culpability, demonstrates a propensity and a capacity to cause harm. Where the conduct of D does not show any potential for harm, liability rests solely on an assessment of the badness of D's character.[62] As such it violates the harm principle, even versions that permit the accommodation of remote and contingent harms.

(ii) Exculpation

Subjective and objective approaches. False beliefs, to constitute a form of exculpation, must either lead to a state of mind incompatible with proof of the *mens rea* required for the offence charged or ground an excuse or justification. For many years, there has been an ongoing dispute whether false beliefs sufficient to exculpate should satisfy a test of reasonableness. The intractable disputes between 'subjectivists' and 'objectivists' cannot be engaged with here. Suffice it to say that, to date, there has been no 'knockdown' argument in favour of one approach or the other. Arguments in favour of a subjective or objective approach gain much of their persuasive force from the particular

---

[58] *R v Shivpuri* [1981] AC 1, reversing *Anderton v Ryan* [1985] 1 AC 560. As discussed earlier (nn. 37, 56 above and associated text) it has been held in the context of liability for substantive offences that a belief that Φ may be taken as knowledge that Φ. However, substantive offences, unlike attempts, do not involve liability based solely on a false belief. The *actus reus* for the offence with which D has been charged must be present.

[59] Criminal Attempts Act 1981, s. 1(2).

[60] Antony Duff, *Criminal Attempts* (Oxford, 1996) 398.   [61] ibid., 378–384.

[62] While it is agreed with Duff that, where D buys an item such as a video recorder falsely believing it to be stolen, it does not follow that D should be convicted for an attempt, formulating a provision which makes appropriate discrimination between different forms of impossibility has, to date, proved to be insuperably difficult: see further Glanville Williams, 'The Lords and Impossible Attempts' [1986] CLJ 33.

offence or defence in issue. If the entirely plausible view is taken that the disregard of respect and autonomy implicit in the crime of rape is present when it would be obvious to any reasonable person that V was not consenting to intercourse, then it is justifiable to disregard D's unreasonable belief that V was consenting.[63] By contrast, it may be considered that in the confused and fast moving events that frequently precede outbreaks of spontaneous violence, any genuine belief that force was required by way of self-defence should serve to excuse.[64] That assessment need not hold for societies with easy access to firearms and a high associated death rate. In such countries, a measure of restraint influenced by a reasonableness requirement may be taken to be in the general societal interest notwithstanding the risk of harsh verdicts.[65] It is not necessary to discuss these issues here. The point is that whether a false belief *per se* or a false belief grounded in reasonableness serves to exculpate is a function of many contingent considerations rather than the exclusive product of some *a priori* moral perspective. If, however, one's moral theory will accept as just only those convictions based on subjective appraisals of culpability, considerations such as social protection and civic order which may argue for a different approach will be excluded.

3. Beliefs and Normative Values

This chapter is concerned with knowledge and beliefs that relate to questions of fact; it falls beyond its scope to discuss the extent to which knowledge and beliefs concerning the state of the applicable *law* should be taken into account when assessing the culpability of defendants. Suffice it here to say that an inflexible application of the principle that ignorance or mistake of law does not excuse from liability will produce harsh verdicts.[66] Indeed, a qualified mistake of law defence has been cogently argued for in this volume.[67] It remains to be seen, however, whether a more general mistake/ignorance of law defence can be provided without unduly undermining the obligatory and impersonal character of legal regulation.

When delineating any mistake of law defence, one must confront and negotiate the intractable fact/law divide.[68] One feature of that disputed borderland does require discussion here: normative standards of appraisal. English law makes considerable use of such standards, standards such as reasonable

---

[63] T. Pickard, 'Culpable Mistakes and Rape: Relating Mens Rea to the Crime' (1980) 30 U Toronto LJ 75.

[64] *R v Williams (Gladstone)* [1987] 3 All ER 411 (CA).

[65] *Beard v United States* (1895) 158 U.S. 550; *People v Johnson* (1954) 117 N.E. 2d 91.

[66] Andrew Ashworth, 'Excusable Mistake of Law' [1974] Criminal LR 652; Douglas Husak and Andrew von Hirsch, 'Culpability and Mistake of Law' in Stephen Shute, John Gardner and Jeremy Horder (eds.), *Action and Value in the Criminal Law* (Oxford, 1993) 157.

[67] Andrew Ashworth, Chapter 13 in this volume, 'Testing Fidelity to Legal Values: Official Involvement and Criminal Justice' at 302–310.

[68] Glanville Williams, 'Law and Fact' [1976] Criminal LR 472 and 534.

force, due care and attention, dishonesty, etc. If such standards are not particularized by a subset of rules, it is conventional to regard the application of such standards to particular circumstances as involving a question of fact.[69] However, it is only a question of fact in the sense that the jury rather than the judge makes the evaluation and its decision has no precedential force. But the issue to be resolved by the jury is a normative one.

Characterizing the application of broad standards of appraisal as questions of fact may lead courts to overlook that the appraisal involves *obligatory* normative standards. By so doing, they may allow undue latitude to forms of unworthy beliefs.[70] For example, in *R v Scarlett*,[71] D was allowed a mistake of fact defence on the basis of his belief that the force he employed to expel a trespasser was reasonable force, notwithstanding a jury finding that the force used was excessive. This was an error, corrected in subsequent decisions.[72] Where a normative judgment involves broad community-based standards of value such as reasonable force, there is no scope for the equivalent of a mistake of law defence. We are not dealing with a thicket of regulatory law where even the best advised and well intentioned may make a condonable error as to what is required legally. Rather, we are dealing with values integral to organized community life from which D should not be exempted unless afflicted with some relevant form of disability. D's firm conviction that the force he used was reasonable may merely demonstrate the gulf between his values and those of the community at large.

Shute condones the error of the Court of Appeal in *Scarlett* when, in the context of findings of recklessness, he asks why, for subjectivists, D's belief that the risk he took was justified is not regarded as relevant to judgements of his culpability as is his perception of the facts and circumstances that constituted the risk.[73] But, as indicated above, subjectivists (and, indeed, objectivists) should find no difficulty in distinguishing between beliefs concerning primary facts and circumstances on the one hand and beliefs about values on the other. Consider D, who is practising archery in his garden, a garden abutting a public footpath. He sees a group of ramblers approaching and recognizes the risk of injury to one or more of them should he continue with his practice. Yet he carries on firing at the target in a self-righteous frame of mind as he firmly considers that a property-holder's right to enjoy activities on his property should not be inhibited by the liberties of mere ramblers. Surely, in

---

[69] *Brutus v Cozens* [1973] AC 854 (HL). The decision is followed very erratically: D.W. Elliot, 'Brutus v Cozens: Decline and Fall' [1989] Criminal LR 323.

[70] A principal criticism of the decision in *R v Ghosh* [1982] QB is that it may allow D to be exempted from community standards of honesty if unaware that his conduct fell below those standards. One might remark, however, that the *Ghosh* test will now assist the argument that theft and other offences which rely heavily on dishonesty as the defining core are compatible with Article 7 of the European Convention on Human Rights.

[71] [1993] 4 All ER 629.

[72] *R v Owino* [1996] 2 Cr App R 128 (CA); *R v Armstrong-Braun* [1999] Criminal LR 416.

[73] Chapter 8 above at 181–182.

the event of injury, he cannot claim that he was not reckless. His views about the rights of property-holders merely demonstrate a rebarbative opinion. To allow such an opinion to deflect a finding of recklessness is not to go with the grain of subjectivism but to allow an extreme form of moral relativism.[74]

C. Summary

Summarized below are some of the conclusions reached in the various sections of this chapter.

(1) In terms of culpability, there may, as a matter of law, be reason to assimilate all true beliefs to knowledge even in cases where there is an absence of any epistemological basis for the true belief.

(2) English law would appear to draw a distinction between explicit and tacit knowledge on the one hand and latent knowledge on the other; the former establishes proof of knowledge whereas the latter category does not. A better division is between explicit knowledge on the one hand and tacit/latent knowledge on the other. Only explicit knowledge reliably captures a culpability sufficient for those offences with a *mens rea* requirement expressed in terms of knowledge. Any shortfall in the appropriate criminalization of conduct that may be caused by dispensing with tacit knowledge as a form of *mens rea* should be remedied by objective forms of liability crafted in the light of the nature and policy of the particular offence.

(3) The form of culpability known as wilful blindness is appropriately considered a form of culpability equivalent to proof of explicit knowledge. Accordingly, extension of the legal meaning of knowledge to encompass wilful blindness falls within the legitimate scope of judicial interpretation.

(4) In principle, knowledge of the future falls within the domain of knowledge strictly-so-called alongside knowledge of the present and the past. Nonetheless, it will frequently be impossible to know at the present time the resolution of some future event. In such circumstances the legal conception of knowledge should not be manipulated to attribute knowledge of that event to a defendant. Rather, where appropriate, a different *mens rea* standard should be formulated by legislation.

(5) Where, by specification or interpretation, knowledge is the required culpability standard for an offence, knowledge relating to all the definitional elements of the offence should prima facie be required. This requirement may be legitimately waived where a defendant believes he

---

[74] A relativism that goes further than that allowed by the decision in *Ghosh* (n. 70 above). At least, under *Ghosh*, D will be found dishonest if he is aware of what the community standard of honesty is (albeit that he does not share those values).

is committing a more serious offence than the one with which he is charged. Knowledge of matters extraneous to the definitional elements of the offence may properly be germane to matters of sentencing but should not be made relevant to issues of liability.

(6) Belief, in contradistinction to knowledge, becomes important in terms of criminal liability where a defendant is possessed of a false rather than a true belief.

(7) The inculpatory force of false beliefs *per se* is for practical purposes confined to the law of attempts. Liability should not be incurred for beliefs which have no engagement, and could have no engagement, with forces in the world as presently understood. Neither should a false belief incur liability where no harm is threatened and the causing of harm plays no part in the defendant's practical reasoning.

(8) The question whether a false belief *per se* or a false belief that satisfies a test of reasonableness should be required to accord exculpation cannot be resolved exclusively by reference to any *a priori* moral perspective. The specifics of the crime or defence and current policy and social concerns may be allowed to determine the choice of culpability standard.

(9) The objective application of normative standards of conduct is entirely compatible with a subjective approach to questions of criminal liability.

10

Recklessness and the Duty to Take Care

VICTOR TADROS *

A. A PROBLEM CONCERNING RECKLESSNESS

Recklessness is concerned with risks, in particular the risk that the *actus reus* of an offence will come about. It is common ground that it is at least sometimes acceptable for the criminal law to deal with those who risk the performance of the *actus reus* of an offence if that *actus reus* comes about. At least in some circumstances, if A takes a risk that B will be killed and B dies, A's action is sufficiently blameworthy to warrant criminal liability, even if A's action is not as blameworthy as an intentional killing. The narrowest common definition of recklessness, what is called *subjective* recklessness, is concerned with risks that are deliberately taken. Some writers, including both J.C. Smith[1] and Glanville Williams,[2] think that this is the only appropriate construction of recklessness. Subjectivists argue that a defendant ought to be considered reckless for the purpose of imposing criminal liability if and only if (a) her action was sufficiently risky to warrant a criminal sanction; and (b) she was aware that her action was that risky.[3] By contrast, objectivist writers argue that it is appropriate to find a defendant criminally liable where (a) her action was sufficiently risky to warrant a criminal sanction; and either (bi) she was aware of that risk or (bii) although she was not aware of that risk, she *ought* in some sense to have been aware that there was such a risk.

* Many thanks to those who participated in seminars at the University of Aberdeen and the University of Birmingham at which an earlier draft of this chapter was given. It has benefited in particular from the comments of Stephen Shute, Andrew Simester and Neil Walker.

[1] See his scathing note to *R v Caldwell* [1981] Criminal LR 392 and further, though rather unreflective, discussion in *Criminal Law* (9th edn., London, 1999) 63–67.

[2] cf. in particular G. Williams, 'The Unresolved Problem of Recklessness' (1988) 8 Legal Studies 74.

[3] Although Stephen Shute questions the point in Chapter 8 in this volume ('Knowledge and Belief in the Criminal Law'; see too the reply by G. R. Sullivan, Chapter 9 in this volume, 'Knowledge, Belief, and Culpability'), I assume that the defendant need not have believed her action was worthy of criminal sanctions, and that it suffices that she believed her action was risky to the degree that is recognized in law as being sufficiently serious to warrant criminal sanctions. There are good reasons to think that this is the better view: we are interested in our, not her, assessment of the reasons for action. See V. Tadros, 'Practical Reasoning and Intentional Action' (2000) 20 Legal Studies 104 at 104–106.

Subjectivists argue that a risky action is only morally significant if the risk is not only taken but also *chosen*. And one cannot choose to take a risk unless one is aware of that risk. Consequently, they conclude, it is only where the defendant was aware of the risk she was taking that criminal liability ought to ensue. Objectivists, on the other hand, argue that it is the responsibility of the defendant to find out about the risks of the actions that she performs. They suggest that this is both a limited and a warranted burden to place on citizens. Consequently, *mens rea* ought to be attributed where the defendant failed to realize that the action that she performed involved serious risks that she ought to have realized may come about as a result of her action.

Various ways have been suggested in which we might go about determining whether or not a defendant ought to have realized that the action that she performed carried risks with it. For example, we might say that the defendant ought to have realized that there were risks if the ordinary person would have known of those risks. Or it might be that the defendant ought to have realized that there were risks, in the sense appropriate for the attribution of *mens rea*, only if an individual with similar characteristics to her would have known of those risks. And then there is the thorny question of which characteristics are important.[4] Alternatively, we might only say that the defendant ought to have recognized that there were risks if her failure to observe them resulted from some blameworthy attitude, say indifference,[5] or some blameworthy emotion, say contempt.[6] Finally, we might say that an individual ought to have realized that there were risks if she did not take sufficient care in determining what risks her action involved.[7] There seems to be no consensus amongst objectivists either as to which is the best theory of objective recklessness or even as to the foundations upon which a theory might be built.[8]

This chapter arises out of a concern that if recklessness is going to be extended beyond subjective principles, a full theoretical discussion of the extent to which this is justifiable is required. This theoretical discussion ought to develop from a general discussion of the limits of the criminal law. For whilst it may be right that an individual ought to be held responsible for ensuring that her actions do not pose serious risks to the public, it does not follow that *criminal liability* is

---

[4] This is closely related to what are called 'capacity' tests which ask whether the defendant had the capacity to have been aware of the risks. cf. H. L. A. Hart, *Punishment and Responsibility* (Oxford, 1968) chs. 2 and 6 and A. Ashworth, *Principles of Criminal Law* (3rd edn., Oxford, 1999) 197–200.

[5] See, e.g., R. A. Duff, *Intention, Agency and Criminal Liability* (Oxford, 1990).

[6] J. Horder argues that the extent to which the agent is to blame for negligence resulting from a mistaken belief is related to emotion in 'Cognition, Emotion and Criminal Culpability' (1990) 106 Law Quarterly Review 469.

[7] See, e.g., S. Gardner, 'Recklessness Redefined' (1993) 109 Law Quarterly Review 21.

[8] A. P. Simester, in 'Can Negligence be Culpable?' in J Horder (ed.), *Oxford Essays in Jurisprudence*, Fourth series (Oxford, 2000), argues that no theory can replace piecemeal examination of various ways in which a defendant fails adequately to form their beliefs. I agree with that analysis, though my understanding of the appropriate failures is different from that of Simester.

appropriate where she fails to achieve that standard. In relation to some serious offences recklessness marks the boundary between civil and criminal liability. Hence, the limits of recklessness form part of the limits of criminal law as a whole. This entails that the justification of recklessness as a *mens rea* term is bound up with the justifiable limits of the criminal law.

The structure of this chapter is as follows. In the first section I will discuss two of the necessary conditions that must be fulfilled if criminal liability is justly to be imposed upon a defendant. The first is that the defendant is responsible for a particular prohibited consequence, action or state of affairs; the second is that the defendant's action is a manifestation of one of a narrow range of vices: primarily, vices that show that the defendant has insufficient regard for the interests of others.[9] As we shall see, there are different reasons why each condition is necessary for the just imposition of criminal liability. Furthermore, different limitations on criminal liability flow from each necessary condition. From this, in the second section, I will show the extent to which these considerations ought to limit criminal liability for risks arising from the action of the accused but of which she was not aware. This will involve a discussion of the extent to which one can be held responsible for one's beliefs and the extent to which the fact that one has certain beliefs might be a manifestation of a vice in which the criminal law is interested. The necessity of a philosophical analysis of beliefs rests on the fact that in cases of objective recklessness, the defendant is typically not sufficiently at fault for the resulting harm *given her beliefs*. If her beliefs were true, if there was in fact no or little risk in her action, there would not have been sufficient reason to make her criminally responsible for any resulting harm (and, in most cases, there would have been no harm). Hence, if she is criminally responsible for the harm, this must be derived, at least in part, from her moral responsibility for the beliefs that she has and acts upon. Finally, in the conclusion, I will construct a general test of recklessness.

B. RESPONSIBILITY AND VICE IN CRIMINAL LAW

In moral philosophy and in ordinary language it is common to use the phrase 'moral responsibility'. The phrase is sometimes used quite loosely, but I think that it often combines two ideas which I will divide into questions of responsibility and questions of vice. Questions of responsibility concern which actions, states of affairs, and consequences rightly reflect on a particular agent. Questions of vice, at least in the narrow sense that is relevant to criminal law, are concerned with failures to be motivated by morally salient reasons. Manifestation of a vice and attribution of responsibility, as I hope to

---

[9] I say 'primarily' because it may be that there are other vices that do not concern the interests of others, but that are also relevant to whether or not we ought to impose criminal liability upon the defendant. Nothing important turns on that question for the purposes of this chapter.

show, are necessary conditions for the just imposition of criminal liability. Consequently, these conditions also impose limits upon the correct definition of recklessness. Let us begin with a sketch of some of the central features of responsibility.

1. Attribution-Responsibility and Role-Responsibility

There are a number of different senses of the term 'responsibility' and, although they are connected, it is worth separating them out analytically. Two of these senses are important here and I will restrict my discussion to them. They can be understood by seeing different ways in which a claim of responsibility might break down. First, a claim of responsibility might break down because the occurrence of an act, consequence, or state of affairs (hereafter C), did not have the appropriate relationship to the agent (hereafter A). If the chain of causation is broken, for example, A will not be responsible for C even if C was intended by A. For the sake of clarity, I shall call this sense of responsibility *attribution-responsibility*. (Since it is concerned with the attribution of responsibility for particular events, this is the sense of responsibility that is of primary concern in the criminal law and, unless the context indicates otherwise, references to responsibility in this chapter are references to attribution-responsibility.) At the same time, a claim of attribution-responsibility for C might break down for a different and less obvious reason: because C is not within A's range of duties. For example, when we say that a professor is responsible for delivering a particular course of lectures, we are speaking about the duties that the professor has. However, if it is not within his range of duties to ensure that the doors are locked after he leaves, he will not be responsible for failing to lock the doors even if it was in his power to do so. Responsibility of this sort is not merely concerned with actual events but can also be prospective, in that it can underpin duties to act in the future. I will call this second sense of responsibility *role-responsibility*.[10]

As a general definition of attribution-responsibility, the following is appropriate: to say that A is responsible for C is to state that C rightly reflects upon A as an agent.[11] There are two aspects to this proposition. The first is that A is an appropriate target for responsibility as an agent; that he is not

---

[10] The term 'role-responsibility' receives attention in Hart (n. 4 above) particularly at 212–214. It should be noted that, unlike me, Hart is not clearly committed to including all prospective senses of responsibility within the concept 'role-responsibility'. Hart suggests that the concept is limited to particular social roles, though he does not define the concept of 'social role' precisely.

[11] It might be thought that there are instances of attribution-responsibility that do not reflect upon agency. For example, there are cases of vicarious liability that are the responsibility of the corporation even if the action of the employee in no way reflects upon the corporation in and of itself. I think that it is not appropriate to say that the company is responsible for the consequence in such instances but only that they are responsible for making up the loss. In other words, this is a question of role-responsibility rather than attribution-responsibility.

insane or a child. I will not say anything about that here.[12] The second is that C has the appropriate relationship to A. This will often, though not always,[13] mean simply that C was brought about by A in the appropriate way. For example, if C was brought about intentionally by A we normally hold A responsible for C. On the other hand, if A brought about C due to an involuntary muscle spasm, barring unusual circumstances, we do not hold A responsible for C. This is why, in my general definition, I suggested that C ought rightly to reflect upon A *as an agent*. There are many things that might reflect upon A in other ways. The concept of attribution-responsibility is not apt to describe them. For example, it might reflect upon me in some way that I am quite tall. But this reflection says nothing about me as an agent. Consequently, although my height reflects on me, it is not something for which I am responsible.

That A is attribution-responsible for C does not entail anything about what kind of judgement ought to be made about A in respect of C.[14] Usually, though it is not always the case,[15] if C is good, A's responsibility for C makes A deserving of praise. If C is bad, A's responsibility for C makes A deserving of blame.[16] From this it might be argued that questions of responsibility are somehow *prior* to questions of morality; that in order to praise or blame we first have to find attribution-responsibility. That is a little misleading. For we are not always required to investigate the attribution-responsibility of the agent A for C before we determine whether or not a moral error has been made in respect of C, and one that governs our assessment of A. An example might be as follows:

> (1) a charity worker comes to A's door asking her to sponsor a particular child who is starving in Africa. A declines out of meanness. The child later starves to death, no one having sponsored him.

In that case, it may be wrong to hold A attribution-responsible for the child's death. Be that as it may, A has failed adequately to consider the life of the child as a reason for action. And this involved the manifestation of a vice by A. Hence, C can be intimately related to A's vice, without A being responsible for C:[17] A is responsible for failing adequately to be motivated by the fact

---

[12] For discussion, see V. Tadros, 'Insanity and the Capacity for Criminal Responsibility' (2001) 5 Edinburgh Law Review 325–354.

[13] For example, A might be guilty of failing to correct C even though she did not bring C about.

[14] cf T. M. Scanlon, *What We Owe to Each Other* (Cambridge, Mass., 1998) 248. At this stage, we need not follow Scanlon in restricting our account to *moral* responsibility.

[15] One can be deserving of praise despite the fact that the consequences of one's actions are ordinarily the subject of blame. The complexities of the relationship are unravelled in M. Stocker, *Plural and Conflicting Values* (Oxford, 1990) chs. 1 and 2.

[16] In one of a number of senses to be elaborated later.

[17] For a related analysis, see G. Watson, 'Responsibility and the Limits of Evil' in J. M. Fischer and M. Ravizza, *Perspectives on Moral Responsibility* (Ithaca, 1993), particularly at 125. Watson shows that attributing responsibility involves more than merely recognizing vice, it involves finding something to respond to.

that C would occur without being responsible for C if and when it does occur. For this reason, it is wise not to prioritize too strictly questions of responsibility over questions of vice. As I hope to show, in order for criminal liability to be appropriate it must be the case both that A is responsible for C and that A manifested an appropriate kind of vice in bringing C about.

That A is responsible for C usually entails that there is an appropriate response for A to make, or to have made, with respect to C or for others to make with respect to A following C. Following C it may be appropriate for A to have certain attitudes or emotions with C (or sometimes, A's *conduct* with respect to C) as their object: pride or satisfaction about C if C is praiseworthy, guilt or shame about C if C is blameworthy.[18] Alternatively, it may also be that an action is required of A: recompense or apology if A has caused loss by C, for example. Further, it may be that there are appropriate emotions or attitudes for others to have or actions for others to perform concerning A. If C is praiseworthy it may be appropriate to praise A and it may also be appropriate to reward her, to thank her, and to feel gratitude towards her. In example (1) the fact that virtually all of the responses listed in this paragraph are inappropriate with regard to A is intimately bound up with the fact that we do not regard him as responsible for the death despite his vice.

In our definition of attribution-responsibility, we have seen that it is concerned with the agent *qua* agent. The consequences, states of affairs, and actions for which the agent is responsible are those that reflect upon the agent as an agent. If that definition is right, we can see that responsibility is usually important only when agency is in question. There are a number of ways in which agency might become important. It might be that there is a connection with the will of the agent. What the agent has done intentionally is obviously a manifestation of agency. But it may be merely that something of the agent's character is made manifest where an exercise of the will is not in question. Consider the following example:

(2) A unintentionally drops a vase as a manifestation of his clumsiness.

In that case we hold A attribution-responsible for the dropping of the vase even though he did not drop it intentionally. Because clumsiness is a characteristic that tells us something about the agent *qua* agent, it is still rightly the subject of attribution-responsibility.[19]

---

[18] cf. B. Williams, *Shame and Necessity* (California, 1993). There are complications. If C is, all things considered, praiseworthy but nevertheless involves a violation of another's interest, it may be appropriate for A to feel regret. cf. Stocker (n.15 above) 28–32.

[19] One reason to think that clumsiness tells us something about the agent *qua* agent is that one can become more or less clumsy through agency. Furthermore, clumsiness is intimately connected with the way in which actions are performed. The corresponding virtue is dexterity. Some definitions of virtue and vice seem to rule out dexterity and clumsiness. I see no reason to limit the definition of virtue and vice in this way. I think that the tendency to limit the definition in this way stems from focusing too strongly on the intellectual faculties.

This shows that choice is not a necessary condition for attributing responsibility. In deciding that A is attribution-responsible for C we need only show that C reflects on A as an agent. And this need not involve choosing. Choosing is only one of the attributes of agency. Nevertheless, if a particular C is completely outwith the control of A, we tend not to attribute responsibility for C to A. Even in the example of clumsiness, it seems important that A's vice is not the result of some abnormal condition that he had no part in bringing about. For example, if A's clumsiness is induced by involuntary intoxication we might not hold him responsible for C. In that case, his clumsiness is no longer *truly* an attribute of *his* agency. Notice the difference with voluntary intoxication where clumsiness is brought about through the agent's will. In the latter case we have no difficulty in attributing responsibility for the broken vase. And this is so even though the agent did not choose to break the vase in either case. Hence some minimal degree of control, over either the particular consequence or the attribute to which C relates, is a necessary condition of A's being attribution-responsible for C. Without this it appears that C says nothing about A *qua* agent.[20]

Conversely, that C is under A's control is not a sufficient condition for attributing to A responsibility for C. There are many events, actions, and consequences in the world which are under my control for which I am not responsible. Consider the following example:

(3) Every week my neighbour, being slobbish, lazy and forgetful, fails to put his rubbish out. If I bang on his door on rubbish days, he will put his rubbish out.

In (3), whether or not my neighbour's rubbish is put out is within my control. But does that make me responsible for whether his rubbish is put out? True, if I do bang on his door I might deserve praise for doing a good deed. And then it might be true that I am at least in part responsible for his rubbish being put out. But if I don't bang on his door I am not responsible for his failure to put the rubbish out. That is his responsibility, not mine.

It is here that the concept of role-responsibility becomes important. A's role-responsibility describes which consequences, states of affairs, and actions

---

[20] There is a philosophical tradition that examines the extent to which virtues can be acquired. It begins with Aristotle who contrasts natural capacities, such as hearing, with virtues. According to him, the latter, unlike the former, can be acquired by habituation. cf. *Nicomachean Ethics* (trans. T. Irwin, Indiana, 1985) Bk 2. Some writers think that, as virtues and vices are *constitutive* of character, we do not have to show any control over our virtues or vices for us rightly to be held to account for the manifestation of those virtues and vices (e.g., R. A. Duff tentatively defends this position in 'Choice, Character, and Criminal Liability' (1993) 12 Law and Philosophy 345–383, at 367). But if this is so, it is difficult to see why we ought to draw a distinction between vices such as clumsiness or stupidity, which are not normally within our control, and disorders, impairments and other forms of defect. Notice that, in contrast to vices, we do not normally regard agents as responsible for the manifestation of those defects in action. Of course it may be that we ought to abandon attributing responsibility in the absence of control *over the action*. I doubt whether this is so, though there is not space to argue the case fully here.

rightly reflect upon A *qua* agent, where the other conditions of responsibility are fulfilled. That I am not role-responsible for ensuring that the rubbish will be put out entails that I cannot be held attribution-responsible for any failure on the part of my neighbour to put his rubbish out. We might say that where an occurrence of C is capable of reflecting upon A as an agent, say because C was within A's control, A will be responsible for C only if C was within A's 'sphere of responsibility'. For convenience, I will use the phrase 'C-type consequences' to designate the *kind* of consequences, actions, or states of affairs of which some occurrence of C is an instance. So, for example, 'that the rubbish is put out' is a C-type consequence that does not fall within my sphere of responsibility whereas, say, 'the behaviour of his child' is a C-type consequence that falls within the parent's sphere of responsibility.

Now, A's intentional actions and their consequences are clearly within the agent's sphere of responsibility. Consequently, in evaluating the extent of an agent's sphere of responsibility our attention naturally turns to questions of omission. Here A's role-responsibility is limited at least in part by particular social roles that A might have. For example, parents are responsible for the upbringing of their children. That is a part of their role. But the same is not normally true of uncles and aunts. Hence, bad behaviour of A's children rightly reflects upon A, as a parent, but it does not rightly reflect on the child's uncles and aunts. This is primarily determined socially. In different societies, or in different sections of our society, it may be that uncles and aunts have significant responsibility for the upbringing of their nieces and nephews. It may be that there are C-type consequences that fall within A's sphere of responsibility simply by virtue of A's being a citizen of a particular state, a member of a community, or even by virtue of being a human being.[21]

That C-type consequences fall within A's sphere of responsibility does not necessarily entail that A will be attribution-responsible for a particular instance of C. In order rightly to be held attribution-responsible it must be shown not only that there is role-responsibility but also that the other conditions of attribution-responsibility are fulfilled. Take the following example:

> (4) A is the father of B. In general he takes steps to ensure that B has good manners. However, on a particular occasion, without A's knowledge, B is hypnotized by a third party into swearing at guests.

In this example although the manners of his child are within A's sphere of responsibility, he is not attribution-responsible for this particular instance in which his child swears. B's swearing is entirely without A's control, and,

---

[21] There is an extent to which one's social role develops according to the responsibilities that one has voluntarily undertaken or willingly embraced. Duties arise from the fact that one has *taken* responsibility. However, not all instances of role-responsibility arise from voluntarily adopting or embracing one's social roles. There are situations in which responsibility is simply thrust upon us. cf. S. Scheffler, 'Relationships and Responsibilities' in *Boundaries and Allegiances: Problems of Justice and Responsibility in Liberal Thought* (Oxford, 2001).

furthermore, would be out of the control of A even if he had all of the virtues of a good parent.

Let us reflect upon this last claim a little. Contrary to some philosophical writing on the matter, control over C itself is not a necessary condition either of attribution-responsibility or role-responsibility. A parent may lack control over a particular instance of behaviour of his child because he does not have all of the virtues of a good parent. Furthermore, he may lack control over the whole range of C-type consequences for that reason. In that case, he is rightly held attribution-responsible for the poor behaviour of his child despite his lack of control. However, if A did in fact have control over C, that may be sufficient to fulfil the condition of responsibility with which we are concerned here even if most reasonable agents would not have had that control.

To summarize this claim: it is a necessary condition of attribution-responsibility either that an agent with all of the appropriate virtues would have had at least minimal control over C or that the agent *did in fact* have at least minimal control over C. This can also be cast in terms of role-responsibility. C falls outwith A's sphere of responsibility if C-type consequences are both outwith A's control *and* would be outwith A's control had he had all of the appropriate virtues.

A final aspect of role-responsibility is worth noting at this stage. There are limits not only to the *nature* of our duties but also to the extent of the requirements that they impose upon us. Consequently, in common usage we talk of *fulfilling* one's responsibility. That we have fulfilled our responsibility normally warrants us not to respond to any bad consequences that result from our action or inaction.

Take the following example:

(5) I am responsible for the teaching of the criminal law course. I take considerable care to ensure that the course is delivered at an appropriate level. It turns out that one of the tutors has delivered the course at too high a level, despite my instructions. This could have been avoided had I spent several days writing a detailed handbook for tutors about the level of the course.

In that case, although I am role-responsible for the teaching of the course, I may not rightly be held attribution-responsible for a particular failure that occurs in the teaching of the course. And this may be true even though it is within my control to ensure that this failure does not occur. Although I have responsibility for the course, there are limits to the duties that I have to ensure that the course is appropriately delivered. I can avoid responsibility for failings in the course simply by doing my duty, at least in some cases,[22] even if I could have avoided those failures by supererogatory acts.

---

[22] This is not a strict rule. There may be some cases where, despite taking all precautions to fulfil my responsibility, I am rightly held responsible for a harm. This conception of responsibility underlies the justification of strict liability in the law of tort: it rests on the claim that some activities, whilst worthwhile, also carry with them burdens of responsibility even in the absence of

2. Responsibility and Criminal Liability

To what extent are these different conceptions of responsibility made manifest in the criminal law? Let us take attribution-responsibility first. Attribution-responsibility is central to determining whether an agent is answerable for a particular action, consequence, or state of affairs at all. At its heart is the doctrine of causation. Where C is a part of the *actus reus* of an offence, it is not sufficient merely to show that A had sufficient *mens rea* and that C actually came about. It is also necessary to show that A caused C.[23] If C was an abnormal or unforeseeable event, A may not be answerable for C. For example, suppose that A intends to kill B and strikes B with a knife, causing a minor injury. B then goes to hospital where he is injected with a fatal dose of pain-killer due to gross negligence on the part of the hospital staff. In that case, A is not criminally responsible for the death of B even though he intended that death. This has nothing to do with questions of vice. A is as vicious as if he had caused B's death. Nevertheless, he is not responsible for B's death. For this reason his crime is rightly labelled as *attempted* murder rather than murder.

Attribution-responsibility is central to the doctrine of automatism. That doctrine is concerned with defendants who are in general to be regarded as responsible agents but who are not responsible for the particular action that they have performed because that action was not performed in the appropriate way or with the appropriate state of mind. Hence, if A assaults B in a state of involuntary intoxication, if that intoxication is sufficiently severe[24] then A is not criminally responsible for assaulting B.

Considerations of attribution-responsibility also inform the distinction of offences by result even where the *mens rea* is the same. Hence, manslaughter is distinguished from assault even though the *mens rea* of the two offences may be identical: an intention to assault. A failure to see the role of responsibility is at the root of the mistake made by those who favour the 'correspondence principle' in criminal law. They think that A's criminal responsibility ought to reflect A's choice of harm, not harms which occur over and above A's choices.[25] However, whilst the fact that the defendant has chosen to perform a wrongful action is rightly considered important in the determination of criminal liability, this is only one principle of the criminal law. Where A has chosen to assault but has in fact caused death, A is responsible for *killing*.

fault. cf. T. Honoré, 'Responsibility and Luck' in *Responsibility and Fault* (Oxford, 1999), particularly at 23 for a similar construction.

[23]   Or, in cases of complicity, assisted or encouraged another to cause C.

[24]   The rules on the severity of intoxication have been applied harshly in both Scotland and England. Their application in both jurisdictions is unclear (see *Brennan v HMA*, [1977] JC 38 and *R v Kingston* [1995] 2 AC 355 respectively). There may be reasons to soften the rules. See G. R. Sullivan, 'Making Excuses' in A. P. Simester and A. T. H. Smith, *Harm and Culpability* (Oxford, 1996) and V. Tadros, 'The Characters of Excuse' (2001) 21 Oxford Journal of Legal Studies 495–519.

[25]   A. Ashworth, (n. 4 above) 89 and B. Mitchell, 'In Defence of the Correspondence Principle' [1999] Criminal LR 195.

That he has not chosen to kill may influence the identity of the offence for which he ought to be convicted. It may even militate against making him guilty of an offence concerned with causing death. But this principle must work against the principle of attribution-responsibility, the principle that one must answer not only for the vices that one has *but for the consequences that one brings about in manifesting those vices*. For correspondence theorists the principle of attribution-responsibility does no work in fair labelling. However, labelling must be fair not only with regard to the degree and kind of vice manifested by A but also with regard to A's responsibility.[26]

We can see, then, that attribution-responsibility informs some of the central doctrines of the criminal law. This is unsurprising, for the concept of attribution-responsibility is also central to our ordinary practices of blaming. Without considerations of responsibility our ordinary practices of blaming make little sense. For when we blame, we blame *for something* and that something is usually an event. Where moral criticism is warranted without attaching itself to any particular event, this is derivative of the ordinary situation in which blame is a response to an event.[27]

Role-responsibility is also central to the conception of responsibility in the criminal law. Why ought the criminal law to be concerned specifically with role-responsibility? In considering whether a particular type of consequence falls within A's sphere of responsibility, we consider what limits we ought to put on the duties that a citizen might have to act. We recognize it is not the case that duties ought to be imposed in respect of C *wherever* A has control over C. For example, that one could prevent the *actus reus* of an offence from being committed does not entail that one ought to have a duty to prevent the *actus reus* of an offence from being committed, breach of which justifies the imposition of criminal liability.

Why should the law put a limit on the duties that we have in this way? One important reason has to do with the project of liberalism. The criminal law ought to be sufficiently restricted that it allows individuals to pursue their own well-being. Well-being is often fulfilled only where one has acted for one's own reasons and not as a result of coercion.[28] For this reason it would be a mistake for the criminal law always to impose the optimal action upon citizens, even if this were attainable. Consequently, the criminal law must tolerate some degree of wrongdoing, and sometimes quite serious wrongdoing, in order to

---

[26] This contributes to the defence of the 'proximity principle' developed by J. Horder in 'A Critique of the Correspondence Principle' [1995] Criminal LR 759 and 'Questioning the Correspondence Principle—A Reply' [1999] Criminal LR 206.

[27] This idea is reminiscent of the celebrated account developed by P. F. Strawson in 'Freedom and Resentment' in G. Watson (ed.), *Free Will* (Oxford, 1982).

[28] For example, one's well-being might be enhanced by choosing to help build shelters for the homeless. If one is forced to help build shelters for the homeless, one's well-being might not be enhanced as much. For although the activity is the same, it is not so intimately *one's own*; it is not so much expressive of one's own agency. And expressing agency is one of the ways in which well-being is enhanced.

preserve autonomy.[29] Reflecting about the limits of role-responsibility is one way in which we might reflect about the impact of liberal political theory on the criminal law.

3. The Vices of the Criminal Law

Whilst the criminal law is limited by considerations of responsibility, it is also limited by considerations of vice. Responsibility alone may be a sufficient condition for civil liability to be justified.[30] However, it is not a sufficient condition for the just imposition of criminal responsibility. In order for criminal liability to be appropriate, it must be the case that the defendant has committed a relatively serious moral wrong. Such a moral wrong, I will argue, has been committed only if the action of the defendant manifests one of a narrow range of vices. Those are the vices that display that one is inadequately motivated by the moral reasons that in fact apply to actions (or beliefs).[31] In other words, in order to show that an individual is worthy of the imposition of criminal liability it is insufficient to show that some vice was manifested in action. Some vices, such as clumsiness and irrationality, are not proper targets for criminal liability. They are to be distinguished from vices such as cruelty, indifference and dishonesty, vices that show that the agent has an insufficient regard for the interests of others. A good introduction to this problem will be to consider the activities of blaming, and the different content that there might be to blame.

We have already seen that responsibility has a role to play in the attribution of blame. This is because we usually blame someone *for* something. But in blaming, we do more than simply attribute responsibility. We make a judgement about the characteristics that an individual has displayed. Blaming is often, though not always, to make a moral judgement about that individual. I use the phrase 'moral judgement' loosely here. The claim is not that blaming generally entails that the person is bad, wicked or evil all things considered. It is simply that blaming involves finding ethical fault of some kind. For example, after dropping the vase, I might be admonished with the following: 'you should have taken more care'. A reprehensible characteristic is being referred to, carelessness, but it is not of the most serious moral kind. It is often the case that there is ethical content to these statements. Often it is implied that had I

---

[29] cf. J. Raz, *The Morality of Freedom* (Oxford, 1986) and 'Liberalism, Scepticism and Democracy' in *Ethics in the Public Domain: Essays in the Morality of Law and Politics* (Oxford, 1994). See also A. P. Simester's defence of the limitation on criminalizing omissions in 'Why Omissions are Special' (1995) 1 Legal Theory 311–335.

[30] cf. Honoré (n.22 above). For a contrary view see E. Weinrib, *The Idea of Private Law* (Cambridge, Mass., 1995).

[31] These are a species of 'guiding reasons' or 'normative reasons', on which see J. Raz, *Practical Reasons and Norms* (Oxford, 1999), J. Gardner, 'Justifications and Reasons' in A. P. Simester and A. T. H. Smith, *Harm and Culpability* (Oxford, 1996), and Tadros (n.3 above). They are only a species because guiding or normative reasons need not be moral, they may be prudential, say, or aesthetic.

had more respect for the property of others I would have taken more care. And a lack of respect for the property of others shows some moral fault on my part.

However, blame is not always of a moral kind and it does not always have a moral target. Blame generally refers to some reprehensible characteristic, but that characteristic need not be of the kind identified in the previous example involving the vase. It may be that blame is simply directed at a vice of the agent, a vice which he ought not to have, but one which does not show that the agent is not sufficiently motivated by the interests of others.

We can see this from the variety of ways in which one might blame. Consider the following discussion which might follow example (2): 'you should have taken more care', to which I reply, 'I did but I'm just clumsy. I took all the care I could but I still dropped the vase'. Now, it might be appropriate to respond with 'you shouldn't be so clumsy'. But in this latter statement, it is not so much my moral failing at the time of acting that is the target of blame. The target is simply a vice, the vice of clumsiness. And whilst clumsiness might be considered a reprehensible characteristic, that one is clumsy does not necessarily establish that one is morally at fault. Because vices are sometimes directly the target of blame, and not all vices reflect moral failings, we can also see that blame is not especially moral.

It may be helpful to illustrate this with a couple of further examples. Suppose that I am being exploited by my employer. It is open to me to stand up to him but I am too cowardly to do so. The next time that I am exploited, one of my colleagues says 'it's your own fault, you ought not to have been such a coward'. Undoubtedly cowardliness sometimes shows moral fault: sometimes the cowardly fail to consider the interests of others before their own. But in this case the only victim of my cowardliness is myself: it is odd to say that I have *moral* fault. In fact, the claim is that standing up to my employer would have been advantageous to myself; the vice here has prudential rather than moral implications.[32] Or suppose that I fail to punish a student who has plagiarized in an essay. I say to my colleague that I could not bear to punish him because he was already in tears. I am accused of being too soft. In this case it is not clear that blaming me for my inaction has any moral content.[33] The claim may simply be that 'to get on in this world' one has to make harsh decisions. Hence in the business world it is common to be accused of not being sufficiently ruthless. Blame is appropriately attributed even though no moral mistake,[34] only a prudential mistake, has been made.

---

[32] Of course the issue may be complicated somewhat. My failure to stand up to my employer may also have some moral fault attached to it. In standing up to my employer I may not just benefit myself but also other employees who are being exploited. In this case there are both prudential and moral reasons not to be cowardly. But we can leave these complications aside for the purpose of the argument.

[33] Though it may. As Andrew Simester has pointed out to me, it may be that I am being accused of failing to respond to reasons of fairness or deterrence. And those reasons are moral reasons.

[34] What I mean by 'moral mistake' is that the agent has made a mistake concerning the balance of morally salient reasons.

How are we to distinguish analytically between moral and non-moral vices? As I hinted above, the basis of the distinction reflects the difference between failures that show a fault of motivation and failures that do not. The paradigm case of the former kind of failure occurs where the defendant has sufficient morally salient facts available to her that oblige her to act (or not act) one way and yet she chooses not to be motivated in the right way by those morally salient facts, leading to a contrary action (or inaction).[35] Choosing against the balance of morally salient reasons is at least the paradigmatic way in which faulty motivation becomes manifest. And it is normally manifest in wrongful action.

We saw in the previous section that choice is not a necessary condition of attribution-responsibility. However, choice *is* paradigmatically connected with moral vices. In the central cases, when one exhibits a moral vice, one chooses not to respect the morally salient reasons against one's action. One chooses to be cruel or vicious.[36] Similarly one might choose to be lazy or careless. These latter characteristics might involve the agent choosing not to trouble herself where there are morally salient reasons to do so. But when one is clumsy, one might take all the trouble in the world and still cause an accident. Or when one is oblivious, one might not notice the feelings of others however much one tries. Hence, manifesting those vices does not show that one has failed adequately to consider the interests of others in one's actions.

There are some vices that almost always reflect faulty motivation at the time of action. There are other vices that rarely do so, if ever. Finally, there are vices that sometimes reflect faulty motivation and sometimes do not. An example of the first set of vices is cruelty. Whether or not an action is cruel is at least in part determined by the motivation with which that action is done. And it is in part determined by a failure to respond appropriately to suffering. Both elements normally show a failure properly to be motivated by morally salient reasons. An example of the second set of vices is stupidity. A paradigm example of stupidity is the failure to draw proper inferences from facts. But failures of that kind tell us little about the motivations of the stupid. The stupid are commonly just as *motivated* as others are to find the truth, but simply lack the same capacity to find the truth. Finally, in the third set of vices we might find cowardice. Sometimes cowardice shows that the coward is insufficiently motivated by the interests of others. Sometimes it does not. For example, A's fear to speak up in the face of racism might show that he is not appropriately motivated by the wrong of racism. B's fear to ask his boss for a

---

[35] I leave aside the debate between cognitivists and non-cognitivists here which complicates the issue somewhat. Cognitivists claim that the agent cannot know all of the relevant facts, as properly knowing the facts properly entails being motivated by them. Non-cognitivists deny that. My claim is intentionally ambiguous regarding that debate.

[36] Though not necessarily under those descriptions. One may be cruel by choosing to v where ving is cruel even if one does not accept that ving is cruel. Hence, morality has a cognitive aspect. This can be accepted even if we do not accept that cognitivism tells the whole story about vices. See further Tadros (n.24 above).

discretionary pay rise, on the other hand, does not show that he is insufficiently motivated by morally salient reasons. To clarify the terminology of this chapter, when a vice shows a failure properly to be motivated by morally salient reasons I call that vice moral. When a vice does not show a failure properly to be motivated by morally salient reasons I call that vice non-moral.[37]

What conclusions can we draw from this discussion of vices? Perhaps the most important is that it is not sufficient for the criminal law simply to tie it-self to the ordinary practice of blaming. A distinction has been drawn in this chapter between blaming in a moral way and the kind of blame that attaches to manifestations of vice that have no moral content. The kind of response that criminal liability exemplifies has the *moral* content to which I referred. The imposition of criminal liability is unjust, therefore, if it is predicated upon a vice that has no moral content. Those who are merely clumsy ought not to be punished for breaking vases. Insufficient consideration for the interests of others[38] is a minimum condition for the imposition of criminal liability.[39]

Why should criminal law be particularly concerned with moral blame rather than blame for other vices? After all, we have seen that non-moral vices are usually considered to be failings in an individual. Why are they not an appropriate target for criminal liability? There are at least two reasons. The first concerns 'the rule of law'. An important principle of the criminal law is that individuals ought to be able to adjust their behaviour according to the rules of the criminal law. Those who are unable to conform to the regulations that the criminal law imposes ought not to be subject to it.[40] If one's vice reflects one's motivations, even if one has the inclinations to act viciously, one can be discouraged by rules. One can be motivated by the rules, counterbalancing one's contrary inclinations. This is particularly true when one's vice is sensitive to practical reasoning. For example, it may be that A is inclined to act dishonestly. The rules of the criminal law can discourage those who otherwise would act dishonestly from acting dishonestly. But one cannot easily motivate, through rules, the clumsy or the irrational not to behave clumsily or irrationally. Hence, vices such as dishonesty and cruelty are amenable to a central purpose of the rule of law where clumsiness and irrationality are not.

The second reason is that the criminal law has an expressive function. The act of punishment is, at least in part, an expressive act. There are a number of

---

[37] Although this is put stipulatively here, I think that it is at least broadly consonant with ordinary usage as can be seen from the discussion above. The distinction that I make is somewhat similar to the distinction that T. M. Scanlon makes between the narrow part of morality, 'what we owe to each other', and the broader compass of morality that concerns other failures of virtue. cf. *What We Owe to Each Other* (n.14 above) 6–7. Scanlon's scheme doesn't map exactly onto mine, however, as I might include the reasons arising out of friendship or loyalty as moral reasons.

[38] Or possibly other morally salient reasons: cf. n. 9 above.

[39] I suspect that a failure properly to recognize this lies behind some of the more extreme forms of objectivism.

[40] This, in my view, lies at the heart of the insanity defence. See Tadros (n.12 above).

different ways in which the content of that expression has been described. Andrew von Hirsch suggests that punishment expresses disapprobation, censure, disapproval, or blame.[41] Douglas Husak defends the stronger view that punishment expresses condemnation.[42] Perhaps more instructive than von Hirsch and less controversial than Husak is the claim that punishment expresses indignation. Indignation, at least according to P. F. Strawson,[43] is a vicarious form of resentment. Where resentment is appropriate on the part of the person who has been wronged, indignation is appropriate on the part of third parties. The relationship between emotional structure and the nature of punishment is central to Strawson's persuasive argument.

But such indignation, and consequently punishment, is appropriate only when the defendant has failed to show adequate consideration for the interests of others. That one has wronged another is not in and of itself an adequate reason for such indignation even if that wrong stems from a vice. Indignation naturally attaches to the bad motivations of the agent, to his will, and not merely to wrongful action. Strawson implicitly takes this line. He suggests that attitudes such as resentment are 'essentially reactions to the quality of others' wills towards us, as manifested in their behaviour: to their good or ill will or indifference or lack of concern'.[44] Implicitly in Strawson's account, indignation, as expressed through punishment, is a reaction to the quality of another's will towards a third party.

Non-moral vices do not show the kinds of motivation to which indignation appropriately attaches. We can see that non-moral vices do not manifest such a lack of motivation from the fact that one often deeply regrets one's own clumsiness or irrationality, and not because of a sudden change of heart, change of motivation, or change of perspective. On the other hand, in acting cruelly one acts in accordance with practical reasoning; one merely shows that one's practical reasoning is insufficiently guided by morally salient reasons. If one regrets a cruel action, it is because one has undergone a change of heart, a change of motivation, or a change of perspective. Any claim by the defendant that he was properly motivated at the time of action automatically fails where his action was cruel. Hence, the fact that the defendant has acted cruelly provides us with a deep insight into his moral character, and his attitude towards others at the time of acting, in a way that clumsiness and irrationality for the most part do not.

To sum up, the basis of the distinction between blameworthiness due to a moral fault and blameworthiness for non-moral vices rests on whether the agent's action is a reflection of her motivations. Where the agent has manifested

---

[41] *Censure and Sanctions* (Oxford, 1993). Each of these terms is used at 9.

[42] See Chapter 2 in this volume, 'Limitations on Criminalization and the General Part of Criminal Law'.

[43] In 'Freedom and Resentment' (n.27 above). For an account of punishment that builds on Strawson's account of the emotional features of punishment, see J. Feinberg, 'The Expressive Function of Punishment' in *Doing and Deserving* (Princeton, 1970).

[44] 'Freedom and Resentment' (n. 27 above) 70.

the kind of vice that reveals her motivations, and in that shows that she is insufficiently motivated by the interests of others, she might be an appropriate target for criminal liability. Where such motivations of the agent are not clearly revealed by the action, criminal liability is inappropriate. The question that arises out of this discussion, in the context of objective recklessness, is whether such motivations are revealed with regard to the false beliefs that defendants might have about risk.

C. BELIEF, RESPONSIBILITY AND VICE

As we have noted, objective recklessness concerns actions that the agent ought to have realized, but did not realize, carried a risk of the *actus reus* of an offence coming about. Hence, objective recklessness is concerned with actions which would not rightly have been the subject of criminal liability, had the beliefs of the agent been true.[45] This suggests that if we are to find responsibility and vice (the two necessary conditions for the imposition of criminal liability defended previously) in situations in which the defendant was not aware of the risks of her action, we need to find that the defendant is responsible and vicious[46] with regard to her false belief.

Some might question this. Need it not simply be shown that the agent is responsible with respect to her actions? Can we do without showing that she is responsible for her beliefs as well? After all, we have already seen that an agent is generally responsible for her actions and the outcomes of those actions. Surely, then, we can find her responsible for a harm caused by her action even where she is not responsible for the belief that made her ignorant of the risk of that harm coming about. Surely we don't have to find responsibility twice: once for the belief and once for the action?

This line of argument involves a mistake about the extent of the requirement of responsibility. We saw that one of the reasons that role-responsibility is a necessary condition for the just imposition of criminal liability derives from a concern with liberty. An individual cannot justly be punished for failing to go beyond her social duty, for the reason that citizens ought to have sufficient options to pursue their own well-being. This reason has equal force in respect of beliefs as it does in respect of actions. An individual ought not to be made criminally liable for failing to do more than is required socially in respect of ensuring that she has true beliefs. Hence if A has fulfilled her responsibility for forming the false belief, or is not responsible for her false belief, she cannot

---

[45] We ought to include cases where the defendant forms no belief, rather than a false belief, about the risks. Everything that I say about false beliefs could equally be said about lack of true beliefs, but I tend to use the former rather than the latter expression for reasons of fluency. Nothing important turns on the distinction for the purposes of this chapter.

[46] 'Vicious' in the sense that she manifested the kinds of vice distinguished in the previous section. I will continue to use the word in this technical sense.

rightly be made responsible for bringing about a risk which would not have been generated if her belief had been true.

We can see this if we consider cases in which the defendant has caused a harm as a result of a false belief about the risks, and has manifested the appropriate vice, but has fulfilled his responsibility in the formation of his belief. Consider the following example:

> (6) I am driving home to watch the football and I come to a junction. I am about to rush out, not caring that a pedestrian might be killed. However, I suddenly realize that I might damage my lovely new car and consequently look either way, just as a responsible driver would. I form the belief that there is no danger but I fail to notice a pedestrian who unexpectedly dashes in front of my car, and run her over.

In this case, I have displayed the vice of indifference towards others. The only thing that prevented me from rushing out was my love of my car. I was not sufficiently moved by the interests of others to refrain from rushing out. Nevertheless, I have fulfilled my responsibility to look either way. I have done all that is required of me responsibly to form a belief about the risks. That I am responsible for my action in driving on, and that I have displayed the vice of indifference, are surely insufficient to make me criminally liable for the death of the pedestrian.[47]

1. Responsibility and Belief

We have seen that in order to find A responsible for C two things must obtain. The first is that C is within A's sphere of responsibility. The second is that C is attributable to A in the appropriate way. I will begin by developing some lines of argument that tend to show that agents are role-responsible for their beliefs.

There appears immediately to be a difficulty in the claim that we are role-responsible for our beliefs. Role-responsibility, I suggested, is only present to the extent that A would have had control over a particular sphere of actions, events, or states of affairs had he had the appropriate virtues. Now, it might be objected that we are not role-responsible for our beliefs by virtue of the fact that *no one* has control, in the relevant sense and to the relevant degree, over their beliefs. There are two stages of belief formation either of which might provide foundation to the claim that we are role-responsible for our beliefs. Founding responsibility upon either stage, however, might be open to objection.

My objector might argue first that there is a difficulty at the moment at which we form our beliefs, given the evidence with which we are presented.

---

[47] This is one problem of using indifference to determine the limits of recklessness, a practice that is common in Scots criminal law and is defended by R. A. Duff in *Intention, Agency and Criminal Liability* (n.5 above).

The difficulty can be seen when we compare action: whereas we commonly choose our actions, and hence can rightly be held responsible for them, we do not, at least ordinarily, choose our beliefs.[48] In forming our beliefs we are not presented with a range of options between which we choose. Rather, in being presented with convincing evidence, we normally form beliefs directly, without the will being involved in some intermediate stage. Once again, compare action: after being presented with convincing reasons for action it is normal for the will to play some intermediate role in our deciding whether to act. Belief, it might be objected, is directly sensitive to the presentation of convincing reasons in a way that action is not.

Perhaps, it may be thought, this ought to direct us away from the moment of belief formation given the evidence to the moment at which we gather evidence. If we do not have an active part to play in the formation of belief, given the evidence, we might still be held responsible for our beliefs if we have an active part to play in the gathering of evidence. But this, it might be argued, leads to a further objection: we do not normally have a great deal of control over the evidence with which we are presented. Normally, evidence is presented to us directly without our playing any active role in gathering that evidence. And that is just as it should be, for it would be unreasonably burdensome to have to investigate whether there is evidence for all of our beliefs. I think that both of these objections are overstated. I will argue that belief formation is active in the appropriate way and that we do have sufficient control over the evidence before us, at least some of the time.

The first thing to note is that the claim that we are not responsible for our beliefs is counterintuitive.[49] We commonly assume that both we ourselves and others are responsible for beliefs. Responsibility for our beliefs is a necessary condition for it to be appropriate to praise or blame others for their beliefs, and also for it to be appropriate to attempt to persuade others that their beliefs are mistaken. Furthermore, it is a necessary condition for us to be right to attribute to others (and to ourselves) virtues associated with belief formation. That we attribute the virtues of perception, open-mindedness, and honesty, and the corresponding vices of obliviousness, obduracy, and dishonesty, in respect of belief formation, assumes a certain degree of responsibility for beliefs that most of us share. Moreover, fundamental virtues of wisdom, intelligence, acuity, and knowledge all rest on our responsibility for our beliefs. If we are not role-responsible for our beliefs, we are simply mistaken in regarding these central virtues as virtues. This gives us good prima facie reasons to see whether the two objections to holding us role-responsible for our beliefs can be deflated. Let us take the two counter-arguments in turn.

---

[48] We do sometimes say that we choose to believe p. I think that such a psychological state is more concerned with acceptance than belief. See, further, Shute, Chapter 8 above.

[49] For a more detailed defence of this claim than I can offer here, see P. Pettit and M. Smith, 'Freedom in Belief and Desire' (1996) 9 *Journal of Philosophy* 429.

The first objection that I posited against holding us role-responsible for our beliefs concerned the question of control. It was suggested that as we do not choose (hence, the objection assumed, control) our beliefs, so we cannot rightly be held responsible for them. But, as I argued earlier, the ability to choose whether or not C occurs is not a necessary condition for A rightly to be held responsible for C. It is only necessary that C reflects upon A as an agent. Hence, in respect of example (2), I argued that we can rightly be held responsible for breaking a vase due to clumsiness even if breaking the vase was not chosen. That we have some control over whether we have the vice of clumsiness makes dropping the vase reflect our agency sufficiently to attribute us with responsibility for doing so. Similarly with beliefs. Because we are responsible for developing the virtues of correct belief formation referred to above, we are also responsible for our beliefs even though we do not choose them. Because our beliefs are sensitive to our virtues, and we can develop virtues, we are also responsible for our beliefs.[50] Belief formation is not primarily passive. As Joseph Raz and Christopher Hookway have noted,[51] whilst we do not choose our beliefs, belief formation is responsive to reason. Hence, it is best thought of as active, or at least that is ordinarily the case.[52]

A related point concerns the extent to which beliefs cohere in a system. For some, it is a necessary condition of being a believing agent that one has a network of beliefs. There is an analytical connection, for these writers, between holding a particular belief and one's system of beliefs. A mental state is wrongly identified as a belief if it occurs without the presence of other beliefs to which it is appropriately related.[53] If this is right, and I think it is, the formation of a belief is not simply a question of an experience (for example, a perceptual experience) being affirmed by an agent. Belief formation takes place holistically through the development of a whole system of beliefs. If my claims about responsibility are correct, to argue that we are not responsible for our beliefs would be to deny that this developing system of beliefs reflects upon us as agents and that seems implausible. Rather, our belief structure is central to agency.

The second argument against our responsibility for our beliefs rested on the claim that we do not normally control the evidence with which we are presented for our beliefs. Again, this claim fails to convince. We are at least

---

[50] On the deep connection with correct belief formation and virtue see J. McDowell, 'Virtue and Reason' in *Mind, Value and Reality* (Cambridge, Mass., 1998). McDowell limits his consideration of virtue to characteristics that make the agent responsive to particular sorts of reasons. His conception of virtue is narrower than mine.

[51] 'When We are Ourselves: the Active and the Passive' in *Engaging Reason* (Oxford, 1999) and 'Epistemic Norms and Theoretical Deliberation' in J. Dancy, *Normativity* (Oxford, 2000) respectively.

[52] Hookway notes some odd counterexamples in 'Epistemic Norms and Theoretical Deliberation' (ibid.).

[53] e.g., D. Davidson, 'Rational Animals' in B. McLaughlin and E. LePore, *Actions and Events: Perspectives on the Philosophy of Donald Davidson* (Oxford, 1985) 473–480, particularly at 475; see Shute, Chapter 8 above.

sometimes in control over the evidence with which we are presented for our beliefs, since we can choose to investigate carefully whether some proposition is true or to take it on face value. Furthermore, we are often in control of the clarity and force with which the reasons for or against a belief present themselves to us. We can take the trouble to think carefully about our beliefs or be relatively unreflective about them. Norms apply to these processes. There are some questions that are so important that we ought to do everything in our power to ensure that our beliefs about the answers are true. Other questions, being less important, do not have this requirement.[54] An important aspect of having the intellectual virtues amounts to having the correct set of policies regarding belief formation: to investigate each belief to the right degree, in the right way, at the right time. Because we have some control over these belief policies we also have some control over which evidence we are presented with.

Obviously, though importantly, we may end up holding false beliefs even if we have and manifest all of the appropriate virtues that are connected to beliefs. Even those with all of the intellectual virtues in optimum balance will not have a complete set of true beliefs. Being intellectually virtuous does not guarantee that one's beliefs are true, though it may increase the probability that one's beliefs are true. This loose relationship between the intellectual virtues and the truth of one's beliefs creates a difficulty for those who wish to focus recklessness around the truth or falsity of beliefs in themselves. That one holds a false belief about something is not sufficient evidence of an intellectual vice, let alone a moral vice.[55] Hence, that one wrongly believes that there was no risk is not in and of itself sufficient evidence of vice at all, let alone of the kind of vice in which the criminal law is interested. And this is true even if that belief would not be held by most reasonable observers. For example, it may be that the belief was formed in relation to another false belief which was acquired for perfectly good reasons.

To sum up, there are at least some good reasons to reject the objections to the claim that we are role-responsible for our beliefs. The beliefs that we have ordinarily reflect upon us as agents. Furthermore, as the beliefs that we have are central to every aspect of our lives, they are also the proper object of responsibility. In fact, I would go further and claim that beliefs, like actions, are central to the notion of responsibility in and of itself. But it is not necessary to defend that grander claim for the purposes of this chapter.

---

[54] The situation is more complex than I have suggested here. It may be that there are some questions that are very important but which we ought not to investigate carefully. For example, it may be very important for a climber to know whether or not the next rock is loose, but investigation may expose the climber to further risks. See also C. Hookway, 'Epistemic Norms and Theoretical Deliberation' (n.51 above).

[55] A leap that Duff sometimes appears to think unproblematic. cf. *Intention, Agency and Criminal Liability* (n.5 above) 161–163.

2. Vice and Belief

We are responsible for our beliefs. That idea, it seems to me, is part of the motivation of many of those who argue for objective recklessness. Some who argue for a very strong form of objective recklessness seem to think that it is the falsity of the defendant's belief that provides the target for criminal liability. But, as we have seen, that one has all of the virtues associated with belief formation in proper balance does not guarantee that one's beliefs will all be true. One can have all of the virtues associated with believing and yet hold false beliefs, even beliefs that most ordinary reasonable people would not hold. For this reason, our responsibility for our beliefs is not sufficient ground for imposing criminal liability in cases where the defendant had a false belief that there was no risk involved in the action that she performed. Consequently, our attention turns from the nature of the belief that is held to the process of belief formation.[56]

To see this, let us return to example (6). In that example, I formed a belief that there was no danger to pedestrians, but that was not a response to my concern for pedestrians but rather my concern for my car. However, I did all that was required of me to ensure that the way was clear; I fulfilled my responsibility. In that case it is wrong to make me criminally liable for the death of the pedestrian. I had *done* as much as could be expected of a truly virtuous person, even though I was not truly virtuous. That I was indifferent to the fate of the pedestrian is not sufficient reason to hold me criminally liable. Fulfilling my responsibility to ensure that the way was clear ought to absolve me of criminal liability even if false beliefs are formed.[57] The falsity of the belief itself is not sufficient evidence of fault. If we are to find fault, we must find it in the process of belief formation. Furthermore, it may be that the defendant has not formed his belief in the way that he ought and yet criminal liability may still be inappropriate. For it must be shown that, in holding a false belief, the defendant manifests the appropriate kind of vice.

It might be thought that the appropriate kind of vice is displayed whenever the defendant has formed an irrational or unreasonable belief about the risks. If that were the case, irrationality or unreasonableness would not simply be descriptions of the nature of the belief itself, regardless of who holds it, but descriptions of the way in which the belief was formed. Such a view might be supported by Joseph Raz's recent analysis of irrational beliefs. 'A belief is irrational', Raz writes, 'if and only if holding it displays lack of care and

---

[56] See also Simester (n.8 above) 95–96.

[57] Compare C. Wells, 'Swatting the Subjectivist Bug' [1982] Criminal LR 209 who claims that *the fact that D had a false belief* about a woman's consent to intercourse ought to be sufficient grounds for attributing *mens rea* because he 'should take more care to ensure that his sexual partner is willing' (at 213). However, it may be that although D took as much care as could reasonably be expected, he still formed a false belief that she was consenting. See my related discussion in 'No Consent: A Historical Critique of the *Actus Reus* of Rape' (1999) 3 Edinburgh Law Review 317–340.

diligence in one's epistemic conduct'.[58] Showing lack of care and diligence, it might be argued, displays a vice that is central to the imposition of criminal liability. After all, that one fails to take care or be diligent also shows that one is insufficiently motivated by the interests of the individuals who might suffer from one's lack of care and diligence.

However, it is not at all clear that the fact that one holds an irrational belief necessarily shows a vice of this kind. That one holds an irrational belief is not itself evidence of a lack of care on the part of the believer. A number of other vices might result in the formation of an irrational belief. It might be that the defendant is merely stupid or illogical; vices which, whilst in themselves warranting blame, do not give rise to the kind and degree of blame that the imposition of criminal liability expresses.[59] If one has such vices, one can take all the care that is required and yet fail to form rational beliefs. In fact, this argument might even be stretched to include some other failings, such as some instances of arrogance.

Consider *R v Shimmen*,[60] in which a martial arts expert attempted to perform a kick near to a window without breaking it. Suppose that he formed the belief that there was no risk involved at all due to an arrogant belief in his own ability. We might conclude that he had manifested a vice in breaking the window, and consequently attribute responsibility to him for breaking the window. But is it correct to attribute criminal liability to him? The difficulty in doing so is that the criminal law should not be interested in the kinds of vice that Shimmen manifested. That Shimmen was arrogant does not show clearly that Shimmen was 'insufficiently different'[61] to the interests of others. It may be that he cared deeply about the shopkeeper and his window, and was sincerely mortified at having broken it (and not because of a change of heart, motivation, or perspective), but truly (though arrogantly) believed that he was doing nothing to put the window at risk. Shimmen may have been responsible for breaking the window but, at least on this presentation of the facts, he did not display an appropriate vice in breaking the window and consequently he ought not to be made criminally liable for it.[62] He did not show an insufficient

---

[58] J. Raz, 'Explaining Normativity: On Rationality and the Justification of Reason' in *Engaging Reason* (n.51 above) 75.

[59] Raz's definition does not even appear to include some of his own examples of irrational beliefs. He discusses the example of Sylvia, who upon leaving the house goes back time and time again to check that the front door is locked, and yet forms an irrational belief that the door is not locked. That belief is irrational. But it is not formed due to a lack of care or diligence on her part.

[60] (1986) 84 Cr App Rep 7.

[61] This formulation is preferable to 'indifferent' for the reason that a defendant might be motivated by a particular concern, but not to a sufficient degree. In that case he is not rightly called indifferent. He is only insufficiently different to that concern.

[62] Of course, in reality it is not plausible that the defendant did think that there was no risk. See Williams (n.2 above) for a discussion of the conditionals that would help to decide whether this was so. Furthermore, it may have been that Shimmen ought to have done more to investigate the risks, by first seeing whether or not he could perform the kick next to something unbreakable, or his own window.

regard for the interests of others. And that, as I argued above, is central to the concerns of the criminal law.

These considerations militate against many popular constructions of objective recklessness. For example, accounts that rely on the risks that the defendant ought to have recognized, even those such as Hart's that restrict liability to the capacity of the accused to recognize the risks involved in performing a particular action,[63] are too broad. Defendants such as Shimmen, on my construction of the facts, ought to recognize the risks and have the capacity to recognize the risks. Nevertheless, they ought not to be made criminally liable.

This should help to guide us in formulating an appropriate definition of objective recklessness. An appropriate definition of objective recklessness would focus on the process of belief formation. And it would be required to distinguish between cases of mere irrationality, stupidity, or arrogance and cases where the formation of an irrational belief shows that the defendant was not adequately motivated by the interests of others. In an earlier part of the discussion,[64] I suggested that our responsibility for our beliefs is grounded on two facts. The first fact is that belief formation is governed by norms. There are norms that govern the ways in which we ought to see the world, and to interpret what we see. One important aspect of the intellectual virtues has to do with the system of norms that we ought to apply to the formation of beliefs. The second fact is that we have some control over which evidence we are presented with. There are also norms that apply to evidence-gathering; the intellectual virtues relate to the system of norms we apply to evidence-gathering as well. Might these two facts provide grounds upon which we can construct a test for objective recklessness? It will be no surprise that I think that they can.

However, one caveat is in order. My claim is not that these are the only ways in which belief formation is sufficiently vicious to warrant criminal liability. It may be that the test of objective recklessness can be extended to include other cases, in particular cases where the offending belief is derived from a further belief that was viciously formed. Space does not permit me fully to discuss such cases here, though I will try to illuminate some potential problems for assessing liability in such cases. The two cases that I will concentrate on here are, I think, the central cases. The first is where the individual has sufficient information at his fingertips to form the belief that there is a significant risk of a wrong being done to another but, due to a motivational reason of a particular kind, fails to form the belief that such a wrong will be brought about. The second is where an individual knows that a situation that he is in, or the activity that he is performing, might give rise to particular risks and fails to investigate whether there are such risks. In the next section I will show how these two cases might be appropriate targets for the imposition of criminal liability.

---

[63] cf n.4 above.   [64] See section C above.

3. Beliefs Formed for Non-Evidential Reasons

One of the difficulties with objective recklessness concerns the kind of vice that forming false beliefs displays. Forming a false belief after being presented with adequate evidence to form a true belief usually gives rise to a charge of irrationality. But, I have suggested, the criminal law ought not to punish the irrational simply for being irrational, even if their irrationality results in the performance of a prohibited action. Irrationality, I suggested, is simply not the kind of vice which deserves the stigma that the imposition of criminal liability attaches to the agent. Furthermore, the irrational cannot usually help being irrational. Consequently, rule of law objections hold against criminalization.

However, this does not entail that we cannot find the appropriate kind of fault at the moment of belief formation. For it is not always the case that, in forming a false belief given adequate contrary evidence, the defendant displays merely the vice of irrationality. This is because there are reasons other than evidential reasons that motivate individuals to hold beliefs.[65] There are some cases where the defendant forms a belief against the balance of evidential reasons not simply because of irrationality but because he is motivated by those other kinds of reasons. In such a case the defendant might not have been irrational in the formation of his belief but might have manifested some other kind of vice (or he might have been both irrational *and* have manifested that other vice). It is as well to begin such a discussion with a familiar example outside the setting of the criminal law.

Take Charlie, a smoker, who forms the belief that smoking is not bad for his health despite overwhelming evidence to the contrary. In such circumstances, a belief that smoking is not bad for one's health might normally (though, as we shall see, not always) be irrational. But suppose that in forming that belief Charlie was motivated not simply by evidential reasons. He was also motivated by non-evidential reasons; in this case, say the fact that he enjoyed smoking.

It might be thought that the formation of such beliefs is always irrational. However, this is clearly untrue. Even in Charlie's case, it may be perfectly rational for him to form the belief that smoking is not bad for his health. Suppose that Charlie knows that even if he were to believe that smoking was bad for his health he would continue to smoke just as much, but his enjoyment would be impaired. In this case, it is rational to hold the belief that smoking is not bad for his health despite all of the evidence to the contrary. Holding a true belief about smoking would make no difference to his habits, but would impair his enjoyment.

---

[65] The term 'motivating reasons' means the same as what J. Raz and J. Gardner call 'explanatory reasons' (see n. 31 above for references). Elsewhere, in 'Practical Reasoning and Intentional Action' (n.3 above) I have used the term 'explanatory reasons'. For the reasons given in J. Dancy, *Practical Reality* (Oxford, 2000) 6–7, I now prefer the former term.

For reasons of clarity it is briefly worth exploring the difference between evidential and non-evidential reasons for holding a belief. Evidential reasons for belief are reasons that make it more likely that a belief will be true. Non-evidential reasons for a belief are reasons that do not make it more likely that a belief will be true. There are (at least) two types of non-evidential reasons that might motivate an agent to form beliefs. First, the agent might be motivated by the desire to experience a particular emotion or attitude. For example, one might form the belief that one is slim because one wants to feel better about oneself. Secondly, the agent might be motivated by the desire to perform a particular action. For example, one might form the belief that there are no bills coming because then one can buy a new guitar. In the latter example, without the belief that there are no bills coming, one would not buy the guitar. Non-evidential reasons are sometimes, slightly misleadingly, called *pragmatic*.[66] I say slightly misleadingly because non-evidential reasons might also be moral reasons. These include the reason that one ought to give others the benefit of the doubt, or the reason that one ought to think modestly about one's own achievements. Both are non-evidential reasons for belief, but it is odd to call such reasons pragmatic.

In the previous example, there is little to say morally about Charlie. That he holds a false belief about smoking is not an appropriate reason for moral criticism, if criticism of any sort. However, the same cannot be said for all beliefs that are formed for non-evidential reasons. That one has formed a belief for non-evidential reasons sometimes matters morally. In forming a belief for non-evidential reasons, one sometimes displays the kind of vice in which the criminal law rightly takes an interest. And this is often the case where the defendant, for non-evidential reasons, forms a false belief about risks. Take Cathy, a football fan, who is rushing to see her team play in the cup final. She comes to a junction and looks both ways but, against all of the evidence, forms the belief that there is no risk in failing to stop. She does this because she is motivated by her desire to arrive on time. In this case, she has displayed the kind of vice in which the criminal law is rightly interested. She has failed to show sufficient regard for the interests of others, namely those other citizens whose health might be endangered by her action. She was not sufficiently motivated by their interests to form an evidentially-justifiable belief concerning the risk of harm to them. Hence, her state of mind is rightly called reckless.

Most cases in which an individual forms a belief for non-evidential reasons might be captured in the criminal law if the phrase 'wilful blindness' were appropriately used. Where the defendant is wilfully blind, at least in the ordinary language use of that term, he either forms a belief, or fails to form a belief that he would otherwise form, through an exercise of his will that reflects his non-evidential reasons for doing so. The phrase has most commonly been

---

[66] See G. Harman, 'Pragmatism and Reasons for Belief' in *Reasoning, Meaning and Mind* (Oxford, 1999). Harman confusingly calls evidential reasons 'epistemic'. Thanks to Stephen Shute for helping me to see the confusion.

used in criminal law as an alternative *mens rea* to knowledge and belief in handling stolen goods (or reset, in Scotland), although its legal validity has been questioned. In my view, along the lines that I have proposed here, the concept does have some distinctive content as a mental state separate either from belief or suspicion, although the criminal courts in England have had difficulty appreciating what that content is. I think that the concept ought to be returned to its meaning in ordinary language. If this could be done it would usefully pick out something important in some cases of objective recklessness.

An objection to this line of argument might come from Stephen Shute. In Chapter 8 above[67] he argues that it would be better to do away with the concept of wilful blindness in the criminal law altogether. He gives two reasons. First, the explanation of wilful blindness has proved complex and confusing. Secondly, wilful blindness is anomalous given that suspicion is not equivalent to belief in the criminal law. In my view, these two arguments ought to be resisted. Whilst it is true that the jurisprudence surrounding the term in English law has become confused, that ought not to lead us to abandon the term, but rather to rethink its use. If it could be returned to its meaning in ordinary language, it would have value in the criminal law, and in offences beyond that of handling stolen goods.

Against Shute's first point, wilful blindness is a common everyday notion and, whilst it may be difficult to explicate, that is no less true of other concepts and terms that are central to *mens rea*, most notably 'intention'. In most cases there appears to be little reason not to leave the concept of wilful blindness to the jury directly, as is done in Scotland.[68] Where it needs special attention and explanation, I think that this is not beyond the power of the courts. On his second point, wilful blindness, in the ordinary sense of the term, appears to have little to do with suspicion. Wilful blindness occurs where a belief is formed (or fails to be formed) for non-evidential reasons despite the presence of sufficient evidential reasons to the contrary, reasons that the agent would, in the absence of those non-evidential reasons, accept. Suspicion, on the other hand, occurs where the agent does not regard herself as having sufficient evidential reasons to form a belief. It occurs when the reasons for a belief, as far as the agent is concerned, tend to support the formation of a certain belief but are not conclusive.[69] If, contrary to the current practice of the English courts,

---

[67] Chapter 8 above at 196–198.   [68] cf. *Latta v Heron* 1967 SCCR Supp. 18.

[69] G. R. Sullivan notes in Chapter 9 of this volume, 'Knowledge, Belief and Culpability', that there might be cases in which, in terms of culpability, D's suspicion that p is in the same moral category as D's belief that p, where p would entail that an *actus reus* was being committed by D. That, I think, is sometimes, though not always, the case. Sullivan's examples seem plausible. However, there are some instances where, in the absence of a belief that p, the defendant is entitled to assume that not-p. For example, suppose that the *actus reus* of an offence against the person will have been committed by D if D has sexual intercourse with V and transmits the HIV virus to V (as has been confirmed in Scotland in *HMA v Kelly* (unreported); cf. V. Tadros, 'Recklessness, Consent and the Transmission of HIV' (2001) 5 Edinburgh Law Review 371–380). We might wish to include within the *mens rea* of the offence 'knowing or believing that he was HIV positive or wilfully blinding himself to that fact'. We might, on the other hand, wish to exclude

the term was used in the way I have outlined, wilful blindness would pick out a psychological state that is of particular moral significance.

The term 'wilful blindness' has another advantage. If it is used carefully, it has the correct sort of normative content: it distinguishes between beliefs that are formed (or fail to be formed) for bad non-evidential reasons and beliefs that are formed (or fail to be formed) for good non-evidential reasons. One would not normally call the person who merely *sees the best in someone* wilfully blind. The term normally suggests that the blindness to a fact is caused by selfish (or otherwise morally vicious) motivations of the agent.[70] This suggests one limb of a test of objective recklessness: if the defendant did not believe that there was a risk that was in fact present because he had wilfully blinded himself to the existence of that risk, he ought to be regarded as reckless for the purposes of the criminal law.

4. Failing in One's Duty to Take Care

A second set of circumstances in which objective recklessness might be justified concerns a failure adequately to investigate the risks that one's actions might involve. There are some circumstances in which one forms a false belief because one has taken inadequate care to investigate whether or not that belief is true. And that inadequacy might display the kind of vice in which the criminal law is appropriately interested.

There are different ways in which one might fail adequately to investigate whether or not a particular belief is true. For example, one might take inadequate practical steps to discover what evidence there is for a particular belief. Alternatively, one might simply fail to think sufficiently carefully about the evidence with which one is presented. Some cases of inadequate investigation

---

suspicion, even if the means of finding out whether or not he was HIV positive were available to D. Suppose that D had completed an HIV test but was too afraid to open the results. One position that we might wish to adopt is that, in the absence of the firm belief that he is HIV positive, D is entitled to assume that he is not, even though he suspects that he is; the existence of his suspicion creates no duty on him to open the letter. Hence, if he has sexual intercourse with V and transmits the HIV virus to her, we might not wish to make him guilty of the offence. If, on the other hand, D reads the letter but wilfully blinds himself that he is not HIV positive (say by pretending to himself that there must be a mistake in the results), then we might wish to make him guilty of the offence.

[70] There are some cases in which this is not so. For example, we might call A trusting if there are some small evidential reasons that her boyfriend is being unfaithful but she does not believe that he is unfaithful. However, once those evidential reasons become overwhelming we might call her wilfully blind to the fact that he is being unfaithful; but there is no reason to think that she is motivated by a lack of concern for others. This might have a role in the criminal law. Suppose that, because she trusts him, D forms the belief that the watch her boyfriend has given her is not stolen. We might not call her wilfully blind. And yet we might say that, and blame her (and contemplate criminal liability) because, she is insufficiently motivated by the interests of others to investigate. That there are such troublesome borderline cases ought not to prevent us from using the term, however. Troublesome cases on the border are the staple diet of the criminal law.

ought to be considered reckless for the purposes of the criminal law. Let us begin by considering *Elliot v C (a minor).*[71]

In that case, the defendant, a 14-year-old girl, poured white spirit onto the carpet of a garden shed and threw two lighted matches upon it. The shed was destroyed and she was charged with reckless criminal damage.[72] In the light of *R v Caldwell,*[73] and despite the expressed contrary inclinations of the Court of Appeal, she was convicted of the offence even though, had she thought about it, she might not have recognized the risk of destroying the shed.

It seems to me that there might be good grounds for attributing recklessness to the defendant. For in failing to investigate the risks, she might have shown a lack of regard for what happened to the property of others.[74] If she knew that playing with fire was dangerous[75] and, despite that, she failed to investigate what risks there might be in this instance of playing with fire, she might also have shown, in performing that action, that she was not sufficiently motivated by the interests that others have in their property. Hence, she might have displayed the kind of vice in which the criminal law is appropriately interested.

Had she not known that playing with fire is a risky activity, on the other hand, she would not have shown any such vice in failing to investigate the risks. In failing to investigate the risks, one has not shown an insufficient regard for the interests of others if one believed that the activity that one has performed was not risky in and of itself. In failing to investigate the risks in such a case, one has shown no more disregard for the interests of others than one shows when one fails to investigate the risks in performing actions that are in fact perfectly safe: actions such as opening jam-jars, turning on the lights, and so on. If she had believed that playing with fire was just like playing with water in terms of the risks attached to it, she could not rightly have been called reckless in failing to investigate the risks involved in her activity.[76]

On the other hand, it may be that a defendant has special knowledge about which kinds of activity are risky. In that case, a failure to investigate the risks might make an attribution of recklessness appropriate even if ordinary citizens would not have been aware of the risks involved. Suppose, for example, that a doctor has special knowledge that a certain type of operation might have particular risks associated with it where ordinary doctors would think it routine. In that case, if the doctor failed to investigate the risks involved in that operation, resulting in the *actus reus* of an offence, recklessness might

---

[71] (1983) 77 Cr App R 103.   [72] Contrary to the Criminal Damage Act 1971, s. 1(1).
[73] [1982] AC 341. cf. n. 1 above.   [74] Despite Goff LJ's claim to the contrary at 118.
[75] And in her evidence she admitted that she knew that fire was dangerous (at 108).
[76] Of course it may have been that she was not sufficiently able to be regarded as criminally responsible at all. For it may have been that she did not have the ability to make an adequate response to the requirements of the criminal law (for an analysis of such questions, see Tadros (n. 12 above)). But that question is only relevant to the question of recklessness in a *sine qua non* fashion. Questions of *mens rea*, like excuses and justifications (see Gardner (n. 31 above)), apply only to the able.

appropriately be attributed. The doctor manifested that he was insufficiently motivated by the interests of his patient by performing the operation without investigating the risks. Had he been sufficiently motivated by the interests of the patient, knowing that this is the kind of activity that might have risks associated with it, he would have carried out the investigation.[77]

Hence, whether one investigates the risks associated with one's actions is only relevant if one has the requisite knowledge that one's action is of the kind that has risks associated with it. One is not required to investigate the risks of one's actions if those actions are thought to be safe. One is not required to investigate the risks of opening jam-jars or switching on lights, for these are things that one can ordinarily perform with no risk to others. Furthermore, if one has a mistaken belief that an action is of this kind, criminal liability ought not to be imposed. For one's failure to investigate the risks would not manifest an appropriate vice in that case but only a lack of knowledge.[78]

Now, it might be thought that we ought to investigate whether or not the defendant was appropriately responsible and manifested the appropriate vice in the formation of that prior belief, the belief as to whether the action was of a kind that required one to investigate the risks. Let us return to a previous variation on *Elliot v C*. In the variation, the facts are identical to *Elliot v C*, except that D believed that playing with white spirit was just like playing with water. In that case, I have argued, she ought not to be regarded as reckless, even though she failed to investigate the risks. For, according to her beliefs, she would have been doing the sort of thing that was very unlikely to carry with it any risks that the *actus reus* of an offence would come about. However, it might be argued that we ought then to investigate whether or not she was responsible and manifested the appropriate vice in forming the belief that playing with white spirit was just like playing with water. Let us call those prior beliefs 'background beliefs'.

There might be cases where we ought to investigate whether the defendant was at fault for the formation of background beliefs. However, in my view, it is normally (though not always) the case that any fault for the formation of

---

[77] As Simester notes in 'Can Negligence be Culpable?' (n.8 above) at 96, the law recognizes that, if the defendant has superior knowledge, she must be judged against that standard. The argument presented here applies that notion to an earlier stage in belief investigation: if the defendant had superior knowledge about whether or not this was a risky situation and fails to investigate the risk she might rightly be considered reckless even if most reasonable citizens would not have considered the situation risky.

[78] Compare S. Gardner, who, in his analysis of *R v Reid* [1992] 1 WLR 793 (n.7 above) writes: 'their Lordships may feel that it is only when someone embarks on a particular activity which is known to be risky that he can be expected to go the extra length of taking the trouble to perceive and avoid the dangers, rather than just avoiding any which he does foresee. But this limitation may well be unjustified. Should not attending to the dangers of one's control be a duty required of everybody, in regard to all their activities, as a concomitant of their partaking in the life of the planet?' (at 27). In my view, their Lordships, if Gardner interprets them properly, were correct and Gardner's question ought to be answered in the negative.

such background beliefs would be too remote from the *actus reus* to warrant the imposition of criminal liability. In my hypothetical variation on *Elliot*, D might have formed the belief that white spirit has the same property as water some time previously, and even if she had some fault in forming that belief, it is not clear that that fault can be transferred to *this* action. Suppose, for example, that she formed her false belief about the properties of white spirit because she had misread her chemistry textbook. She might have been at fault for her misreading, but is that fault sufficiently connected to the *actus reus* of this offence to impose criminal liability for criminal damage? I think not.

Furthermore, an investigation into the defendant's fault for her background belief about whether the action was risky would often be very difficult evidentially. Background beliefs, such as beliefs about the properties of white spirit, are commonly formed over a period of time, with a number of events and actions contributing to the formation of those beliefs. It is often unclear, even to the agent herself, when a belief was formed. It would be difficult, then, to isolate the fault in the formation of those beliefs. If the defendant builds on that false belief to form the belief that there was no risk in the activity performed in this case, for the most part at least, she ought not to be regarded as reckless.

There are cases, however, where the background belief is not only false but also abhorrent in itself: abhorrent not because of the way in which it was formed but because of its very content. An example of this kind might be racist beliefs. Ordinarily, the defendant who holds such a belief immediately shows the kind of attitude in which the criminal law is interested. Furthermore, there might be policy reasons to expand the test in such cases. That might not often be important for questions of recklessness, but it might be important in the related field of mistaken beliefs in self-defence. For example, if D attacks V believing that he himself is being attacked, but D's belief is formed because V is black and D is a racist who believes that all black people are very violent, D ought not to be entitled to a defence. Cases in which the content of a background belief shows something abhorrent about the attitudes of the defendant might provide cases over and above the test proposed here where we ought to find that the defendant is reckless.

D. Conclusions

From this discussion, we can derive a test of recklessness that can be applied where the agent has failed to realize the risks that his action created. The agent will be reckless if the following conditions are fulfilled:

(a) the action was of a kind that might carry risks with it according to the beliefs of the individual;

and either:

(bi)   given those beliefs the agent failed to fulfil his duty of investigating the risks; or

(bii) the agent wilfully blinded himself to the existence of the risks.

Where these conditions are not fulfilled it might well be appropriate to make the defendant civilly liable for any harm that is caused through his risky action. But, for the most part at least, criminal liability is inappropriate. This is because the criminal law, unlike the civil law, is concerned not with distributing losses but with punishing the defendant for harms both for which he is responsible and which manifest the appropriate kind of vice.

This test proposed marks a middle way between purely objective and purely subjective accounts. In favour of objective accounts, there are at least some cases where one can attribute *mens rea* to the defendant despite the fact that she does not recognize the risks involved in what she is doing. If her background beliefs are such that she ought to investigate the risks and she does not perform that investigation adequately, or if she forms a belief that there is no risk for a non-evidential reason, it is appropriate to regard her as reckless for the purposes of the criminal law. On the other hand, the test is sensitive to considerations of the rule of law that subjectivists are concerned with. Citizens are given a fair opportunity to know when they are and are not breaching the criminal law, without being required to go far beyond the call of duty in investigating the risks involved in acting day-to-day. It is only those actions that are already recognized by the defendant as risky that have attached to them burdens of investigation, at least as far as the criminal law is concerned. Furthermore, the central purpose of the criminal law, of punishing those who manifest vices such as cruelty or indifference, is achieved without also making criminals of the stupid, the ignorant, or the clumsy.

11

Battered Women Who Kill Their Sleeping Tormenters: Reflections on Maintaining Respect for Human Life while Killing Moral Monsters

JOSHUA DRESSLER *

Women are often killed by persons whom they know, in particular by husbands or other males with whom they are sexually intimate.[1] In fewer numbers, but perhaps with increasing frequency, abused women kill their victimizers,[2] usually during a physical confrontation,[3] but occasionally while

* Many persons, too many to list here, have helped me work out my ideas on the subject of this chapter. Special thanks go to various persons on both sides of the Atlantic and on various sides of the issue: Robert Batey, Paul Eden, Herbert Fingarette, Jerry Gordon, Peggy Nelson, and Robert Schopp. I also received valuable criticisms and insights (not all of which could find their way into this chapter) from the faculties of McGeorge School of Law, Cleveland-Marshall College of Law, Ohio State University, and University of the Michigan, where I had the opportunity to present versions of this chapter, as well as from the participants at the conference on 'Criminal Law: Doctrines of the General Part' at the University of Birmingham. This chapter was written almost exclusively while I was a member of the faculty at McGeorge School of Law. I express my gratitude to McGeorge Dean Gerald Caplan for the support the school provided me in this regard. Douglas H. Smith, my research assistant at McGeorge School of Law, provided thorough and perceptive assistance.

[1] In 1994, 28 per cent of all female murder victims in the USA were killed by a husband or boyfriend. In contrast, only 3 per cent of male victims were killed by a wife or girlfriend: US Department of Justice, Bureau of Justice Statistics, *Criminal Victimization in the United States* (May 1997, NCJ-162126) vii. Approximately 1,800 persons in the USA were killed in 1996 by persons with whom they were sexually intimate; about three-quarters of the victims were women: US Department of Justice, Bureau of Justice Statistics, *Violence by Intimates* (Mar. 1998, NCJ-167237) 6. Encouragingly, the intimate partner homicide rate in the USA has declined over the past two decades: L. Dugan, D. S. Nagin, and R. Rosenfeld, 'Explaining the Decline in Intimate Partner Homicide' (1999) 3 Homicide Studies 187. The decline appears to be the result of three factors: declining domesticity (an increase in the divorce rate); the improved economic status of females; and an increase in domestic violence services: ibid.

[2] The general belief is that most women who kill their partners were themselves battering victims: H. Maguigan, 'Battered Women and Self-Defense: Myths and Misconceptions in Current Reform Proposals' (1991) 140 U Pennsylvania L Rev 379, at 397.

[3] According to one survey of appellate court decisions involving battered women who killed their abusers, about three-quarters involved confrontational homicides: ibid.

the batterer is asleep or in some other passive condition. This chapter considers the latter situation—in which the victim of ongoing physical abuse kills her abuser in non-confrontational circumstances—and reflects on how the criminal law should deal with these homicides.

The traditional rule in the USA[4] is that a person may not use deadly force unless she reasonably believes that it is necessary to protect herself from imminent use of unlawful deadly force by an aggressor.[5] In this context, 'imminent' means 'at this particular instant',[6] or 'impending, and present, and not prospective or even in the near future'.[7] Therefore, according to this rule,[8] when a battered woman kills her abuser while he sleeps, she is not entitled to a self-defence instruction in a murder prosecution.[9]

But, this rule is undergoing attack. At least a few American jurisdictions—apparently resulting in a 'surprising number of acquittals'[10]—now permit a defendant to introduce expert testimony that she is a battered woman suffering from 'battered woman syndrome' (BWS), and to assert the claim of self-defence notwithstanding the passive condition of the decedent.[11] BWS testimony increasingly is permitted in other common law jurisdictions, as well.[12] Canada[13]

---

[4] Except where otherwise noted, my summary of the law relates only to American jurisprudence. Of course, the moral issues raised (if not necessarily their resolution) have no geographical or cultural limitations.

[5] J. Dressler, *Understanding Criminal Law* (2nd edn., New York, 1995) 199. 'Deadly force' typically is defined as force likely to cause death or serious bodily injury: ibid. at 201. Although some American courts use the term 'immediate' rather than 'imminent' in self-defence law, the terms are at times used interchangeably: R.F. Schopp, B.J. Sturgis and M. Sullivan, 'Battered Woman Syndrome, Expert Testimony, and the Distinction Between Justification and Excuse' (1994) U Illinois L Rev 45, at 65. Any differences between the terms are of no moment in non-confrontational homicide cases.

[6] *People v Dillon* (1962) 24 Ill2d 122, 125–26, 180 NE2d 503, 504.

[7] J. Miller, *Handbook of Criminal Law* (St Paul, Minnesota, 1934) 202.

[8] As discussed later, the Model Penal Code provides a more expansive version of the defence not based on the imminency of the threat. However, the 1985 Commentary to the Code's self-protection provision states that although '[s]ome jurisdictions have followed the Code on this point . . . more have retained the [traditional imminency] formulation': American Law Institute, *Model Penal Code and Commentaries*, Comment to Section 3.04 (1985) 40.

[9] e.g., *State v Norman* (1989) 324 NC 253, 258–60, 378 SE2d 8, 12–13.

[10] S. Graff, 'Battered Women, Dead Husbands: A Comparative Study of Justification and Excuse in American and West German Law' (1988) 10 Loyola Los Angeles International & Comparative LJ 1, at 17.

[11] e.g., *State v Hennum* (1989) 441 NW2d 793, 797–99 (Minnesota) (refusing to rule out, as a matter of law, self-defence claims in sleeping abuser cases); *State v Leidholm* (1983) 334 NW2d 811, 813–14 (North Dakota) (permitting a self-defence claim in which defendant stabbed her abusive husband with a butcher knife while he slept); cf. *State v Gallegos* (1986) 104 NM 247, 251–52, 719 P2d 1268, 1272–73 (allowing self-defence instruction in a case in which defendant shot and then stabbed her abusive husband while he was lying awake on the bed, despite the absence of a threat at that moment); *State v Allery* [1984] 101 Wash2d 591, 592–95, 682 P2d 372, 313–15 (allowing self-defence instruction when defendant shot decedent while he was lying on the couch, following a verbal threat by the decedent to kill her at some unspecified time).

[12] See S.I. Gatowski, S.A. Dobbin, J.T. Richardson, and G.P. Ginsburg, 'The Globalization of Behavioral Science Evidence About Battered Women: A Theory of Production and Diffusion' (1997) 15 Behavioral Science and Law 285, at 286–289.

[13] *R v LaVallee* [1990] 1 SCR 852, 856–59, 889–90 (L, a battered woman, shot V in the back of the head as he left her room during a party in which V warned her that after everyone left, 'either

and South Australia[14] now allow battered women to introduce BWS testimony in support of self-defence pleas where the circumstances are non-confrontational or arguably so. BWS evidence has more limited support in England. It is admissible to mitigate a homicide to manslaughter on the ground of provocation and, one would assume, diminished responsibility, but it has not yet been used to justify a non-confrontational homicide on self-defence grounds.[15]

Is the trend (or, at least, the reform movement) I am describing, which English courts have largely resisted so far, a wise one? It is impossible, of course, not to feel enormous compassion for battered women, and to feel deep revulsion regarding the acts of batterers. These emotions may explain the trend of courts to admit BWS evidence in non-confrontational cases and, as a result, to expand the contours of self-defence law. I submit, however, that this trend is mostly wrong-headed.

The thesis of this chapter may be summarized as follows. First, properly understood, BWS evidence should only play a limited role in self-defence cases. Secondly, BWS evidence disguises what is probably the true basis for the self-defence claims of battered women. What I believe animates the reform movement is the belief that battered women, *syndrome or no syndrome*, are justified in killing their abusers, much as a person is justified in putting to death an insect or vermin.

Thirdly, if society genuinely believes that human life is special—even sacred—we should not justify non-confrontational killings, even of batterers. The law, quite simply, should not authorize homicides that are not necessary on the immediate occasion. I concede at the outset that the argument for my position here is not unassailable. My task is not to convince the reader beyond a reasonable doubt of my position. My goal is more modest, namely, to offer readers—and courts and legislators—reasons to pause and reflect on the matter.

Fourthly, and finally, I submit that battered women are on better theoretical footing if they seek to defend themselves in non-confrontational circumstances

---

you [will] kill me, or I'll get you'; held: BWS testimony was admissible in support of L's self-defence plea, in order to dispel the myths that battered women are not beaten as badly as they claim or have a masochistic desire to be beaten, as well as to assist the jury in evaluating L's ability to determine whether physical harm would occur on the present occasion).

[14] *R v Kontinnen* [1992] 16 Crim LJ 360 (Supreme Court, South Australia, 26 March 1992, unreported) (BWS testimony admissible in sleeping-abuser homicide case).

[15] *R v Ahluwalia* [1992] 4 All ER 889, at 897–899 (BWS is an abnormal mental characteristic of sufficient permanence that it may be considered in determining whether a reasonable person with such a characteristic would have lost her self-control in the face of provocation); see S. Yeo, 'Battered Women Syndrome in Australia' [1993] 143 New LJ 13 (stating that English law treats BWS as an abnormal state of mind, whereas 'a growing number of common law jurisdictions' treat the condition as a normal state of mind); Gatowski *et al.* (n. 12 above) 288 (in comparison to the USA and Canada, 'English courts have been reluctant to entertain evidence of self-defense' in battered woman cases).

by asserting an *excuse* defence not directly based on self-defence.[16] I will defend here a theory of excuse that advocates for battered women have not generally articulated in the legal literature, and that courts and law-makers have not considered. If my arguments are persuasive, a battered women could seek to excuse her conduct absent the use of BWS testimony without falling back on mental illness claims that make her appear irrational.

Sometimes we reach the right outcome in the law, but for the wrong reasons. A defendant and her lawyer may not care how they obtain an acquittal,[17] but we in the academy should care. It should now go almost without saying that there are important moral and practical reasons for distinguishing between justification and excuse defences, and for caring about the underlying moral theories of the criminal law.[18] And, if I am right to be concerned, the likely effect of permitting battered women to claim self-defence in non-confrontational situations will be a coarsening of our attitudes about human life, and perhaps even the promotion or condonation of homicidal vengeance. England and other jurisdictions should reflect long and hard before they continue down the road some American courts are taking.

A. Role of BWS Evidence in Self-Defence Cases

Dr Lenore Walker, the first person to describe and advance the concept of BWS, has identified three distinct and repetitive cycles in a typical battering

[16] I treat self-defence as a *justification* defence in this chapter, as it is commonly considered in modern law. Some commentators advocate characterizing self-defence as an excuse, e.g., C.O. Finkelstein, 'Self-Defense as a Rational Excuse' (1996) 57 U Pittsburgh L Rev 621; C.J. Rosen, 'The Excuse of Self-Defense: Correcting a Historical Accident on Behalf of Battered Women Who Kill' (1986) 36 American U L Rev 11.

Some scholars reason that self-defence, although a justification defence, is converted to an excuse if the actor kills on the basis of an objectively false, although reasonable, belief that she is responding to an imminent deadly threat, e.g., G. Fletcher, *Rethinking Criminal Law* (Boston, 1978) 762–769; P. Robinson, *Criminal Law Defenses*, Vol. 2 (1984) 8. This is not the traditional view of the matter, and elsewhere I have argued against such a narrow view of justification: J. Dressler, 'New Thoughts About the Concept of Justification in the Criminal Law: A Critique of Fletcher's Thinking and *Rethinking*' (1984) 32 UCLA L Rev 61, at 92–95.

Some American jurisdictions recognize an imperfect or incomplete form of lethal self-defence, which reduces the offence to manslaughter, if an actor kills on the basis of an *unreasonable* belief that a deadly attack is imminent, e.g., *In Re Christian S* (1994) 7 Cal 4th 768, 771, 872 P2d 574, 575. Battered women have uncontroversially been convicted of manslaughter on this basis, e.g., *State v Norman* (1989) 324 NC 253, 378 SE2d 9 (probable basis of jury verdict); *People v White* (1980) 90 Ill.App3d 1067, 1070–71, 414 NE2d 196, 198–200. This defence, which ought to be viewed as a partial *excuse* and which I favour, is not the focus of this chapter.

[17] I.B. Nodland, 'Defending Battered Women: Everything She Says May Be Used Against Them' (1992) 68 North Dakota L Rev 131, at 138 (warning fellow lawyers representing battered women not to become 'bogged down in endless . . . battles over (1) differences between what is a justification and what is an excuse; [and] (2) is this self-defense or diminished mental capacity'; and stating that '[t]he only important thing is to get [the battered woman's] story told and to educate the jury on the battered woman syndrome').

[18] J. Dressler, 'Justifications and Excuses: A Brief Review of the Concepts and Literature' (1987) 33 Wayne L Rev 1155, at 1167–1174.

relationship.[19] First is the 'tension-building' phase when minor battering incidents occur and the woman attempts to placate the batterer. Phase two is the 'acute battering incident', when the tension that has built up during the first phase explodes in violence. This is followed by the 'loving and contrition' period when the male seeks forgiveness (perhaps genuinely) and promises to amend his ways. Over time, the tensions rebuild and the cycles repeat. Abuse victims 'live in a state of constant "[a]gitation and anxiety bordering on panic" as they await the next assault'.[20] The cycle of violence explains in part why battered women do not leave their abusers:

[S]imply put, the third stage of the cycle reaffirms the woman's hopes that her mate's behavior will change. In addition, since the woman cannot predict or control the occurrence of acute outbreaks of violence, she sinks into a 'psychological paralysis' [which Walker has termed 'learned helplessness'] in which she feels helpless to change her situation.[21]

Walker has explained 'learned helplessness' further: 'We found that battered women suffer from . . . distortions of perception. A battered woman often believes that the batterer is omnipotent, that no one can help her, and thus she limits the number of responses she feels are possible or safe to make'.[22] A battered woman feels 'paralyzing terror' manifested by 'chronic apprehension of imminent doom, of something terrible always about to happen'.[23] She is demoralized, suffers from depression, and feels unable to cope. The abuse victim is so convinced of the omnipotence of her batterer that, in one case, a woman shot her husband six times as he lay in bed, and then told the police when they arrived, '[b]e careful, he has a lot of guns in there. He's going to be very angry and will shoot you'.[24]

Despite non-trivial criticisms of Walker's research,[25] American courts generally permit defendants in self-defence cases to introduce expert BWS testimony

[19] L.E. Walker, *The Battered Woman* (New York, 1979) 55–70.
[20] K. Kinports, 'Defending Battered Women's Self-Defense Claims' (1988) 67 Oregon L Rev 393, at 399 (quoting Hilberman and Munson, 'Sixty Battered Women' (1977–78) 2 Victimology 460, at 464).
[21] A.E. Thar, 'The Admissibility of Expert Testimony on Battered Wife Syndrome: An Evidentiary Analysis' (1982) 77 Northwestern U L Rev 348, at 351.
[22] L.E. Walker, R.K. Thyfault, and A. Browne, 'Beyond the Juror's Ken: Battered Women' (1982) 7 Vermont L Rev 1, at 8–9. Notwithstanding their supposed emotional paralysis, one study of battering victims reported that over 80 per cent of them were divorced or were in the process of divorcing the abuser: A. Jones, 'When Battered Women Fight Back' (Fall 1982) 9 Barrister 12, at 14.
[23] E. Hilberman and Kit Munson, 'Sixty Battered Women' (1977–78) 2 Victimology 460, at 464.
[24] L.E.A. Walker, 'Understanding Battered Woman Syndrome' (1995) 31 Trial (No. 2) 30.
[25] e.g., R.F. Schopp, B.J. Sturgis and M. Sullivan, 'Battered Woman Syndrome, Expert Testimony, and the Distinction Between Justification and Excuse' (1994) U Illinois L Rev 45, at 53–59; D.L. Faigman, 'The Battered Woman Syndrome and Self-Defense: A Legal and Empirical Dissent' (1986) 72 Virginia L Rev 619, at 630–643; see D.L. Faigman, and A.J. Wright, 'The Battered Woman Syndrome in the Age of Science' (1997) 39 Arizona L Rev 67, at 75 (noting that '[s]urprisingly, no proponent of the [BWS] has responded' to Faigman's 1986 methodological critique).

for various purposes.[26] First, learned helplessness testimony may offset the belief of jurors that claims of prior abuse are untrue ('If all of this had really happened, wouldn't she have left?') or that, even if true, a woman who remains in an abusive relationship has a masochistic desire to be beaten. Secondly, BWS testimony may support the defendant's claim that she subjectively believed that she had to kill her abuser at that moment. For example, experts claim that a battered woman becomes 'attuned to her abuser's pattern of attacks', and she 'learns to recognize subtle gestures or threats that distinguish the severity of attacks and that lead her to believe a particular attack will seriously threaten her survival'.[27] Thirdly, BWS evidence is sometimes used to support the objective prong of self-defence: that the defendant's belief that she needed to act at that moment was reasonable to a person in her circumstances, that is, to a person suffering from BWS. One court has explained this as follows: 'The standard is whether the circumstances were such as would excite the fears of a reasonable person possessing the same or similar psychological and physical characteristics as the defendant'.[28]

B. The *Norman* Case: Killing a Moral Monster

Consider the marriage of Judy and J.T. Norman. I purposely have selected their story[29]—probably the homicide case most commonly cited or discussed in the relevant American battered-woman self-defence literature[30]—not because it represents an average battering relationship, but because it perhaps does *not*. The circumstances leading up to the homicide were extreme and extraordinarily shocking. Indeed, if *anyone* ever deserved to be killed while he slept, it surely was J.T. Norman. Therefore, at the risk of focusing on one of the worst cases, even while trying to determine the proper rule for the somewhat more typical battering situation, let us consider their story.

The defendant, Judy Norman, and J.T. Norman had been married 25 years at the time of J.T. Norman's death. Norman was an alcoholic. He had begun

---

[26] H. Maguigan, 'Battered Women and Self-Defense: Myths and Misconceptions in Current Reform Proposals' (1991) 140 U Pennsylvania L Rev 379, at 461–478; R.A. Schuller and N. Vidmar, 'Battered Woman Syndrome Evidence in the Courtroom' (1992) 16 Law and Human Behavior 273.

[27] 'Developments in the Law—Legal Responses to Domestic Violence' (1993) 106 Harvard L Rev 1498, at 1582.

[28] *Smith v State* (1997) 268 Ga 196, 199–201, 486 SE2d 819, 823.

[29] *State v Norman* (1988) 89 NC App 384, 366 SE2d 586, *reversed* (1989) 324 NC 253, 378 SE2d 8.

[30] e.g., J.M. Cohen, 'Regimes of Private Tyranny: What Do They Mean to Morality and for the Criminal Law?' (1996) 57 U Pittsburgh L Rev 757, at 786–790; G.P. Fletcher, 'Domination in the Theory of Justification and Excuse' (1966) 57 U Pittsburgh L Rev 553, at 555–556; R.A. Rosen, 'On Self-Defense, Imminence, and Women Who Kill Their Batterers' (1993) 71 North Carolina L Rev 371; B.C. Zipursky, 'Self-Defense, Domination, and the Social Contract' (1996) 57 U Pittsburgh L Rev 579, at 583–584.

to drink and to beat defendant five years after they were married. The couple had five children, four of whom are still living. When defendant was pregnant with her youngest child, Norman beat her and kicked her down a flight of steps, causing the baby to be born prematurely the next day.

Norman, himself, had worked one day a few months prior to his death; but aside from that one day, witnesses could not remember his ever working. Over the years and up to the time of his death, Norman forced defendant to prostitute herself every day in order to support him. If she begged him not to make her go, he slapped her. Norman required defendant to make a minimum of 100 dollars per day; if she failed to make this minimum, he would beat her.

Norman commonly called defendant 'Dogs', 'Bitches', and 'Whores', and referred to her as a dog. Norman beat defendant 'most every day', especially when he was drunk and when other people were around, to 'show off'. He would beat defendant with whatever was handy—his fist, a fly-swatter, a baseball bat, his shoe, or a bottle; he put out cigarettes on defendant's skin; he threw food and drink in her face and refused to let her eat for days at a time; and he threw glasses, ashtrays, and beer bottles at her and once smashed a glass in her face. Defendant exhibited to the jury scars on her face from these incidents. Norman would often make defendant bark like a dog, and if she refused, he would beat her. He often forced defendant to sleep on the concrete floor of their home and on several occasions forced her to eat dog or cat food out of the dog or cat bowl.

Norman often stated both to defendant and to others that he would kill defendant. He also threatened to cut her heart out.[31]

In the 36 hours immediately preceding J.T.'s death at Judy's hands, Judy was the victim of physical and verbal abuse typical in their relationship. J.T. slapped Judy, threw a bottle at her, smeared food on her face, burned a cigarette on her chest, and threatened at one point to 'cut her breast off and shove it up her rear end'.[32] During the last day, the police were called to the house three times. Once, no help arrived. A second time, an officer observed that Judy was bruised and advised her to file a complaint against her husband, but she stated that he would kill her if she did. A third time the police came when Judy Norman took an overdose of 'nerve pills'. Later, after J.T. went to sleep, Judy went to her mother's house, retrieved a gun, returned home, and shot her tormenter while he slept. At trial, Judy claimed self-defence, supplemented by expert testimony that she suffered from BWS. The trial court refused to instruct the jury on the defence, and the jury convicted Judy of manslaughter.

Now, for a moment, assume that this had been a confrontational case. Suppose that Judy Norman had shot J.T. while he was beating her with a baseball bat. This would be a straightforward self-defence case. BWS testimony would

---

[31] *State v Norman* (1988) 89 NC App 384, 385–87, 366 S.E.2d 586, 586–87.
[32] ibid., 387, 366 SE2d at 588.

be unnecessary. But, now suppose that the facts were more ambiguous. Assume that one day J.T. is watching a football game on television. His team is losing. J.T. gets drunker and drunker, and angrier and angrier. Finally, he rises, lumbers toward the kitchen where Judy is working and, while holding the empty beer bottle by its neck and waving it above his head, yells, 'Hey bitch', at which instant Judy takes a butcher knife she is coincidentally holding and lunges toward him, stabbing him to death.

Consider this version of *Norman* from the defence perspective at trial. If the jury knows nothing about the Norman marriage, there is relatively little basis for it to understand how Judy could have believed that her bodily integrity was in jeopardy at that moment. J.T.'s actions—calling her a bitch and holding the bottle up—could have various meanings including, simply, that he was a vulgar drunk man expecting Judy to get him another beer. Therefore, in order for an attorney to persuade the jury that Judy subjectively believed that J.T. was going to beat her badly with that bottle, and that such a belief was reasonable, the defence *should* be entitled to introduce evidence of J.T.'s prior abuse, to show that he was a violent man, someone reasonably to be feared, particularly when he was drunk.[33] Perhaps there were even incidents where he beat her in similar circumstances—drunk, during football games, with an empty beer bottle; or, perhaps Judy can testify that J.T. typically beat her when he used the word 'bitch'. Such abuse evidence would make her self-defence claim highly credible. But, it should be noticed, a case for self-defence can be made here without introducing evidence of BWS; what is needed, simply, is evidence that she was a battered woman.

Nonetheless, in ambiguous confrontational cases such as the hypothetical one, there may be justification for introducing syndrome evidence, but its proper use is far more limited than current law suggests.[34] BWS testimony should be limited to enhancing the battered woman's credibility, particularly if the prosecution casts doubt on the defendant's claims of prior abuse. For example, in the absence of BWS testimony, jurors might believe a prosecutor's insinuations (or even in their absence) that 'if she really had been abused, she would have left him long ago'—'learned helplessness' testimony would answer this concern. Or, suppose that the prosecutor introduces testimony of third parties that the defendant and the decedent acted as a seemingly 'normal couple'. BWS testimony would demonstrate that batterers do not beat their partners unceasingly (although this actually seems to be the case in the Norman relationship), and that typically there is a loving/contrition stage that belies the domestic violence.

---

[33] A jury is entitled to consider all of the circumstances surrounding an incident, including the conduct of the decedent prior to the homicide, in determining whether the actor had reasonable grounds to believe that a deadly attack was imminent: *State v Wanrow* (1977) 88 Wash 2d 221, 234–36, 559 P2d 548, 555–56.

[34] See S.J. Morse, 'The "New Syndrome Excuse Syndrome" ' (Winter/Spring 1995) 14 Crim Justice Ethics 3, at 10–13.

These may be the only valid grounds for permitting BWS testimony in self-defence cases.[35] The reason for this is foundational. Self-defence is a justification, not an excuse. The claim of a defendant asserting any justification claim is that she acted properly or permissibly—that she was right, or at least not wrong, in doing what she did.[36] She is not claiming, as she would be if she were asserting the defence of insanity or any other excuse, that her conduct was wrong, but that she should not be blamed for her actions.[37] Yet, battered woman syndrome evidence—*indeed all syndrome evidence*—speaks to the actor's state of mind, rather than to the act itself.[38] It provides reasons why we should treat the syndrome-suffering actor differently than we do others, and why we should not blame her when we would hold others morally accountable for similar conduct. This point is more evident once one turns to non-confrontational cases, specifically to Judy Norman's decision to kill her husband while he was sound asleep.

There is simply no basis for suggesting that J.T. Norman, as he slept in bed, *in reality* represented an imminent threat to Judy Norman.[39] It is even hard to

---

[35] Some contend BWS evidence should be admitted to show that a battered woman is hyper-vigilant and can identify an imminent attack from a seemingly innocuous act, e.g., *People v Humphrey* (1996) 13 Cal 4th 1073, 1083–87, 921 P2d 1, 7–9. But, it is at least debatable whether syndrome evidence is necessary to make this valid point. As commentators have observed, 'some battered women may well be able to predict forthcoming abuse with sufficient accuracy to support a reasonable belief, but these beliefs are the product of neither a special capacity nor the [BWS]. They reflect an ordinary process of inductive inference from past behavior in similar circumstances': R.F. Schopp, B.J. Sturgis, and M. Sullivan, 'Battered Woman Syndrome, Expert Testimony, and the Distinction Between Justification and Excuse' (1994) U Illinois L Rev 45, at 73. In the ambiguous Norman hypothetical, for example, Judy could testify that the word 'bitch' or the beer bottle above the head was an ordinary precursor to an imminent beating. Or, consider the following example:

V and D are mobsters. V drives D to a cabin in the woods, tells him to sit in a chair at a table, and gives him a hot bowl of oatmeal to eat. For 20 years, D has accompanied V to this cabin with other persons who were similarly given a bowl of oatmeal to eat. In every case, V pulled out a gun and killed the person while he ate the oatmeal. On several occasions, V did this to his former partners. This was a murder ritual for V. D shoots and kills V before he completes the oatmeal: B.C. Zipursky, 'Self-Defense, Domination, and the Social Contract' (1996) 57 U Pittsburgh L Rev 579, at 604.

Putting aside for now the issue of *when* D is entitled to shoot V, this is a case in which non-expert evidence of the murder ritual is enough to explain why D reasonably believed his life was in jeopardy.

[36] J. Dressler, 'New Thoughts About the Concept of Justification in the Criminal Law: A Critique of Fletcher's Thinking and *Rethinking*' (1984) 32 UCLA L Rev 61, at 81.

[37] J. Dressler, 'Justifications and Excuses: A Brief Review of the Concepts and Literature' (1987) 33 Wayne L Rev 1155, at 1162–1163.

[38] See L.E.A. Walker, 'Battered Women Syndrome and Self-Defense' (1992) 6 Notre Dame Journal of Law, Ethics and Public Policy 321, at 324 ('[B]attered women are so heterogeneous that there really is no one typical way for them to act. Rather each woman's thinking, feeling, and acting must be explained in the context of her life as well as the way the abuse has specifically impacted on her state of mind').

[39] R.A. Rosen, 'On Self-Defense, Imminence, and Women Who Kill Their Batterers' (1993) 71 North Carolina L Rev 371, at 375 (although critical of the imminency requirement, the author concedes that at the time Judy shot J.T., the threat of death or serious bodily injury was not imminent according to any reasonable interpretation of the term).

believe that she *subjectively* believed this. She may have believed that she had to kill J.T. while he slept if she wanted him dead, but did she *really* believe that he represented an instantaneous threat?[40] Indeed, if Judy Norman *did* believe this because of BWS, this raises serious doubts about her contact with reality—and, *that* is a potential argument for excusing Judy Norman, but not for justifying the homicide.

The conceptual—and even practical—effect of BWS evidence is to pathologize the Judy Normans of the world.[41] It replaces the stereotype of the hysterical woman with the battered one.[42] BWS 'marks the woman as a collection of mental symptoms and behavioral abnormalities'[43] who lacks the psychological capacity to remove herself from her abusive partner. Indeed, the term 'syndrome' itself suggests an abnormality.[44] It presupposes the existence of a disease-state, or something akin to it.[45] The language used by BWS advocates and courts to describe a battered woman's condition frequently demonstrates that the self-defence claim sounds as much in mental incapacity excuse terms as it does in justification.[46] Thus, ironically, BWS bring the courts back full circle (albeit under the umbrella of 'self-defence') to the early American battered women cases, in which defendants sought full or partial exculpation on the grounds of temporary insanity or diminished capacity.[47]

---

[40] In fact, the defence presented no expert testimony to support such a claim.

[41] A juror simulation suggests that 'the presence of expert evidence providing a diagnosis of [BWS], compared to a no expert control, [causes] the jurors to view the defendant as more distorted in her thinking, less capable of making responsible choices, and less culpable for her actions': R.A. Schuller and P.A. Hastings, 'Trials of Battered Women Who Kill: The Impact of Alternative Forms of Expert Evidence' (1996) 20 Law and Human Behavior 167, at 169.

[42] P.L. Crocker, 'The Meaning of Equality for Battered Women Who Kill Men in Self-Defense' (1985) 8 Harvard Women's LJ 121, at 137.

[43] A.M. Coughlin, 'Excusing Women' (1994) 82 California L Rev 1, at 76; see also P. Margulies, 'Identity on Trial: Subordination, Social Science Evidence, and Criminal Defense' (1998) 51 Rutgers L Rev 45, at 48 (the BWS theories 'pathologize women by making them seem passive, emotionally volatile, and irrational').

[44] *Merriam Webster's Collegiate Dictionary* (10th edn., Springfield, Mass. 1993) 1196 ('a group of signs and symptoms that occur together and characterize a particular abnormality').

[45] In the USA, BWS is not now recognized as a mental disease, but domestic battering is treated as an 'interpersonal stressor' that often results in symptoms related to post-traumatic stress disorder: American Psychiatric Association, *Diagnostic and Statistical Manual of Mental Disorders* (4th edn., Washington, 1994) 425.

[46] e.g., *R v Runjanjic & Kontinnen* (1991) 56 SASR 114, at 117 ('there are certain behaviour patterns displayed by women who are battered . . . and it leads to certain *inabilities* to handle situations in the way *ordinary* people would') (emphasis added); *United States v Marenghi* (1995) 893 F Supp 85, 87 (Maine) (the defendant 'was a *victim* of [BWS] that prohibited her from *forming the requisite capacity* to commit the crimes as charged') (emphasis added); *Chester v State* (1996) 267 Ga. 9, 16, 471 SE2d 836, 841–842 (Sears J concurring specially) (describing a person with BWS as one who is 'afflicted' and a victim who may 'experience a change in cognitive thinking ability' or act in a 'dissociative state' as a result of her 'deeply troubled state of mind'); *People v Torres* (1985) 128 Misc2d 129, 132, 488 NYS2d 358, 361 (Sup. Ct.) (BWS creates such a '[n]umbed . . . dread of imminent aggression, [that] these women are *unable to think clearly* about the means of escape from this abusive family existence') (emphasis added).

[47] See D.R. Follingstad, 'Forensic Evaluations of Battered Women Defendants: Relevant Data to be Applied to Elements of Self-Defense' (1996) 5 Applied and Preventive Psychology 165, at 167.

And, today, feminists—who sought to move the battered women cases away from these sometimes stigmatizing excuses—increasingly appreciate this fact.[48] One feminist scholar has gone so far as to characterize the BWS cases as promoting a 'misogynist defense'.[49]

The BWS cases are not only potentially demeaning to women, but are conceptually incoherent. Even if syndrome evidence is properly introduced to support a battered woman's subjective belief that the sleeping abuser is an imminent threat to her life, there is no basis for claiming that such a belief is reasonable unless the 'reasonable person' is characterized as a 'reasonable battered woman suffering from BWS'. Although some subjectivization of the 'reasonable person' standard is appropriate—for example, inclusion of the actor's physical size and capacity for self-defence, and her relevant experiences with the abusive decedent[50]—it is a contradiction in terms to describe the 'reasonable person' as one who suffers from emotional paralysis or whose fear causes her to misperceive reality (the 'reality' being that the abuser represents a long-term threat to the woman's safety, but that while asleep he does not represent an imminent threat). Put simply, without distorting the meaning of reasonableness beyond sensible recognition, a 'reasonable person' does not fear instantaneous death from a sleeping person.

C. Seeking a Moral Theory of Justification

If I am right so far, BWS evidence is of only limited relevance in non-confrontational self-defence cases. This does not mean, however, that there is no potential non-consequentialist basis for justifying Judy Norman's conduct.[51] Indeed, I believe that the unreflective view of many persons, including some courts, is that a battered woman, with or without the syndrome, *is* justified in killing her abuser, for the simple reason that he deserves it. Consider, for example, these remarks expressed in the *Norman* case:

---

[48] E.M. Schneider, 'Describing and Changing: Women's Self-Defense Work and the Problem of Expert Testimony on Battering' (1992) 14 Women's Rights Law Reporter 213, at 230–235.

[49] A.M. Coughlin, 'Excusing Women' (1994) 82 California L Rev 1, at 70.

[50] S.J. Morse, 'The "New Syndrome Excuse Syndrome" ' (Winter/Spring 1995) 14 Crim Justice Ethics 3, at 11 (the reasonable person should only be endowed with the normal, non-culpable characteristics of the defendant that are relevant to the situation).

[51] It is doubtful that utilitarian arguments justify non-confrontational homicides. Although an act-utilitarian might justify Judy Norman's actions, a rule-utilitarian would have difficulty supporting a redefinition of self-defence to include non-confrontational killings. It is hardly clear that, as a rule, it is socially beneficial for battering victims to kill their abusers in non-imminent, especially non-confrontational, circumstances. Presumably, the preferred outcome is one that would deter preemptive strikes by women while simultaneously according battered women protection from their abusers (e.g., through confinement and/or treatment of the batterers). Furthermore, a rule permitting or encouraging non-confrontational homicides could not easily be cabined. *Norman* is an extreme version of marital violence: where would the line be drawn in others cases of familial abuse, and would other women and children be encouraged to kill in less extreme circumstances? One virtue of the bright-line common law rule is the relative clarity of the message it sends.

By his barbaric conduct over the course of twenty years, J.T. Norman reduced the quality of the defendant's life to such an abysmal state that, given the opportunity to do so, the jury might well have found that she was justified in acting in self-defense for the preservation of her tragic life.[52]

And consider one justice's comments in a battered child syndrome case, in which a teenager, after years of alleged abuse, ambushed his father in the garage, and then sought to claim self-defence:

This case concerns itself with what happens—or can happen—and did happen *when a cruel, ill-tempered, insensitive man roams, gun in hand, through his years of family life* as a battering bully—a bully who, since his two children were babies, beat both of them and his wife regularly and unmercifully.[53]

What may animate these two justices (and clearly explains the views of many persons with whom I have conversed about *Norman*) is an implicit acceptance of the moral theory of forfeiture, namely, that a person by his wilful, egregious conduct may forfeit his right to life; therefore, termination of his life constitutes no socially recognized harm to society.[54] Judy Norman and the teenager who killed his abusive father were justified (according to this view) in killing their tormenters, not because their conduct was reasonable to the clouded mind of a syndrome victim, but because the victim had it coming. By acting as a monster for years, the abuser forfeited his right to life—his death constituted a mere blip on society's social-harm moral radar screen.[55] As Hugo Bedau has critically explained the forfeiture principle, '[the wrongdoer] no longer merits our consideration, any more than an insect or a stone does'.[56]

As with any moral argument of this sort, I cannot demonstrate conclusively that it must be rejected.[57] It should be noted, however, that the forfeiture principle runs counter to the traditional view that the focus of criminal trial is not supposed to be on 'the blame attaching to the dead man'.[58] The purpose

[52] *State v Norman* (1989) 324 NC 253, 275, 378 SE2d 8, 21 (Martin J dissenting) (emphasis added).

[53] *Jahnke v State* (1984) 682 P2d 991, 1011 (Wyoming) (Rose J dissenting) (emphasis added).

[54] The fact that many persons expressly or implicitly justify non-confrontational 'self-defence' homicides on forfeiture grounds is of more than simple sociological interest. If I am correct, this view permeates the minds of some (I believe, many) American judges and legislators and, therefore, represents a point of view with explanatory force that must be confronted head-on. See n. 57 below.

[55] See J.M. Cohen, 'Regimes of Private Tyranny: What Do They Mean to Morality and for the Criminal Law?' (1996) 57 U Pittsburgh L Rev 757, at 790–791 (comparing domestic abusers to public tyrants) ('So evil are these [persons] for what they take away from the capacity to lead good lives that . . . [their] death may be a misfortune but it has no effective cost').

[56] Hugo Bedau, 'The Right to Life' (1968) Monist 550, at 570.

[57] From conversations, I have found that the forfeiture concept does not resonate well to English ears. Among many persons in the USA, unfortunately, it does. The idea of forfeiture is not foreign to a society that executes a good number of its murderers and which, until relatively recently, in some states permitted police officers to kill non-violent fleeing felons: *Tennessee v Garner* 471 U.S. 12 (1985) (declaring unconstitutional statutes that authorize the use of deadly force against non-violent fleeing felons).

[58] *R v Duffy* [1949] 1 All ER 932, at 933.

of the trial is not to stand in moral judgement of the decedent's character, but rather to evaluate the propriety of the defendant's conduct in relation to the decedent. Indeed, forfeiture runs counter to the proposition that 'all human lives must be regarded as having an equal claim to preservation simply because life itself is an irreducible value'. The proposition here is not that life may not be taken but that 'in making the judgment certain considerations [should] be ruled out. The life of the good man and the bad stand equal, because how a man has led his life may not affect his claim to continued life'.[59]

The implications of the forfeiture principle are troubling. It suggests that a human life is expendable. Persons can swat the wrongdoer like a fly and toss his remains in the garbage. The logic of an unvarnished version of the forfeiture principle is that a battered woman has a moral claim against her abuser, *in infinitum*. She—or others at her behest—may kill him at any time. Consider a battered woman who hires a contract killer to take her husband's life, and then asserts self-defence.[60] No court has allowed such a claim to go to the jury,[61] but the logic of forfeiture suggests otherwise. Or, more sympathetically, suppose that a battered woman turns to her brother to kill her tormenter, and then claims self-defence. If J.T. Norman's death is tantamount to throwing out the garbage, or swatting a fly—if he is not recognized as a human being deserving of the law's protection while he sleeps—what basis is there for prosecuting the woman or, for that matter, the contract killer or brother who kills J.T. for her?[62] A moral theory that could justify a contract killing, even of someone as miserable as J.T. Norman, should be rejected. And, I would submit, even a moderated forfeiture principle, that would limit the right to kill to the abuse victim (or her family), is not one society should countenance.

The forfeiture justification is sometimes restated slightly. Rather than argue that the batterer has no right to life, some defenders of battered women prefer to characterize the woman who executes the sleeping abuser as a 'spontaneous vigilante' 'punishing a deserving felon',[63] rendering the sleeping batterer 'his

---

[59] S.H. Kadish, 'Respect for Life and Regard for Rights in the Criminal Law' (1976) 64 California L Rev 871, at 880.

[60] e.g., *People v Yaklich* (1991) 833 P2d 758 (Colorado Ct. App.); *State v Leaphart* (1983) 673 SW2d 870 (Tennessee Ct. Crim. App.).

[61] Lenore Walker is critical of this refusal. She suggests that abused women who hire contract killers should not be treated as premeditated killers but rather should be understood as 'women, [who] because of sex role conditioning or other factors, cannot use sufficient force to protect themselves'. She views the law's rejection of the defence in these circumstances as still another example of the law's '[b]iases . . . against women': L.E. Walker, 'A Response to Elizabeth M. Schneider's Describing and Changing' (1986) 9 Women's Rights Law Reporter 223, at 224.

[62] Indeed, imagine the case of a burglar-thief who enters the Norman house believing it is unoccupied, discovers J.T. sleeping in bed, and decides to kill Norman to avoid detection. Does the forfeiture principle suggest that even *this* killing is socially harmless because J.T. is expendable? I assume that nobody would accept the 'logic' of forfeiture taken to *this* level, and certainly no court would.

[63] E. Ayyildiz, 'When Battered Woman's Syndrome Does Not Go Far Enough: The Battered Woman as Vigilante' (1995) 4 Journal Gender and Law 141, 148, at 166.

due',[64] and thereby repairing the social order.[65] From a rule-utilitarian perspective, of course, private vigilantism is dangerous because of the risk of unleashing unnecessary violence and of undermining essential social norms. The idea of self-defence as a form of retributive punishment also conflicts with the *lex talionis* proportionality principle: the batterer's punishment is death, whereas his prior offences necessarily exclude the actual taking of life.[66] And even in the case of murder, there can be mitigating factors that justify the belief that death constitutes excessive, undeserved punishment.[67] If the 'penalty' of death is going to be imposed—if the judgement that a person deserves to die is going to be made—it ought to come from society as a whole, upon conviction by a jury.

By far the best justificatory explanation of self-defence—one sounding in a right of autonomy—can be seen in the Hobbesian claim that the obligation of citizens to their government lasts 'as long, and no longer, than the power lasteth by which [the government] is able to protect them'.[68] One can argue for a similar justification to kill aggressors by applying John Rawls' 'veil of ignorance'.[69] Surely, a rational person in the 'original position' would retain the right to use deadly force in those circumstances in which the government cannot protect her. As Professor Claire Finkelstein has demonstrated,[70] however, Anglo-American law has never taken the right of self-preservation as far as Hobbes did, who maintained that the right of a self-interested individual to kill could even be exercised against other justified actors, including the sovereign. Indeed, early English law only *excused* deadly self-defence, in part because a defender's actions *are* self-interested rather than performed for the social good. And, although, the law now justifies deadly force in self-defence, it is evident that we do so cautiously. Lethal self-defence is probably the weakest justification defence the law recognizes,[71] and is very narrowly defined in

---

[64] M.J. Willoughby, 'Rendering Each Woman Her Due: Can a Battered Woman Claim Self-Defense When She Kills Her Sleeping Batterer?' (1989) 38 Kansas L Rev 169.

[65] Ayyildiz (n. 63 above) 149.

[66] G.P. Fletcher, *A Crime of Self-Defense* (New York, 1988) 29. In the USA, the Supreme Court has held that death is an unconstitutionally excessive penalty for rape on the ground that the rapist, by definition, has taken no life: *Coker v Georgia* (1977) 433 U.S. 584.

[67] *Woodson v North Carolina* (1976) 428 US 280, 303–04 (the view that every murderer should be executed, no matter what the circumstances, improperly 'excludes from consideration in fixing the ultimate punishment of death the possibility of compassionate or mitigating factors stemming from the diverse frailties of humankind. It treats all [murderers] . . . not as uniquely human beings, but as members of a faceless, undifferentiated mass to be subjected to the blind infliction of the penalty of death'). It may be hard to imagine that there are any reasons for mitigating J.T. Norman's punishment. However, even in this extreme case, there may be an explanation for how he became the moral monster that he was—perhaps he was horrendously abused as a child—that might call for a 'compassionate' response.

[68] T. Hobbes, *Leviathan* (London, 1651) ch. XXI, para. 21.

[69] J. Rawls, *A Theory of Justice* (Oxford, 1971) 17–21.

[70] C.O. Finkelstein, 'Self-Defense as a Rational Excuse' (1996) 57 U Pittsburgh L Rev 621, at 635–641.

[71] A self-defender's act of killing is more aptly described as permissible, tolerable, or not wrongful, rather than as affirmatively good. P.H. Robinson, 'A Theory of Justification: Societal

order to maintain the principle that all human life, even that of an aggressor, should be preserved if at all possible. The requirement of imminency sets the rigid common law parameters of the right of self-defence.[72]

Of course, it is precisely this imminency requirement that advocates for battered women, and many feminists generally, criticize. Although Susan Estrich has demonstrated that it is an overstatement to suggest that *all* self-defence rules are designed to define and protect 'manly behavior',[73] feminists have quite rightly argued that the traditional rules of self-defence are based on male experiences.[74] In general, the defence contemplates the situation of two men of roughly equal strength in a one-time conflict, perhaps in a bar or on a street. Self-defence rules do not recognize the experiences of women and, in particular they do not contemplate the problems inherent in domestic violence circumstances, namely, the dissimilar strength of the parties and the fact that the victim and her aggressor may be in nearly unceasing contact with each other.

Do these differences suggest that we should abandon the imminency rule, as is certainly required at a minimum if we are going to justify the killing of a sleeping or otherwise passive abuser? Put differently, how broadly should the law define a person's right to kill in order to protect her bodily integrity? Currently, defensive force must be proportional and necessary: a person may not kill to protect a less valuable right than human life; and the right to kill is limited to those circumstances in which deadly force is the only option. Would abandonment of the imminency requirement undermine the necessity requirement, which (again) is founded on the principle that human life is sufficiently valuable that the life of even a 'bad guy' should not be terminated intentionally unless essential to save an innocent life?

The Model Penal Code[75] has moved away from a strict imminency requirement. The Code provides that deadly force may be inflicted (assuming certain other requirements, not relevant here, are satisfied) if it is 'immediately necessary . . . on the present occasion'. For example, suppose that J.T. Norman informed Judy, who is standing in the kitchen with a knife preparing dinner, that he is going to the bedroom to get a gun to kill her. In a Model Penal Code state, Judy could justifiably stab J.T. in the back as he turns to leave the kitchen.[76] In a strict common law jurisdiction, Judy would

---

Harm as a Prerequisite for Criminal Liability' (1975) 23 UCLA L Rev 266, at 284; J. Dressler, 'New Thoughts About the Concept of Justification in the Criminal Law: A Critique of Fletcher's Thinking and *Rethinking*' (1984) 32 UCLA L Rev 61, at 84–85.

[72] G.P. Fletcher, 'Domination in the Theory of Justification and Excuse' (1966) 57 U Pittsburgh L Rev 553, 569.

[73] S. Estrich, 'Defending Women' (1990) 88 Michigan L Rev 1430, at 1431–1432.

[74] P.L. Crocker, 'The Meaning of Equality for Battered Women Who Kill Men in Self-Defense' (1985) 8 Harvard Women's LJ 121, at 123–128.

[75] Model Penal Code s. 3.04.

[76] See American Law Institute, *Model Penal Code and Commentaries* (1985) Comment to s. 3.04, 39–40. For another example, see the oatmeal hypothetical in n. 35 above.

seemingly have to wait to see if he really did return with a gun, at which point she would have little hope of protecting herself from her armed husband.

By dispensing with the strict imminency requirement, the Model Penal Code provides a battered woman and all others who are threatened with a broader defence, namely with the right to act when the need appears urgent, although not imminent. The Code's approach increases the risk that, in the hypothetical, J.T.'s threat on this occasion was bluster—it might not be bluster over the long haul, but the Code requires that the force be immediately necessary *on the present occasion*—but this is a risk that sensible people should be willing to accept, because, in the first place, as between the threatening party and the innocent person, it is fair to provide the latter with some leeway, and because the full defence does not apply unless the defender's (Judy's) belief that force is immediately necessary is a reasonable one.

But, the Code provision, as sensible as it is, does not provide protection to women who kill batterers while they are asleep, watching television, or are otherwise in a passive condition at the time of the incident. In these circumstances, some defenders of battered women argue it should be sufficient that deadly force is necessary to prevent *eventual* use of deadly force by the batterer. According to this view, the social problem of male domination of women—physical, psychological, political, and sexual—justifies dispensing with any temporal limitation on the right of self-defence.[77] In essence, what is sought is 'not a mere modification of self-defense, but an extension in kind as well as degree'.[78] Essentially, the legal claim is that 'what the woman faces at the time she kills . . . is in fact the sum total of all batterings she has received in the past *as well as those which are sure to come in the future*'.[79] One scholar has tentatively proposed that deadly force be legally justified if the batterer's prior conduct presents a 'menace of inevitable death or grievous bodily harm',[80] or even if such harm is not inevitable, if the actor reasonably believes that it is.

Other issues aside, the danger of this defence lies in its speculativeness. Once the temporal limitations are gone—once we move past imminent or 'immediately necessary . . . on the present occasion' threats—how well can one predict what human conduct is inevitable? As one scholar has observed, 'even funnel clouds sometimes turn around, and human beings sometimes defy predictions'.[81] Human beings are far less predictable than funnel clouds because they possess the capacity for free choice. They are the 'wild cards'[82]

---

[77] B.C. Zipursky, 'Self-Defense, Domination, and the Social Contract' (1996) 57 U Pittsburgh L Rev 579, at 581.

[78] A.D. Eisenberg, and D.A. Dillon, 'Medico-Legal Aspects of Representing the Battered Woman' (1980) 5 Oklahoma City U L Rev 645, at 654.

[79] ibid. (emphasis added).

[80] Zipursky (n. 77 above) 609 (emphasis omitted).

[81] A.W. Alschuler, 'Preventive Pretrial Detention and the Failure of Interest-Balancing Approaches to Due Process' (1986) 85 Michigan L Rev 510, at 557.

[82] S.H. Kadish, 'Complicity, Cause, and Blame: A Study in the Interpretation of Doctrine' (1985) 73 California L Rev 323, at 360.

in any predictive game. This does not mean that human beings *always* defy predictions, or even that specific humans *usually* defy predictions; it is enough to say that they *sometimes* defy predictions, and the likelihood of error rises dangerously when one is merely predicting some 'inevitability', well down the road.[83] When the law justifies a battered woman killing a sleeping abuser—when it justifies the certainty of his immediate death—on the basis of some 'inevitable' future event, and when one takes the defence the further step of justifying the killing, even if the harm is *not* inevitable, if a reasonable person would incorrectly predict it, we have moved a long way from the principle that human life should be maintained as often and as long as reasonably possible.[84]

Issues of proof of inevitability aside, even if we assume that a certain harm X *is* inevitable in 10 years, or five years, or five months, why should the law justify a preemptive strike 10 years, five years, or five months before it becomes necessary? I fully agree that it is unfair to wait until an 'inevitability' is imminent—it is unfair to put the entire risk of error on the battering victim rather than on her attacker[85]—but the Model Penal Code's solution of waiting until the force is immediately necessary on the present occasion strikes me as a suitable compromise. Moreover, there is no conceptual basis for limiting any expanded defence to battered women or even to other categories of persons who might be identified as victims of domination.[86] We should hesitate long and hard before we promote a criminal defence that categorically justifies the taking of life before it is immediately necessary.

D. Excusing Homicide by Battered Women

So far I have made the following claims. First, BWS evidence should play only a minor role in battered women self-defence cases, and surely less of one than it is currently accorded in many American jurisdictions. Secondly, as a theoretical matter, a claim of self defence in a non-confrontational battered woman case *can* plausibly be justified in the absence of BWS evidence. However, one of the arguments that probably underlies such self-defence claims

---

[83] Also, as the roads gets longer, the possibility of a non-lethal solution, e.g., the abuser is jailed for unrelated reasons, he becomes infirm, or enhanced-domestic-violence services mitigate the problem, is enhanced.

[84] 'Even the most optimistic behavioral scientists and legal commentators now seem to believe that the accuracy of predictions of dangerousness, whether made clinically or statistically, is "probably no better than one valid assessment out of two"': C.P. Ewing, 'Preventive Detention and Execution: The Constitutionality of Punishing Future Crimes' (1991) 15 Law and Human Behavior 139, at 141 (quoting C. Slobogin, 'Dangerousness and Expertise' (1984) 133 U Pennsylvania L Rev 97, at 117).

[85] J.M. Cohen, 'Regimes of Private Tyranny: What Do They Mean to Morality and for the Criminal Law?' (1996) 57 U Pittsburgh L Rev 757, at 793–794.

[86] G.P. Fletcher, 'Domination in the Theory of Justification and Excuse' (1966) 57 U Pittsburgh L Rev 553, at 575–576.

(forfeiture) is morally unacceptable. A second basis largely founded in political theory (a 'rights' theory) adequately explains the justification in paradigmatic self-protection circumstances, and justifies broadening the right of self-protection to circumstances when a threat, although not imminent, requires an immediate response. But the rights theory cannot easily or, I think, wisely justify ordinary non-confrontational homicides.

None of this suggests that Judy Norman may not be entitled to exculpation. Rather, the significant point is that the law should avoid the treacherous moral path of promoting or, at least, tolerating as 'not wrongful', preemptive strikes inflicted on sleeping batterers by their victims. There may be a better path to take: that of potentially *excusing* some battered women who kill their sleeping abusers.[87]

In the realm of excuse, one could return to use of BWS evidence, but this may suggest that the battered woman is sick or abnormal and may result in defence attorneys making potentially demeaning arguments. However, there is an alternative. I have previously written about excuses this way:

Desert [of punishment] is based on the principle that a specific blameworthy act can be imputed to the person—not just to the body of the person—who is in court if, but only if, he had the capacity and fair opportunity to function in a uniquely human way, *i.e.*, freely to choose whether to violate the moral/legal norms of society.

'Free choice' exists if the actor has the substantial capacity and fair opportunity to: (1) understand the pertinent facts relating to his conduct; (2) appreciate that his conduct violates society's moral or legal norms; and (3) conform his conduct to the law. Unless all three conditions for free choice are present, blame does not attach to the wrongdoer [and an excuse should be recognized], as he lacks a critical attribute of personhood.[88]

As this explanation suggests, there are two different types of excuse claims. Sometimes the actor claims a lack of capacity to satisfy one or more of the

---

[87] I am considering here only the question of whether a battered woman should be *fully* excused for her actions. There are various grounds for partially excusing (convicting of manslaughter) the battered woman. First, she may be able to raise an imperfect self-defence claim, see n. 16 above. Secondly, in a Model Penal Code jurisdiction in the USA, she could seek to reduce her offence to manslaughter on the ground that she killed as the result of an 'extreme mental or emotional disturbance' for which there is a 'reasonable explanation or excuse': Model Penal Code s. 210.3(1)(b). A strict heat-of-passion claim might be ruled out on the ground that the battering victim had reasonable time to cool off while her abuser slept. However, the cumulative impact of a series of beatings may arguably cause an ordinary person to become and remain enraged while the batterer sleeps. See *Commonwealth v McCusker* (1972) 448 Pa 382, 389, 292 A2d 286, 289–90 (permitting a heat-of-passion case to go the jury based on three provocative acts over a three-week period); *R v Thornton* [1992] 1 All ER 306, 313–314 (provocative acts in the course of domestic violence over a period of time may be considered by a jury as context or background, in judging a defendant's response to a final provocation); see also J. Greene, 'A Provocation Defence for Battered Women Who Kill?' (1989) 12 Adelaide L Rev 145. Thirdly, in some jurisdictions, a diminished capacity defence might be available.

[88] J. Dressler, 'Reflections on Excusing Wrongdoers: Moral Theory, New Excuses and the Model Penal Code' (1988) 19 Rutgers LJ 671, at 701; see also H.L.A. Hart, *Punishment and Responsibility* (Oxford, 1968) 152.

three preconditions of free choice set out above. An incapacity excuse is one that suggests that, at least at the time of the prohibited act, the actor lacked the attributes of a moral agent because of internal malfunctioning or non-functioning. Insanity, involuntary intoxication, and infancy are incapacity excuses. This is the category of excuse that attorneys representing battered women pled before they 'discovered' self-defence.

There is an entirely different basis for excuse, however. An actor may assert that there is nothing wrong with *her*—her capacity to function as a moral agent is unimpaired—but that (on a specific occasion) she lacked a *fair opportunity* to demonstrate one or more of the three criteria of personhood. Here, it is an *external* event or circumstance, acting upon the moral agent, that frees her from moral blame. Duress and mistake of law are examples of no-fair-opportunity excuses.

Incapacity excuses are, in some sense, empirical. That is, there will be a need to introduce evidence, often of an expert variety, regarding the internal (mal)functionings of the actor, in order to show that she substantially lacked the ability to reason properly and/or to control her conduct. In stark contrast, no-fair-opportunity defences are primarily moral or normative in nature. Although an empirical issue is raised (what opportunities did the actor have?), the ultimate question is normative: is it *fair* or morally just to hold the person accountable for her actions in view of the circumstances called to the fact-finders' attention?

Whereas incapacity claims call for syndrome-type evidence and may seem potentially demeaning to an accused, a no-fair-opportunity excuse provides a potential syndrome-free zone in which an accused can show that she did not act culpably because, in essence, she acted as an ordinary individual might have behaved in similar circumstances. In an extreme case, a plausible claim can be made by a battered woman—enough of a claim to go to a jury—that she should be excused for killing the monster lying in bed next to her, on the ground that, at the time of her unjustified actions (I stress, the actions remains unjustified), she did not have a fair opportunity to conform her conduct to the dictates of law.

Imagine a jury considering the BWS-free evidence that was or could have been presented on Judy Norman's behalf if a jury had been asked, essentially, 'Did Judy have a fair opportunity *not* to kill J.T. on the day she shot him?' The jurors would presumably ask themselves, 'What else could she have done other than take the extreme step of violating the law by killing him?' Could she have left him while he slept? Since this is a syndrome-free case and, consequently, learned helplessness is irrelevant, the answer is 'yes'. But, even granting this, was walking out the door too hard an option for Judy to exercise? That question, in turn, requires further reflection. Did Judy have children? Yes, she had five. What, then, were her options? She could have left the children with J.T. A jury would likely find such an alternative unthinkable: it would be equivalent to abandoning her offspring, and such desertion might have resulted in their mistreatment at J.T.'s hands, in view of studies that have shown a correlation between spousal and child abuse.[89] So, could Judy have left *with* them? That would lead the jury down still further paths, requiring them to consider the feasibility of Judy supporting her children alone, the adequacy of domestic violence services in the community, and the risk that J.T. could have found them had she fled with them in tow.

Were there other options? Perhaps she could have called the police to seek help. But, the facts show that the police came to the Norman residence on more than one occasion during the final hours, and she received no immediate help. It is possible a defence attorney could introduce evidence of prior spurned efforts to obtain help from the police or other social agencies.

This would be a start toward making a plausible no-fair-opportunity excuse claim. The point here is *not* that a jury necessarily would—or even should—excuse every battered woman who kills her abusive partner in non-confrontational circumstances. The more grave the offence, the more society has a right to expect a law-abiding person to avoid violating the law. The thrust of my claim is, simply, that in a just system of criminal laws, a jury should be given the opportunity in some, perhaps many, non-confrontational cases to consider a battered woman's excuse claim.

If I am right that a battered woman should often be able in non-confrontational circumstances to plead excuse for her conduct, and that the basis for such an excuse is that she did not have a fair opportunity to act within the restrictions of the law, the issue is whether there is any current excuse defence she may claim. At least in the USA, it is recognized that there is a need for a residual justification defence—in the Model Penal Code, it is the choice of evils defence sometimes described as 'necessity'[90]—to which a person can turn when no ordinary justification claim applies. Conceptually, there may also be a need for a residual *excuse* defence that exculpates actors who lack a fair opportunity to understand the attendant facts or law or (as in the case of some abused women or children) to conform their actions to the law's dictates.

As it turns out, the no-fair-opportunity claim suggested here looks a great deal like the rationale for the existing defence of duress. A duress defence is based on the principle that compelling circumstances can impair a moral agent's freedom of choice to a point that it is, quite simply, unjust to punish her.[91] As I have written elsewhere, '[a]t its core, the defense of duress requires us to determine what conduct we, a society of individual members of the human race, may legitimately expect of our fellow threatened humans'.[92] The

[89] V.M. Mather, 'The Skeleton in the Closet: The Battered Woman Syndrome, Self-Defense, and Expert Testimony' (1988) 39 Mercer L Rev 545, at 552.

[90] Model Penal Code s. 3.02.

[91] R. Cross, 'Murder Under Duress' (1978) 28 U Toronto LJ 369, at 372; I.H. Dennis, 'Duress, Murder and Criminal Responsibility' (1980) 96 LQR 208, at 230–237.

[92] J. Dressler, 'Exegesis of the Law of Duress: Justifying the Excuse and Searching for Its Proper Limits' (1989) 62 Southern California L Rev 1331, at 1366.

essential test in the battered woman's situation is 'not whether the actor made the right or a permissible decision, not even whether the choice was expected as a predictive matter, but rather whether, in light of the nature of the [situation] and the expected repercussions from [not acting], we could fairly expect a person of nonsaintly moral strength to resist'[93] killing her abuser.

A battered woman who kills in non-confrontational circumstances cannot presently plead duress in jurisdictions that apply the common law duress defence. First, in the paradigmatic duress case, the coerced party will commit an offence against an innocent person or her property, rather than to commit an act of violence on the coercer himself. Secondly, the defence only applies to *imminent* human threats. Thirdly, duress is not a defence to criminal homicide.[94] Because common law duress does not apply in the Judy Norman context, a jurisdiction that intends to provide a just system of laws will need to recognize a residual no-fair-opportunity defence or, far preferably,[95] broaden its present duress defence.

Some American states already recognize a broader version of duress. In states that have adopted the Model Penal Code standard, a woman arguably could assert the duress defence in Judy Norman's circumstances. The Code provides in part that it is a defence to any offence, *including murder*, that 'the actor engaged in the conduct charged . . . because [she] was coerced to do so by the use of, or a threat to use, unlawful force against [her] person . . . that a person of reasonable firmness in [her] situation would have been unable to resist'.[96] The defence abandons the imminency requirement and applies not only to conduct stemming from a threat of future force but also in response to prior applications of actual force, as long as the threat or force would cause a person of reasonable firmness—not a person suffering learned helplessness as a result of BWS[97]—to commit the offence charged.[98]

---

[93] ibid., 1367.   [94] *R v Howe* [1987] 1 All ER 771, at 778.

[95] Elsewhere, I have warned against the tendency of some to excuse everyone for whom we legitimately feel compassion: J. Dressler, 'Reflections on Excusing Wrongdoers: Moral Theory, New Excuses and the Model Penal Code' (1988) 19 Rutgers LJ 671. Thus, I would like to avoid the need for the law to recognize a residual excuse defence. However, a just system of laws should be more generous with its excuse defences than with its justifications; we should be less willing to say that homicides are permitted than to say that they are wrong but that sometimes the actors are excusable.

[96] Model Penal Code s. 2.09(1).

[97] When battered women have assisted their abusive partners to commit crimes against third parties and have then pled duress, many courts have refused to incorporate BWS into the standard of the 'person of reasonable firmness': L.K. Doré, 'Downward Adjustment and the Slippery Slope: The Use of Duress in Defense of Battered Offenders' (1995) 56 Ohio State L J 665, at 716. An actor's conduct is compared to the objective touchstone of 'men in general'; liability does not 'depend upon the fortitude of any given actor': American Law Institute, *Model Penal Code and Commentaries* (1985) Comment to s. 2.09, 374. In contrast, the Court of Criminal Appeal in South Australia has held that BWS evidence *is* admissible for the purpose of showing, *inter alia*, that a woman of reasonable firmness would have succumbed to the pressures of the abuser: *R v Runjanjic & Kontinnen* (1991) 56 SASR 114, at 120.

[98] Professor Andrew von Hirsch has pointed out to me that a similar defence may be possible under the German Penal Code. Section 35(1) of that Code provides that '[a] person acts without

A possible conceptual obstacle to application of the Model Penal Code in the battered woman context is that the defence does not fit the paradigm of coercer demanding coerced to commit a criminal act against the person or property of innocent third party. But, the language of the Code does not demand such a narrow reading: it requires only that the defendant explain her decision to engage in certain conduct (here, the killing of the abuser) on the ground that she was coerced to do so by another person's (here, the abuser's) prior use of force, threats of future force, or both; and that a person of reasonable firmness in the defendant's situation would have responded similarly. The Commentary to the Code states that the law is ineffective and 'divorced from any moral base and is unjust' if it 'imposes on the actor . . . a standard that his judges are not prepared to affirm that they . . . could comply with if their turn to face the problem should arise'.[99] It would seem that the community's representatives, the jurors, should be permitted to decide whether they, but for the grace of God, would have acted differently. The jurors' answer (I hope) will often be that they would *not* have taken the extreme step of killing the abuser while he slept, but the opportunity to make the claim is consistent with the rationale of the Code's duress defence.

From the perspective of the battered woman, of course, this is a vastly preferable excuse claim than one based on temporary insanity or some other mental disability claim. Less obviously, it is a better way to handle non-confrontational cases than through the justification route of self-defence. First, it avoids the pressure otherwise placed on legislatures and courts to expand self-defence beyond morally acceptable parameters (and, certainly, beyond the lines any legislature would draw but for the claims of battered women or, perhaps, children). Secondly, this approach *adds* to the possible claims of a battered woman in court. She retains the right to claim self-defence in confrontational circumstances and, in theory, can still plead insanity or some other incapacity excuse.

Thirdly, by shifting the claim in sleeping-abuser cases from one of justification to that of excuse, we preserve acoustical separation between, on the one hand, conduct rules, which are addressed to the public and intended to guide personal behaviour and, on the other hand, decision rules, which are not addressed to the general public because they are intended for use in relation to a criminal trial and not meant to affect public conduct.[100] Thus, the criminal

guilt [is excused] where he commits an unlawful act in order to ward off a present, not otherwise preventable danger of life, limb, or freedom to himself or a person close to him' (translation by Professor von Hirsch).

[99] American Law Institute, *Model Penal Code and Commentaries*, Comment to s. 2.09 (1985) 374–375. In the context of necessity, presumably a justification defence, Lord Coleridge took a contrary position when he stated that '[w]e are often compelled to set up standards we cannot reach ourselves, and lay down rules which we could not ourselves satisfy': *R v Dudley and Stephens* (1884) 14 QBD 273, at 288. But a decision rule does not need to be as rigid as a conduct rule. See n. 100 below.

[100] M. Dan-Cohen, 'Decision Rules and Conduct Rules: On Acoustic Separation in Criminal Law' (1984) 97 Harvard L Rev 625, at 625–630, 737–738. Of course, true acoustical separation

law would continue to set out a clear, almost bright-line, moral principle that killing aggressors is unjustifiable except in very narrow circumstances, while maintaining an escape hatch for excusing those who violate the strict moral rules in compelling circumstances.

Fourthly, there may be strategic reasons for sounding the claim in no-fair-opportunity excuse, rather than in justificatory, terms. To the extent that jurors are sensitive to the distinction, a jury might find it easier to excuse a woman for killing a sleeping man than to seek to justify her actions.[101] One commentator has suggested that self-defence cases, at least those that have been founded on BWS testimony and claims of 'learned helplessness', apply more readily to ' "respectable", relatively passive and middle-class women … than [to] women with a documented history of aggressive behavior'.[102] An excuse defence that focuses on compelling circumstances may be less susceptible to economic class distinctions. And, some battered-woman advocates are beginning to see the wisdom of this change in focus. Some have argued that trial 'testimony should shift from a focus on learned helplessness and the woman's psychological state to a greater emphasis on the defendant's circumstances and alternatives'.[103] This, of course, is precisely the direction of the law I am urging, albeit in duress, rather than self-defence, terms.

E. Conclusion

Twenty years ago, famed professor Yale Kamisar had occasion to honour a fellow professor (although scholarly combatant) who was known for taking strident published positions on police interrogation law. With his tongue probably only slightly in his cheek, Kamisar wrote:

Professors, it seems, are supposed to tiptoe, not crash. They are supposed to be troubled and tentative, not take very strong and very clear positions on anything (except,

---

does not exist except in an imaginary world. The public is at least minimally aware of excuse defences, although they often misunderstand their nature and scope. The absence of total separation sometimes serves as an argument for abolishing all excuses defences, on the ground that their existence may undermine the conduct rules by convincing some persons that they can escape liability and punishment by feigning an excuse. This is not the place to rehearse the arguments why such a claim may be wrong from a utilitarian perspective, and certainly is unacceptable to any non-consequentialist.

[101] Of course, jurors may not know that the law categorizes homicides as 'justifiable' and 'excusable', but they are likely to be sensitive in an untutored way to the difference between saying that an act is right and proper, on the one hand, and saying that it is wrong but that they do not want to punish the actor because they do not blame her. The fact that feminists early on sought to shift the legal debate from claims of incapacity to self-defence demonstrates that there *is* an intuitive understanding in the public between excusing actors and justifying acts.

[102] E. Stark, 'Re-Presenting Woman Battering: From Battered Woman Syndrome to Coercive Control' (1995) 58 Albany L Rev 973, at 1019.

[103] R.A. Schuller and P.A. Hastings, 'Trials of Battered Women Who Kill: The Impact of Alternative Forms of Expert Evidence' (1996) 20 Law and Human Behavior 167, at 171.

perhaps, right down the middle). Their stock in trade is not supplying answers but asking questions . . . They earn points, it seems, by showing how *agonizingly subtle and complex* an issue or problem actually is, not by suggesting how *simple* it might really be.[104]

As Kamisar has recently acknowledged, he too has been known in his career for taking strong, clear, not-right-in-the-middle, positions about police interrogation law. But, when it has come to another topic of Kamisar's concern, physician-assisted suicide, he has effectively cried uncle:

Of course, when I spoke of [the other professor] declining to take the conventional route, I had myself in mind as well. But I never promised, or at least I never meant to promise, that I could *always* show how simple seemingly subtle and complex problems really are. Sometimes, I am afraid, what appear to be agonizingly subtle and complex problems turn out to be just that.[105]

Any thoughtful commentator must feel similarly chastened when considering the plight of battered women. I stated at the outset, and I reaffirm here, that there are possible theoretical grounds for justifying the homicidal actions of the Judy Normans of this world. But, those arguments, I think, are not as simple and obvious as some might make them appear. Again, Yale Kamisar has said it well:

Here, as elsewhere, it is very hard to maintain absolute prohibitions. But here, as elsewhere, problems arise when one starts carving out exceptions. I venture to say that, however great the care with which one formulates the exceptions, 'hard' cases are bound to emerge on *the other side* of the line and with it the pressure to extend the outer boundaries of the exceptions to embrace these new 'hard' cases.[106]

When he wrote this, Kamisar was considering whether the law should punish physician-assisted suicide. His concerns in that realm apply here, too: once we start shifting the lines of justifiable self-defence beyond their present fairly narrow confines, we very quickly reach a disquieting point. In the case of physician-assisted suicide, Kamisar suggested that one solution is to prohibit the conduct and yet, in the 'heartbreaking' cases, simply to allow it to occur underground. The moral principles against killing would be upheld, and yet we would resolve the individual case 'satisfactorily'.

In the battered woman cases, there is another solution. We can stick by our relatively narrow rules of justification, and yet recognize an excuse defence (ideally, a broad version of duress) that permits jurors, if occasionally inclined to do so, to hold blameless those women who kill in truly heartbreaking and compelling circumstances. There is good conceptual reason to follow this path.

[104] Y. Kamisar, 'Fred E. Inbau: "The Importance of Being Guilty"' in Y. Kamisar, *Police Interrogation and Confessions: Essays in Law and Policy* (Ann Arbor, Michigan,1980) 95, at 104.
[105] Y. Kamisar, 'Physician-Assisted Suicide: The Problems Presented by the Compelling, Heartwrenching Case' (1998) 88 Journal Crim. Law and Criminology 1121, at 1146.
[106] ibid., 1145–1146.

12

Killing The Passive Abuser: A Theoretical Defence

JEREMY HORDER *

A. No Self-Defence Justification for Killing a Passive Abuser?

In 'Battered Women Who Kill Their Sleeping Tormenters . . .', Joshua Dressler focuses on legal and ethical difficulties posed by cases in which a woman (it is normally a woman) kills her partner whilst he is asleep, or otherwise in a passive and unthreatening state, following (characteristically) many years of violent abuse at his hands. Even if, when she killed, she was not in what could be called a 'calm' frame of mind, she may well not have spontaneously lost self-control at the crucial moment, and will thus be thwarted in a plea of provocation, or its equivalent.[1] Further, she will frequently be found not to have been suffering from a mental abnormality, of the kind that would entitle her to plead insanity or diminished responsibility. What other defences, if any, are open to her? Dressler raises some important questions about the campaign to categorize such killings of an abuser by the person abused as self-defensive (this categorization would, of course, entitle the defendant to an acquittal on the grounds of justifiable homicide).[2] He argues, instead, that if a defence to murder in such circumstances is appropriate, the killing of a passive abuser might best be regarded as excusable because committed under duress.

Dressler divides his argument into four theses. First, properly understood, evidence of so-called 'battered woman syndrome' (BWS) should play only a limited role in self-defence cases. This claim will be considered in section E below. His second thesis is that the inflated claims made for the wide-ranging relevance of BWS evidence probably conceal the real basis of the pressure to categorize the killing of passive abusers as justifiable homicide. This is that the battered woman is putting to death a person whose right to life is

* I am particularly grateful to the editors of this volume for their painstaking work and extensive comments on successive drafts of this chapter.

1 See, e.g., the facts in the much discussed English case of R v Duffy [1949] 1 All ER 932.

2 He is in distinguished company: see the remarks of Sir John Smith in his Justification and Excuse in the Criminal Law (London, 1989) 114–117.

regarded, by some American theorists who write and campaign in support of her, as effectively forfeit in the light of his abusive behaviour. I shall not be much concerned with this thesis, even though in American society capital punishment is widely thought to be legitimate, and its numerous adherents implicitly accept that someone can in some circumstances forfeit his or her right to life. In common with many other liberal democracies, the USA is a society governed by the rule of law. The rule of law demands that those who have forfeited the right to life are not—in virtue of that fact alone—now to be regarded as 'fair game' in the sights of any more-or-less aggrieved citizen. That argument disappeared with the rise to peremptory status of the notion of due process of law, and with the abolition of the rules making manifest felons a legitimate target for any citizen who came across them.[3] The motivations of those taking part in campaigns for reform of the law may be of sociological interest; but they cannot shed light on the analytical question of whether (as presently conceived) the defence of self-defence does indeed cover some—although clearly not all—cases in which X kills Y when Y is not posing an immediate or imminent danger. That question is the subject of Dressler's third and most important thesis: that if we are committed to regarding human life as special, we should not regard the deliberate taking of life in self-defence as justified unless it was absolutely necessary on the immediate occasion. This restriction effectively bars battered women who kill passive abusers from pleading self-defence, because the abuser will not, *ex hypothesi*, at that moment have been posing an imminent danger of the kind that called for an immediate response. Dressler's fourth thesis is that, if complete acquittal, without categorizing the case as justified, is none the less warranted in such cases, then the defence of duress provides a neglected but promising line of defence for the abused woman who kills a passive abuser. In this chapter, I shall try to cast some doubt on Dressler's view that self-defence is an inappropriate plea for a battered woman who has killed a passive abuser. My view departs from his because I think that, in certain respects, his account of the nature, and limits, of self-defence is unnecessarily restrictive.

B. SELF-DEFENCE AS A JUSTIFICATION

I will start with some abstract considerations. For Dressler, the distinction between justification and excuse depends on the 'acoustic separation' argument.[4] This is the argument that justifications are part and parcel of conduct rules, designed to guide personal behaviour *ex ante*, whereas excuses are part

---

[3] For the historical picture see, further, T.A. Green, *Verdict According to Conscience* (Chicago, 1985) 30.

[4] See M. Dan-Cohen, 'Decision Rules and Conduct Rules: On Acoustic Separation in Criminal Law' (1984) 97 Harvard LR 625, cited by Dressler in Chapter 11 of this volume, 'Battered Women Who Kill Their Sleeping Tormentors: Reflections on Maintaining Respect for Human Life while Killing Moral Monsters', text at n. 100.

and parcel of decision rules by which judges assess the culpability of defendants *ex post facto*.[5] On this view, self-defence, being a justificatory defence, is rightly located only in the conduct-guiding part of the criminal law. I can see that those who take this line would be made uneasy by any suggestion that the law might give *ex ante* guidance on when one may permissibly kill someone, when that person is not posing an imminent or immediate danger. There is always a risk that one is in error in perceiving a need to use lethal force in self-defence. In the absence of immediate danger, the argument runs, the law cannot credibly give *ex ante* guidance that one may use lethal force, when such force is not obviously necessary (if such force is mistakenly thought to be necessary, it may be excused *ex post facto*). The problem of force used in error is an issue addressed in section C below, but the objection described here seems to be in part what drives Dressler's reluctance to permit that self-defence be used as a defence for violence employed against a passive abuser.

However, viewed as a totality, the rules governing self-defence are too complex to be neatly categorized as either a set of (*ex ante* justificatory) conduct-guiding rules or a set of (*ex post facto* excusatory) decision-making rules. It is true that, in certain circumstances, some of the rules of self-defensive 'engagement' may indeed be of a kind rightly regarded as conduct-guiding. So if, for example, police officers are required by law, whenever possible, to issue a warning to a suspect before opening fire, even in self-defence, this operates as a conduct-guiding rule that they are meant to follow.[6] It is functionally equivalent to other guides to conduct that are based on *ex ante* justificatory considerations, such as the need to show a householder a warrant that has been obtained to search the premises before the search begins. Such rules are there to be followed and relied on. They are, though, to be contrasted, not just with excuses, but with justificatory rules of self-defence that operate by way of *ex post facto* vindication rather than by way of *ex ante* guidance. If I have done only what I reasonably thought to be necessary and proportionate to defend myself, when attacked, I will come to the court seeking vindication for my actions, on the grounds of their necessity, proportionality, and reasonableness. I will *not* be seeking to show that, at the relevant time, I was guided by a *legal* rule that made my conduct permissible. Moreover, accepting this point does not weaken the case for regarding self-defence as a justification. As I shall now try to explain, one can sometimes be legally justified even if one is guided solely by moral considerations.

In this regard, we must turn our attention to a jurisprudential distinction, the relevance of which has gone unnoticed by most criminal lawyers.[7] The

---

[5] See also P. Robinson, 'Rules of Conduct and Principles of Adjudication' (1990) 57 University of Chicago LR 729.

[6] See J. Rogers, 'Justifying the Use of Firearms by Policemen and Soldiers: A Response to the Home Office's Review of the Law on the Use of Lethal Force' (1998) 18 Legal Studies 486.

[7] The distinction was first drawn by Jules Coleman: see now his 'Incorporationism, Conventionality, and the Practical Difference Thesis' (1998) 4 Legal Theory 381.

legal significance of some laws consists merely in the fact that they incorporate into the *actus reus* moral rules or principles that already bind citizens to act in certain ways, rather than in the fact that they provide additional guides to conduct, separate from morality itself. An obvious example would be a law making 'insulting' behaviour an offence. In this example, one cannot simply look to the law for *ex ante* practical guidance on what one ought to do; that guidance is provided by the social and moral norms governing what counts as 'insulting'. Laws like this simply systematize such moral guidance—making it simultaneously legal guidance—through incorporation. With other laws, by contrast, legal significance is to be found mainly in the fact that they make a practical difference to the rules or standards by which we should be guided. An obvious case is that of so-called 'regulatory offences'. A by-law permitting me to smoke only in the smoking compartment of a train is a law the legal significance of which is that it makes a practical difference to the kinds of conduct that are and are not permissible. It is there to be relied on, through its provision of *ex ante* guidance to citizens. Into which category do the laws of self-defence fall? The laws of self-defence typically say, at the core, that I may take such self-defensive steps as are necessary and proportionate in blocking, or warding off, dangers that cannot reasonably be met by other means. At the core of self-defence is thus a law whose permission is shaped by the contours of the moral permission. It amounts, more or less, to a re-statement of moral norms that do not depend on the law for their existence. Especially from the point of view of the ordinary citizen, this is how things should be. It is not reasonable to expect citizens to do more, in such extreme and exceptional situations, than follow the guidance of morality, in the expectation that they will, *ex post facto*, be vindicated at law.[8]

Suppose that there is a distinction between aspects of justification whose function is to provide *ex ante* legal guidance, and aspects of justification that give *ex post facto* legal vindication to conduct appropriately guided by morality. Whilst it does not yet prove anything one way or the other, this supposition at least sheds a somewhat more favourable light on the killing of passive abusers by abused victims. If such cases are seen as turning on aspects of justification relevant to *ex post facto* legal vindication, rather than as cases where the issue is whether *ex ante* legal guidance was followed, the acoustic separation argument is sidelined. The focus is now not on the kind of special justificatory rules that the law should itself provide explicitly to guide people,

---

[8] See further, J. Horder, 'On the Irrelevance of Motive in Criminal Law', in J. Horder (ed.), *Oxford Essays in Jurisprudence*, 4th Series (Oxford, 2000). Matters are, as I have already indicated, not quite so simple where one is concerned with those who are not ordinary citizens, such as law enforcement officers who, acting in that capacity, are entitled to expect *ex ante* guidance from the law; but I am not concerned with them here. Even where the conduct of ordinary citizens is in issue, it may occasionally be appropriate for the law to specify standards—particularly negative ones—explicitly to guide the citizen *ex ante*. It may be important, for example, for the law to seek to avoid misapprehensions by stating clearly what cannot be done to repel an attack on one's property, as opposed to one's person.

but on the ordinary justificatory standards morality provides: standards—
like reasonableness—that have been incorporated into the law. In this chapter, I shall claim that the killing of passive abusers may, in exceptional cases,
be morally (and hence, through incorporation, legally) justified, in the sense
of being worthy of legal vindication, on the grounds of defensive reasonableness in all the circumstances.

C. The Right and the Reasonable in Self-Defence

With these considerations in mind, we can turn to a major theoretical issue,
touched on in the preceding section. This issue is whether, to be justified, one
needs to show that one was actually right to do as one did; or whether one can
still be justified if one acted on a reasonable mistake as to the justificatory
facts. Those theorists who insist that justifications are confined to right
actions[9] tend to be those who also insist on the importance of the 'acoustic
separation' argument; for the following reason. On the 'acoustic separation'
argument, justifications are there to provide legally authoritative *ex ante*
conduct guidance. Accordingly, it might seem hard to accept that *the law* (as
opposed to morality) should authorize conduct *ex ante* (rather than regarding it as excusable, *ex post facto*) when that conduct involves the invasion of
another's rights prompted by a mistake, however reasonable, as to the existence of the justificatory facts. The reasonableness of the mistake, on this view,
seems more naturally regarded as furbishing the case in law for an excuse,
rather than as doing anything to clothe the conduct in question with (*ex ante*)
justificatory legal import. If I have interpreted it correctly, the problem with
this view is that it has never been plausible to confine instances of justification, in law or morality, solely to cases in which the defendant was right to act
as he or she did. For example, suppose a known psychopath (X) is rushing towards me with a raised knife, shouting that he is going to kill me; so I hit him
with a brick to meet what I perceive to be an imminent danger. Whether I am
really in imminent danger may turn, of course, on factors going beyond what
appearances clearly suggest. Unbeknown to me, X might have been engaged
in a practical joke, in which it was important that there appeared to be a very
real danger to me, but at the end of which X fully intended to drop the knife
and reveal the joke to me. In such a case, whether I am justified in acting self-
defensively cannot intelligibly turn on whether X is, or is not, in fact a danger
to me, something that turns on his secret intentions. It must turn on what, in
all the circumstances of which I ought to have been aware, I reasonably believed.[10]

---

[9] The most famous example being Paul Robinson: see, e.g., his *Structure and Function in Criminal Law* (Clarendon Press, 1997) ch. 5C.

[10] See, in this regard, the arguments of Russell Christopher, in his 'Self-Defence and Objectivity: A Reply to Judith Jarvis Thomson' (1998) 1 Buffalo Criminal LR 537. Christopher rejects

Now, as we saw in the last section, Dressler supports the 'acoustic separation' argument. However, he also (rightly) denies that the defence of self-defence *must* be excusatory when the putative defender is acting on a reasonable but mistaken belief in the need to act defensively, as in the example just given where X appears to be attacking me.[11] The way in which these two strands in his argument are joined has important implications for the way he treats 'passive abuser' cases, since it introduces a tension that remains undissolved. On the one hand, the 'acoustic separation' argument, according to which justifications such as self-defence must be capable of guiding conduct *ex ante*, inclines Dressler towards the view that attacks must be imminent before they can justifiably be met with self-defensive force. Only then, in Dressler's view, is it most likely that a putative defender will be sure of her (justificatory) ground for striking with lethal intent, in a way that would make it appropriate for the law to give her an *ex ante* permission so to act. This argument effectively excludes the defence of self-defence in 'passive abuser' cases, except in the most improbable instances (where V is currently passive but, for whatever reason, is rightly judged to be on the point of springing into action). Accordingly, Dressler argues that killers of passive abusers can, at best, be excused (on the grounds of duress). On the other hand, Dressler is rightly keen to emphasize the need, in appropriate cases, to furnish the defendant who has killed a passive abuser with a defence that focuses, at least in part, on the reasonableness of her response. So he argues that duress, with its reliance on a judgement of how the person of reasonable firmness may have responded in the defendant's situation, fits the bill (an argument addressed in section F below). Remember, though, as we saw just now, that Dressler rightly says that one can act justifiably—not merely excusably—when one acts wrongly but reasonably. The troubling question for Dressler is now why the focus on the reasonableness of the defendant's response, in killing the passive abuser, does not lead him to modify or abandon the 'acoustic separation' argument. Why not say that a defendant who kills a passive abuser could conceivably be vindicated *ex post facto*, on the grounds of self-defence? These issues are explored in the sections below.

---

the well-known view of Paul Robinson that whether one was justified turns simply on whether one was 'objectively' in the right, whatever the reason(s) for which one acted: see Robinson (n. 9 above). I am not suggesting here that there is never moral or legal significance in just being right, as things turn out. For example, in cases where one acts on a 'hunch' that turns out to be correct, one can be regarded as fully justified in having so acted; whereas, if one acts on a 'hunch' that turns out to be wrong, one may well not even be excused if the hunch was not based on reasonable grounds: see J. Horder, 'Self-Defence, Necessity and Duress: Understanding the Relationship' (1998) XI Canadian Journal of Law and Jurisprudence 143, at 147–148.

[11] See J. Dressler, 'New Thoughts about the Concept of Justification in the Criminal Law: A Critique of Fletcher's Thinking and Rethinking' (1984) 32 University of California LA L Rev 61, at 92–95.

D. THE REASONABLENESS OF BELIEFS AND THE 'IMMINENCE' REQUIREMENT

The argument in section B above suggested that actions can be justified (vindicated as self-defensive) *ex post facto*, on the grounds of their conformity to moral standards, like reasonableness, incorporated into the law. It follows that if the beliefs of at least some abused killers that they are in danger from a passive abuser can be regarded as reasonable, then they may prima facie be entitled to plead self-defence as a justification for their actions. In perhaps the most important part of his chapter, Dressler confronts this argument head on, as part of his case that self-defence is an inappropriate defence for the killer of the passive abuser. He argues that the belief of an abused woman that she is in real danger at the hands of a passive abuser is not reasonable. At best, her false and unreasonable belief is one she is not to be blamed for holding and acting on; thus, he concludes, it is a belief having excusatory, and not justificatory significance. Dressler's argument depends on a conjunction between two points. First, he takes it as axiomatic that one does not act in self-defence, for legal purposes, unless one is seeking to ward off an imminent or immediate danger. Building on this point, he makes a second point. If one accepts the first point, namely that self-defence requires an imminent danger, one must also accept the need to show that the abused killer *reasonably* believed that she was faced with an imminent or immediate danger posed by the passive abuser. It is this, he claims, that supporters of abused killers who kill passive abusers cannot do. His second point is that, at best, an abused killer may have believed honestly that the passive abuser posed an imminent danger, a claim that might be bolstered by evidence that the killer was suffering from BWS. Dressler believes, though, that such evidence would, by its nature, be evidence of an excusatory and not of a justificatory kind. For him, such evidence is focally concerned with the lack of blame to be attached to the killer, given her distorted perception of the situation, something that in turn was brought about by prolonged abuse. As Dressler puts it: 'Put simply, without distorting the meaning of reasonableness beyond sensible recognition, a "reasonable person" does not fear instantaneous death from a sleeping person'.[12]

The force of this argument depends, however, on the legitimacy of taking as one's premise the first point, namely that the belief with which we are concerned must be a belief that the danger posed by the passive abuser is an imminent or immediate one. Here, we may have to accept that there are significant differences between American and English law. American law closely confines the limits of conduct regarded as defensive: it must be conduct that meets a danger that is 'impending, and present, and not prospective or even in the near future'.[13] It may be doubted, however, whether this has

---

[12] Chapter 11 above, text following n. 50.
[13] Chapter 11 above, text at n.7, citing J. Miller, *Handbook of Criminal Law* (1934) 202.

ever been a universal requirement in English law. As Aileen McColgan has pointed out in her discussion of self-defence against passive abusers,[14] in English and Irish law the relevant rules are flexible and context-dependent. It has been held that a soldier in Northern Ireland was entitled to shoot someone whom he (mistakenly) believed to be a terrorist, to prevent him committing terrorist crimes in the near future even though there was no suggestion that any such crime was imminent.[15] In *R v Cousins*,[16] D produced a shotgun and threatened V that he (D) would use it at some point in the future, unless a close relative of V's withdrew a threat to kill D. It was held that D should have been entitled to plead that his conduct was self-defensive or action in prevention of crime. Finally, in *A-G's Reference (No. 2 of 1983)*,[17] it was held that D could be lawfully in possession of petrol bombs when he had prepared them solely for the purpose of defending his property against possible looting during a city riot.

In some situations, of course, such as the example given earlier where X charges at me with the knife, the imminence of the danger dictates the nature of my reaction, and leaves me with no choice or time to choose. As the cases just cited show, however, it does not follow that the legal understanding of a self-defensive situation, in which force is permissibly used, is one that revolves around the need for an imminent threat that leaves the defender with no choice or time to choose. Rather, the legal understanding of a self-defensive situation, in which force is permissibly used, includes, *inter alia*, a requirement that any alternative course of (avoiding) action was a choice we could not reasonably expect the defender to make. Situations where the danger was imminent present one—but only one—way in which this requirement can be met. One should not fall into the trap of assuming that one-off adversarial encounters set the entire agenda governing the legitimate use of defensive force. The use of such force may be legitimate in other sets of circumstances. The rules governing the so-called 'imminence' requirement are (in England and Wales at least), and ought to be, flexible, to account for the wide range of circumstances in which the need to use defensive force may arise. In short, what should matter is not whether the threat was imminent, but whether the defendant had a fair and reasonable opportunity to do other than he or she did, in meeting the threat. This can be illustrated by adapting one of McColgan's own examples.[18] Suppose that D is being held hostage by dangerous terrorists who let

---

[14] A.McColgan, 'In Defence of Battered Women Who Kill' (1993) 13 Oxford Journal of Legal Studies 508, at 517–518.

[15] *R v Kelly* [1989] NI 341; but for criticism see A.P. Simester and G.R. Sullivan, *Criminal Law: Theory and Doctrine* (Hart Publishing, 2000) 623. The ensuing discussion of the case law is taken directly from Simester and Sullivan's helpful exegesis.

[16] [1982] QB 26 (CA), discussed by Simester and Sullivan (n. 15 above) 624.

[17] [1984] QB 456 (CA), discussed by Simester and Sullivan (n. 15 above) 624. It should be noted that, as the authors point out, in both *Cousins* (n.16 above) and in *A-G's Reference (No. 2 of 1983)*, the steps taken in self-defence were not intended to be lethal.

[18] McColgan (n. 14 above) 518.

her know, expressly or by implication, that she is 'in all probability' to be killed 'shortly', or 'in the near future'. That night, catching her sleeping guard unawares, she intentionally kills him with a blow on the head, as the only way of making her escape undetected. Even on the Model Penal Code's more generous definition of the so-called imminence requirement, in terms of a requirement that an attack be 'immediately necessary . . . on the present occasion',[19] it is unclear that D satisfies this test. There is no clear temporal sense in which there is a threat to her life that calls for an attack on the guard *there and then*. So, it cannot be said that her action is, strictly speaking, 'immediately necessary on the present occasion'. Yet, it seems doubtful that any English court (or, I would add, any reasonable legal system) would deny her a defence of self-defence, on facts such as those just given. The reason for this is that she quite properly took the view that although her chosen course of action was not the only one open to her, she could not reasonably be expected to take another course of action that involved further delay and hence risk to herself. In other words, there was no opportunity to do other than she did that she could fairly have been required to take up.

There are, it seems to me, important similarities between hostage situations and the relationships of domination, unpredictability, and violence in which battered women find themselves trapped. Many such women learn that if they attempt to leave, they will be followed and forced to return, to face even greater hostility and more serious violence.[20] In any event, a concern for the welfare of children of the family will often make these women the equivalent of hostages. That is why the example just given provides more than an academic debating point. Research has found that the most significant difference between cases in which battered women did kill their abuser, and cases in which they did not, lay not in the psychological states of these women but in the abusiveness of their situation. The abusive partners of women who killed have been found to have been more frequently and more violently abusive, more likely to have threatened to kill, and more likely to have abused a child or children as well as their partners.[21] None of this evidence, of course, can raise even a prima facie case that the abusers in question 'forfeit' their right to life. What it does do, however, is give some substance to the view that, in certain exceptional cases, women whose partners are increasingly violent and possessive abusers are in a situation similar to that faced by hostages facing an unpredictable but seemingly escalating threat. They may (reasonably)[22]

---

[19] Model Penal Code s. 3.04; discussed by Dressler in Chapter 11 above, text at n. 75.

[20] See, e.g., the research discussed by McColgan (n. 14 above) 517 n. 46.

[21] See ibid., 517 n. 48.

[22] English law requires no more than an honest belief in the existence of such an opportunity: see *R v Gladstone Williams* (1984) 78 Cr App Rep 276. It has been argued that this contravenes the human rights of persons *unreasonably* mistaken as aggressors (at least where it is law enforcement officers who make such unreasonable mistakes): see A. Ashworth, *Principles of Criminal Law* (3rd edn., Oxford, 1999) 149.

take the view that there was no fair opportunity to do other than they did, in using lethal force against the abuser or hostage-taker while he was in a passive state, in order to escape the predicament.

Dressler's argument against this line of reasoning is that the defence of self-defence is narrowly defined in order to uphold 'the principle that human life should be maintained as often and as long as reasonably possible'.[23] We can agree on this, but it does not by itself point to an immediacy basis, rather than to a 'fair opportunity to do otherwise' basis, for setting the limits to justifiable self-defence. A strictly construed imminence or immediacy requirement is the optimum rule for aggressors in general. It shifts the burden of risk (the defender may lose a chance to make a pre-emptive strike, or may lose the chance to incorporate a necessary element of surprise in his or her response, and so forth) on to the defender. It shifts the burden in this way by insisting that defenders stay their hand until it appears there can be no reasonable doubt about the (putative) aggressor's intentions. Conversely, a rule requiring only that (putative) defenders subjectively believe, whether reasonably or not, in the need for defensive action at the point when they use it, would be the optimum rule for defenders in general. Such a rule would shift the burden of risk—the aggressor changes his mind; an opportunity for the defender not to use force crops up; the 'aggressor' turns out to be innocent after all, and so forth—on to (the person believed to be) the aggressor. It would shift the burden in this way because it would take no account of the objective plausibility of regarding the (putative) aggressor's actions as requiring a self-defensive response.[24] The need to preserve human life ought, in this as in other contexts, to be interpreted in such as way as to accommodate principles of equal concern and respect governing *both* these possible outcomes. A requirement that the (putative) defender have no fair and reasonable opportunity to do other than use defensive force is meant to exhibit an equal concern and respect for both the putative defender and the supposed aggressor. Through the insistence on the need for 'fairness' and 'reasonableness', the requirement seeks to distribute evenly the burden of risks faced respectively by (putative) defenders and (putative) attackers. The mistaken defender's subjective perceptions will carry weight, in so far as there were good grounds for forming them (i.e. they were reasonable). However, they will carry no more (but no less) weight than the actions of the person mistaken as the aggressor, in so far as these gave good grounds for the perception that they amounted to a danger calling for the use of defensive force.

What is meant to be Dressler's clinching argument, in this regard, runs as follows. Even if, in a particular case, one accepted that a battered woman would be very likely to suffer grave harm or death at the hands of her abuser at some point, it could not be right for her to make a pre-emptive strike

---

[23] Chapter 11 above, text at n. 84.

[24] See, in this regard, the comments about English law in n. 22 above. For criticism, see S. Uniacke, *Permissible Killing* (Cambridge, 1994) 42–47.

months or even years before it is 'actually necessary' (i.e., for Dressler, imminent). For that would be to make the abuser bear the entire risk of any error, i.e. the risk that there will never in fact be a fatal attack by the abuser, and the longer it is before the (imminent) attack is anticipated, the greater the risk of that error. I believe that this is an example of what I referred to earlier as the tension in Dressler's argument between two views of self-defence as a justification. To be justified in acting in self-defence, must one be in the right, in that one is actually facing danger, or it is enough that one reasonably believes oneself to be facing danger that is effectively inescapable, even if one is in fact mistaken?[25] I hope to have provided an argument, brief though it was, to show that, to be justified and not merely excused in using force self-defensively it is enough that one reasonably believed that one was in danger, even if one was, as it turns out, in error; provided there was no reasonable alternative to doing as one did. Accepting this point is important, because it will then be incorrect to say that pre-emptive strikes made in response to anything other than an impending attack throw too much of the burden of justificatory error onto the person thought to be about to attack. The burden will in fact be shared roughly equally between (putative) aggressor and (putative) defender, if what the law requires is that there has been no fair and reasonable opportunity to do other than the (putative) defender did, in the way I have explained. In some, wholly exceptional, cases, the killing of a passive abuser might well meet this criterion.

Dressler's argument at this point is also vulnerable to the accusation that it is too insensitive to its context. To support his argument about the risk of error when a battered woman judges that she needs to make a pre-emptive strike against a violent abuser, he cites the evidence of behavioural scientists that clinical or statistical predictions of dangerousness can do no better than one valid assessment out of two.[26] The error rate for the untrained lay person is, no doubt, much higher than this; but that overlooks two points. First, someone caught in the domestic equivalent of a hostage situation cannot be required to act as if they were in the same position as a detached expert observer, weighing to a nicety the exact level of risk posed by the abuser. In any event, statistical predictions about dangerousness drawn up by behavioural scientists have a public, bureaucratic significance quite different from—indeed incommensurable with—the personal significance of a similar prediction made by a person who is herself the focus of the danger. Secondly, the risk of error in one's predictions decreases in normative significance as the normative significance of the gravity of the danger increases. Suppose X decides to play 'Russian roulette' with me (without my consent) by putting one bullet in an empty revolver that can hold up to six bullets, spinning the barrel, pointing it at my head and then preparing to fire. Now, assume that if I am to prevent X firing at all, I must use lethal force to prevent her. If so, then

---

[25] See text to n. 9 above.   [26] Chapter 11 above, text at n. 84.

whether or not I am entitled to kill X is unlikely to be affected by the fact that, as I know, there is only a one-in-six chance that, when X fires, the gun will go off. The *gravity* of the danger involved means that I do not have to concern myself with the fact that, in all probability, when X pulls the trigger nothing will happen and so my pre-emptive strike will not (on this particular occasion) have averted a truly 'live' danger.[27] Going back to the point made at the outset, if I am right (and putting it very simply), what we need to have in focus is whether it was fair and reasonable, in all the circumstances, to do the harm that was done in self-defence. The gravity of the danger that D reasonably perceives herself to be facing, just as much as the likelihood that that danger will turn into reality, is a key issue affecting the question of whether D's response was fair and reasonable.

E. The Relevance of Evidence of Battered Woman Syndrome

It is in relation to a claim of reasonableness respecting D's response, that battle is likely to be joined over the admissibility of evidence of battered woman syndrome. Dressler suggests that 'learned helplessness' is of relevance in self-defence cases only to explain why the defendant did not leave, in spite of years of battering, and why, given the cyclical nature of long-term abuse, there may be periods in which abuser and abused appear to be acting as a normal couple.[28] He thus regards such evidence as essentially only suitable for rebutting any attack on the defender's credibility and character, and perhaps also for underpinning some kinds of excusatory claim on her part. Dressler resists the view that such evidence can also be relevant to the objective question in self-defence cases, the question of the reasonableness of her use of force in all the circumstances. Suppose one were prepared to accept, however, that in the exceptional situation of a battered woman trapped in an abusive relationship it is sometimes reasonable to believe, as the leading expert Lenore Walker put it, that 'the batterer is omnipotent, [and] that no one can help her'.[29] Accepting this makes a battered woman's belief in the need to use lethal pre-emptive force of potentially crucial significance to the objective question in self-defence cases. For then the issue can be framed as Wilson J framed it, in the famous decision in *R v Lavallee*:[30]

---

[27] In this example, of course, the danger looming is immediate harm, whereas this is not true of the case in which a battered woman kills her sleeping abuser; but there is clearly a distinction between the immediacy of a danger, whatever the probability that it will turn into reality, and the degree of that probability in itself. So the difference between the examples, in point of immediacy, is not significant.
[28] Chapter 11 above, text following n. 34.
[29] L.E. Walker, R.K. Thyfault and A. Browne, 'Beyond the Juror's Ken: Battered Women' (1982) 7 Vermont LR 1, at 8–9, cited by Dressler in Chapter 11 above, text at n. 22.
[30] [1990] 1 SCR 852, at 888–889.

If, after hearing the evidence . . . the jury is satisfied that the accused had a (reasonable) apprehension of death or grievous bodily harm and felt incapable of escape, it must ask itself what the 'reasonable person' would do in such a situation.

In this regard, it is still an open question whether evidence of BWS is always evidence of some kind of mental abnormality. As some scholars have claimed on the basis of empirical research,[31] such evidence may equally well be argued to be part of a broader picture of how *ordinary* people, be they long-term hostages or battered women, tend to think and act in a certain kind of exceptional situation.[32] And that will be evidence, in that kind of situation, of the reasonableness of their beliefs.

F. DURESS: THE RIGHT ALTERNATIVE FOR THE BATTERED WOMAN?

If one accepts the claim made in the last section, then I think my argument to this point could be summarized thus:

(a)   one can justifiably act in self-defence when one reasonably believes in the circumstances of justification;

(b)   the circumstances of justification depend, *inter alia*, upon whether one had no fair and reasonable opportunity to do other than use force to avert a danger;

(c)   these circumstances may exist even when the alleged danger is posed by a passive abuser, because (in some cases) the danger the abuser poses must be assessed in the light of the fact that he is effectively holding the abused person hostage, in a situation in which the abuser's violence and unpredictability may be worsening;

(d)   rather than being assumed to be evidence of mental abnormality, evidence of BWS may be evidence of exceptional circumstances in which ordinary and reasonable people might come to believe killing is necessary to protect themselves from an abuser.

---

[31]   See M. Shaffer, 'The Battered Woman Syndrome Revisited: Some Complicating Thoughts Five Years After *R. v. Lavallee*' (1997) University of Toronto LJ 1, at 12–13.

[32]   Dressler discusses this point in Chapter 11 above, at n.35. He suggests, in effect, that what a jury may conclude about an abused woman's sensitivity to her abuser's likely behaviour is a matter of ordinary inductive inference, and is not assisted by 'syndrome' evidence; but that seems open to question. Sometimes, people may only reach certain conclusions about what ought to be done under special conditions or circumstances. It could be, e.g., that reasonable people would not typically conclude that X should be done, in the light of behaviour Y, unless inclined to this conclusion through constant exposure to instances similar to Y. Evidence of BWS is evidence of how, *given her continual exposure to behaviour Y (V's behaviour to date)*, a woman quite reasonably concluded that X should be done (V must be killed whilst passive), a conclusion that might, equally reasonably, not be drawn by someone who had not been continually exposed to behaviour Y. There is every reason to think that expert 'syndrome' evidence may assist the jury in its evaluation of this point.

Now, one way of countering these arguments, other than showing simply that they are wrong, is to say that they are unnecessarily tortuous. This will be so if a defence of duress provides a simpler, more elegant, and more just solution when a battered woman has killed her passive abuser. Dressler makes this argument, suggesting that the excusatory defence of duress is much more appropriate, in such situations, than self-defence. He says, with approval, that the Model Penal Code requires that:

the actor engaged in the conduct charged . . . because [she] was coerced to do so by the use of, or a threat to use, unlawful force against her person . . . that a person of reasonable firmness in [her] situation would have been unable to resist.[33]

What is important about this passage, however, is that it is correctly envisaged that in duress cases the actor is *coerced* into action, by the use or threat of force.[34] Some dangers can only be met, if self-preservation is to be secured, by actions that avoid, block, or ward off the danger. When such dangers are directly met by such actions—avoiding, blocking, warding off—then those actions are 'self-defensive' by nature; they are not 'coerced'.[35] By way of contrast, duress cases involve dangers in the specific form of coercive threats ('do this or else'). When a danger takes the form of a coercive threat it may be unwillingly *complied with* by the victim, and it is the response of unwilling compliance that brings the defence of duress into play. So, for example, suppose that D is verbally threatened with grave harm unless she commits theft. She could defy the threatener and risk the consequences, or comply with his demand in the face of the threat and plead duress. The latter response would, however, be qualitatively different from a response that sought to avoid, block, or ward off the threat: this would involve, say, disabling the threatener, 'trumping' his threat with a counterthreat (both 'blocking' actions) or, alternatively, persuading him that the demand made is impossible to fulfil or that someone else is better placed to fulfil it (both 'avoiding' or 'warding off' actions). These latter responses—blocking, avoiding, or warding off the threat—are, as I would have it, by their nature self-defensive, whereas it is compliance in the face of the threat that is characteristic of duress cases. This being so, it will be misleading to characterize the response of the battered woman who kills a passive abuser as a response made under duress, because ordinarily she cannot credibly be described as complying with a demand in the face of a coercive threat. Whatever we make of her actions in terms of

[33] Model Penal Code s. 2.09(1).
[34] I can be coerced by the use of, as well as by the threat of, force: suppose I twist your arm behind your back and continue to twist it until you decide to give in to my demands. For discussion, see Sir John Smith, 'Individual Incapacities and Criminal Liability' (1998) Med L Rev 138, at 159–160.
[35] J. Horder (n. 10 above) 149–150. By speaking of 'directly' meeting the danger, I do not have physical directness in mind. If I set a trap for a pursuing attacker, this is a direct blocking action, in a normative sense, even though it is physically indirect. A danger is met indirectly in a normative sense when a person who is *not* posing the danger has *their* interests invaded in order to avoid, block, or ward off the threat. See the text immediately following n. 36 below.

immediacy, proportionality, and so forth, there seems to me to be little doubt that she seeks, in killing the abuser, to block a danger (rather than unwillingly to comply with a threat); thus her action is, in principle, self-defensive in nature.

For English lawyers, part of the difficulty here may be generated by the fact that the English defence of 'duress of *circumstances*'[36] may arise in respect of actions that involve circumstantial duress *vis-à-vis* X, but which are simultaneously defensive *vis-à-vis* Y. Suppose I run into X's house without his or her permission, in order to avoid my attacker, Y. In this example, *vis-à-vis* Y my action is self-defensive (it is 'normatively direct' avoiding action).[37] *Vis-à-vis* X, however, my action is taken under conditions of circumstantial duress, albeit duress explained by my self-preservatory conduct in responding to the danger posed by Y. In this example, what makes it right to describe my conduct as taken under circumstantial duress *vis-à-vis* X, rather than as self-defensive, is that X is an *innocent* person whose interests are invaded as a means of avoiding the danger. In so describing my conduct, in this example, we should not be distracted by the fact there is someone, the attacker, respecting whom the self-same action can be described as self-defensive (a 'normatively direct' avoiding action). Duress of circumstances is generated by the need to defend one's own or another's interests;[38] but to describe an action as taken under circumstantial duress, *as opposed to* being self-defensive, is to mark out its impact on the interests of an innocent person. Thus one typically says, 'In defending myself [against Y], it was unfortunately necessary to invade X's interests'. Dressler notes this point,[39] but does not pursue it further, perhaps because he regards the passive abuser as 'innocent' in the relevant sense; but if that is the reason, it might be thought to beg the question. The passive abuser (like the hostage's captor, in McColgan's example) is killed because it is he who poses the danger. He is not an innocent person who has become the instrument through which danger from a different source is being blocked or warded off. It follows that, as least in some cases, the correct jurisprudential characterization of the actions of an abused woman who kills her passive abuser is as the normatively direct blocking of a danger to which she was unjustly exposed, an action that is in principle self-defensive.

---

[36] It fact it is a wrongly classified species of necessity: see the discussion in Ashworth (n. 22 above) 226–236, and in Horder (n. 10 above) 160–163.

[37] See discussion in n. 35 above.

[38] Necessity or duress of circumstances may also be invoked when someone acts to promote, not merely to defend, another's interests, but I am not concerned with such cases here.

[39] Chapter 11 above, text following n. 98.

13

Testing Fidelity to Legal Values: Official Involvement and Criminal Justice

ANDREW ASHWORTH*

When one considers the range of defences typically open to persons accused of crime in what might be broadly termed Anglo-American legal systems, they emerge as diverse and heterogeneous. It is well known that some defences, such as duress and necessity, do not rest on the absence of *mens rea* or *actus reus*. It is also well known that various defences, or 'defences', derive their strength chiefly from the absence of *mens rea* but have been developed so as to incorporate limiting conditions from other sources, for example, mistake and intoxication. One of the more curious aspects of English law, and of some other legal systems, is that a defence may be rejected as such and yet indirectly be allowed, in practice, if and to the extent that the elements of that same defence can be regarded as negativing a key fault element for a particular crime. For example, it is arguable whether there is a general defence of necessity, but if by chance the offence requires proof of 'dishonesty' or includes the phrase 'without reasonable excuse' it may be possible to allow the fact of necessity to exculpate.[1] There is no general defence of mistake of (civil) law, but if by chance the offence requires proof that the defendant knew that the property damaged 'belonged to another' it should be possible to allow the mistake of law to exculpate.[2] This approach has been taken further—some would say, too far—on some occasions when appellate courts have been construing the requirement of 'intention'. Thus in *Gillick v West Norfolk and Wisbech Area Health Authority*[3] the House of Lords held that a doctor

* An early version of this chapter was given as a paper to a staff seminar at Nottingham Law School. A more developed version was presented at the seminar at the University of Birmingham on which this volume is based. That seminar was generously funded by the *Modern Law Review*, which exercised its option to publish the paper: (2000) 63 MLR 633–659. I am grateful to participants at both seminars for their suggestions, to Paul Roberts and Andrew von Hirsch for detailed comments, and to the editors of this volume for perceptive comments and queries which have led to further revisions.

[1] For elaboration and examples, see the classic article by P.R. Glazebrook, 'The Necessity Plea in English Criminal Law' [1972] Camb LJ 87.

[2] *R v Smith (D.R.)* [1974] QB 354; see further nn. 13–15 below.

[3] [1986] 1 AC 112 (dealing with the point incidentally to a non-criminal appeal).

would not have intended a consequence that she knew would follow from her action, if her purpose was the clinical one of preserving the patient's health and well-being: this was tantamount, in a sense, to the creation of a defence of 'clinical balance of evils', but it was wrapped up rather clumsily as a mere interpretation of the term 'intention' and therefore none of the broader questions about such a defence were addressed.[4] Similarly, in *R v Steane*[5] the Court of Criminal Appeal held that the defendant did not intend to assist the enemy if his reason for doing the acts was to save his family from a concentration camp: insofar as Steane realized that assisting the enemy would be a virtually certain consequence of his acts, the decision may be characterized as recognizing an extension to the defence of duress, but presented as an interpretation of the 'with intent' requirement and thus avoiding discussion of the broader questions of policy.

These familiar features of the English legal landscape have been revisited in order to suggest that, at least in uncodified systems of criminal law,[6] there is considerable ambiguity about the boundaries of defences to criminal liability. One advantage of this ambiguity, no doubt, is that it enables the system to respond flexibly to individual cases, without throwing open the doors to all manner of supposed grounds for exculpation. The corresponding disadvantages are that the broader issues of principle raised by certain arguments for exculpation are unlikely to be considered thoroughly, and that the law cannot function properly as a source of guidance for conduct if the boundaries of permissible conduct are systematically undefined. Those disadvantages may be particularly weighty in some spheres, which brings me to the focus of this chapter. Three topics are to be discussed, with a view to probing the foundations and the boundaries of the relevant doctrines and their place in a system both of criminal law and, more widely, of criminal justice. The three topics may be described, in a preliminary fashion, as officially-induced mistake of law, entrapment, and law enforcement motivation. The first deals with cases in which a defendant has based conduct on a view of the law, implanted by an official, that turns out to be erroneous. The second relates to cases in which a defendant's conduct followed instigation by an official, or by someone acting under the direction of an official. And the third deals with cases in which a defendant's conduct was motivated by a desire to bring someone else to justice or to restore property to its lawful owner or the police.

None of these topics lies in the mainstream, and their links may not be immediately apparent. I believe that, among the strands of reasoning attached to each of the three claims for recognition, one common element is fidelity to

---

[4] For discussion, see A. Ashworth, 'Criminal Liability in a Medical Context: the Treatment of Good Intentions', in A.P. Simester and A.T.H. Smith (eds), *Harm and Culpability* (Oxford, 1996).

[5] [1947] KB 997.

[6] And probably in some codified systems: see clauses 4(4) and 45(4) of the draft English criminal code, in Law Commission No. 177, *A Criminal Code for England and Wales* (London, HMSO, 1989).

legal values—by which I mean, broadly, the importance of recognizing that the criminal justice system ought to welcome conduct that promotes its integrity and ought to refuse to act upon conduct that undermines its integrity. To take official legal advice and to follow it is generally the conduct of a good citizen, as is conduct motivated by the purpose of enforcing the law. These activities demonstrate fidelity to the rule of law, and to values that form part of a sensible political morality. Conversely, for the courts to entertain a prosecution arising from an act of entrapment by an official is to undermine the integrity of the criminal justice system, as it is for the courts to entertain the prosecution of a citizen who was reasonably relying on official legal advice. Now the latter claim is probably more novel and more difficult to sustain, and the arguments will be developed as the chapter proceeds. It assumes that coherence is an important value in the criminal justice system—coherence not merely as the absence of contradiction, but more positively as a network of mutually supporting rules and principles.[7] It also assumes that it is fair to regard the acts of the courts as systemically connected to the conduct of police officers on which prosecutors seek to rely. And it assumes that decisions of the courts carry a social symbolism which is rightly used to affirm legal values.[8]

These arguments will be taken further below. If we grant that the three claims should be recognized, how ought the legal system to respond? Much criminal law scholarship assumes that the answer to this question would lie in the recognition or non-recognition of one or more of the three claims as a defence to liability. Is there a version of each of the claims that is so compelling as to warrant recognition as a full defence? If not, then there might be the possibility of a qualified defence; otherwise, the claim might be reflected in mitigation of sentence. However, it would not be right to dismiss the claims of a full defence until all the possible categories and rationales have been examined. There are different types of rationales for admitting what are termed 'defences', for example, simple failure of proof (mistake and intoxication, at least in their unrestricted form); preconditions of liability (e.g. the 'defences' of insanity and infancy); justifications (such as self-defence and the prevention of crime); excuses (e.g. duress); and even 'non-exculpatory public policy defences'.[9] More will be said later about this fifth category, which raises the question whether it is more appropriate to deal with a claim procedurally than through the substantive law: if convincing arguments can be made for

---

[7] cf. the discussion of coherence by J. Raz, *Ethics in the Public Domain* (Oxford, 1994) ch. 13, recognizing it as a formal value and arguing in favour of 'local coherence' within particular branches of the law.

[8] cf. J. Gardner, 'Crime: in Proportion and in Perspective', in A. Ashworth and M. Wasik (eds.), *Fundamentals of Sentencing Theory* (Oxford, 1998) especially at 49–52.

[9] Four of these five categories of rationale derive from the work of Paul H. Robinson: for a recent restatement see his *Criminal Law* (New York, 1997) 379–381. However, the second, 'preconditions of liability', is identified in the writings of R.A. Duff, 'Law, Language and Community: Some Preconditions of Criminal Liability' (1998) 18 Oxford Journal of Legal Studies 189, and J. Gardner, 'The Gist of Excuses' (1998) 1 Buffalo Crim LR 575.

one or more of the three claims, would it be more fitting to stay the prosecution, rather than leave the defendant to raise a defence at trial? What factors should determine the answer to this question?

Having ventilated these possibilities in this preliminary fashion, we now pass to a discussion of each of the three claims, beginning with cases in which the defendant has acted in reliance on a view of the law implanted by an official.

A. Reliance on Official Legal Assurance

1. Outline of the Current Legal Position

English criminal law has traditionally shown a reluctance to admit any defences based on mistake of law.[10] The maxim *ignorantia juris neminem excusat* has often been cited by judges when refusing to allow both defences of simple ignorance of the law and defences based on erroneous legal advice. The draft English criminal code thus provides that 'ignorance or mistake as to a matter of law does not affect liability to conviction for an offence except (a) where so provided, or (b) where it negatives the fault element for the offence'.[11] This restatement is doubly unfortunate: first, there had been some recognition by the Law Commission of the arguments for a defence based on officially-induced mistake of law but they had not been pursued because this might require 'a major exercise in law reform' beyond the codification project;[12] secondly, the recognition that mistake of law might occasionally negative one or more offence requirements perpetuates an unprincipled variation among situations where the defence is or is not admitted, since it is highly unlikely that those who drafted the offences were intending by their chosen words to include or exclude a defence of mistake of law.[13]

In England the judicial decisions are no longer all in one direction. In *Cambridgeshire and Isle of Ely County Council v Rust*[14] the defendant had made enquiries of local and national authorities before setting up a stall on a grass verge beside a highway. None of them suggested that it was unlawful, and indeed he used the stall and paid rates on it for three years. Eventually the county council decided that the stall must go, and prosecuted Rust for pitching a stall on the highway. He pleaded 'lawful excuse', but the Divisional

---

[10] See A. Ashworth, *Principles of Criminal Law* (3rd edn., Oxford, 1999) 243–248.

[11] Law Commission No. 177 (n. 6 above) cl. 21.

[12] The view of the code team who drew up the first draft of the code: Law Commission No. 143, *Codification of the Criminal Law: A Report to the Law Commission* (London, 1985) paras 9.4–9.6.

[13] A well-known contrast is that between the two House of Lords decisions, *Grant v Borg* [1982] 1 WLR 638 ('knowingly remaining beyond the time limited by leave', ignorance of law held irrelevant) and *Secretary of State for Trade and Industry v Hart* [1982] 1 WLR 481 ('knows that he is disqualified for appointment to that office', ignorance of law held relevant).

[14] [1972] 1 QB 426.

Court held that, despite all the enquiries he had made, there can be no 'lawful excuse for conduct because one is mistaken as to the law; every one is supposed to know the law'. In *R v Arrowsmith*[15] the Court of Appeal rejected the defence of reasonable belief that the conduct did not amount to an offence, stemming from a letter sent by the Director of Public Prosecutions. The court held that 'a mistake as to the law would not avail the appellant except perhaps in mitigation of sentence'. In *R v Bowsher*[16] the defendant's driving licence was returned to him by court officials earlier than it should have been, and he was still within a period of disqualification. On a prosecution for driving whilst disqualified, the Court of Appeal held that his reasonable mistake could not be a defence since all the elements of the crime were fulfilled.

More recently, however, in *Postermobile plc v Brent London Borough Council*[17] representatives of the defendant company were told by officials from the Brent planning department that it would be within the law to erect advertising hoardings on a particular site so long as they were erected for less than a month. Brent Council prosecuted the company soon after the advertisements were erected. The defence argued that the prosecution should be stayed for abuse of process, since the council was going back on a promise not to prosecute. The council replied that the company should have known that it was unwise to rely on statements by junior and inexperienced planning officers. The Divisional Court held that the prosecution should be stayed: it is 'important that the citizen should be able to rely on the statements of public officials', and 'it was not as though they had requested planning advice from one of the council's gardeners'. Since this case involved advice given before the defendant did the act complained of,[18] it is in substance a case of officially-induced mistake of law. The decision does not create a defence as such, but effectively pre-empts the need for such a defence by allowing the whole prosecution to be stayed in certain circumstances.

In Canadian law there is a defence of 'officially induced error'. Its elements were spelt out by the Ontario Court of Appeal in *R v Cancoil Thermal Corporation*,[19] where the defendants had relied on advice from an official of the government agency that subsequently prosecuted them. Lacourciere JA held that:

---

[15] (1974) 60 Cr App R 211. [16] [1973] RTR 202.

[17] *The Times*, 8 December 1997; cf. *Environment Agency v Stanford*, unreported, 30 June 1998, where the Divisional Court held that a similar claim (based on the words and actions of inspectors) failed on the facts, and *South Tyneside Borough Council v Jackson*, unreported, 14 February 1997, where the Divisional Court held that a man who had obtained both advice from the police and counsel's opinion had not taken 'all reasonable precautions' within the wording of the statute.

[18] Several of the earlier authorities on staying a prosecution because the prosecutor has reneged on a promise not to prosecute involve promises made *after* the offence, and relate (for example) to promises not to prosecute in exchange for providing evidence against another: see *R v Croydon Justices, ex parte Dean* (1994) 98 Cr App R 76, *R v Bloomfield* [1997] 1 Cr App R 135, and *R v Townsend, Dearsley and Bretscher* [1998] Crim LR 126.

[19] (1986) 52 CR (3d) 188, building on comments in the Supreme Court of Canada in *R v MacDougall* (1982) 31 CR (3d) 1, at 10.

The defence of 'officially induced error' is available as a defence to an alleged violation of a regulatory statute where an accused has reasonably relied upon the erroneous legal opinion or advice of an official who is responsible for the administration or enforcement of the particular law. In order for the accused to successfully raise this defence, he must show that he relied on the erroneous legal opinion of the official and that his reliance was reasonable. The reasonableness will depend upon several factors, including the efforts he made to ascertain the proper law, the complexity or the obscurity of the law, the position of the official who gave the advice, and the clarity, definitiveness and reasonableness of the advice given.[20]

Turning to the USA, the Model Penal Code (MPC) does not recognize a general defence of mistake of law, although it does acknowledge that such a mistake may negative the culpability requirements of certain offences.[21] However, the MPC provides for a limited defence of officially-induced error of law, in cases where a defendant relies on an erroneous statement of the law made by a person or body responsible for the interpretation, administration, or enforcement of the law, provided such reliance is reasonable.[22] It will be observed that this defence does not extend to reliance on a lawyer's advice, largely because of the alleged dangers of collusion and fabrication.[23] The formulations of the defence vary among different American states, and some require reasonable belief in the legality of the conduct and reliance on an official statement—two separable elements that may be combined in the single requirement of 'reasonable reliance', but which ensure that a person who relies on an official statement even though he thinks it is erroneous does not have a defence.[24]

2. Rationales for Recognizing the Claim

From that sketch of the law we now pass to consideration of the principal rationales for recognizing the claim of officially-induced error of law. The first rationale brings out the elements of the excuse in the claim, the second establishes a connection with the principle of legality, and the third and fourth relate the claim to the logic of the criminal justice system.

The first possible rationale is that it should be regarded as reasonable, in the light of what the state may fairly expect of individual citizens, to place reliance on official advice. This rationale may be related to John Gardner's illuminating distinction between excuses as denials of responsibility and excuses as assertions of reasonable response to the circumstances

---

[20] (1986) 52 CR (3d) 199; for a subsequent development in Canadian law, see the decision in *Jorgensen*, n. 30 below and accompanying text.

[21] American Law Institute, *Model Penal Code* (1962), s. 2.02(9); for judicial authority, see *Raley v Ohio* (1959) 79 SCt 1257 and *US v Laub* (1967) 87 SCt 574.

[22] ibid., s. 2.04(3)(b).

[23] The English decision in *Cooper v Simmons* (1862) 7 H & N 707 is to the same effect.

[24] For discussion, see Paul H. Robinson, *Criminal Law Defenses* (St Paul, Minnesota, West Publishing, 1984) para. 183(d).

prevailing.[25] The claim of reliance on official advice is not a denial of responsibility. Its essence lies in an assertion of responsible and reasonable—and hence blameless—conduct. It is surely reasonable for a citizen to rely on an interpretation of the law proffered by an official (assuming that the citizen is a layman in the matter). The defendant has behaved as a good citizen, and has done what it was reasonable to do, approaching the relevant authorities in *Cambridgeshire and Isle of Ely County Council v Rust*, asking planning officers in *Postermobile v. Brent LBC*, and so forth. This is behaviour that the state ought to value, and certainly ought not to punish. Whatever the merits of the argument that to allow mistake of law as a general defence would be to encourage ignorance of the law,[26] the reverse is true of the claim of officially-induced error: to recognize this would signal the value of citizens checking on the lawfulness of their proposed activities.

Since the essence of this rationale lies in the reasonableness of the defendant's conduct, it is important to consider what factors might make the reliance more or less reasonable, where an official has offered an assurance.[27] One question is when it is reasonable to assume that the official has the authority to offer guidance: it is possible to rule out extreme cases, as where the official does not work in the relevant department[28] or where the official is manifestly too junior,[29] but a fairer general test is whether a reasonable citizen would consider the particular official to have responsibility for the enforcement or administration of the relevant law.[30] Another question is when it might not be reasonable to rely on the assurance of an apparently authoritative official. One possibility is that D herself is an expert and she knows that the advice is probably wrong. A further possibility is where the assurance encourages a course of conduct that is so patently wrong that it is unreasonable to follow it. In the controversial case of *United States v Barker*[31] the defendants, recruited by a White House official who assured them that he had the appropriate authority, broke into an office in order to obtain certain files, as part of the Watergate conspiracy. The Circuit Court held that the defendants should be granted a defence of reasonable reliance on the advice of a

---

[25] J. Gardner, 'The Gist of Excuses' (1998) 1 Buffalo Crim LR 575, particularly 578–579 and 588.

[26] And it has few, as A.T.H. Smith demonstrates: 'Error and Mistake of Law in Anglo-American Criminal Law' (1984) 14 Anglo-American LR 3, at 17–19.

[27] Some relevant factors are set out in the quotation from Lacourciere JA in the Canadian case of *Cancoil Thermal Corporation* (n. 19 above).

[28] As in Schiemann LJ's example of asking a gardener about planning law: see n. 17 above.

[29] This was the unsuccessful argument of the council in the *Postermobile* case (n. 17 above).

[30] ibid., repeated in *R v Jorgensen* [1995] 4 SCR 55, per Lamer CJ at 79 (Supreme Court of Canada); cf. the English provision in s. 3(4) of the Control of Pollution Act 1974, creating a defence to the crime of unlicensed waste disposal where a person 'took care to inform himself from persons who were in a position to provide information'. Presumably this might support an argument based on mistake as to the authority of the person to provide information, where D mistakenly believed that there was such authority.

[31] 546 F 2d 940 (1976).

government official. Critics have argued that where the conduct in question is *malum in se* or otherwise manifestly illegal the grounds for regarding the reliance as reasonable are much weaker.[32] There is some plausibility to this response and, while the area of uncertainty it leaves (what are the *mala in se*? how does one divine the boundaries of manifest illegality?) detracts significantly from rule of law values such as fair warning, it is a familiar feature of excuse-based defences that they rely on relatively open-textured concepts such as reasonableness. There are a couple of analogies that might be mentioned briefly in this context. One is that the doctrine of entrapment (considered below) is confined by the Model Penal Code to offences not involving physical injury: if Barker and his associates had been told that they were authorized to beat and injure a particular person, would and should the court have been willing to grant the defence? Secondly, the doctrine of superior orders is subject to a similar limitation. Although the boundaries of that doctrine remain open to debate, one view is that a soldier ought to have a defence when following the commands of a superior officer in a military setting, unless the commands were 'manifestly illegal'.[33] The foundations of the defence lie in excuse rather than justification, it appears, and so the soldier is excused on the basis that it is reasonable to rely on superior orders unless those orders command conduct that is so plainly wrong that the soldier ought to resist, despite the breach of military discipline involved in disobeying orders.[34] The 'fair warning' deficit in the *Barker* ruling could be reduced by drawing on these two analogies.

Thus far we have discussed an excuse-based rationale for relying on officially-induced mistake of law, with possible restrictions. But if the matter is viewed entirely as a question of lack of culpability, it might be asked why the discussion has been confined to *officially* induced mistakes. A citizen might have a mistaken view of the law implanted or confirmed by a lawyer or by a respected colleague, and if she acts in good faith on that belief she is surely not culpable. Since the focus of this chapter is upon the role of officials, this point will not be pursued to a conclusion here. Some commentators have taken the view that reliance on a lawyer's advice is not a sound basis for allowing excuses, even though qualified lawyers are 'officers of the court', the argument being that lawyers can be hired and fired, and that some defendants, including wealthy corporations, might then be able to shield themselves from some deserved criminal liability.[35] On the other hand, arguably it might be far

---

[32] e.g. Comment, '*U.S. v. Barker:* Misapplication of the Reliance on an Official Interpretation of the Law Defence' (1978) 66 Calif LR 809; J. Dressler, *Understanding Criminal Law* (2nd edn., 1995) 146.

[33] The words used by the Supreme Court of the Cape of Good Hope in *R v Smith* (1900) 17 Cape of Good Hope Reports 561.

[34] G. Williams, *Criminal Law: the General Part* (2nd edn., London, 1961) 296–301.

[35] ibid., 298; Robinson (n. 24 above) para. 183(c).

more reasonable in some circumstances for a citizen to rely on the advice of a respected lawyer than that of a junior official.[36]

The second possible rationale connects the claim of reasonable reliance on official legal advice with the principle of legality. That principle, as declared (for example) in Article 7 of the European Convention on Human Rights, holds that 'no-one shall be held guilty of any criminal offence on account of any act or omission which did not constitute a criminal offence . . . at the time when it was committed'. The reason behind this strong statement of principle is that the criminal law is a censuring institution and conviction may have far-reaching consequences, which make it so unfair as to constitute a breach of human rights if a person is convicted for contravening a law about which he did not know (and could not reasonably have been expected to know) and to which he could therefore not adjust his conduct.[37] In cases where a person is advised by an official that the law is such-and-such, and adjusts her conduct to that advice, it seems plainly unfair to convict her of an offence if the court decides that the legal advice was erroneous. All the reasons supporting the principle of legality apply, by way of strong analogy, to reasonable reliance on official legal advice.[38] It can be conceded that the mistaken citizen is not being punished 'on account of an act or omission which did not constitute a criminal offence' when done; it did constitute an offence, but the official mis-understood its implications. However, from the point of view of the mistaken citizen, it is *as if the conduct did not constitute an offence*, because of the of-ficial source of the assurance on which she reasonably relied. The connection with the 'fair warning' element of the principle of legality is particularly strong because of the involvement, on the one hand, of a state official and, on the other hand, of a citizen conscientious enough to follow official advice.

It should be noted that some have argued the legality point from the other direction. Jerome Hall maintained that to allow a defence of mistake of law would be to substitute the opinion of the official for the court's own decision about the law,[39] which raises rule of law concerns about officials dispensing with the law. Such concerns must be taken seriously, but the way to do so is to create forms of corruption offence aimed at officials. The question here is whether a citizen does wrong by reasonably following official advice: in res-ponse, the argument has been put for an excuse based on the idea of reason-able reliance, and the defendant would certainly be convicted if he did the act

---

[36] A.J. Ashworth, 'Excusable Mistake of Law' [1974] Criminal LR 652; at least, 'taking coun-sel's opinion' is a well-known practice, which a solicitor might well advise in other spheres of conduct. But the hapless busker in the *South Tyneside* case (n. 17 above) was refused a defence despite relying on counsel's opinion.

[37] The principle of legality sustains three more detailed principles (fair warning, maximum certainty, and strict construction of penal laws): see Ashworth (n. 10 above) 70–85.

[38] D. Husak and A. von Hirsch, 'Culpability and Mistake of Law', in S. Shute, J. Gardner and J. Horder (eds.), *Action and Value in Criminal Law* (Oxford, 1993) 166–167.

[39] J. Hall, *General Principles of Criminal Law* (2nd edn., Indianapolis, 1960) 388.

again. A version of the Hall argument found its way into proposals for an Australia-wide criminal code: the review committee accepted that there should be a defence of reliance on a decision of a competent court, but held that 'to allow a defence when the accused acted on advice given by a Government official would . . . in effect give a dispensing power to administrative officials, contrary to fundamental constitutional principle'.[40] The 'dispensing power' argument seems to be connected with the suggestions of corruption that led some to disallow a defence based on reasonable reliance on a lawyer's advice, but the Australian report fails to mention any of the arguments set out above to the effect that seeking official advice amounts to good citizenship.

The third rationale is of a different kind: that if the state, through its officials, implants or confirms a particular view of the law, it is a breach of good faith for its officials then to bring a prosecution founded on a different view of the law. This has sometimes been cast as an estoppel-based rationale, arguing that the state should be estopped from prosecuting someone to whom it has given advice that turns out to be mistaken.[41] A few critics have taken this point literally, comparing the claim with the doctrines of estoppel in equity and public law and pronouncing that there is a lack of fit.[42] However, the estoppel argument is intended to function extra-legally, at a moral and political level, where the concept of estoppel rather than any technical legal doctrine would be relevant.

Similar in some respects is the fourth rationale, grounded in the integrity principle: that for the criminal justice system to produce a conviction of a person who has been advised by an official that the conduct would be lawful would involve the system in a disreputable self-contradiction, and would compromise its integrity. Fuller discussion of the integrity principle will be deferred until the next section of the chapter.[43] For the present, we should recognize that both this rationale and the estoppel rationale may require at least one further assumption, about 'the unity of the criminal justice system': there can only be a self-contradiction (or an estoppel) if the official who gave the advice and the court before which the prosecution is subsequently listed can properly be regarded as part of the same entity, referred to broadly as 'the state'.[44] Or, if that were thought too question-begging, one could focus on the courts and argue that their integrity would be compromised if they convicted someone who reasonably relied on official advice. The integrity principle is

[40] Review of Commonwealth Criminal Law, *Interim Report: Principles of Criminal Responsibility* (Canberra, Australian Government Publishing Service, 1990) para. 6.24.

[41] A.J. Ashworth, 'Excusable Mistake of Law' [1974] Criminal LR 652; Robinson (n. 24 above) para. 183(c).

[42] See P.G. Barton, 'Officially Induced Error as a Criminal Defence: a Preliminary Look' (1980) 22 Crim LQ 314, at 329–331.

[43] See nn. 82–89 below.

[44] The state is now shedding several tasks, through deregulation and privatization, so a full elaboration of this point would require some carefully drawn distinctions.

that the legal process should signify its insistence that those who enforce the law should also obey the law,[45] and that where the police cross the line between acceptable and unacceptable methods of detecting criminals it would damage the integrity of the criminal justice system if the courts were to act on the fruits of that investigation.[46] Criminal justice must carry moral authority and legitimacy, and this would be significantly compromised if courts were able to convict citizens for acts which originated in an official error or other official misconduct.

3. The Response of the Criminal Justice System

Acceptance of a rationale based on estoppel or judicial integrity would have two significant implications. One is that it may be applicable only to cases of reliance on *official* statements of the law, and may not extend to reliance on legal advice from a lawyer.[47] That, in turn, suggests that reasonable reliance is not the sole foundation: a doctrine of reasonable reliance on an official legal assurance may be based partly on the culpability-related element of reasonable reliance and partly on the source of the advice relied upon.[48]

The other implication of the estoppel and integrity principles is that they do not point necessarily towards the creation of a *defence* of reasonable reliance on an official assurance. Rather, they point towards the procedural remedy that no prosecution should be allowed where there was reasonable reliance on official legal advice: even if it is difficult to regard the criminal courts as part of the same entity as officials in the planning departments of a local council, for example, it is less difficult to regard the prosecution service thus.[49] If a prosecution is brought and the defendant claims reasonable reliance on official advice, this ought properly to be a ground for staying a prosecution for abuse of process rather than simply a defence to be assessed during the course of a trial. The system-related elements of the doctrine of reliance on official legal advice, emphasized by the integrity principle, are no less important than the culpability elements. It may be said that the element of 'reasonable

---

[45] See, e.g., Stephen and Aickin JJ in *Bunning v Cross* (1978) 141 CLR 54, at 75.

[46] Supreme Court of Canada in *Amato v R* (1982) 69 CCC (2d) 31.

[47] This point requires full argument in another context. In England and Wales a solicitor is an officer of the court and, insofar as the rationale of judicial integrity is promoted, one might argue that it would be easier to sustain the argument for a solicitor's advice than for that of a public official.

[48] A.T.H. Smith, 'Error and Mistake of Law in Anglo-American Criminal Law' (1984) 14 Anglo-American LR 3, at 21; cf. A.P. Simester and W.J. Brookbanks, *Principles of Criminal Law* (Wellington, Brookers, 1998), whose comment that 'a principal rationale of the doctrine is that the offender was misled about the scope or content of the law by one who, in the nature of her office, ought to have been better informed—a very different explanation than absence of fault' (408), is not intended to deny the dual nature of the rationale. See also W.J. Brookbanks, 'Officially Induced Error as a Defence to Crime' (1993) 17 Crim LJ 381.

[49] The courts belong to the judiciary and the officials (one might assume) belong to the executive branch of government, but the status of prosecutors is often said to be 'quasi-judicial', and might therefore be partly executive too.

reliance' is excuse-based, and therefore closely related to certain defences to liability and suitable for adjudication by the tribunal of fact; but the whole concept of reasonable reliance in this context is constructed around public policy elements of good citizenship and the principle of legality, with personal excusing conditions playing a secondary (if essential) role. The judicial integrity argument leads in the same direction: the courts simply should not lend themselves to prosecutions based on official error or misconduct. All these points are developed more fully in relation to entrapment below. For present purposes, the reasoning here can be related back to the decision in *Postermobile v Brent LBC*, discussed above.[50] In that case the Divisional Court held that the prosecution should be stayed for abuse of process, where the defendants had acted on advice given by officials from the planning department of the local council and then found themselves prosecuted by the local council. This procedural remedy of staying the prosecution is surely more appropriate than either a substantive defence or the exclusion of evidence: it is timely, conclusive, and closely tied to the rationale of estoppel or judicial integrity.

B. Entrapment by Law Enforcement Officers

1. Outline of the Current Legal Position

On the question of entrapment we find considerable variation of approach among legal systems. In current English law the furthest-reaching response to a finding of entrapment is the exclusion of evidence thereby obtained, at the discretion of the court;[51] more broadly, courts have allowed entrapment as a ground for mitigation of sentence. The hesitancy of the English courts in this area means that there is no developed doctrine of entrapment, and so for doctrinal discussion it is preferable to look to the USA and elsewhere. The American Law Institute's Model Penal Code provides that entrapment may constitute a defence to crime. Its essence is that a law enforcement officer has employed 'methods of persuasion or inducement that create a substantial risk that such an offence will be committed by persons other than those who are ready to commit it'.[52] It will be noticed that this formulation focuses primarily on the conduct of the officer and its probable consequences, rather than upon the situation of the particular defendant and whether he or she was actually instigated by the officer's conduct to commit the offence. To reflect this, the approach will be referred to here as the official-centred model.

---

[50] See n. 17 above and accompanying text.
[51] One decision has recognized that it would be possible to stay the prosecution for abuse of process: see *R v Latif and Shahzad* [1996] 1 WLR 104.
[52] American Law Institute, *Model Penal Code* (Final draft 1962), s. 2.13.

Towards the opposite end of the spectrum lie those definitions of entrapment that focus on the dynamics of the particular incident giving rise to the criminal charge. In opinions handed down by the US Supreme Court, this approach has been developed so as broadly to turn on two requirements, inducement or instigation by the police and innocence on the part of the defendant.[53] The first requirement looks to the part played by the official: was it active rather than passive? Did it cause the commission of the offence? The second requirement, which must also be satisfied, has been encapsulated in the term 'pre-disposition'. Thus, if it can be established that the defendant was pre-disposed to commit the offence, the fact that the particular incident was instigated by an official is not sufficient to found the defence. In blunt terms, pre-disposed persons are fair game, whereas the virtue of previously 'innocent' citizens should not be tested. To mark the distinction from the first model, this approach will be referred to here as the defendant-centred model.

Although the two models lie towards opposite ends of a spectrum, each of them may be modified in the light of other policies, preferences, and principles. Thus the Model Penal Code definition excludes from the entrapment defence all cases of causing or threatening bodily injury, on the basis that defendants who are prepared to go so far should be liable to conviction and punishment, and that the proper way of dealing with the over-zealous official is to prosecute him or her for incitement.[54] On the other hand, the defendant-centred model can be expanded, so that in cases of egregious misconduct by police officers or their agents the defence should be available whether or not the defendant was 'pre-disposed': the argument here would be that, even if the primary rationale of the defence is not the promotion of proper standards of conduct by officials, it is right to place some limits on the type of conduct that may lawfully be employed in pursuit of suspected offenders, even those believed to be pre-disposed. A doctrine of entrapment may, therefore, draw on elements of both models.

Returning to English law, the judicial decisions have not pursued a single course. However, now that the Human Rights Act 1998 is in force, English courts are required to act in conformity with the European Convention on Human Rights, and to take account of the decisions of the European Court of Human Rights. In *Teixeira de Castro v Portugal*[55] the European Court held that there was a breach of the Article 6 right to a fair trial where a person who was not known to the police, and who was approached twice by undercover police officers to supply them with heroin, succumbed to the temptation and obtained heroin to sell to them. The court made it clear that the decision

---

[53] See the majority opinions in *Sorrells v US* 287 US 435 (1932) and in *Sherman v US* 356 US 369 (1958).

[54] ALI, *Model Penal Code: Text and Commentary*, Vol. ii, 420. One might maintain that this limitation is insufficiently extensive, and one might question why it is only in this type of case that officers who go so far as to incite criminality should be prosecuted.

[55] (1999) 28 EHRR 101.

would have been otherwise if there had been evidence to show that the defendant was known to be pre-disposed to such conduct. When the House of Lords came to deal with two appeals on the question of entrapment, after a series of appellate decisions which had failed to develop a clear and convincing approach, their Lordships stated that the Strasbourg Court's decision in *Teixeira de Castro* is consistent with the common law. Thus in *R v Looseley; Attorney-General's Reference No. 3 of 2000*,[56] the House of Lords held that the proper remedy for entrapment is to stay the proceedings for abuse of process; that it is not entrapment if a law enforcement officer provides a person with an opportunity to commit an offence, merely by acting as a normal customer might act in the circumstances;[57] that the essence of entrapment is the instigation of an offence, by offering a person some kind of inducement that would not be present in the ordinary run of transactions;[58] and that the presence or absence of 'predisposition' on the part of the person entrapped is not important, since the focus is on the conduct of the law enforcement officer.[59]

This decision suggests that the English courts are adopting an official-centred model of entrapment. Moreover, the analysis regards test purchases as a central case.

In *DPP v Marshall and Downes*[60] undercover officers tried to buy liquor in individual bottles from defendants whose licence was restricted to the sale of liquor by the case, and when the defendants sold the bottles to them they brought a prosecution. No evidence of 'pre-disposition' was adduced in this case, but the Divisional Court held that the test purchase was not so unfair that the evidence ought to be excluded. Presumably one might argue that persons granted official licences ought to obey the terms of those licences at all times and that, unless some extra inducement was offered in the test purchase, no important values are compromised. It seems that such cases would fall outside the Model Penal Code's entrapment defence, because a test purchase does not create a substantial risk that the offence will be committed by persons other than those ready to commit it. However, these cases demonstrate the complexity of the issues here, and the need to examine the various possible rationales lying behind any entrapment doctrine.

2. Rationales for Recognizing the Claim

There are many serious crimes that it is difficult or almost impossible to detect and solve without the use of some techniques of pro-active policing. In many crimes the police may find it easier, or more cost-effective, or even necessary, to adopt a subterfuge whereby an opportunity for someone to commit

---

[56] [2001] UKHL 53.   [57] ibid., paras 23, 102, 112.
[58] ibid., para. 70.   [59] ibid., para. 68.
[60] [1988] 3 All ER 683; it should be noted that there are a few statutory provisions that expressly authorize test purchases, such as s. 27 of the Trade Descriptions Act 1968.

the offence is provided. Such activities raise important *Rechtsstaat* concerns, in terms of both proper respect for citizens and the accountability and transparency of law enforcement agencies. It is in this context that we turn to examine the circumstances in which, and the reasons why, the claim of entrapment should be recognized. Four arguments, which overlap in places, may be considered as possible rationales.

First, it may be argued that citizens should not be liable to conviction if the involvement of law enforcement officers was active rather than passive. A different version of the argument is that it is the function of the police to prevent or detect crime and not to create it. Where the idea for the crime originated with the law enforcement officers, their conduct was wrongful and the defendant should not be liable to conviction.[61] If, on the other hand, it is clear that the idea originated with the defendant and the undercover police simply played along with the scheme in order to obtain evidence of the crime (as in *Smurthwaite*),[62] it cannot be said that the police created the crime. However, one might think that the 'crime creation' argument paints with too broad a brush, whereas the active/passive distinction is more workable because it recognizes that undercover police officers may properly play some role in the planning of an offence, and proposes that the limits should be set by reference to the active/passive distinction.

But the active/passive distinction is no more than a *facon de parler* in the present context. It does not represent the distinction between act and omission, or between action and inaction, but simply expresses the outcome of discussions of what should be acceptable or permissible police conduct in given situations. The *Smurthwaite* case might be offered as an example of police conduct that remained within the bounds of acceptability: there was no active encouragement of the defendant by the officer, even though the latter responded to requests and offered assistance when it seemed appropriate in order to maintain the deception. A case that falls clearly on the other side of the line is *Jacobson v US*,[63] where on 11 occasions the police mailed to the defendant some material advertising pornographic literature, trying to tempt him to place an order; which he did only on the eleventh occasion. It could be contended that the police merely provided an opportunity for the defendant to offend and went no further; the reply would be that they provided this opportunity 11 times, and that this amounted to objectionable 'virtue-testing'. As such, it could not be described as 'passive', and the Supreme Court was right to quash the conviction. But the facts of *Jacobson* show that the test of 'providing an opportunity' may not be sufficient on its own.

One sphere in which the passive/active distinction appears particularly unhelpful is that of test purchases. In a case such as *DPP v Marshall and*

---

[61] For a wide-ranging discussion, see B.G. Stitt and G.G. James, 'Entrapment and the Entrapment Defense: Dilemmas for a Democratic Society' (1984) 3 Law and Philosophy 111.
[62] *R v Smurthwaite and Gill* (1994) 98 Cr App R 437.   [63] 503 US 540 (1992).

Downes[64] one would need to say that, so long as the officers did no more than any other customer would do, in that there was no extra encouragement or inducement to commit an offence, then it could be said that this is not an example of active instigation but simply of passively providing an opportunity for the commission of the offence. A somewhat similar analysis might be applied to the use of decoys, as for example where a policewoman is clothed in the manner of an elderly lady, so that other officers can catch anyone minded to attack and rob the elderly. As a matter of principle, is it objectionable for police officers to dress up so as to test the virtue of citizens? In this case there can surely be no objection: an old lady walking along a street is a perfectly normal occurrence, and no one other than an intending criminal would treat it as an invitation to crime. It provides an opportunity for crime, but hardly one that could be described as out of the ordinary or abnormal.

A further case of virtue-testing is *Williams and O'Hare v DPP*,[65] where the police, as part of an initiative against vehicle crime, left an unattended van with its rear shutter partly open and cartons of cigarettes visible. After about half an hour, during which many passers-by appeared to notice the cigarettes but walked on, two eight-year-old boys took a carton of cigarettes, and they were intercepted and reprimanded by the police. About an hour later two men walked past the van several times until eventually, having decided that it was truly unattended, they began to remove cartons from the rear of the van. They were then arrested. What distinguishes this from other 'sting' operations is that there was no reason to suspect the defendants of any intention to break the law before they succumbed to the temptation: the van was an open temptation to all members of the public, rather like leaving an unattended wallet in full view to see who would pick it up and whether they would try to keep it. Many would argue that this crosses the line into unacceptability. The police are testing the virtue of all-comers, at least in that locality, and are likely to ensnare some people who would not otherwise have committed this or any other crime. The 'sting' is in no way confined to, or targeted at, those who might otherwise commit offences of this kind. This shows the limitations of the judicial observation that, in 'sting' cases, it is the defendants who apply themselves to the trick rather than the police who apply the trick to the defendants.[66] Such a statement draws no distinction between those who can fairly be assumed to have decided to offend before the opportunity is provided by the 'sting', such as thieves or their agents who enter a jeweller's shop

---

[64] See n. 60 above and accompanying text.   [65] (1994) 98 Cr App R 209.

[66] The aphorism of Lord Taylor CJ in *R v Christou and Wright* (1992) 95 Cr App R 264, a case in which the issue was slightly different (in that it was assumed that the 'sting' was to gather evidence of crimes already committed) but where his Lordship was seeking to draw the same distinction. Prosecutors have invoked Lord Taylor's aphorism in several subsequent cases, but when the defence tried to rely on it in *R v Shannon* [2001] 1 Cr App R 168, Potter LJ replied (at 192) that 'it does not seem to us that the aphorism of Lord Taylor amounts, or was intended to amount, to a litmus test of admissibility or a substitute for detailed consideration of the facts of each case'.

to sell stolen jewellery, and those who are merely passers-by who fall prey to temptation. Even if it can be said that the latter group 'applied themselves to the trick', one can maintain that they should not have been subjected to such a degree of temptation, deliberately and by state officials.

The decision in *Williams and O'Hare* was defended rather weakly by Lord Hoffmann in *Looseley*: he stated that because the crime was prevalent in the area, 'it was an authorised investigation into actual crime and the fact that the defendants may not have previously been suspected or even thought of offending was their hard luck'.[67] This is unconvincing. Lord Hoffmann was on much firmer ground when he rejected the active/passive distinction. It does not assist in drawing the line between the permissible and the impermissible: the question is really one of examining the appropriate limits of state action in testing the virtue of citizens. It has been argued that test purchases should fall within the limits of acceptability so long as the test purchaser behaves in the same way as a normal customer. Test purchases are easier to justify because the seller is licensed by the state or subject to known legal controls applicable to the business. Where the virtue-testing has no such definite target, it is much more difficult to justify. State officials should certainly not create opportunities for crime that are abnormal and tempting to all citizens. Thus a distinction should be drawn between the policewoman dressed as an old lady (which is sufficiently normal, and holds out no special inducement to crime) and leaving valuables unattended as in *Williams and O'Hare* (which is hardly normal, and certainly holds out an open inducement to crime). The acceptability of certain intermediate forms of pro-active policing remains to be debated, for example, where a policewoman dresses as a prostitute, in an area of known prostitution, in an attempt to convict men for soliciting or 'kerb-crawling'.

Secondly, it can be argued that the active/passive distinction, or at least the arguments presented above, should not be determinative when the defendant may fairly be said to have been 'pre-disposed' to this type of offence. This concept has been invoked by courts in a number of jurisdictions. Thus in *Jacobson v US*[68] the US Supreme Court held that the defendant could not be said to have been pre-disposed to commit the offence involving the transmission of pornographic material through the mail, on the basis of a single piece of conduct several years earlier at a time when the distribution of such material was not illegal. Similarly in *Teixeira de Castro v Portugal*[69] the European Court of Human Rights held that the conduct of the undercover officers went beyond what was permissible, in that they twice tried to tempt a person whom they had no grounds for suspecting of previous involvement in drug dealing. The court suggested that it might have been otherwise if it had been established that the defendant was known to be pre-disposed to commit such offences.

[67] [2001] UKHL 53, para. 65.   [68] 503 US 540 (1992).   [69] (1999) 28 EHRR 101.

This raises further questions: what is pre-disposition and on what kind of evidence is it proper to base a finding thereof? And why should pre-disposition be relevant to entrapment? The answers to the questions are intertwined, as will become apparent. The judicial decisions certainly differ in their notions of pre-disposition. The clearest cases are those in which the defendant is already involved in the criminal activity at the time that it is infiltrated by the police.[70] Then there are cases in which the police have reasonable grounds for suspecting that D is involved in a certain type of offending: this is the requirement laid down by the Supreme Court of Canada in *R v Mack*,[71] and it is one on which the prosecution could be put to proof. Next come those cases in which the defendant is clearly 'ready and willing' to become involved in the illegal enterprise, as where D responded enthusiastically to the suggestion of an offence.[72] The most troubling issue is whether the existence of previous convictions for like offences is sufficient to establish predisposition. In *Jacobson v US* the Supreme Court had a relatively easy decision to make on this point, since there was only one previous incident and it was not an offence because the conduct was not illegal when the previous incident took place.

The House of Lords struck an important blow against reliance on predisposition in *Looseley*: not only did Lord Hoffmann criticize the doctrine by pointing out that 'the result is that people with criminal records are fair game',[73] but he went on to argue that the presence or absence of predisposition is irrelevant. By adopting an official-centred approach to entrapment, 'the English doctrine assumes the defendant's guilt and is concerned with the standards of behaviour of the law enforcement officer'.[74] There are good grounds for rejecting the notion of predisposition as unduly wide and unfair. For example, there is a strong argument against encouraging the police to target known offenders, since in practice this may lead to unfair harassment and to slipshod police methods unless there is some clear and present connection between D and the type of crime under investigation. Moreover, in principle it contradicts equality before the law by treating convictions as a permanent indication of propensity.[75] However, the main question is whether recent convictions ought to be regarded as proof, without more, of a pre-disposition sufficient to justify the police in taking pro-active measures targeted at D, and the answer ought to be in the negative. This may be thought to strike a proper

---

[70] e.g. *Ludi v Switzerland* (1993) 15 EHRR 173.   [71] [1988] 2 SCR 903.

[72] This was said to be true of Shahzad in the case of *R v Latif and Shahzad* [1996] 1 WLR 104.

[73] [2001] UKHL 53, para. 67.   [74] ibid., para. 68.

[75] This point was made as long ago as 1958 by Frankfurter J, dissenting in *Sherman v US* 356 US 383 (1958). It is repeated in the Commentary to the Model Penal Code (n. 52 above), Pt I, 421. However, it is to be noted that English law generally places greater emphasis on some types of previous convictions. The one purpose of the Sex Offenders Register, introduced by the Sex Offenders Act 1997, is to require offenders to register their names and addresses so that the police know where they are; no doubt if sex offences of a particular kind are committed in a certain locality, the police will consult the Register and visit any registered offender who has a record of similar offending.

balance between the need for pro-active policing to detect certain crimes[76] and the protection of citizens from random virtue-testing. The Supreme Court of Canada surely has it right, in requiring proof of reasonable grounds to suspect D of being involved presently in this kind of unlawful activity.[77] 'Reasonable suspicion' should not be founded on rumour or unspecified 'information received',[78] and ought ideally to be supported by surveillance reports or similar evidence, although the Supreme Court of Canada has held that to target people dressed in a certain way and frequenting a 'known' area can satisfy the test.[79]

Thirdly, there is the question whether the deterrence of improper conduct by law enforcement officials is the true reason for having an entrapment doctrine. Thus the American Law Institute, adopting arguments advanced in the early US Supreme Court decisions, states that the rationale of the doctrine is to deter police behaviour that would be 'shocking to the moral standards of the community'.[80] This rationale led the ALI to propose an official-centred definition that focuses on the conduct of the officer rather than the response of the actual defendant. Others have insisted on the link between official-centred (sometimes termed 'objective') definitions of entrapment and a deterrent rationale.[81]

However, there are difficulties with this link. It is by no means clear that an entrapment doctrine, with either procedural or substantive consequences in the criminal process, does operate as an effective deterrent to law enforcement officers.[82] Of course it would rarely be the case that the entrapment doctrine would be the only mechanism for preventing unacceptable pro-active policing, since there would be internal police guidance backed by internal disciplinary proceedings. Yet, even accepting that, it seems statistically rare for courts to recognize entrapment as a chilling factor in prosecutions. Neither in Canada nor at federal level in the USA, where the entrapment doctrine is clearly recognized, has it been allowed to prevail on many occasions. Since the operation of deterrence requires the persons who are to be deterred to believe that there is a significant risk of being caught and of being 'punished'

[76] Note that if this 'need' is relied upon as part of the justification, the prosecution ought to show that this type of crime was not reasonably open to detection by other available methods: per Lamer J in *R v Mack* (1988) 67 C.R. (3d) 1, at 50.

[77] In *Mack*, ibid.

[78] Reliance on such inferior grounds for suspicion was criticized by Stewart J, speaking for the majority in *US v Russell* 411 US 423 (1973).

[79] *R v Barnes* (1991) 3 CR (4th) 1; see the discussion by D.R. Stuart, *Canadian Criminal Law* (3rd edn., Scarborough, Ontario, Carswell, 1995) 532–536.

[80] *Model Penal Code: Text and Commentary*, Vol. ii, 406.

[81] e.g. Robinson (n. 24 above) Vol.1, 209(d)(3).

[82] Under existing law, most entrappers commit the offence of incitement, but are not prosecuted. A specific offence of entrapment might prove to be a more powerful deterrent if prosecutions were brought with some frequency: this was recommended by the Law Commission in Law Commission No. 83, *Defences of General Application* (London, 1977) para. 5.48, but its proposals on entrapment were flawed on other grounds (see A.J. Ashworth, 'Entrapment' [1978] Criminal LR 137) and have not been adopted.

for the misconduct,[83] it seems unlikely that a doctrine of entrapment adds greatly to the forces of dissuasion. A further difficulty in asserting the link between an official-centred definition and a deterrent rationale is that other rationales might equally well support a doctrine of entrapment that focuses on the conduct of the official. One such rationale is the preservation of the integrity of the criminal justice system, to which we now pass.

Fourthly, it can be argued that the principle of judicial integrity supplies the rationale for the entrapment doctrine. The principle, as we saw earlier,[84] is that the legal process should signify its insistence that those who enforce the law should also obey the law. The moral authority and legitimacy of the courts would be undermined if they were to 'countenance behaviour that threatens . . . the rule of law'.[85]

As Lord Nicholls put it in *Looseley*:

> It is simply not acceptable that the state through its agents should lure its citizens into committing acts forbidden by the law and then seek to prosecute them for doing so. That would be entrapment. That would be a misuse of state power, and an abuse of the process of the courts. The unattractive consequences, frightening and sinister in extreme cases, which state conduct of this nature could have are obvious. The role of the courts is to stand between the state and its citizens and make sure this does not happen.[86]

Some would add that to act on the fruits of entrapment would involve the legal system in self-contradiction:[87] thus the American philosopher Gerald Dworkin has argued that, if we accept 'the system of criminal sanctions as a choosing system and as the enforcement of law, i.e. authoritative rules backed by sanctions', then:

> it is not consistent with such a system that law enforcement officials attempt to see if they can cause a person to commit a crime by suggesting or encouraging in any way that a crime can be committed . . . It is not the purpose of officers of the law to encourage crime for the purpose of punishing it.[88]

This is a strong affirmation of the coherence or integrity principle which would, as it stands, rule out the provision of opportunities for offending, even to those reasonably suspected of being presently disposed to commit this kind of offence. However, it has been argued above that there are justifications for

---

[83] For a recent thoughtful review of deterrence and its operation in criminal law, see A. von Hirsch, A.E. Bottoms, E. Burney and P.-O. Wikstrom, *Criminal Deterrence* (Oxford, 1999).

[84] See n. 43 above and accompanying text.

[85] Per Lord Griffiths in *R v Horseferry Road Magistrates' Court, ex parte Bennett* [1994] 1 AC 42.

[86] [2001] UKHL 53, para. 1.

[87] The estoppel argument was examined above in relation to the doctrine of reasonable reliance on official legal advice. It was raised by Glanville Williams in his analysis of entrapment in *Criminal Law: the General Part* (n. 34 above) 781–782.

[88] G. Dworkin, *The Theory and Practice of Autonomy* (New Haven, 1988) 142–143.

allowing limited pro-active police conduct towards such persons, whilst insisting that in all other respects the legal system should refuse to act on cases involving the instigation of crime or the virtue-testing of persons. Thus the contention here is for a modified version of the integrity principle.

If a principle of judicial integrity is to be sustained, persuasive arguments need to be found on two points. The first is that the criminal process, or criminal justice system, has such a unity that a court deciding whether or not a defendant should be convicted can be said to have its integrity compromised if it acts upon evidence resulting from an investigative procedure, carried out well before the trial, that amounted to entrapment. One reason in favour of accepting this point is that the court's judgment is a solemn and public pronouncement, representing the culmination of the criminal process and carrying considerable symbolic significance. It should therefore declare that entrapment is wrong, and prevent the prosecution from relying on it. This leads to the second point: critics would argue that this symbolism can cut both ways. If the result of the court's ruling is that the prosecution fails, even though it appears plain that the defendant was (factually) guilty of the offence, this may put the criminal justice system in a disreputable light so far as some sections of the public are concerned.[89] They may contend that acquitting the apparently guilty is likely to undermine the integrity of the system, not to enhance it. However, that would be to place the reputation of the criminal justice system with the general public (and/or sections of the media) above the significance of fundamental legality values, notably the need for investigators to keep within the law, which the court ought surely to reaffirm.[90] If the media and the public construct the reputation of the courts on false premises, that problem should be addressed directly, rather than the courts compounding the error. The true principle of judicial integrity is one based on rule of law values and on principle. Arguments grounded in versions of public opinion[91] introduce several rogue elements—incomplete information, failure to consider counterarguments, manipulation by the mass media—which are unworthy foundations for public policy, even though they must sometimes be acknowledged as constraints on public policy. Arguments that avoid this reliance on public reactions, such as that of Dworkin,[92] are more convincing.

[89] A point made forcefully by the Chief Justice of Singapore in *SM Summit Holdings v Public Prosecutor* [1997] 3 SLR 922, although he went on to exclude the evidence in that case. For discussion of these issues in the Singapore context, see A. Ashworth, 'What is Wrong with Entrapment?' [1999] Singapore JLS 293.

[90] On the reasons on which judges should act, as distinct from reasons that may underpin the criminal justice system as a whole, see J. Gardner, 'Crime: in Proportion and in Perspective', in A. Ashworth and M. Wasik (eds), *Fundamentals of Sentencing Theory* (Oxford, 1998) 37.

[91] See the distinction made by P. Mirfield, *Silence, Confessions and Improperly Obtained Evidence* (Oxford, 1997) 23–28, between 'court-centred' and 'public attitude' versions of the integrity principle.

[92] See n. 85 above and accompanying text.

Lastly, it is worth reflecting briefly on the question whether the doctrine of entrapment should be applicable only where an official or a person working for an official (as an informant or *agent provocateur*) is involved in instigating the offence, or whether it should extend to cases of journalists or private citizens who set out to tempt others into law-breaking. The judicial integrity rationale does not apply to non-official entrapment,[93] and the thrust of the discussions surrounding the active/passive distinction was that it concerns the proper limits of state action towards citizens. So far as non-official entrapment is concerned, the most pertinent principle is that in criminal law individuals are treated as autonomous beings who are capable of making choices of their own in all but a few extreme situations (e.g., duress, necessity).[94] If one citizen is approached by another with a plan for a crime, and the two of them go ahead and commit it, the fact that the one was tempted by the other, and would not have committed the crime if the other had not come along, is regarded as irrelevant. The law treats them both as responsible individuals: anyone who fails to resist temptation must take the consequences. If there is evidence of exploitation or pressure falling short of duress, mitigation of sentence might be granted. Should it matter, therefore, that those who hold out the temptation are working for a newspaper in order to produce an *expose*?[95] The rationales for not convicting on the basis of official entrapment are not relevant, and if it then becomes a question of the culpability of the defendant, it is difficult to see anything stronger than an argument for some mitigation of sentence. (In such cases it may also be important to consider the criminal liability of the entrapper, and in particular whether the entrapper might have some form of 'public interest' defence for otherwise criminal conduct. This is considered in section C below.)

3. The Response of the Criminal Justice System

The arguments considered in the previous section do not point unequivocally to one formulation of the doctrine of entrapment, although the use of the concept

[93] More exactly, it does not apply in the same terms. There might be room for an argument that, if the entrapper committed a criminal offence (such as incitement) in the course of entrapping the defendant, the court's integrity would be compromised if a conviction of the entrapped person were based on the fruits of the entrapper's crime. Even if that argument were sustainable, it would depend on whether the entrapper did commit a crime or had a form of public interest defence: see section C below.

[94] For general discussion, see Ashworth (n. 10 above) 27–29 and 250–262; for a critique that regards the exceptions as contradictions, see A. Norrie, ' "Simulacra of Morality"? Beyond the Ideal/Actual Antinomies of Criminal Justice' in R.A. Duff (ed), *Philosophy and the Criminal Law* (Cambridge, 1998).

[95] See *R v Morley and Hutton* [1994] Criminal LR 919 (incitement by journalist treated on same basis as incitement by police officer for purpose of exclusion of evidence); *R v Tonnessen* (1998) 2 Cr App R (S) 328 (incitement by journalist and subsequent humiliation of defendant by publication of photographs warranted mitigation of sentence); *R v Shannon* [2001] 1 Cr App R 168 (journalist set up the opportunity, but no evidence of instigation or incitement sufficient to warrant either exclusion of evidence or stay of the prosecution); *R v Hardwicke and Thwaites* [2001] Criminal LR 218 (same journalist as in *Shannon*, similar reasoning).

of 'pre-disposition' and the rationale of deterrence were rejected. If we were to proceed on the basis of judicial integrity as the rationale, that would indicate that the response of the criminal justice system should be to prevent prosecutions based on official entrapment from going ahead. As was argued above in relation to reasonable reliance on official legal advice, the involvement of a law enforcement official in the creation of the offence should be regarded as a bar to trial. The prosecution ought not to be launched and, if it is, it ought to be stayed. This reasoning derives support from the decision of the European Court of Human Rights in *Teixeira de Castro v Portugal*,[96] where the court expressed the point strongly by stating that the applicant had been 'deprived from the outset of a fair trial'. That may be taken to indicate that the trial should not have taken place. This is now the position adopted in English law following the decision of the House of Lords in *Looseley*.[97]

On the footing that the offence was occasioned by the law enforcement official, it is surely right that no prosecution should be brought or that any prosecution brought should be stayed. The doctrine of abuse of process appears to be a tailor-made remedy for such gross defects in the early processes of law enforcement as improper conduct that instigates or generates an offence. The exclusion of evidence is inadequate: even if it were automatic rather than discretionary, it would leave the possibility that the prosecution might succeed by virtue of real or circumstantial evidence. Mitigation of sentence is plainly inadequate to reflect true entrapment, since there would have to be a conviction before the case ever reached the sentencing stage. Why not, alternatively, allow a defence to liability, as in many American jurisdictions? The answer must be that, inasmuch as the rationale for the defence lies in *official* involvement in the *creation* of the crime, this imports the integrity principle and its supporting arguments; and that, where the integrity principle is engaged, it is wrong for a prosecution to be brought and inappropriate to allow the case to proceed so far as to require a defence to be advanced. There is some debate in the American literature about whether entrapment issues ought to be laid out for a jury decision, and anyone with strong preferences for jury adjudications might argue that a defence is more fitting on that ground. However, the reasons in favour of staying the prosecution seem more powerful, even if the conclusiveness of the remedy—which means that the prosecution case is never opened, and the jury has no opportunity to consider the matter—might create a risk that judges allow it so infrequently as to weaken its practical effect.[98]

Finally, it will be observed that the focus of the whole discussion of entrapment has been upon the source of the inducement held out to the citizen, i.e. an 'official' source. The emerging preference has been for a hybrid model, with official-centred elements that rule out unacceptable conduct by officials

---

[96] (1999) 28 EHRR 101. [97] [2001] UKHL 53.
[98] A warning note sounded by Stuart (n. 76 above) 537.

and defendant-centred elements which refer to the defendant's present dispositions rather than his culpability on the occasion when the law enforcement officer approached him. The latter may be regarded as an unusually explicit nod towards the character theory of criminal liability,[99] probably stemming from the pragmatic argument that law enforcement agencies would be intolerably handicapped if they were unable to undertake some proactive work. However, it is notable that the rationale for recognizing entrapment does not rest to any significant extent on a reduction in the culpability of the defendant on normal principles. Insofar as culpability is engaged, it is in the modified causal sense that, since the crime was caused by the entrapper and would (probably) not have happened otherwise, the defendant should not be held to account for it. But this is very much a modified or attenuated sense of causation, since the defendant chose to commit the crime and was not coerced to do so.

C. Law Enforcement Motivation

1. Outline of the Current Legal Position

A claim based on what is here termed 'law enforcement motivation' arises where a person does a prohibited act, apparently with the required fault element, but with the purpose of bringing another person to justice, handing prohibited goods to the authorities, or exposing wrongdoing. The link with pro-active policing will be obvious, since undercover police officers or their informants would need to rely on this kind of claim if prosecuted for their involvement in ongoing offences; for this reason, it is clear that any recognition of a doctrine of 'law enforcement motivation' must be subject *inter alia*, to the limitation that such a defendant has not gone so far as to do acts amounting to entrapment.[100] However, there are many cases of law enforcement motivation which have nothing to do with pro-active policing, and concern acts by private citizens.

There is no standard pattern of response to claims of this kind. It appears that in the USA arguments based on law enforcement motivation have little prospect of success unless they can be brought within the confines of an existing doctrine. The closest of these appears to be the defence of 'public authority justification',[101] but that seems to be restricted to defendants who hold, or can claim to hold, some position (parent, teacher, ship's captain, etc.) that makes it necessary for them to use force so as to preserve good order.

---

[99] On which there is a considerable literature: for a thoughtful contribution which discusses entrapment, see G.R. Sullivan, 'Making Excuses', in A.P. Simester and A.T.H. Smith (eds.), *Harm and Culpability* (Oxford, 1996).

[100] For the Law Commission's proposal to create an offence of entrapment, see n. 80 above.

[101] Model Penal Code, s.3.08, discussed in conjunction with s.3.03 by Robinson (n. 9 above) 421–435.

This is much narrower than the claim considered here. English law has been more responsive, but is still patchy and confused. There are some scattered statutory provisions, such as section 5(4) of the Misuse of Drugs Act 1971, which allows an accused a defence to drugs charges on proof that his intention in keeping possession of the drug was to prevent another from committing an offence or to hand it over to the authorities, in both cases provided he took steps as soon as possible to hand the drugs in. More recently the Protection from Harassment Act 1997, introduced to penalize 'stalking', provides defences where the course of conduct 'was pursued for the purpose of preventing or detecting crime',[102] so as to shield from liability those seeking to enforce the law. If we turn to the draft criminal code, we find a specific provision in clause 27(6) which allows a defence to a person alleged to have been an accomplice to an offence where his purpose in giving assistance was to frustrate the commission of the substantive offence. A parallel provision protects defendants whose purpose was to avoid or limit the harmful consequences of an offence. The aim of these provisions is to ensure that police officers and their agents are not liable to conviction in such cases. The Law Commission recognized that there would be other situations in which a claim of law enforcement motivation might be advanced, and stated that 'the common law on this topic . . . can be further developed under clause 45(c)', the clause preserving the courts' liberty in this respect.[103]

The common law is little developed because, as the Law Commission recognized, prosecutions are relatively rare in this type of case, particularly where an informant or police officer has been involved in an offence. Five judicial decisions might be mentioned briefly. Probably the best known is *R v Smith*,[104] where the defendant had offered a gift to the Mayor of Castleford and was charged with corruption. He admitted the offer but stated that his purpose was to expose the corrupt practices which he believed to be rife in the local council. The Court of Criminal Appeal dealt with the case as one of statutory interpretation: the key term 'corruptly' was held simply to require proof of a deliberate offer and an intention that the offeree should enter into a corrupt bargain, and not to require any proof of dishonesty. The defendant's alleged beneficent motive was therefore no defence. In *R v Clarke*,[105] however, the Court of Appeal faced the issue without hiding behind the wording of the charge. The defendant had participated in a burglary, apparently in order to frustrate the outcome. At trial, he was acquitted of burglary, which includes the requirement of dishonesty, to which the jury clearly thought that his defence (that he was working for the police and passing on

---

[102]   Protection from Harassment Act 1997, ss. 1(3)(a) and 4(3)(a).

[103]   Law Commission No. 177, *A Criminal Code for England and Wales* (1989), Vol. 2, para. 9.33. It is nevertheless surprising that a specific defence was provided in complicity cases but not, for example, in conspiracy cases, where there is nothing other than a passing reference in cl. 50(3) to the common law. See also n.6 above.

[104]   [1960] 2 QB 423.

[105]   (1984) 79 Cr App R 344; cf. the earlier Canadian case of *R v Ormerod* [1969] 4 CCC 3.

information about the other offenders) was relevant; but the judge directed the jury to convict of aiding and abetting burglary, and it was against this conviction that he appealed. The court held that it would be wrong to state 'that conduct which is overall calculated and intended not to further but to frustrate the ultimate result of the crime is always immaterial and irrelevant'. In the 'exceptional and rare' type of case where it could be said that the defendant's acts were done in order to allow 'the police to make use of information concerning an offence that is already laid on', a jury might conclude that the defendant had been acting lawfully, and a defence to crime should therefore be recognized.

The Court of Appeal returned to the narrower approach in *R v Shaw*,[106] where the defendant was charged with inciting another employee dishonestly to obtain property by deception. His defence was that the whole scheme was intended to demonstrate how easy it would be to pass bogus invoices through the company's accounting system, and that he hoped to obtain some career advancement from this exercise. The Court of Appeal quashed his conviction, stating that the judge had misdirected the jury as to proof of Shaw's dishonesty, to which his explanation was relevant. No reference was made to an independent defence of law enforcement motivation. One point, to which we will return later, is that this was not a case of public law enforcement so much as a private endeavour with beneficial motives.[107] The high water mark of the narrow literal approach is the decision of the Privy Council in *Yip Chiu-Cheung v R*.[108] A drugs enforcement agent, working undercover, agreed with the defendant to import heroin. The plan was that the agent would transport the heroin: the defendant appealed against his conviction for conspiracy with the agent, arguing that the agent would not have committed an offence by transporting the heroin because he would lack the necessary fault element for the offence. 'It was urged on their Lordships that no moral guilt attached to the undercover agent who was at all times acting courageously and with the best of motives in attempting to infiltrate and bring to justice a gang of criminal drug dealers'. But, held Lord Bridge, the agent would still have been committing an offence when he imported the heroin and, even though the officials may have agreed to turn a blind eye, they had no authority to absolve him from the criminal offence. Now the result of this reasoning was to sustain the defendant's conviction for conspiracy, which doubtless was what the courts wanted. But if the agent had been prosecuted, would they have adopted the same strict line, or would they have found a personal defence for the agent along the lines adumbrated in *Clarke*, a decision not cited by the Privy Council?

---

[106] [1994] Criminal LR 365.

[107] For another case of private endeavour (on this occasion, to save a bank from ruin by speculators), see *Wai Yu-Tsang v R* [1992] 1 AC 209, where the conviction for conspiracy to defraud was upheld.

[108] [1995] 1 AC 111.

Brief mention may be made, finally, of the decision in *R v Pommell*,[109] where the defendant's answer to charges of possessing a firearm and ammunition was that he had just taken them off another person, who was intending to commit a crime with them, and that he intended to pass them to his brother for surrender to the police. The Court of Appeal held that a defence should be available if those facts were established, that 'balance of evils' reasoning was relevant, and that the closest defence was the species of necessity known as duress of circumstances. In principle, a court should therefore decide whether the defendant acted as he did because he reasonably believed that death or grievous bodily harm might be caused to someone, and whether a person of reasonable firmness would have reacted similarly to the situation.[110] It would also be important to determine whether the defendant intended to hand in the gun at the first reasonable opportunity.

The law discloses no clear pattern. The varying facts extend from the prevention of crime (*Pommell*) to entrapment (*Smith, Yip Chiu-Cheung*, perhaps *Clarke*) and the detection of offenders (Protection from Harassment Act 1997). The Court of Appeal's willingness to adapt the law in *Clarke* and in *Pommell* so as to develop a distinct defence has not been followed up, and it remains easy for courts to retreat into a kind of literal interpretative mode that allows them to avoid the issue of principle, and to try to reflect their conception of the merits of each case under the cover of mere statutory interpretation.

2. Rationales for Recognizing the Claim

We may focus on three arguments in favour of establishing a distinct doctrine of law enforcement motivation. The first of these exploits a link between the claim and the general principles of justification. It is well known that the criminal law recognizes a number of doctrines, most of which function as defences, that justify conduct otherwise criminal: among these are self-defence, prevention of crime, and the apprehension of suspected offenders, all of which may afford a defence to the use of force. A number of controversies surround the justifications, and some of them are mentioned in the paragraphs that follow. The fundamental notion is that justified conduct is right, or at least permissible and tolerable.[111] The justifications may be said to exempt certain categories of behaviour from the general prohibitions of the law,[112] although the reasons for doing so may be differently conceptualized. Some

---

[109] (1995) 2 Cr App R 607, not following *Woodage v Moss* [1974] 1 WLR 411; see also the subsequent decision in *R v Pommell* [1999] Crim LR 576 when the same defence was raised.

[110] These tests were laid down in *R v Martin* (1989) 88 Cr App R 343.

[111] For brief explanation, see e.g. P.H. Robinson, *Fundamentals of Criminal Law* (2nd edn., Boston, 1997) 453–454, or, more fully, G.P. Fletcher, *Rethinking Criminal Law* (Boston, 1978) ch. 13.

[112] R.F. Schopp, *Justification Defenses and Just Convictions* (Cambridge, 1999) 30.

would say that the justifications recognize conflicts of private rights and resolve them on morally appropriate principles, e.g., that in self-defence situations the aggressor has to forfeit limb or life if there is no other reasonable choice; others would contend that it is in the public interest that certain acts be done, such as conduct in order to prevent crime or to apprehend suspected offenders, at least within limits compatible with the public interest (e.g., proportionality and necessity). These rationales may overlap or even be complementary, applying in different circumstances. If we consider some of the contexts in which the claim of law enforcement motivation might be raised, it is evident that they come close to the public interest rationale. The provision in the Misuse of Drugs Act 1971 exempting persons who possess drugs in order to deliver them into police custody chimes well with a 'prevention of crime' rationale, as does the claim in *Pommell* of an intent to surrender the gun to lawful authority. The provision in the Protection from Harassment Act 1997 explicitly mentions the prevention of crime and detection of offenders, and the latter reason was also prominent in the Court of Appeal's acceptance of the collaborative activities of the defendant in *Clarke* (although rejected, for instrumental reasons, in *Yip Chiu-Cheung*). It is certainly compatible with a sensible political morality for the law to recognize the value of behaviour aimed at the prevention of crime and the detection and/or apprehension of suspected offenders.

Whereas the public interest rationale establishes the connection with legal and social grounds of justification, that would be insufficient to sustain the claim of law enforcement motivation without a second rationale—that the purpose with which the defendant acted supplies a good reason for exculpation. One obvious difficulty with this might stem from the maxim that 'motive is irrelevant to criminal liability', still stated as a principle in some leading texts[113] but rightly regarded as an unsatisfactory overstatement by other writers.[114] It might be possible to state that motive (suitably distinguished from intent) is usually irrelevant when a court is determining whether or not a person intended a certain result, but the adverb 'usually' demonstrates the flexibility that the courts have insisted on retaining for themselves. Moreover, what might be termed anti-law-enforcement motivation is constitutive of certain offences, such as doing an act with intent to impede the apprehension or prosecution of a suspected offender[115] and wounding or causing grievous

---

[113] e.g. J.C. Smith and B. Hogan, *Criminal Law* (9th edn., London, 1999) 77–79—motive is irrelevant because it is not an element of most offences.

[114] e.g. in such disparate writings as A. Norrie, *Crime, Reason and History* (London, 1993) 37–57; N. Lacey, 'A Clear Conception of Intention—Elusive or Illusory?' (1993) 56 MLR 621; A. Ashworth, 'Criminal Liability in a Medical Context: the Treatment of Good Intentions', in A.P. Simester and A.T.H. Smith, *Harm and Culpability* (Oxford, 1996); and J. Horder, 'On the Irrelevance of Motive' in J. Horder (ed), *Oxford Essays in Jurisprudence*, 4th series (Oxford, 2000).

[115] Criminal Law Act 1967, s.4(1).

bodily harm 'with intent to resist or prevent the lawful apprehension or de-
tainer of any person',[116] so there can hardly be any compelling reason why
such a motive should not be the basis of a defence.

The reason why law enforcement motivation should be recognized as exculpatory is because, and to the extent that, it shows that the defendant acted
as a good citizen. Just as the motivation of someone who acted on official
legal advice shows an intention (indeed, an effort) to abide by the law, the
motivation of someone who acted for the purpose of enforcing the law shows
an intention (indeed, an effort) to enforce the law or to bring about compliance. However, the difference between the two types of case does raise questions. A sensible political morality should certainly look with favour on
citizens who act on official legal advice, but there may be dangers in encouraging people to act out of law enforcement motivation—dangers of vigilantism, of unfair virtue-testing, and even of hindering the activities of the official
law enforcement agencies. To revert to the five cases set out above, it is far
easier to regard as permissible the conduct of the defendants in *Clarke* and
Yip Chiu-Cheung,[117] and perhaps *Pommell,* than that of the defendants in
Smith and *Shaw*—one might say that the latter two ought to have brought
their suspicions to the notice of the authorities rather than embarking on conduct of dubious legality.[118] This leads into the question of who should determine what counts as the motivation and behaviour of a law enforcer: to be
congruent with the standard of the good citizen, it ought surely to be required
that the defendant acted for a purpose that is a recognized law enforcement
purpose, and not for a purpose that he or she thought should be so recognized.[119]

A third rationale might be provided by the doctrine of lesser evils. In the
USA it is well established that conduct might be justified if it can be regarded
as the lesser evil in a given situation, subject to various limitations. Thus the
core of the Model Penal Code defence is that 'the evil sought to be avoided
by such conduct is greater than that sought to be prevented by the law defining the offense charged'.[120] English law has never espoused such a general
defence: the 'lesser evils' rationale is evident in English defences such as
duress of circumstances[121] but, as we saw in *Pommell,*[122] that defence is
only available where there is reasonably believed to be a threat of death or

[116] Offences Against the Person Act 1861, s.18.

[117] Subject to appropriate safeguards, such as proper authorization: see the provisions in Part
II of the Regulation of Investigatory Powers Act 2000, introduced in an attempt at compliance
with the European Convention on Human Rights.

[118] These reflections are relevant to the discussion above of non-official entrapment, by individuals or by newspaper reporters: see n. 92 and accompanying text above.

[119] On this view, the principle in *Chandler v DPP* [1964] AC 763 (that it is not for the defendants to determine what is a purpose 'prejudicial to the State') should be applicable.

[120] American Law Institute, Model Penal Code, s. 3.02; see further Robinson (n. 9 above)
407–420.

[121] cf. now *Re A (children) (conjoined twins: surgical separation)* [2000] 4 All ER 961.

[122] Discussed at n. 109 above and accompanying text.

serious injury to someone. Irrespective of the arguments for a general 'balance of evils' defence, the notion itself provides support for the claim of law
enforcement motivation, in cases where the defendant's well-motivated act
is not more destructive than the danger which it is his purpose to avert.

3. The Response of the Criminal Justice System

We have seen that law enforcement motivation involves a purpose that
chimes well with existing justifications for otherwise criminal conduct. Such
a purpose is also consistent with the motivation of a model citizen. How,
then, should the criminal justice system respond? In principle this should be
treated as a justification, at least in those cases where a law enforcement officer acts for this purpose and has whatever authorization is necessary. The
Protection from Harassment Act 1997 is one of the few provisions to recognize this explicitly; the normal position is that law enforcement officers are
simply not prosecuted for conduct of this kind.

English statutes contain scattered defences of law enforcement motivation,
in the Misuse of Drugs Act 1971, the Protection from Harassment Act 1997
and (in relation to complicity) in the draft criminal code, and the judicial decisions lack consistency. This piecemeal approach is unsatisfactory, and there
seems no good reason for selecting some offences rather than others. Whenever a proposal for a new defence is made, one hears the response that the
floodgates will open and the courts will be unable to prevent numerous false
defences from succeeding. A version of this objection is to be found in the
approach of the Law Commission to the idea of recognizing, in relation to the
offences of offering or receiving a bribe, a defence based on the intention to expose corruption. The Commission was persuaded by those who suggested that
such a defence would be abused by unscrupulous people and others who might
be encouraged to take the law into their own hands, and recommended against
introducing the defence.[123] Where individual citizens are concerned, as distinct from law enforcement officers, it is pertinent to ask whether they should
be encouraged to take their concerns to the police wherever time permits, and
not to set off on their own course of virtue-testing, entrapment, etc. The Law
Commission was not convinced by those who argued that the purpose of exposing corruption is a laudable one, and that private individuals might operate as an independent check on corruption. However, it would have been
preferable to explore the possibility of a limited defence, while making it clear
that the incitement or instigation of an offence is not permissible.

---

[123] Law Commission No. 248, *Legislating the Criminal Code: Corruption* (London, 1998)
para. 5.149; the Commission added that to introduce such a defence would be to create 'a glar-
ing inconsistency between, for example, corruption and conspiracy to defraud' (para. 5.150). No
such inconsistency would exist if a general defence were introduced.

D. FIDELITY TO LEGAL VALUES

It appears that the claims of the three doctrines discussed in this chapter can draw upon at least three distinctive rationales. The first may be found in the concept of good citizenship. A legal system ought to recognize that it is the conduct of a good citizen to seek official legal advice and to follow such advice (unless it is manifestly unreasonable to do so). It should recognize that it is the conduct of a good citizen to hand over drugs, guns or other prohibited articles to the police, and (in limited circumstances) to become involved in an offence in order to expose the offenders and ensure that the offence is frustrated. This rationale can also be used to demonstrate why conduct of these kinds is not blameworthy: it is reasonable for a citizen to believe that it is not just excusable but right thus to act.[124] A second rationale is the principle of integrity, which insists that those who enforce the law should obey the law, and that it would undermine the integrity of the criminal justice system if courts were to entertain prosecutions resulting from the entrapment of citizens by officials or resulting from the defendant's following of official advice which the prosecution now claims to have been mistaken. A third rationale emphasizes the connection with 'rule of law' values, notably the absence of fair warning of the legal position in cases where a defendant reasonably relies upon official (but mistaken) legal advice, and the abuse of authority involved in cases of entrapment by law enforcement officials. This rationale may also suggest that conduct in these circumstances is less blameworthy. These rationales interact so as to establish that recognition of the three doctrines would support legal values, whereas the failure to recognize one or more of them may be said to undermine legal values.

If these arguments about fidelity to legal values are accepted,[125] we then move to the instrumental and institutional question about the most appropriate response of the criminal justice system to each doctrine. There are at least four possible responses: to stay the prosecution, to exclude the resulting evidence, to recognize a defence to criminal liability, or to rely on mitigation of sentence. It might be thought that, since the first two are procedural responses whereas the third is a matter of substantive law, the relevant question would be whether the doctrines relate to substance or procedure. The usual distinction is that matters relating to outcomes are regarded as substance, whereas matters relating to earlier processes such as investigations are regarded as procedure. That distinction gives no clear pointers to the classification of the three doctrines considered here. As Galligan has observed:

---

[124] See the reference at n. 25 above to Gardner's development of this approach.

[125] In using the concept of 'fidelity to legal values', I have avoided reference to Lon L. Fuller's concept of 'fidelity to law', in *The Morality of Law* (New Haven, 1964), especially ch. 2, which has some rather different features. However, Fuller does describe his notion of fidelity as reciprocal, i.e. that both the state and the citizen should respect the values which he outlines, which also forms part of the notion developed here.

Values like these are protected because they are important in the life of a society wherever they occur. It is difficult to see what is served or gained by designating them as procedural values, and the same may be said of the modern tendency to call them process values. If the term 'process values' is meant to indicate only that some of the standards governing legal processes are separate from outcomes, no harm is done; if the term means more, then its significance is unclear.[126]

If there is no clear distinction between substance and procedure to indicate which of the four responses might be most appropriate, we should turn our attention to the place of those responses within Anglo-American law. It is probably true in practice that many instances falling within the three doctrines would not result in a prosecution: the authorities would simply decide, by reference to the law or the public interest, that a prosecution would not be appropriate. But we have seen that prosecutions have been brought and, as such, it is emphatically not sufficient to leave the three claims to be dealt with at the sentencing stage, by way of mitigation. The strength of the rationales set out above indicates that it would be unfair to register a conviction in a clear case where one of the three doctrines applies. Neither is it sufficient to leave the claims to be resolved by the vagaries of legislative drafting, whether a particular statute has a relevant defence or qualification, whether the wording of an offence can be interpreted so as to deal with the claim, and so forth.

The proper course is to assess the strength of the rationales for each doctrine, and then to identify the most appropriate response to the claim in view of the rationale. Where government officials have played a part in creating an offence, it seems appropriate to consider a procedural response that prevents a trial from taking place, notably, a stay of the prosecution on grounds of abuse of process. On this view, both entrapment and reliance on official legal advice should be taken out of the trial and dealt with at the earlier stage of arraignment. This is now the position adopted in English law in entrapment cases, following the decision of the House of Lords in *Looseley*.[127] The House accepted that, in some cases in which a prosecution is not stayed for abuse of process, it might be appropriate to consider excluding evidence obtained by entrapment by invoking the discretion in section 78 of the Police and Criminal Evidence Act 1984. However, the primary remedy is to stay the prosecution for abuse of process, on the ground that 'the court will not permit the prosecutorial arm of the state to behave in this way'.[128] Some may argue that in practice the courts would be likely to construe it narrowly, because it is such a conclusive remedy, and so the possibility of a defence to liability (determined by a jury) should be retained. But to concede that would not be to concede the primary suitability of staying the prosecution.

---

[126] D.J. Galligan, *Due Process and Fair Procedures* (Oxford, 1996) 51.
[127] [2001] UKHL 53.   [128] ibid., para. 16, per Lord Nicholls.

Index of Subjects

Name Index

Printed in the United Kingdom
by Lightning Source UK Ltd.
119727UK00001B/55